Accounting for Alcohol

AF840943

Consumption of alcohol is a globally ubiquitous, often controversial activity, and business organizations in this sector are of significant social and economic relevance. This book draws on accounting records from the sector to reveal fresh and unique insights into the historical development of the production of alcoholic beverages.

Offering a historic overview of the three major areas of the alcohol industry – brewing, distilling and wine – this book reveals the commonalities and differences which are present in the industry, while also highlighting its social impact. The editors bring together contributions from around the world, including five European countries, Japan, Mexico and Russia to demonstrate how accounting has developed over time. Offering diverse geographical and historical perspectives, it explores multiple aspects of accounting within the industry, including internal control, earnings management, competition and regulatory aspects. The fascinating insights into breweries, wineries, spirit distillers, vineyards and other related organizations provide a unique historic perspective of accounting systems, techniques and practices.

Drawing on an international range of examples and rich archival material, this valuable research collection will be of great interest to researchers and advanced students of accounting and business history.

Martin Quinn is Associate Professor in Accounting at DCU Business School, Ireland. He has published widely on management accounting, accounting change and accounting history. His articles on accounting in the brewing sector from contemporary and historic perspectives have been published in journals such as Management Accounting Research, Accounting History Review and Accounting History.

João Oliveira is Assistant Professor in Management at FEP.UP – School of Economics and Management, University of Porto, Portugal. He has published on management accounting, accountants' roles and shared services centres and is conducting historical research on accounting and control rules at the Society of Jesus.

Routledge New Works in Accounting History
Series Editor: John Richard Edwards, Richard Fleischman, Garry Carnegie, Salvador Carmona

This innovative series contains volumes on accounting history, auditing, bibliography, development of accounting principles and standards, education and ethics, financial reporting, law and regulations, management accounting and the theoretical works of leading scholars. Providing students, teachers and researchers with the opportunity to learn more about the discipline of accountancy and its past, this series is a vital addition to any accounting library.

Curtis Jenkins Cornwell & Company
S. V. Cornwell

Contributions of Limperg & Schmidt to the Replacement Cost Debate in the 1920s
Frank L. Clarke, Graeme Dean

Accounting and Food: Some Italian Experiences
Edited by Massimo Sargiacomo, Luciano D'Amico, & Roberto Di Pietra

Memorial Articles for 20th Century American Accounting Leaders
Edited by Stephen A. Zeff

The Italian and Iberian Influence in Accounting History
The Imperative of Power
Edited by Michele Bigoni and Warwick Funnell

The Origins of Accounting Culture
The Venetian Connection
Edited by Massimo Sargiacomo, Stefano Coronella, Chiara Mio, Ugo Sostero, and Roberto Di Pietra

Accounting for Alcohol
An Accounting History of Brewing, Distilling and Viniculture
Edited by Martin Quinn and João Oliveira

For more information about this series, please visit: www.routledge.com

Accounting for Alcohol

An Accounting History of Brewing, Distilling and Viniculture

Edited by Martin Quinn and João Oliveira

Routledge
Taylor & Francis Group
LONDON AND NEW YORK

First published 2019
by Routledge
2 Park Square, Milton Park, Abingdon, Oxon OX14 4RN

and by Routledge
52 Vanderbilt Avenue, New York, NY 10017, USA

First issued in paperback 2020

Routledge is an imprint of the Taylor & Francis Group, an informa business

© 2019 selection and editorial matter, Martin Quinn and João Oliveira; individual chapters, the contributors

The right of Martin Quinn and João Oliveira to be identified as the authors of the editorial material, and of the authors for their individual chapters, has been asserted in accordance with sections 77 and 78 of the Copyright, Designs and Patents Act 1988.

All rights reserved. No part of this book may be reprinted or reproduced or utilised in any form or by any electronic, mechanical, or other means, now known or hereafter invented, including photocopying and recording, or in any information storage or retrieval system, without permission in writing from the publishers.

Trademark notice: Product or corporate names may be trademarks or registered trademarks, and are used only for identification and explanation without intent to infringe.

British Library Cataloguing-in-Publication Data
A catalogue record for this book is available from the British Library

Library of Congress Cataloging-in-Publication Data
A catalog record for this book has been requested

ISBN 13: 978-0-367-58691-1 (pbk)
ISBN 13: 978-1-138-73733-4 (hbk)

Typeset in Bembo
by Apex CoVantage, LLC

Contents

Figures

Tables

Editors' acknowledgements

This book emerged out of a conversation – in a pub in Glasgow – with two editors from Taylor & Francis, namely Terry Clague and Jacqueline Curthoys. Thanks to both of you, and a special thanks to Jacqueline as the commissioning editor. Thanks also to the editorial assistants during the project – Isobel Fitzharris, Laura Hussey and Jessica Harrison. Thanks also to the reviewers who provided feedback and encouragement when we first proposed organizing this volume. Of course, this book would not have come into existence without the chapter contributors, who also played a fundamental role as reviewers. To each of you, a sincere thanks from both of us, and we do hope you enjoy reading the final volume.

Accounting for alcohol

An accounting history of brewing, distilling and viniculture

Martin Quinn and João Oliveira

Introduction to the book

Accounting history scholarship and research cover many topics and many types of organisations. However, this book was particularly motivated by a lack of research on what we might term a very particular but at the same time quite ubiquitous setting: the alcoholic drinks sector. As an example of a similar situation in another particular yet ubiquitous setting, Funnell (2009, pp. 561–562) comments on the relative lack of historic accounting research on the military sector, which is surprising given not only expected specificities in such a setting but also the occurrence of wars and military activities throughout time across the world. Similarly, the making and consumption of alcohol are quite ubiquitous throughout the years and around the world; moreover, the topic has been the subject of numerous controversies and regulations, and has involved organisations that not only tend to have specific characteristics but may also be of significant economic and social relevance. Despite this, the accounting history literature is surprisingly scarce of research on the sector and organisations within.

In this book, we cover the industries of brewing, distilling and viniculture. Beer has been brewed in some form for about 3,000 years (for example: Haydon, 2001; Talbot, 2006) and wine pre-dates Christianity (to around 5,000 BC), with the distillation of alcohol arriving later, around the 12th century (Forbes, 1970). Across their long history, alcoholic beverages also have been the subject of controversies, both within the social and political realms and across many geographies and cultures. Their production, distribution and consumption have been often subject to regulations, some promoting it, others constraining it, others even prohibiting it, either totally or partially. Major economic, political and social issues, ranging from wars and taxes to religion and moral, have been at stake and related with these markets, industries and organisations. Some organisations in this industry have a rich history spanning across centuries, sometimes under a stable ownership of a single family, sometimes involved in drastic reorganisations. Accounting records and other accounting-related documents of organisations from this industry may provide unique and fruitful insights into accounting practices, business practices and even social issues and movements, some specific to the sector and others a reflection of the surrounding context in each period, and may reveal commonalties and differences that spurn further research. While the chapters vary considerably, this book does reveal some previously untouched archival sources on accounting at breweries, distilleries and wineries. Even merely creating an awareness of such sources, we hope, will inspire on-going research.

The specific aims of this book are two-fold. The first aim is to provide a general historic view of accounting in the brewing, distilling and viniculture industries, considering an extended time frame and from a wide range of jurisdictions across three continents. With such a view, accounting history scholars will have a base to study accounting practices and changes in the sector and a base to compare to other organisations, business sectors and geographies. The second aim of this book is to provide a highly contextualised analysis of accounting. Throughout this book, the reader will gain an appreciation of not only how accounting was influenced by issues around the organisations, industries and societies at stake but also how accounting was instrumental in sometimes subtle and other times drastic changes in those organisations, industries and societies. These two aims provide a wide scope to the book, and hence we hope that it will appeal not only to accounting historians but also to business historians and, more broadly, to accounting and business academics in general.

Before we summarise the content of the book, we should point out that we consider 'accounting' a broad concept, not limited to accounting techniques or accounting reports, or to typical categories such as financial accounting or management accounting. For example, the book contains chapters with content on counting of goods; controlling of assets, transactions and consumption; reporting flows and duties; accountability relations and practices; accounting information systems; accounting in product development; accounting and government; and accounting and markets. Some chapters provide extensive detail on accounting techniques within organisations, others focus on how accounting supported business growth or on interactions both within the organisations and between organisations and stakeholders. This broad definition of accounting contributes to a diverse set of chapters, which illustrates the rich possibilities available to researchers in this area.

As suggested by the book title, this volume is divided into three equal parts, each one reflecting three broad types of alcoholic beverage: beer, spirits and wine. Part 1 contains five chapters on accounting for beer and brewing. Then, Part 2 has five chapters on accounting for spirits and distilling. Finally, Part 3 has five chapters on accounting for wine and viniculture. We summarise each of the chapters next.

Summary of content

As mentioned earlier, Part 1 contains chapters on the subject of beer and brewing. Chapter 1 analyses a technological change at the world-famous Guinness brewery in Dublin, Ireland. The chapter details the introduction of accounting machines to the Accountant's Department at the brewery in the late 1920s. In essence, these machines were typewriters that could add figures, reducing the work of clerks in the accounting department. Although this took place almost a century ago, the authors reveal some similarities to findings of studies on the introduction of contemporary information technology, such as Enterprise Resource Planning systems. They also present some differences, a key one being the ability of Guinness to customise the machines – an aspect addressing contemporary debates about whether organisations should adapt to technology, or the other way around.

Chapter 2 analyses how optimism was present in the Annual Report of a Spanish brewery, *El Alcázar*, over the period 1928–1992. More specifically, the chapter performs content analysis to identify the positive and negative tone of a document called the *Memoria*. This document is a management report containing non-standard narrative information on the most important events of the company for each reporting year. By analysing several variables and using software to ascertain the tone of words used in the *Memoria*, the results are broadly in line with previous research. Positive references are consistently preferred, irrespective of performance, as measured by return on assets (ROA), a finding that is in line with impression management. However, there is an increase in negative references when ROA decreases, which is not in line with impression management. Overall, though, there is a constant predominance of positive references, and hence the tone of the report is consistently positive.

Chapter 3 provides insights from a previously unexplored archive, namely that of Macardles Brewery in Dundalk, Ireland. The chapter details how accounting information was utilised to value the brewery by the British government in its efforts to acquire control of the licensed liquor trade in Britain and Ireland. In essence, the method used to determine a value for any brewing business was based on an averaging of profits and an agreed multiplier. The chapter analyses the economic and political context in which various valuation proposals emerged and were discussed. The government objective came from an increasing temperance movement, and the chapter concentrates on a 1917 scheme and its proposals for the purchase of brewing interests – a policy also influenced by the events of World War I. On the other hand, brewers were opposed to any move to nationalise or close their trade, and this chapter also reveals how directors at Macardles engaged in an exercise to tidy the company balance sheet prior to the 1917 valuation. The chapter describes why ultimately the scheme did not proceed, and it reveals that some valuation measures similar to today were used, as well as political processes and managerial approaches that could well be found in contemporary organisations.

Chapter 4 describes how the post-war construction of the Orion Brewery in 1957 contributed to the social and economic development of the island of Okinawa, Japan, and it also details accounting in new product development. The brewery founder aimed to brew an inexpensive beer that the public could drink daily. Therefore, costs and production capacity were important, and budgetary controls during the construction of the brewery were important to achieve a cost-effective factory at a scale lower than typical. Sales were increased mainly through increasing Orion's product range, through a new product development process including value engineering, cost tables and more cooperation between departments. In addition, the chapter explains how relations with banks, the local community and the local government were important to foster tax legislation favouring Orion over competition and how these relations were indispensable for Orion's success.

Chapter 5 details accounting controls around alcohol in the British Royal Navy from 1793 to 1815. While these controls related to both beer and stronger alcohol like rum, this chapter was located in Part 1 given its greater focus on the former drink. The chapter provides details of rules set out for Royal Navy ships in terms of daily alcohol allowances and how the purser on each ship had to account for alcohol and for expenses such as cask repairs. The accounting carried out was basic recording and listing of detail, and the creation of simple cash accounts. A simple system of internal control was also applied in terms of the more senior officers needing to sign records, accounts and certificates of the purser, as well as the control and certification of wastage. The authors then draw upon Foucauldian ideas on governmentality to interpret the mechanisms in place as a way to create control through knowledge and centrally administrated regulations.

Chapter 6 bring us to the first of our chapters on spirits and distilling. It analyses the Watercourse Distillery, Cork, Ireland, and details how accounting information was used and reported by this distillery between 1792 and 1864. The distillery was founded by Thomas Hewitt, one of Cork's 'Merchant Princes' of the time, who were often involved in local government, promoting cultural activities and investing in local business. The chapter notes an emphasis on financial accounting–type information, with a focus on the overall profit amount – typical of merchants' accounting. Although some literature suggests that cost accounting techniques developed from the early 1800s, no evidence of any such techniques is revealed. Although the distillery remained generally profitable during the research period, the profit levels did fluctuate, and through a combination of legislation governing distilling and a lack of detailed (cost) accounting information, the distillery was effectively a price-taker.

Chapter 7 details accounting for vodka in the Russian empire from the 17th century to 1914. The production of vodka (and its predecessors) was highly regulated. As early as the 17th century, *kabaks* (places for production and distribution of bread wine and beer) had books recording procurement and consumption of raw materials and other production costs, product yields and information about cash proceeds from sales. Such records were then compiled at the municipal and state level, and the chapter describes in detail the complex reporting and accountability processes set up within a comprehensive regulatory framework. By 1800, double-entry accounting was introduced for private companies. By 1895, while private production was permitted, the state controlled distribution, allowing it to account for all sales (from the municipal to the national level) and collect the corresponding excise taxes.

Chapter 8 explores accounting and the Scotch whisky industry from its early days through to the 2000s. The chapter provides commentary on production planning, international taxation issues, profit optimisation and investments in the sector. The chapter thus focuses on accounting at the level of the industry, as opposed to individual firms. The importance of accounting concepts such as investment and the role of taxation in the development of the Scotch whisky market are emphasised. The level of investment required has resulted in a small number of large companies being dominant, although financing options are becoming easier for smaller operators in recent times, with the chapter analysing the optimisation opportunities presented by financial innovations in the capital market.

Chapter 9 also adopts a macro-level, now with a mainly sociological perspective, to analyse the development of tequila from a drink of the Mexican poor to a highly sought-after beverage. The chapter details the development of tequila from the early 18th century to about the 1950s, following the drink's cultural development and how it made the journey from a primitive to a socially accepted and even popular and profitable drink, in particular within the U.S. market. Shifts in social perceptions about the drink, as well as a lowering of prices in the 1940s, led to a tequila boom, increasing the revenues and profits of tequila producers. The chapter also briefly explores how policies about tequila, shifting from prohibition to regulation and taxation, may have created a role for accounting information.

Chapter 10 concludes the analysis of the distilling sector, exploring the rise of the Distillers Company Limited (DCL) from 1850 to 1925. The chapter provides details of how DCL came about through several mergers and acquisitions in the early 1900s, with DCL keen to purchase other distillers which were undervalued or had fallen on hard times. The end result of this process was a whisky industry with an effective monopoly of DCL, it being the sixth largest manufacturing company in the United Kingdom by 1930. The chapter also mentions creative accounting practices which brought about the downfall of the business of the Pattison brothers around the turn of the century, depicting a story which may resonate with some contemporary accounting and corporate failures.

Chapter 11 is the first of the five wine-related chapters. The chapter describes the accounting records of two *Maisons de vin*, that of René-Jean Goubault-Lambert at Rochefort-sur-Loire and that of Jean-Baptiste Ackerman-Laurance at Saumur – both in the Maine et Loire wine region, in France. The records date from the 19th century and include several books of accounts, including a *Grand livre*. These books not only recorded the daily transactions of each business but also provided the owners with summary information which assisted in expansion decisions. The chapter also highlights the importance of trust between trading partners and accountability towards company owners, to which accounting records and reports were fundamental, and relates some management difficulties with shortcomings in the accounting records.

Chapter 12 provides an account of the *en primeur* trading system and the Bordeaux Place. These are essentially sales and marketing devices to guarantee the perceived quality and the commercialisation of Bordeaux wine. Their origins are traced back to the Middle Ages, and the analysis continues to the present day. To maintain quality and price, wine sales are carefully controlled and managed within the trading systems, which protect incumbents and enforce transactional behaviour and where reputation and trust are key. A key feature is a regulated classification of wine producers according to their 'growth', and the system in place has in effect allowed some Bordeaux wine producers to be price makers. Within this complex and possibly discreet system, accounting plays a role, albeit a probably minor one, to enable the comparison of prices and costs, and more particularly to support cash management.

Chapter 13 details accounting in Spanish wine co-operatives during the 20th century, closely relating the significant political changes during this period with changes in the co-operatives and their accounting. The chapter draws on elements of institutional theory and a model of the co-operative life cycle to explore the development of accounting practices. During the first third of the 20th century, accounting was not regulated and it was based on simple groupings of items, yet providing a relatively accurate idea of liquidity, inventories, fixed assets, debt and share capital. During Francoism (1939–1971), the co-operative model expanded, increasing the development and homogenisation of accounting methods, including some more developed cost and management accounting. After Francoism, accounting homogenised further as new laws and European Union (EU) regulations led to standardised financial accounting practices.

Chapter 14 describes accounting and accountability within the wine cellar of the Benedictine monastery of Silos, in Spain, in the 14th, 18th and 19th centuries. The authors provide a quite detailed explanation of the accounting reports from these three periods, starting by showing how the Rule of Saint Benedict established general principles with regard to a moderate consumption of wine (or even abstinence), to be implemented by each Superior according to local circumstances. In the 19th century, multiple controls were in place, both visits and weekly, half-year and quadrennial accountability processes. Overall, we find an increased accountability, and a detailed recounting of a visit by the Father General – in effect within the context of an audit – is given. The main focus of the chapter is the Wine Cellar Book, which reveals the procedures to prepare the accounts, the people involved, the amounts involved and the sources of income and expenditure related to wine harvesting and production.

Finally, Chapter 15 details accounting at a Port wine chartered trade company from 1756 to 1826. The double-entry accounting records of the *Companhia Geral da Agricultura das Vinhas do Alto Douro*, in Portugal, are thoroughly analysed. The authors frame the accounting numbers, books and practices within the institutional context of the organisation, in particular with regard to its relations with the state, shareholders, board members, creditors and other stakeholders. The chapter includes a map of all books kept by the company, describes the preparation of statements of financial position and provides detail of reported earnings and dividends. The authors identify a clear practice of earnings smoothing, particularly after 1784, which promoted an 'institutional fit' that ensured the continuity and sustainability of the *Companhia* itself.

To summarise, the 15 chapters in this book cover a time period from the 14th century to the 20th century, draw on qualitative and quantitative methods and explore multiple topics related to brewing, distilling and viniculture, from many countries around the world. They also reveal detail on multiple aspects of accounting, providing both micro-level and macro-level perspectives, analysing how accounting was influenced by organisational, industry and society-level issues, and also how accounting influenced those issues. We do hope you enjoy reading it, and we also hope it has given a taste of the material about the alcohol industry that is available in many archives around the world. A toast to more research in this area of accounting history!

References

Forbes, R. J. (1970). *A Short History of the Art of Distillation: From the Beginnings Up to the Death of Cellier Blumenthal*. Leiden: EJ Brill.

Funnell, W. (2009). Military accounting. In: J. R. Edwards and S. P. Walker, eds. *The Routledge Companion to Accounting History*. London: Routledge.

Haydon, P. (2001). *Beer and Britannia: An Inebriated History of Britain*. Stroud, England: Sutton Publishing.

Talbot, P. A. (2006). *The Accounting History of the English Brewing Industry 1700–1939: An Exploration of Foucauldian Disciplinarity*. PhD thesis, University of Warwick.

Part 1

Accounting for beer and brewing

1 The introduction of accounting machines at Guinness

Carmen M. Martínez Franco and Martin R. W. Hiebl

Introduction

In contemporary research, the introduction of new technology is viewed as often leading to organisational improvements and advantages. To gain such benefits, it seems essential for organisations to *adapt* such technology and to *adapt to* such technology (Orlikowski, 1993; Szulanski, 2000). Such adaptation processes seem challenging, as organisations may have to develop new behaviours and organisational routines to reap the full benefits of new technology. In many cases, organisations have to go through a learning process that allows new technology-related routines to evolve or to change existing routines through an evolutionary process (Nelson and Winter, 1982). In such processes, collective participation of organisational actors is often required (Edmondson et al., 2001).

Historically, the most common goal of the introduction of new technologies has been cost reduction (Wilson, 1989). Since a significant share of management accountants' daily work is described – both in the contemporary and the historical accounting literature (e.g., Granlund and Lukka, 1998; Hiebl et al., 2015; Johnson, 2002) – as being focused on accounting for and reducing costs, we can argue that management accountants should be very open to the introduction of new technologies. However, to an important degree, management accountants' work routines can also be affected by new technologies. For instance, management accountants may benefit from new technology by gaining easier and faster access to data they need to analyse, which may enable them to speed up reporting processes. Besides such direct effects, there can also be indirect effects on management accountants. For example, new technology may lead to changes in management practices, organisational structure and business processes, which in turn affects the work of management accountants who have to reflect such broader organisational changes in their accounts and reports (Granlund and Malmi, 2002).

Thus, it may be argued that technology and technological change are of high importance for management accounting and management accountants. Nevertheless, there is a debate in the contemporary accounting literature on whether or not new technology has strong effects on management accountants and management accounting routines. In this context, most contemporary studies are focussed on the effects of Enterprise Resource Planning (ERP) systems on management accounting. Two main positions have emerged from this literature. While some studies conclude that new technology such as ERP systems has only a relatively moderate impact on management accounting (e.g., Granlund and Malmi, 2002), others find more significant changes in the role of management accountants following the introduction of new technology (e.g., Scapens and Jazayeri, 2003). Although we do not aim to resolve these opposing positions in this chapter, we argue that the literature on technological change in management accounting has been remarkably singular as to the form of technological change – that is, the introduction of ERP systems.[1] However, historically, other technological innovations have affected management accountants, and historical accounts offer a rich and more complete source for studying this topic. In this chapter, we study an early form of technological change: the introduction of typewriters in the first half of the 20th century. We do so by presenting a historical case study on the introduction of Smith Premier accounting machines at Arthur Guinness, Son & Company Limited (hereafter Guinness).

With this study, we aim to provide a historical answer to the question on the effects of new technology on management accounting and the work of management accountants. We also aim to provide a more complete picture on management accounting in the brewing industry during the first half of the 20th century. While a series of studies in this field have been published recently (e.g., Hiebl et al., 2015; Kristandl and Quinn, 2017; Martínez Franco et al., 2017; Quinn, 2014; Quinn and Jackson, 2014), such studies do not yet illuminate the role of technological change. Our chapter, however, shows that technological change was an important driver of management accounting change, even in the early 20th century. More specifically, this chapter paints a picture of the direct and indirect effects of new technology and the implications for management accountants at Guinness. This contributes to the extant historical literature but also provides some counterbalance to the contemporary literature, which sometimes suggests that new technology has only a relatively moderate impact on management accounting. Our findings reveal that the introduction of Smith Premier accounting machines facilitated and reinforced processes of management accounting change at Guinness.

The remainder of this chapter is organised as follows. In the next section, we review the extant literature on new technology and management accounting change, which is the background in which we position this chapter. The following section then describes our historical research methods, and afterwards we detail the introduction of Smith Premier accounting machines at Guinness. In the final section, we conclude the chapter with a discussion of our findings and we provide suggestions for future research.

New technology and management accounting change

Throughout history, the business environment has been changing constantly. Such change may have various effects on firms. It may increase the pressure to lower total costs, reduce inventories, shorten processing times, provide more reliable delivery dates and better customer services, expand the product range, improve quality and efficiently coordinate global demand, supply and production. If such pressures materialise, organisations are sometimes forced to reinvent themselves and ignite organisational change. One way to drive change is by adopting new technology in order to sustain competitiveness and to adapt to the changing environment (Edmondson et al., 2001; Umble et al., 2003).

Information technologies are thus often conceptualised as drivers of change that can transform organisational structures and social contexts. Such transformation can be observed both at the micro and at the macro level and is considered to have significant effects on individual actors and organisational structures (Applegate, 1996; Caglio, 2003; Hiltz and Johnson, 1990). At the same time, the social contexts of actors and organisations are known to be important factors in driving the adoption and use of new information technologies (Davis and Taylor, 1986; Noble, 1984; Wynne, 1988). Since actors' behaviour is significantly shaped by organisational culture (e.g., Allaire and Firsirotu, 1984; Meek, 1988), we can follow that organisational culture plays an important role in the successful implementation of new technology. Schneider (2000) defines organisational culture as the character or the personality of an organisation and the ways things are done in an organisation. There is reason to believe that organisational culture is crucial for employees' general acceptance and understanding of a technological change. Park et al. (2004) suggest some key cultural attributes which have moderate-to-high positive correlation with the success of new technology implementation. These attributes include team-oriented work, trust, working closely with others, sharing information freely, fairness and enthusiasm. However, there are also cultural attributes which are known to hinder successful adoption of new technology, such as stability, compliance, attention to detail and being calm.

Researchers such as Quinn and Jackson (2014) suggest that organisational change, in general, and management accounting change in particular, should be viewed as a process rather than a static event. Similarly, Scapens and Jazayeri (2003) find the process of introducing new technology to be evolutionary than rather revolutionary, implying that such change occurs slowly and in certain stages over time. Such slow change may be explained by the routine nature of accounting. Changing institutionalised accounting routines may only be possible over time since more abrupt change may face severe resistance. In this vein, new technology may again be an important factor. Edmondson et al. (2001) suggest the introduction of new technology to be a premier trigger for changing routines. In line with this notion, Granlund and Malmi (2002) found that organisational practices such as management accounting are typically changed to fit new technology, not vice versa.

As described earlier, changes in management accounting may be triggered and explained by technological innovation. The literature provides well-developed concepts and a large body of empirical results on the adoption and implementation of technology. For instance, Fichman (1992) defines an innovation as any idea, practice or object that is perceived as new by the adopter. The adoption of such innovations is contingent on factors which determine the ultimate rate and pattern of adoption. Amongst such factors are personal characteristics of adopters (e.g., their level of education and their level of cosmopolitanism), the stages of the adoption decision and the actions of certain individuals who can influence the adoption (e.g., to accelerate adoption). For technological innovation that affects organisational routines deeply ingrained in organisational structures, as is the case for many management accounting practices, further implementation characteristics are important factors for the adoption and diffusion of innovation. These implementation characteristics are organisational complexity (number of people and functions affected), divisibility (ability to divide implementations by stages or sub-populations) and transferability (communicability and maturity) (Leonard-Barton and Deschamps, 1988).

For centuries, accounting was a manual process. In large organisations, prompt access to financial information was basically impossible due to a need to conduct extensive and time-consuming manual searches through bound ledgers. Starting in the late 19th century, a series of technological innovations emerged that not only changed the way accounting processes were conducted but also dramatically changed the information that was provided, and indeed the accounting profession in its own right. The mechanical era was dominated by devices which utilised mechanical actions of levers, gears and wheels to process data. While hand-operated initially, later mechanical devices were often driven by a motor. The mechanical period lasted for two more decades until a second major innovation in information processing emerged: the computer (Wootton and Kemmerer, 2007).

In the first half of the 20th century, the introduction of mechanical technology was led by the strong presence of American companies such as Remington Rand and IBM and the favourable disposition of banks to adopt any technology innovation which would enhance their economies of scale. At this time, banks were particularly open to technological innovation since they had significant numbers of employees engaged in repetitive tasks and high wage demands – work that could be largely automated through the introduction of more sophisticated machines. In the particular case of a medium-sized bank in Lille (Crédit Du Nord), the introduction of 25 accounting machines in 1927 reduced the number of employees by 12 percent (Bonin, 2004). At this time, a network of specialists also emerged who were actively involved in the banking sector. This network met regularly at conferences and discussed the best ways of incorporating machines into their organisations and the changes to be implemented in accounting processes (Bonin, 2004). In line with these developments, requirements for accountants changed as well. For instance, the original exam syllabus of the Institute of Cost and Works Accountants issued in 1919 included mechanical knowledge and workshop knowledge, including the relations between costs and design (Bhimani and Bromwich, 2009).

Largely disconnected from these historical findings, a considerable amount of contemporary research has been conducted on the implementation processes of ERP systems in the management accounting literature of the 1990s and early

2000s.[2] This literature has mostly sought to analyse the effect of ERP systems such as SAP, Baan and Oracle, on management accounting practices. An ERP system comprises a set of integrated application modules, which span most business functions, including accounting. Ideally, such systems also enable users to access real-time data from different information bases on all aspects of the business. To enable such benefits, the adoption of ERP systems can require organisations to change their ways of working. This explains why ERP systems can be an important driver for business process re-engineering (Scapens and Jazayeri, 2003). There are studies which claim ERP systems have had an important impact on management accounting and accountants, while others only find moderate such impacts. Advocates of a significant impact of ERP systems on management accounting (e.g., Anastas, 1997; Edmondson et al., 2001; Fichman, 1992; Scapens and Jazayeri, 2003; Umble et al., 2003; Wilson, 1989) argue that ERP systems can support the integration of financial and management accounting data and processes, fostering a unified enterprise view of the business. Regarding the accounting profession, ERP systems may contribute towards the reduction of accounting personnel, they may enhance the role of management accountants, they may create new requirements for accountants and accounting systems and they can eliminate or change accounting routines. They also offer the possibility of online data access without the need to wait for periodic reports, may improve and standardise the flow of information, may offer more forward-looking information and may generally decrease the cost of information. Caglio (2003) suggests that these various impacts of ERP systems on management accounting can be traced back to three structural effects of ERP systems on management: a higher degree of standardisation of practices, a stronger need for integration and inter-functional collaboration and a more prominent role of the accounting department in the management of the information technology system (Caglio, 2003).

Such views of a significant impact of ERP systems on management accounting contrast with other studies which conclude that ERP systems have only little (immediate) impact on management accounting, partly due to the long time needed to fully implement them. In consequence, the impacts arising from ERP systems may be slow to emerge. Such introductions of ERP systems may also come with considerable complexity and the need to adapt the ERP systems to different departments, the need to transfer and integrate information from various prior systems and organisational actors' resistance to change. While all these issues may be challenging for management accountants, studies arguing for only limited impacts of ERP systems on management accountants find that such systems do not change, but only reinforce existing management accounting routines. They conclude that ERP systems may facilitate a change in the way management accounting routines are performed, but not in the underlying nature of these routines (Granlund and Malmi, 2002; Maccarone, 2000; Booth et al., 2000).

As indicated earlier, we obviously do not aim to assess any relation between ERP systems and management accounting, but the previously noted contemporary literature will be drawn upon for our historical study on the introduction of typewriters as an early form of technological innovation in management accounting.

Archival sources

Our research is based on records from the Guinness archive. These archival records generally extend from 1759 to date, with a 30-year hold on document release. The archive holds more detailed records from Guinness' listing on the stock market from 1886 on. We chose Guinness as a case example, as a series of recent studies (e.g., Hiebl et al., 2015; Martínez Franco et al., 2017; Quinn, 2014; Quinn and Jackson, 2014) shows that the Guinness archive covers detailed internal accounting records. Most importantly here, there is also an array of records covering the period of the introduction of Smith Premier accounting machines around 1928–1929.

After initial contacts with the archivist, we were granted access to the archive and with the help of the archivist we searched for documents related to the introduction of Smith Premier accounting machines. In Table 1.1, we present a summary of the archival records that emerged as relevant from this search. We grouped these records into three clusters: (1) documents related to ordering Smith Premier accounting machines, (2) documents related to ordering supplies in connection with the accounting machines and (3) documents related to instructions to ledger-keepers. All the archival records were examined in detail and digitally photographed for ease of analysis.

Generally, the quality of archival documents can be assessed by four criteria: authenticity, credibility, representativeness and meaning (Scott, 1990). As argued by Quinn and Jackson (2014), the archival sources at Guinness comply with

Table 1.1 Archival records related to the introduction of Smith Premier accounting machines at Guinness

Archival Classification	*Brief Description*
Ordering of Smith Premier accounting machines	Records of orders of Smith Premier accounting machines, letters between Guinness and the Smith Premier company requesting changes in machines and stock count.
Ordering of supplies in connection with accounting machines	Records of orders of steel cabinets, chairs, boxes, envelopes, ledger cards, account forms, etc., in connection with accounting machines, statements for use in stock count.
Instructions to ledger-keepers	Files of instructions from the chief accountant to ledger-keepers about the use of the Smith Premier accounting machines, the established period of accounting information, the information format, statement examples of customers and instructions about the implementation of Smith Premier accounting machines in new stores of different districts.

all these criteria, and this applies to our study as well. First, all documents were examined locally at the archive, which grants them authenticity. Second, the records seem credible because they consist of written internal reports, orders, instructions, memoranda and other documents from the Accountant's Department. Third, while we cannot be sure that these records represent the introduction of accounting machines at other firms at this time, we know from related research that the accounting operations at Guinness in the first half of the 20th century can be regarded as typical of this time in history (Hiebl et al., 2015; Quinn and Jackson, 2014). We thus suggest that our findings are representative of the introduction of technological innovation in management accounting in the first half of the 20th century. Finally, the documents examined contained cross-references to other documents and were clearly filed and typed. They thus carried excellent comprehensibility and comply with Scott's (1990) requirement for meaning.

The introduction of Smith Premier accounting machines at Guinness

Company and technological background

Arthur Guinness started to brew ale in Dublin in 1759 with £100 he inherited. He then signed a 9,000-year lease for the St. James's Gate Brewery (Lynch and Vaizey, 1960). The first export of ale to England occurred in 1769, which marks the start of highly successful exporting activities, which today span most countries worldwide. In 1799, Arthur Guinness ceased to brew ale, and instead he focused on improving the brew of his popular black beer "porter". Guinness continued to grow its global market share and in 1886 was listed on the London Stock Exchange (Quinn and Jackson, 2014).

It was around this time, more precisely in 1872, that the first mass-produced typewriter was introduced. It was designed by Christopher Latham Sholes, who worked for the Remington Typewriter Company. The typewriter quickly gained popularity, and from 1889 onwards many typewriter manufacturers appeared, among them the Smith Premier Company. The Smith Premier typewriter appeared in 1890. Key characteristics of this typewriter were "its relief of cattails and flowers and the columns casting into the sides of the machine. Instead of the levers used on earlier machines, this machine was designed with cranks and rods that could be easily adjusted for optimum control" (Early Office Museum, 2017). A second model, the SP2, appeared in 1895. Starting with the SP3 model in 1901, the machine had a total of 84 keys (the SP1 and 2 had 76 keys each) and:

> was available in different carriage widths on the models 4, 5 and 6. In 1908, Smith Premier launched the SP10, the only full-keyboard front strike typewriter ever built. The SP10 was the last of the "real" Smith Premiers. After

> the demise of the company, the brand name was bought by the Remington Typewriter Company, which continued to launch regular office machines and portables with the name Smith Premier.
>
> (The Typewriter Database, 2017)

Until 1940, when Smith Premier production ended, four more models were manufactured (models 30, 40, 50 and 60). The last model – the Smith Premier Typewriter No. 60 "C" – was acquired by Guinness in 1928.[3]

Archival records findings

The Smith Premier accounting machines were introduced to the Accountant's Department at Guinness in 1929. Our findings indicate that this form of technological change was mainly driven by Walter Phillips, the chief accountant of the time. According to Hiebl et al. (2015), Phillips was the chief accountant of Guinness from 1919 to 1938. There is no evidence that Phillips had any professional training qualification, and indeed Martínez Franco et al. (2017) indicate that chief accountants at Guinness fulfilled their roles by "learning on the job" – in particular learning from their predecessors. In the case of Walter Philipps, this was learning from his predecessor J. A. Hayes and serving as deputy chief accountant to Hayes. So, while Philipps had little external training, some literature describes him as an "expert accountant", whose technological contribution marked a new stage in the Accountant's Department of the company (Dennison and MacDonagh, 1998; Hiebl et al., 2015).

From our archival findings, November 13, 1928, marks the first time the Smith Premier Company contacted Walter Phillips. The company thanked Phillips for visiting their stand at a business exhibition the same day and, as promised, enclosed a specimen of a ledger and statement prepared simultaneously on the Smith Premier Ledger Posting Machine. They also indicated to be pleased to call before the end of the week to more fully explain the details of the system as applied to his own work. Three days later, Phillips granted them a meeting and the same day received a quotation for a Smith Premier accounting machine. The cost of the No. 60 "C" Cross Accounting Machine was £212/19/11.[4] It was characterised by a writing length of 12½ inches and fitted with electrical equipment, quick insertion lever, star proof of clearance, palm tabulator and tabulating keys and oblique figures. Furthermore, the machine was equipped with one to eight wheel vertical sterling totalisers with a capacity of printing numbers up to £9,999/19/11 in the debit column; one to nine wheel vertical sterling totalisers with a capacity of printing numbers up to £9,999/19/11 in the credit column; and three dummy totalisers and one to nine wheel vertical sterling totalisers with a capacity of printing numbers up to £9,999/19/11 in the debit and credit balances. The Smith Premier Company indicated the training of operators would be undertaken by them until the operators were satisfied that they were fully competent on the machines and the system. According to Smith Premier Company letters found in the Guinness archive, this was a usual procedure when these machines were installed at that time. The Smith Premier Company also informed Phillips that the machine came with a guarantee for 12 months for full up-keep and repair, and after that period a maintenance contract could be entered for "a small cost per annum". In November 1928, Phillips asked for some potential adaptations to the machines and finally, at the end of the next month, Phillips requested permission to borrow one of their accounting machines to give it a thorough trial under normal working conditions. In the archival records, Phillips signalled that he was convinced that the machines would save a good deal of time when the staff had got familiar with them because, in particular, no separate staff for the actual writing of accounts would be needed and the balancing of the ledgers would be facilitated. For three months, the accounting staff of Guinness tested and worked with the Smith Premier machine. Finally, on March 21, 1929, Phillips ordered two more machines for trial. He confirmed, judging from their experience, it would be wise to adopt this method of keeping their ledgers and they would require a considerable number of machines. At the same time, he argued that it was expedient to go slowly in the matter, since the transition from the old methods to the new could not be effected in a hurry.

In the initial trial runs, there were three loaned machines at the Accountant's Department for a total of almost four months. By April 1929, Phillips seemed to be fully convinced of the usefulness of the machines. On April 16, 1929, Phillips got board permission to pay for the trial machines and he also ordered two more machines. In that order, he informed the Smith Premier Company that it would be necessary to purchase a good many more of these machines before the installation could be regarded as complete. And so it was: in less than a year, the Accountant's Department of Guinness had installed a total of 37 machines. Table 1.2 details this ramp-up of Smith Premier accounting machines in operation at Guinness' Accountant's Department. We found a large order of 20 machines in June 1929. This exceptionally large order can be explained by a 10 percent discount offered by the Smith Premier Company. At the same time, the archival records suggest that it seemed hard for Philipps to accurately

Table 1.2 Ordering of Smith Premier accounting machines at Guinness (1928–1929)

Date	*Newly ordered machines*	*Total machines in operation*
December 21, 1928	1	1
March 6, 1929	2	3
April 16, 1929	2	5
May 13, 1929	3	8
June 20, 1929	4	12
June 25, 1929	20	32
October 17, 1929	4	36
November 14, 1929	1	37

estimate the quantity of work that each machine would be capable of doing. This may explain – besides aiming for a smooth transition, as indicated earlier – why Phillips did not order all the machines at once but approached the eventual number of machines needed step-by-step over 1929.

While the introduction of Smith Premier accounting machines spanned all of 1929, there were quite immediate effects. The number of machines introduced in the Accountant's Department increased; however, the Accountant's Department staff numbers decreased. This decline was also noted by Hiebl et al. (2015), who hinted that the decrease by 11 people (from 61 to 50) at the Accountant's Department from 1929 to 1931 may be due to the introduction of Smith Premier accounting machines. This relatively large reduction in headcount can also be explained by the large amount of paper to be printed by the Accountant's Department. In 1929, all Guinness departments required 1,152 bound ledgers from the Printing Department for the coming year, of which 972 were for direct use by the Accountant's Department. So it seems as if the largest impact by the introduction of typewriters could be observed at the Accountant's Department, since this department accounted for the vast majority of ledgers to be printed.

Besides orders for Smith Premier machines, orders were also made for the purchase of accessories, such as steel cabinets, chairs, boxes, envelopes, ledger cards and account forms. From the archival records, it becomes obvious that tests were carried out and changes were requested to adapt the format to the needs of the work procedures, the required information and the accounting machines. Characteristics such as texture, font size and letters were adapted to the ledger cards, envelopes and account forms. Also, different colours were set to differentiate accounting information for different districts. Boxes were supplied for holding ledger cards of different measures, and steel cabinets were installed to save the machines with locks or keys. These changes following the introduction of Smith Premier accounting machines signal that this form of technological innovation in management accounting not just had an effect on the staff members (in terms of reduced staff members) but also on the additional materials which were part of the accounting routines at Guinness of that time.

These changes in routines and procedures in the Accountant's Department in order to adapt to the use of new technologies and take advantage of them also directly materialised in the archival records analysed. We found letters, memos and reports that contained numerous instructions from Phillips to the ledger-keepers. The ledger-keepers were given instructions on how to calculate the basis for discounts on customer purchases with the help of the Smith Premier machines. It was recommended to rely on standard price rates rather than on the cash value paid for beer, as the difference between the two hardly affected the final results, and therefore customers would not appreciate the extra detail of information. The accounting clerks also received instructions on the frequency of sending accounting information to customers. In this case, we can directly see the effect of the machines on the outputs of the Accountant's Department. In March 1929, Phillips proposed sending out the balances to customers on a *monthly* basis, regardless of whether the level of activity with each customer was high or low. Before this time, customer balances were sent out only when a minimum activity level with the customer was surpassed and, if not, were sent out only every three months. Since the machines now allowed for an automatic calculation of the customer balances with little effort by the Accountant's Department, the new monthly frequency of sending out customer balances was adopted – although this action resulted in some increased costs for envelopes and postage. The majority of the departments expected that the customers would appreciate the receipt of such information on a monthly basis. In addition, the availability of monthly balances would provide better and more recent information in cases of customer doubts regarding the correctness of the numbers. At the end of March 1929, a total of 770 accounts of customer balances were sent out, and from this date, the balances were sent out every month. The individual balances were accompanied by an introductory text whose standardisation indicates the automatic nature of the production of these letters:

> The balance of your account at the end of the period for which this Statement is furnished is the last item shown in the Balance column. If shown in black, the amount is due by you (debit); if in red the amount is due to you (credit). Any beer ordered but not dispatched before the end of the period will be charged in the next Statement.

In this context, a requirement that was agreed to ensure the correct functioning of the machines was that accountants must have all the documentation available at the end of the first business day of the month. This would ensure that they could check the records in the different accounting books that the stock of beer was not fictitious. To do this, following the introduction of the Smith Premier machines, they established that the days of the month included in Table 1.3 must be respected to update the quantities in the respective books.

The archival records show that this new procedure resulted in complaints from some other departments, who argued that they could not meet the deadlines, as they were working with customers from 50 different countries, with half of them having credits granted, and that they needed to wait until the last day of the month to make the records. The chief accountant became aware of the situation and consequently allowed the records to be made no later than between the first and second day of the subsequent month. In addition to these

Table 1.3 Deadlines for sending out accounting information at Guinness in 1929

Department	*Deadline*
Secretary Department Journal	12 noon penultimate working day of the month
Cask Department	12 noon penultimate working day of the month
Cash Books	First day of the month
Emergency Journal	The day before penultimate working day of the month
Charges Keeper	Last two days of the month

automated monthly balances, checks of discount allowances could be automated, thanks to the Smith Premier accounting machines. This automation enabled the Audit Department to omit their manual checking of the discount allowances. The machines gave them a check of the total discount allowed. The records indicate that both the auditor and the chief accountant agreed and recognised the advantage of the extra hours saved with this change. During the implementation period of the machines, the archival records also indicate that not only the accountants at Guinness headquarters but also the stores in the different districts incorporated the machines, albeit only in a gradual process. They, too, received detailed instructions on the changes of procedures and routines by the Accountant's Department. Although we could observe from the archival records how some work in the Accountant's Department was automated due to the use of new technology, there were cases in which errors were discovered in the calculation of customer balances. Consequently, the chief accountant gave instructions on how to inform the customers when an error was discovered beyond the monthly deadlines and how their balance would be corrected in the following statement.

To summarise, we can identify various effects on the accountants' work at Guinness following the introduction of Smith Premier accounting machines. There were mainly time savings and staff and cost reductions due to the automation of accounting tasks. In addition, thanks to automation, an opportunity arose to provide customers with periodic information on their balances on a more regular basis. The Smith Premier accounting machines also provided some benefits for other actors, such as auditors, as they could rely upon the automated calculation of total discounts allowed to customers instead of performing manual checks. Of course, these benefits did not come without a cost. Besides the costs for the machines, there was also the need to adapt various other working material to the needs of the new machines. In addition, the accountants needed additional training by external experts on the functioning of the accounting machines. This applied not just to the Accountant's Department but also to store clerks, who received detailed instructions on how to operate the new machines from the Accountant's Department.

Discussion and concluding comments

This chapter sought to analyse the effects of technological change on management accounting in the brewing industry from a historical perspective. From the archival records of Guinness, we can conclude that the introduction of the Smith Premier accounting machines in 1929 had several effects on the Accountant's Department of Guinness. When comparing our historical case with findings from the contemporary literature – which is mainly focused on the effects of ERP systems on management accounting – we can observe similarities, but also some differences.

First, similar to the introduction of ERP systems (Anastas, 1997; Edmondson et al., 2001; Fichman, 1992; Scapens and Jazayeri, 2003; Umble et al., 2003;

Wilson, 1989), the introduction of Smith Premier accounting machines at Guinness resulted in quite substantial changes to the work of accountants. Some routines were eliminated, such as the audit control on discounts. We can also identify that customers could now get information on a monthly, standardised and automatic basis, which was an important step forward at that time. This automation seemed to lead to a reduction of staff and to lower information costs. This reduction in staff numbers seems to be different from ERP adoptions discussed in the more contemporary literature, suggesting that automation and time savings thanks to ERP systems led accountants to free up time for more "value-adding" tasks such as advising management (e.g., Gärtner et al., 2013). Thus, despite the important role of the chief accountant (see later), we can argue that some of the accounting clerks in the 1920s performed repetitive tasks that could be replaced by machines. Our evidence suggests that freeing up their time using Smith Premier machines did not result in them changing to other tasks – instead they were dismissed. Thus, it seems as if accountants nowadays are better equipped to master technological change since they can revert to other, potentially more value-adding tasks than accountants in the 1920s.

Similar to contemporary studies on ERP system adoption, we can identify problems or disadvantages that come with technological change in accounting (Booth et al., 2000; Granlund and Malmi, 2002; Maccarone, 2000). For instance, this chapter underpins the complexity of the implementation and adaptation of different staff members and departments to new technologies, the need to educate users and initial technical problems associated with technological change. However, our findings suggest that Guinness dealt successfully with these challenges. It is not entirely clear from the archival records what the driver of this change was. The brewing sector potentially was a good place to use such technology due to the large numbers of comparable customers and transactions, and thus the inherent opportunity for standardisation and automation. Moreover, the context of the Economic War in Ireland and the Great Depression gave rise to the need for cost reductions. Finally, the enthusiasm of Phillips and his active role involved in ensuring that the implementation of these machines turned out successful, and that all operators received adequate training, could be another key success factor.

We also observed that implementation was not immediate, but the process was gradual and spread over more than one year. From our findings, it seems as if the department needed time to adapt to the machines for an effective use and, first of all, needed an initial trial to check the suitability of the new technology for their requirements. During this implementation process, the machines were also adapted to the working procedures so that they could be used as effectively as possible. In a contemporary study on the adoption of ERP systems, Granlund and Malmi (2002) argued that it is organisational practices that are changed to fit new technology, not vice versa. In Guinness, we can observe that not only were the practices changed to fit the new machines, but also the machines were somewhat adapted to fit the needs of the Accountant's Department. Therefore, our case suggests that this relationship is not necessarily one-directional, at least historically.

When further comparing our work here with the contemporary literature on ERP systems and accounting, the gradual implementation of the accounting machines at Guinness happened over time, as noted earlier, and thus not in a "big-bang" way sometimes suggested for the introduction of ERP systems (e.g. Gargeya and Brady, 2005; O'Leary, 2000). The gradual process at Guinness can thus be much better compared to so-called "gradual phase-in" ERP system adoptions (e.g., Abdinnour-Helm et al., 2003; Hiebl et al., 2017). The chapter also highlights that this technological change was very much driven by the chief accountant at Guinness. This indicates that it is not only nowadays that chief financial officers and other accounting leadership personnel – who can well be compared to the position of the chief accountant at Guinness in the 1920s (cf. Martínez Franco et al., 2017) – exert decisive influence on technological choices (Hiebl et al., 2017). This reinforces some recent findings in the literature that in the earlier parts of the 20th century, leading accountants were not just "bean counters" but were very much engaged in matters of value-adding activities and organisational change more generally (Hiebl et al., 2015; Martínez Franco et al., 2017).

Our study has some limitations and points to some future research needs. First, the Guinness archive represents a single case study, and our results may not be readily generalisable to other firms of that time. Second, we focussed on a time frame which is virtually devoid of accounting regulation, in comparison with today. Third, we could not observe actual accounting practices in real time and during an extended period, a research approach that yields rich insights; we "just" analysed artefacts from an archive and from a very specific and limited time period, which could possibly not represent a complete picture of the accounting practices, both at that particular time and during a more extended period. It would thus be advisable to study a longer time frame to complete our findings and the evolution of the process over time. Finally, it would, of course, be very interesting to compare this study with the introduction of the same or a similar technology in other companies at the same time in history.

To finish, we believe that much can be learned from historical studies on technological change in accounting, such as our work, that highlights that the challenges and obstacles to be overcome were similar to those faced in contemporary accounting-related technological change. The benefit of historical accounts, however, is that the underlying change can likely be analysed more holistically, as the aftermath of such change should already be well known and/or recorded. We therefore argue that the analysis of historical technological accounting change is not only of value to a more complete understanding of accounting phenomena but may also provide valuable hints for technological change in contemporary organisations' accounting processes.

Notes

1 Recently there have been calls for research on the effects of more recent technological change such as digitalisation (e.g., Quattrone, 2016) or big data (e.g., Gärtner and Hiebl, 2018) on management accounting.

2 Precursors of ERP systems were Manufacturing Resource Planning (MRP) systems, which sought to maximise efficiency in the timing of raw material orders and in the scheduling of machining and assembly in the manufacturing process (Bhimani and Bromwich, 2009). For more detailed information on the development of these systems, refer to Kumar and Meade (2002) who reviewed contemporary developments in planning systems and how ERP emerged.
3 Photographs of some of these typewriters can be seen at http://typewriterdatabase.com/smithpremier.98.typewriter-serial-number-database.
4 To put this cost into perspective, the annual salary of clerks in the Accountant's Department at Guinness ranged from £170 to £540 around the time investigated in this chapter (Hiebl et al., 2015). So the Smith Premier accounting machines can be considered costly, since their cost is roughly comparable to an average clerk's annual salary at that time.

References

Primary sources

Archive of Arthur Guinness, Son and Company Ltd, St. James's Gate, Dublin, Ireland.

Files utilised:

Instructions to ledger-keepers – Ref GDB/FN01/0001.78.3
Ordering of Smith Premier accounting machines – Ref GDB/FN01/0001.78.1
Ordering of supplies in connection with accounting machines – Ref GDB/FN01/0001.78.2

Secondary sources

Abdinnour-Helm, S., Lengnick-Hall, M. L. and Lengnick-Hall, C. A. (2003). Pre-implementation attitudes and organisational readiness for implementing an enterprise resource planning system. *European Journal of Operational Research*, 146(2), pp. 258–273.

Allaire, Y. and Firsirotu, M. E. (1984). Theories of organisational culture. *Organization Studies*, 5(3), pp. 193–226.

Anastas, M. (1997). The changing world of management accounting and financial management. *Strategic Finance*, 79(4), p. 48.

Applegate, L. M. (1996). *Managing in an Information Age*. Cambridge, MA: Harvard Business School Press.

Bhimani, A. and Bromwich, M. (2009). *Management Accounting: Retrospect and Prospect*. Oxford: Elsevier.

Bonin, H. (2004). The development of accounting machines in French banks from the 1920s to the 1960s. *Accounting, Business & Financial History*, 14(3), pp. 257–276.

Booth, P., Matolcsy, Z. and Wieder, B. (2000). The impacts of enterprise resource planning systems on accounting practice – The Australian experience. *Australian Accounting Review*, 10(22), pp. 4–18.

Caglio, A. (2003). Enterprise resource planning systems and accountants: Towards hybridization? *European Accounting Review*, 12(1), pp. 123–153.

Davis, L. E. and Taylor, J. C. (1986). Technology, organisation and job structure. In: R. Dubin, ed., *Handbook of Work, Organization and Society*. Chicago: McNally, pp. 379–419.

Dennison, S. R. and MacDonagh, O. (1998). *Guinness 1886–1939: From Incorporation to the Second World War*. Dublin: Stylus Publishing.

Early Office Museum (2017). *Antique Special Purpose Typewriters*. Available at: www.officemuseum.com/typewriters_office_special.htm [Accessed 19th July 2017].

Edmondson, A. C., Bohmer, R. M. and Pisano, G. P. (2001). Disrupted routines: Team learning and new technology implementation in hospitals. *Administrative Science Quarterly*, 46(4), pp. 685–716.

Fichman, R. G. (1992). Information technology diffusion: A review of empirical research. *ICIS Proceedings*, Association of Information Systems, Massachusetts Institute of Technology, pp. 195–206.

Gargeya, V. B. and Brady, C. (2005). Success and failure factors of adopting SAP in ERP system implementation. *Business Process Management Journal*, 11(5), pp. 501–516.

Gärtner, B., Feldbauer-Durstmüller, B. and Duller, C. (2013). Changes in the role of management accountants following the introduction of ERP systems. *European Journal of Management*, 13(3), pp. 33–44.

Gärtner, B. and Hiebl, M. R. W. (2018). Issues with big data. In: M. Quinn and E. Strauß, eds. *The Routledge Companion to Accounting Information Systems*. New York: Routledge, pp. 161–172.

Granlund, M. and Lukka, K. (1998). Towards increasing business orientation: Finnish management accountants in a changing cultural context. *Management Accounting Research*, 9(2), pp. 185–211.

Granlund, M. and Malmi, T. (2002). Moderate impact of ERPS on management accounting: A lag or permanent outcome? *Management Accounting Research*, 13(3), pp. 299–321.

Hiebl, M. R. W., Gärtner, B. and Duller, C. (2017). Chief Financial Officer (CFO) characteristics and ERP system adoption: An upper-echelons perspective. *Journal of Accounting and Organizational Change*, 13(1), pp. 85–111.

Hiebl, M. R. W., Quinn, M. and Martínez Franco, C. (2015). An analysis of the role of a chief accountant at Guinness c. 1920–1940. *Accounting History Review*, 25(2), pp. 145–165.

Hiltz, S. R. and Johnson, K. (1990). User satisfaction with computer-mediated communication systems. *Management Science*, 36(6), pp. 739–764.

Johnson, H. T. (2002). A former management accountant reflects on his journey through the world of cost management. *Accounting History*, 7(1), pp. 9–21.

Kristandl, G. and Quinn, M. (2017). Internal accounting practices at Whitbread and Company c.1890–1925. *Accounting History*, 23(1/2), pp. 206–230.

Kumar, S. and Meade, D. (2002). Has MRP run its course? A review of contemporary developments in planning systems. *Industrial Management and Data System*, 102(8), pp. 453–462.

Leonard-Barton, D. and Deschamps, I. (1988). Managerial influence in the implementation of new technology. *Management Science*, 34(10), pp. 1252–1265.

Lynch, P. and Vaizey, J. (1960). *Guinness's Brewery in the Economy: 1789–1856*. Cambridge: Cambridge University Press.

Maccarone, P. (2000). The impact of ERPs on management accounting and control systems and the changing role of controllers. In: *23rd Conference of the EAA*, Munich, pp. 29–31.

Martínez Franco, C., Feeney, O., Quinn, M. and Hiebl, M. R. W. (2017). Position practices of the present-day CFO: A reflection on historic roles at Guinness, 1920–1945. *Revista de Contabilidad*, 20(1), pp. 55–62.

Meek, V. L. (1988). Organizational culture: Origins and weaknesses. *Organization Studies*, 9(4), pp. 453–473.

Nelson, R. R. and Winter, S. G. (1982). *An Evolutionary Theory of Economic Change*. Cambridge, MA: Harvard Business School Press.

Noble, D. F. (1984). *Forces of Production: A Social History of Industrial Automation*. New Brusnwick: Transaction Publishers.

O'Leary, D. E. (2000). *Enterprise Resource Planning Systems: Systems, Life Cycle, Electronic Commerce, and Risk*. Cambridge: Cambridge University Press.

Orlikowski, W. J. (1993). CASE tools as organizational change: Investigating incremental and radical changes in systems development. *MIS Quarterly*, 17(3), pp. 309–340.

Park, H., Ribière, V. and Schulte Jr., W. D. (2004). Critical attributes of organizational culture that promote knowledge management technology implementation success. *Journal of Knowledge Management*, 8(3), pp. 106–117.

Quattrone, P. (2016). Management accounting goes digital: Will the move make it wiser? *Management Accounting Research*, 31, pp. 118–122.

Quinn, M. (2014). Stability and change in management accounting over time. A century or so of evidence from Guinness. *Management Accounting Research*, 25(1), pp. 76–92.

Quinn, M. and Jackson, W. J. (2014). Accounting for war risk costs: Management accounting change at Guinness during the First World War. *Accounting History Review*, 24(2–3), pp. 191–209.

Scapens, R. W. and Jazayeri, M. (2003). ERP systems and management accounting change: Opportunities or impacts? A research note. *European Accounting Review*, 12(1), pp. 201–233.

Schneider, B. (2000). The psychological life of organizations. In: N. M. Ashkanasy, C. P. Wilderom and M. F. Peterson, eds. *Handbook of Organizational Culture and Climate*. Thousand Oaks: Sage Press, pp. 17–21.

Scott, J. (1990). *A Matter of Record: Documentary Sources in Social Research*. Cambridge: Polity Press.

Szulanski, G. (2000). The process of knowledge transfer: A diachronic analysis of stickiness. *Organizational Behavior and Human Decision Processes*, 82(1), pp. 9–27.

The Typewriter Database (2017). *Smith Premier Typewriter*. Available at: http://typewriterdatabase.com/smithpremier.98.typewriter-serial-number-database [Accessed 1st June 2017].

Umble, E. J., Haft, R. R. and Umble, M. M. (2003). Enterprise resource planning: Implementation procedures and critical success factors. *European Journal of Operational Research*, 146(2), pp. 241–257.

Wilson, T. D. (1989). The implementation of information system strategies in UK companies: Aims and barriers to success. *International Journal of Information Management*, 9(4), pp. 245–258.

Wootton, C. W. and Kemmerer, B. E. (2007). The emergence of mechanical accounting in the US, 1880–1930. *Accounting Historians Journal*, 34(1), pp. 91–124.

Wynne, B. (1988). Unruly technology: Practical rules, impractical discourses and public understanding. *Social Studies of Science*, 18(1), pp. 147–167.

2 Optimism in annual reports

The case of a Spanish brewery

Alonso Moreno

Introduction

Impression management tries to explain managers' self-serving behaviour of disclosure in an opportunistic attitude (Neu, 1991; Merkl-Davies and Brennan, 2007). The annual report has been traditionally considered one of the main channels used by companies to communicate with stakeholders (Courtis, 1987; Campbell et al., 2006). It consists of both quantitative and narrative information. This latter information is considered to attract wider readership than financial figures, as users are usually interested in forming an opinion about the general situation of the company and its performance (Bartlett and Chandler, 1997). Therefore, narrative information can offer an avenue to companies towards impression management. Impression management can happen if managers offer an optimistic view of the company which is distinct from actual performance. Most extant literature has found that annual reports are overwhelmingly positive, irrespective of performance (Hildebrandt and Snyder, 1981; Gibbins et al., 1990). Although corporate reports usually increase in negative content with bad performance, a positive net tone constantly predominates (Abrahamson and Park, 1994; Merkl-Davies et al., 2011).

The analysis of historical narrative information disclosed by companies can provide more evidence about the evolution and interpretation of these practices, apart from the standardization of such narrative. Historical records provide a longitudinal character that can give more depth to data collected by other means (Cobbin et al., 2013). Longitudinal studies allow one to analyse changes in disclosure over time (Pettigrew, 1990; Burns, 2000). Impression management has not been usually analysed over time. Previous literature has typically analysed differences between the best- and the worst-performing companies in a single period (Courtis, 1998; Clatworthy and Jones, 2006). This chapter analyses the historical narrative information disclosed by a Spanish brewery, *El Alcázar*, over the period 1928–1992, in order to determine if the tone of the corporate reports is related to profitability. Different variables that may affect disclosures are controlled. Specifically, the source of this research is the management report, a non-standardized document issued as part of the annual report, consisting of narrative information that describes the situation and the most important events of the company for the year.

El Alcázar was a medium-sized public limited founded in Jaén (Andalucía) in 1928 (Moreno, 2011). Jaén was at that time an underdeveloped and mainly agricultural region. For that reason, the company was important for its environment from its founding. During the decade 1925–1935, only 77 companies were constituted in the province. *El Alcázar* accounted for 8.2% of the total share capital raised (Hernández Armenteros, 1999). In 1981, the gross value-added of the company accounted for 2.9% of provincial gross domestic product (GDP) in the industrial sector (El Alcázar, 1984; Moreno and Cámara, 2014). In 1990, with nearly 500 direct employees and $60 million in sales, it was among the largest companies in Jaén according to both criteria (AEPJ, 1993; Andalucía Económica, 1991, 1992). By then, it had also become the seventh-largest Spanish brewery measured by production volume (García Ruiz and Laguna Roldán, 1999; Moreno and Cámara, 2016). Finally, in 1993, after different direct and indirect corporate operations, the company was legally dissolved, although the brand still exists. Both Spain in general and the brewing sector in particular – with the latter shadowing the general development of the country – experienced great changes during the research period. The country experienced a range of political regimes, including a dictatorship, a republic, civil war, dictatorship (again), democracy and then joining the European Economic Community (EEC). During this period, beer evolved from a niche to a mass-market product (Moreno and Cámara, 2016).

The rest of the chapter is organized as follows. The next section details an impression management framework and raises the research hypotheses on tone and profitability. The context of the research is then given, consisting of a brief history of Spain and the brewing sector during the analysis period, and also providing information about the studied brewery. The methodology section provides information about the documentary sources, the software used to compute tone and the research design. Next, the results of the multiple regression model are offered, which is followed by some conclusions and additional discussion about impression management.

Framework

Previous literature has found that the tone of annual reports is consistently positive, independent of good or bad performance (Hildebrandt and Snyder, 1981; Gibbins et al., 1990; Merkl-Davies et al., 2011). This behaviour could be related with the psychological communication tendency to use more positive words than negative words (Boucher and Osgood, 1969), known as the 'Pollyanna hypothesis'. In a context of corporate reports aimed at providing useful information to stakeholders – mainly shareholders – to make decisions, this practice can be considered impression management. Alternatively, some research has found that tone can have predictive power. Davis et al. (2012) suggest that managers use tone, at least to some extent, to communicate predictive information in earnings press releases and that stakeholders consider it, at least in part, to be a credible signal despite the potential for managers to behave opportunistically when selecting language. Patelli and Pedrini (2014) also found that optimistic tone is congruent with both past and future performance.

Net tone is composed of positive and negative language. In the case of positive language, in contrast to impression management, a sensible managerial behaviour would suggest a direct relationship between profitability and positive language. Under this approach, an increase (or decrease) in profitability should be followed by an increase (or decrease) in positive references (Clatworthy and Jones, 2003; Merkl-Davies et al., 2011). Otherwise, no or negative relationship between profitability and positive language could be considered impression management. Therefore, behaviour in line with impression management can be expressed as follows:

> H1: There is no or a negative relationship between profitability and positive language.

In the case of negative language, in contrast to an opportunistic behaviour, an incremental information perspective would suggest an inverse relationship between profitability and negative references. Thus, an increase (decrease) in profitability should be followed by a decrease (increase) in negative references. The evidence usually shows this behaviour in corporate reports. However, negative language is overwhelmingly a minority in relation to the positive language (Abrahamson and Park, 1994; Clatworthy and Jones, 2003; Merkl-Davies et al., 2011). In any case, and focusing only on negative language, no or positive relationship between profitability and negative language could be considered impression management. Therefore, a behaviour in line with impression management could be expressed as follows:

> H2: There is no or a positive relationship between profitability and negative language.

Apart from profitability, other different variables can influence tone. Previous literature that has studied different textual characteristics has also measured the possible effect of risk, size, changes in chairperson and changes in titles of documents, among other variables. Performance is directly associated with profitability and inversely with risk. Therefore, in line with impression management, the opposite directions argued for profitability would be argued for risk. Impression management would suggest no or a positive (negative) relationship between risk and positive (negative) references. With regard to size, the direction of its potential association with tone is unpredicted (Moreno et al., 2017). This is the same for the changes in title in the document under study. A change in title is usually a consequence of a major change in the annual report for different reasons, such as strategy, image or regulation, among others (Moreno et al., 2017), and therefore its impact on tone is unpredicted. In the case of the chairperson, extant research associates the use of positive language with a charismatic CEO

(Fanelli et al., 2009; Aerts and Yan, 2017). To the extent that the characteristics of the different managers of the company are beyond the scope of the present research, a specific tone direction for the different managers is also not predicted.

Context

El Alcázar was incorporated in 1928 through the acquisition of another smaller brewery, *El Lagarto*, legally operating from 1921. The company's share capital was provided originally by four family groups and remained quite stable until the 1960s, when two major 'outsider' shareholders entered the company (Courage, Barclay and Simonds in 1964 and *Corporación Industrial* – a *Banco Urquijo* company – in 1966). In 1985, in anticipation of Spain's entry into the EEC, *Cruzcampo*, a larger Spanish brewery, took over *El Alcázar*. After *Cruzcampo* was acquired by Guinness in 1991, most subsidiary companies of *Cruzcampo* legally disappeared in 1993, as was the case of *El Alcázar* (Moreno, 2011). Table 2.1 summarizes the most important events in the history of the company.

Table 2.1 Major events in the history of *El Alcázar*

Year	*Event*
1928	Constitution of *El Alcázar*
1936–1938	No Management Report (MR) is produced because of Spanish Civil War
1939	The company begins to amortize through the indirect method
1940	The beer association agrees upon uniform prices and conditions for the sale of beer
1940	The company begins to create accounting reserves
1949	The new maltery commences operations
1949	*Banco Español de Crédito* extends credit to the company, greatly increasing the level of liabilities
1956	Share capital increases from 3.5 million to 10 million pesetas
1959	Share capital increases from 10 million to 20 million pesetas
1961	Another brewery, *Cervecera Manchega*, is constituted by members of the board of directors
1961	The company relocates to a new factory
1962–1967	Successive issues increase share capital to 100 million pesetas over this time frame
1963	New vice general manager appointed (general manager, 1964; chair of the National Association of Breweries, 1982)
1963	The balance sheet and income statement are reformatted
1964	Courage becomes a shareholder (share capital after increase: 70 million pesetas; share: 14.29%)
1965	An accounting chart of the company was created in 1965
1965	The accounting section is restructured, including billings, deposit control and accounting and statistics

(Continued)

Table 2.1 (Continued)

Year	*Event*
1966	*Corporación Industrial* becomes a shareholder (share capital after increase: 77.8 million pesetas; share: 10%)
1966	The format of the MR is changed, becoming much more structured and comprehensive
1967	Workers form a mutual housing co-operative (100 houses)
1969	A new maltery begins production
1970	*Cervecera Manchega* merges with *El Alcázar*
1971	The format of the balance sheet is changed, with new divisions
1974	The format of the MR is reverted to a format similar to that used before 1966
1978	Commissions are appointed in the board of directors
1979	The company starts to diversify
1980	The administration stops intervening in the beer pricing system
1980	The company evaluates the possibility of being listed
1985	*Cruzcampo* takes over *El Alcázar*
1985	Five managing directors are appointed to the board of directors
1987	A new factory is opened
1991	Guinness takes over *Cruzcampo*
1993	All subsidiaries of *Cruzcampo* are merged into *Grupo Cruzcampo, SA*

Source: Adapted from Moreno (2011) and Moreno and Cámara (2014)

In the first third of the 20th century, the brewing and consumption of beer in Spain was concentrated in large cities. Beer was not very popular among the general population, and its consumption was quite seasonal (Trujillo García, 1989; Moreno and Cámara, 2016). Virtually coinciding with the constitution of *El Alcázar*, the economic, social and political situation of the country was worsening during the 1930s, which gave way to the Spanish Civil War (1936–1939). The effect of the war on different companies, including breweries, was dependent on its geographical area. Following typical Republican practice, many companies were placed in administration. This was the case of *El Alcázar*, although only in the last year of the war did production stop completely (Moreno and Cámara, 2014). For that reason, a lack of accounting information is found in this period. The management report from 1936 to 1938 and financial statements in 1938 were not produced (Moreno, 2011). However, the assets of the company were apparently not significantly damaged:

> During that period, the intervention committee did not constitute an unbeatable obstacle to the good wishes and noteworthy efforts of the [Managing Director] to manage the company's assets, and although he has been able neither to do everything he wished nor to avoid some actions which he was against, [he has got] a highly satisfactory result of

> the conservation and management of the forced operation of the factory since 18 July [1936].
>
> (Minutes of the Shareholder General Meeting, 26 April 1939, translation; Moreno, 2013)

A dictatorship was imposed after the Civil War. The first years of the autocratic regime were particularly difficult. People were divided, the economy weakened, infrastructure destroyed and the country isolated. Shortages and rationing made it difficult for people and companies to survive (Comellas, 1990). The lack of raw materials and consequent stagnation were the most remarkable facts of the brewery sector in the 1940s and 1950s. The regime also controlled matters related to products and pricing. In an attempt to try to alleviate this situation, *El Alcázar* installed its own malting operation in 1949 (Moreno and Cámara, 2014).

In 1959, Spain started to move away from autocracy. It accomplished economic stabilization and liberalization measures, and the regime reduced its intervention in the economy. It joined international organizations and increased relationships with foreign countries (Tamames Gómez, 2005). Coinciding with this opening of the economy, the brewery sector witnessed huge development. In the 1960s, beer production multiplied four-fold in Spain, whereas in Europe it increased by only one third. The Spanish expansion was favoured by the transformation from a rural to an urban society, the relative cheap price of beer and the growth and better distribution of income per capita (Trujillo García, 1989; Moreno and Cámara, 2016). By then, the company built a new factory and improved the management with more qualified staff, which led to advances in accounting, including more attention on costs (Moreno Aguayo, 2013; Moreno and Cámara, 2014).

In 1978, after the death of the dictator (Franco), Spain passed a liberal constitution and turned into a full-fledged democracy. In relation to the economy, the development of stabilization plans allowed the correction of macroeconomic imbalances and the modernization of fiscal and monetary instruments, which later led to the definitive elimination of control of beer prices by the government (Solbes Mira, 2005; Moreno, 2013). This system, together with an international inflation crisis, had been very harmful for breweries in the previous years. It also led to the first years of losses in *El Alcázar*. In 1986, Spain joined the EEC.[1] Increasing liberalization and extensive legislative reforms stimulated domestic and foreign investment. As a consequence, big multinationals entered the market and, after a process of concentration, the number of Spanish breweries reduced drastically (Trujillo García, 1987; Moreno and Cámara, 2014), as was the case of *El Alcázar*.

Methodology

The historical series of *El Alcázar*'s annual reports includes, along with quantitative statements, a document entitled *Memoria*. This document is in essence a management report, containing non-standardized narrative information describing the most important events of the company for the reporting period (Moreno and Casasola, 2016). This is a document usually prepared by medium-sized Spanish companies, quite similar to the president's letter/chairman's address prepared by larger companies. The management report – or *Memoria* – was compiled by the company management, provisionally approved by the board of directors and formally approved by the shareholders' general meeting. Although this document was not initially required by law, it was required by *El Alcázar*'s Articles of Association. It is not mentioned by Spanish law until the Companies Act of 1951, which included the duty to draw up an explanatory report, although it did not specify any minimum content. Only in 1989 did the reform of the Companies Act specify the minimum content to be included in the management report for the first time (Moreno and Cámara, 2016; Moreno and Casasola, 2016). The documentary series used in this chapter covers from the incorporation of the company (1928) to its legal extinction (1993). This chapter analyses longitudinally all the available management reports. This consists of 59 management reports. The reports for the years 1934, 1950 and 1983 were missing, and no reports were produced from 1936 to 1938 because of the Spanish Civil War. The source has been used in previous research: Moreno and Casasola (2016), along with data of another company, analysed the effect of profitability on readability evolution.

To analyse and count for positive and negative references, the LIWC[2] software was used. This software allocates words into one or more categories. We used the pre-defined categories in the software for both positive and negative references.[3] In the first case, the positive emotions (equivalent in Spanish to *love*, *nice*, *sweet*, etc.; 642 words or word stems) are recorded. In the second case, the negative emotions (*hurt*, *ugly*, *nasty*, etc.; 745 words or word stems) are taken into account. In both cases the occurrences were divided by the total number of words in the document in order to consider the relative values.

To test the real impact of profitability on tone, similar to Moreno and Casasola (2016), other variables with a possible influence on tone (risk, size, changes in general manager and changes in document titles) are also controlled for possible simultaneous effects. Therefore, a multiple regression model was developed. With the same database, Moreno and Casasola (2016) initially examined a variety of potential proxy measures for profitability and size. However, to avoid multi-collinearity problems, for profitability they finally selected return on assets (ROA), positive or negative net profit (PLNP) and increase or decrease in net profit from the previous year (IDNP); and for size, sales turnover (TURN). Risk was proxied by the leverage ratio (LEVE); different general managers were identified by dummy variables (GM_i); and different document titles, also accounted for by dummy variables ($TITL_i$), were controlled. In essence, this chapter reproduces the independent variables used by Moreno and Casasola (2016).[4] Table 2.2 shows the variables and proxy measures used in the analysis.

Table 2.2 Variables and proxy measures

Variables	*Proxy measure*	*Name*	*Definition*	*Transformation*
Positive refs.	LIWC 2007 category	POSI	Words of the category/ total words in document * 100	–
Negative refs.	LIWC 2007 category	NEGA	Words of the category/ total words in document * 100	–
Profitability size	Return on assets	ROA	Net profit/total assets * 100	–
	Net profit (+/–)	PLNP	0 = loss; 1 = profit	–
	Net profit (Δ/∇)	IDNP	0 = decreasing; 1 = increasing (compared to the previous year)	–
	Sales turnover	TURN	Sales turnover deflated using CPI[a] with base 1928 (millions pesetas)	Log 10
Risk	Leverage	LEVE	Total liabilities/total assets * 100	–
General manager title	GM	GM_i	Defined as one dummy for each different general manager	–
	different titles	$TITL_i$	Defined as one dummy for each different title of the report	–

a Consumer Price Index based on Maluquer de Motes (2013)

Results

Table 2.3 shows the summary distribution statistics for the variables used in the analysis. The average value for the ROA was 9.1%. The highest ROAs were reached within the period from 1951 to 1958. Only four years showed a negative ROA: 1975, 1976, 1977 and 1992. In relation to the variable PLNP, the company had losses in only four years (those mentioned earlier with regard to the negative ROAs). With regard to the variable IDNP, the company increased net profit in relation to the previous year in 66% of the cases. The average value of the leverage was 22%, and the highest values were found in the second half of the 1960s and from 1988 on. The average of the sales turnover (base 1928) was 8.39 million pesetas. This magnitude was steadily increasing over the period. In relation to the qualitative variables, five different general managers signed the management report (1928–1932; 1933–1961; 1962–1963; 1964–1991; 1992) and two different titles were identified (1928–1989: Report; 1990–1992: Management report).

Table 2.3 Summary distribution statistics

	N	*Mean*	*Std. Dev.*	*Minimum*	*Maximum*
POSI	59	2.70	0.75	1.22	4.54
NEGA	59	0.70	0.43	0.00	1.82
ROA	64	9.06	8.39	−4.75	36.78
PLNP	64	0.94	0.24	0.00	1.00
IDNP	64	0.66	0.48	0.00	1.00
LEVE	64	0.22	0.15	0.00	0.54
TURN[a]	64	8.39	9.73	0.19	39.01
GM_1	65	0.08	0.27	0.00	1.00
GM_2	65	0.45	0.50	0.00	1.00
GM_3	65	0.03	0.17	0.00	1.00
GM_4	65	0.43	0.50	0.00	1.00
GM_5	65	0.02	0.12	0.00	1.00
$TITL_1$	65	0.95	0.21	0.00	1.00
$TITL_2$	65	0.05	0.21	0.00	1.00

a Before transformation

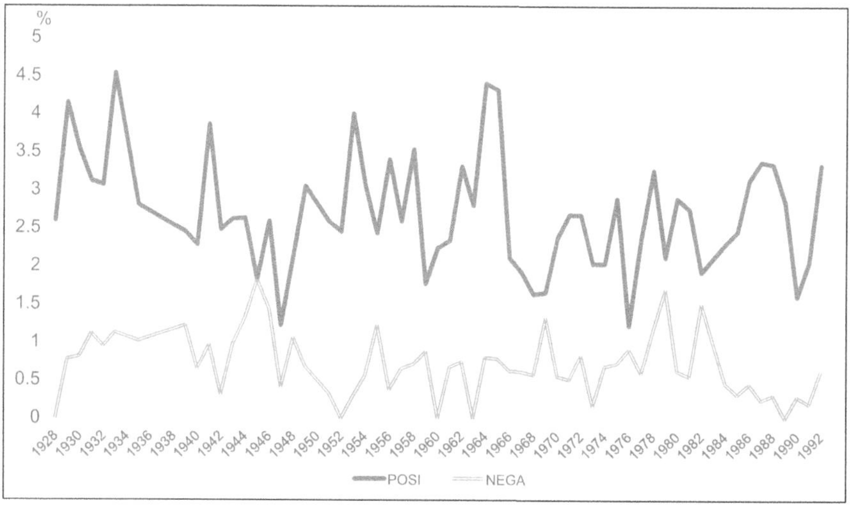

Figure 2.1 Evolution of positive and negative references (1928–1992)

Figure 2.1 shows the evolution of positive and negative references in *El Alcázar*'s management reports. The average of positive references was 2.7% and that of negative references was 0.7%. This implies that, on average, the positive content of the document was approximately four times higher than the negative content. There was no year with a net negative tone. In every year the net tone was positive, with the only exception of 1945, when the net tone was neutral. In no year were the positive references under 1.2%. However, there were no negative references at all in five years and in no year were they over 1.85%. These findings are in line with the Pollyanna hypothesis (Boucher and Osgood, 1969). The tone of the corporate reports is biased. In the years with losses (i.e. 1975, 1976, 1977 and 1992), reasonably the tone should have been negative in an attempt to provide incremental information. However, the tone remained permanently positive.

Table 2.4 shows the correlation coefficients between the variables. The values of the significant correlations are low, both for POSI and NEGA. In relation to POSI, the highest correlation with the quantitative variables is with LEVE (–0.243). The negative sign suggests an inverse relationship between POSI and LEVE, in which an increase in risk is associated with a decrease in positive references. This behaviour would be in line with an incremental information perspective and in contrast to impression management. The other significant correlation (among the quantitative variables) is with TURN (–0.207), also suggesting an inverse relationship between POSI and TURN. In the case of the qualitative variables, there is a direct association with GM_1 (0.278) and an inverse association with GM_4 (–0.216). In relation to NEGA, the highest correlation is with LEVE (–0.337). The sign of this association suggests an inverse relationship between NEGA and LEVE, in which an increase in risk is associated with a decrease in negative references. This is in contrast to incremental information and in line with impression management. There is also an inverse association with TURN (–0.282). The titles are also significantly correlated to the negative content.

For the multiple regression model, GM_1 and $TITL_1$ were dropped. In this case, when the simultaneous effect of different potential variables on tone are controlled, the previous variables proved significant in the univariate analysis do not emerge. Table 2.5 shows the result for both POSI and NEGA models. The POSI model is not significant (*p*-value: 0.302). It does not show any significant relationship between POSI and any independent variable. The results show that the positive tone of management reports is independent of profitability, risk, size, general managers or titles and, particularly, it does not depend on profitability (Hildebrandt and Snyder, 1981). The finding that there is no relationship between profitability and positive references reveals managers' self-serving behaviour, in line with impression management, and therefore H1 is supported (Merkl-Davies et al., 2011).

The situation for the NEGA model is different. This model is significant at 10% and adjusted R^2 is 0.123. There is only one significant independent variable (at a 10% significance level): ROA (–0.017). A decrease in ROA implies an increase in the negative references. Therefore, this variable has a certain ability to explain, moderately, the changes in the negative content of the management reports, and the negative sign of the coefficient is in line with incremental information provision and in contrast to impression management. However, there is no association between NEGA and the other two proxy measures related to

Table 2.4 Pearson correlation coefficients

	POSI	*NEGA*	*ROA*	*PLNP*	*IDNP*	*LEVE*	*TURN*	P/GM_1	P/GM_2	P/GM_3	P/GM_4	P/GM_5	$TITL_1$
ROA	0.000	–0.172											
PLNP	0.090	–0.007	0.375***										
IDNP	–0.150	0.090	0.136	0.086									
LEVE	–0.243**	–0.337***	–0.266**	–0.264**	–0.023								
TURN	–0.207*	–0.282**	–0.358***	–0.265**	0.067	0.673***							
GM_1	0.278**	0.144	–0.160	0.075	0.058	–0.414***	–0.324***						
GM_2	0.012	0.118	0.642***	0.226**	–0.070	–0.473***	–0.737***	–0.226**					
GM_3	0.089	–0.152	–0.011	0.052	0.140	0.084	0.033	–0.052	–0.157				
GM_4	–0.216*	–0.127	–0.487***	–0.152	0.035	0.573***	0.823***	–0.261**	–0.780***	–0.181*			
GM_5	0.110	–0.026	–0.221**	–0.486***	–0.182*	0.276**	0.210*	–0.037	–0.110	–0.025	–0.127		
$TITL_1$	0.116	0.192*	0.152	0.243**	0.156	–0.429***	–0.355***	0.065	0.194*	0.045	–0.091	–0.567***	
$TITL_2$	–0.116	–0.192*	–0.152	–0.243**	–0.156	0.429***	0.355***	–0.065	–0.194*	–0.045	0.091	0.567***	–1.000***

$N = 57$

*$p < 0.1$; ** $p < 0.05$; *** $p < 0.01$

Table 2.5 Regression model for POSI and NEGA

	POSI		*NEGA*	
	B	*p-value*	*B*	*p-value*
Constant	3.189	0.000***	0.781	0.021**
ROA	0.008	0.654	–0.017	0.090*
PLNP	0.427	0.378	0.041	0.871
IDNP	–0.277	0.220	0.169	0.151
LEVE	–0.008	0.455	–0.009	0.101
TURN	–0.195	0.655	–0.280	0.219
P/GM_2	–0.746	0.121	0.233	0.348
P/GM_3	0.014	0.986	–0.011	0.979
P/GM_4	–0.370	0.626	0.413	0.297
P/GM_5	1.584	0.251	0.781	0.276
$TITL_2$	–0.668	0.281	–0.083	0.796
p-value	0.302		0.090*	
Adjusted R^2	0.038		0.123	

$N = 57$

*$p < 0.1$; ** $p < 0.05$; *** $p < 0.01$

profitability. In addition, there is no significant association between NEGA and any other independent variables (risk, size, general managers or titles). Although the association is not strong, there seems to be evidence of a certain negative relationship between profitability and negative references. Therefore, H2 is not supported. This specific finding is not in line with impression management, but more related to a possible attempt to give incremental information. However, this potential attempt to give useful information to make informed decisions would be quite limited, because the increase in the negative references remains diluted in an overwhelming positive net tone (Abrahamson and Park, 1994; Clatworthy and Jones, 2003).

Conclusions

This chapter has analysed, on a longitudinal basis, the positive and negative references contained in the management report disclosed by a Spanish brewery, *El Alcázar*, over the period 1928–1992, with the objective to study the potential relationship between tone and profitability, in the light of impression management. Additional variables that can affect the disclosures were also controlled. In contrast to this study, previous literature has mainly studied impression management comparing the best- and the worst-performing companies in a single period and in Anglophone countries. The management report, issued as part of the annual report, is a non-standardized document with narrative information about the situation and main events of the company during the reporting period.

The results are in line with Moreno and Jones (2015) with regard to tone. On the one hand, positive references are consistently preferred, irrespective of performance, in line with impression management. On the other hand, there is a modest increase in negative references when ROA decreases, which is not in line with impression management. Although the results could be interpreted, to some extent, as contradictory, the relative values of both the positive and negative references shed some light to help interpret the results. Overall, there is a constant predominance of positive references. The relative presence of positive references is permanently higher than the relative presence of negative references. Thus, the tone is consistently positive. The potential effort to give incremental information is indeed very limited when profitability decreases, because the weight of the negative references, even if increased, is dwarfed by the total amount of positive references. This result can be considered very limited, because it was only found (with a 10% significance) with regard to changes in ROA, but not in other measures of profitability tested, as positive or negative net profit or changes in net profit. For these reasons, taken as a whole, the results could be essentially interpreted in line with impression management. Alternative variables such as risk, size, different general managers or different titles have not proved to be significant in explaining changes in tone when their simultaneous effects are controlled.

Extant literature on impression management is mainly based on Anglophone countries (Courtis, 1986; Subramanian et al., 1993; Clatworthy and Jones, 2006). Most of it has also found that annual reports are overwhelmingly positive, irrespective of performance (Hildebrandt and Snyder, 1981; Gibbins et al., 1990). Previous research also argues that different contexts are expected to provide different disclosure (Doupnik and Riccio, 2006; Guillamon-Saorin and Sousa, 2010) and that, therefore, different legal and economic conditions between countries are expected to provide different textual patterns in disclosures (Jones, 1988; Merkl-Davies and Brennan, 2007). Our results, based on a country (Spain) with different characteristics also show that tone is consistently positive in annual reports. The pattern is therefore similar in relation to tone to most previous research.

There is, of course, a limitation to the work presented here. Although the software used for the analysis (LIWC) has been used previously and externally validated (Donohue et al., 2013), this type of study assumes that language, which is in essence qualitative, can be quantified (Patelli and Pedrini, 2014). Long-term longitudinal studies are not common in impression management, so further research could consider the evidence here by analysing the evolution of other impression management techniques over time in other companies.

Notes

1 In 1987, the consumption of beer (66.6 litres per capita) in Spain exceeded the one of wine (55 litres) (Trujillo García, 1989). This was a very significant fact, because traditionally in the Mediterranean countries the consumption of wine had prevailed. Culture and drinking patterns had traditionally differed between Mediterranean countries and northern European countries. However, from the 1960s, there was a progressive convergence in relation to the consumption per capita and choices of drinks (Knibbe et al., 1996).

2 This software analyses different textual characteristics (Pennebaker et al., 2007). It has a range of different language dictionaries, including LIWC 2001 Spanish dictionary. For more information, see www.liwc.net.
3 Loughran and McDonald (2016) sought to measure tone with word lists developed specifically for corporate communication, instead of general tone category dictionaries, such as those used by the software. However, those types of specific lists have been mainly designed for English texts. In addition, Twedt and Rees (2012) found similar results between both types of dictionaries.
4 Their general model also includes different company statuses in order to distinguish between listed/unlisted periods. However, *El Alcázar* was never a listed company.

References

Primary sources

Archive of Heineken España, SA Jaén Factory (formerly *El Alcázar, SA*) – Management reports, 1957–1992

Provincial Historical Archive of Jaén. Administración Central (5), Hacienda, Sociedades. N. 47.570. Administración Central (5), Hacienda, Balances. N. 20.104 – *El Alcázar, SA*. Management reports, 1929–1956

Secondary sources

Abrahamson, E. and Park, C. (1994). Concealment of negative organizational outcomes: An agency theory perspective. *Academy of Management Journal*, 37(5), pp. 1302–1334.

AEPJ (1993). *Anuario Estadístico de la Provincia de Jaén, 1992*. Jaén: Diputación Provincial de Jaén – Instituto de Estudios Giennenses.

Aerts, W. and Yan, B. (2017). Rhetorical impression management in the letter to shareholders and institutional setting: A metadiscourse perspective. *Accounting, Auditing and Accountability Journal*, 30(2), pp. 1–30.

Andalucía Económica (1991). Las pymes mayores de Andalucía. Ranking 300 empresas, 12, pp. 24–44.

Andalucía Económica (1992). En la variedad está el negocio. Ranking 300 empresas mayores, 23, pp. 22–50.

Bartlett, S. A. and Chandler, R. A. (1997). The corporate report and the private shareholder: Lee and Tweedie twenty years on. *British Accounting Review*, 29(3), pp. 245–261.

Boucher, J. and Osgood, C. E. (1969). The pollyanna hypothesis. *Journal of Verbal Learning and Verbal Behavior*, 8(1), pp. 1–8.

Burns, J. (2000). The dynamics of accounting change: Inter-play between new practices, routines, institutions, power and politics. *Accounting, Auditing and Accountability Journal*, 15(5), pp. 566–595.

Campbell, D., Moore, G. and Shrives, P. (2006). Cross-sectional effects in community disclosure. *Accounting, Auditing and Accountability Journal*, 19(1), pp. 96–114.

Clatworthy, M. and Jones, M. J. (2003). Financial reporting of good news and bad news: Evidence from accounting narratives. *Accounting and Business Research*, 33(3), pp. 171–185.

Clatworthy, M. and Jones, M. J. (2006). Differential patterns of textual characteristics and company performance in the chairman's statement. *Accounting, Auditing and Accountability Journal*, 19(4), pp. 493–511.

Cobbin, P., Dean, G., Esslemont, C., Ferguson, P., Keneley, M., Potter, B. and West, B. (2013). Enhancing the accessibility of accounting and business archives: The role of technology in informing research in accounting and business. *Abacus*, 49(3), pp. 396–422.

Comellas, J. L. (1990). *Historia de España contemporánea.* Madrid: Rialp.

Courtis, J. K. (1986). An investigation into annual report readability and corporate risk-return relationships. *Accounting and Business Research*, 16(64), pp. 285–294.

Courtis, J. K. (1987). Fry, smog, lix and rix: Insinuations about corporate business communications. *Journal of Business Communication*, 24(2), pp. 19–27.

Courtis, J. K. (1998). Annual report readability variability: Tests of the obfuscation hypothesis. *Accounting, Auditing and Accountability Journal*, 11(4), pp. 459–471.

Davis, A. K., Piger, J. M. and Sedor, L. M. (2012). Beyond the numbers: Measuring the information content of earnings press release language. *Contemporary Accounting Research*, 29(3), pp. 845–868.

Donohue, W. A., Liang, Y. and Druckman, D. (2013). Validating LIWC dictionaries: The Oslo I accords. *Journal of Language and Social Psychology*, 33(3), pp. 282–301.

Doupnik, T. S. and Riccio, E. L. (2006). The influence of conservatism and secrecy on the interpretation of verbal probability expressions in the Anglo and Latin cultural areas. *International Journal of Accounting*, 41(3), pp. 237–261.

El Alcázar (1984). *El Alcázar. Informe económico social. Año 1983.* Jaén: Artes gráficas.

Fanelli, A., Misangyi, V. F. and Tosi, H. L. (2009). In charisma we trust: The effects of CEO charismatic visions on securities analysts. *Organization Science*, 20(6), pp. 1011–1033.

García Ruiz, J. L. and Laguna Roldán, C. (1999). *Cervezas Mahou, 1890–1998. Un Siglo de Tradición e Innovación.* Madrid: LID.

Gibbins, M., Richardson, A. and Waterhouse, J. (1990). The management of corporate financial disclosure: Opportunism, ritualism, policies and processes. *Journal of Accounting Research*, 28(1), pp. 121–143.

Guillamon-Saorin, E. and Sousa, C. M. P. (2010). Press release disclosure in Spain and the UK. *International Business Review*, 19(1), pp. 1–15.

Hernández Armenteros, S. (1999). *El crecimiento económico en una región atrasada, Jaén, 1850–1930.* Jaén: Instituto de Estudios Giennenses.

Hildebrandt, H. W. and Snyder, R. D. (January 1981). The Pollyanna hypothesis in business writing: Initial results, suggestions for research. *Journal of Business Communication*, 18(1), pp. 5–15.

Jones, M. J. (1988). A longitudinal study of the readability of chairman's narratives in the corporate reports of a UK company. *Accounting and Business Research*, 18(72), pp. 297–305.

Knibbe, R. A., Drop, M. J. and Hupkens, C. L. H. (1996). Modernization and geographical diffusion as explanations for regional differences in the consumption of wine and beer in the European Community. *Substance Use & Misuse*, 31(11/12), pp. 1639–1655.

Loughran, T. and McDonald, B. (2016). Textual analysis in accounting and finance: A survey. *Journal of Accounting Research*, 54(4), pp. 1187–1230.

Maluquer de Motes, J. (2013). *La inflación en España. Un índice de precios de consumo, 1830–2012.* Madrid: Banco de España. Estudios de Historia Económica. N. 64.

Merkl-Davies, D. M. and Brennan, N. M. (2007). Discretionary disclosure strategies in corporate narratives: Incremental information or impression management? *Journal of Accounting Literature*, 26(1), pp. 116–194.

Merkl-Davies, D. M., Brennan, N. M. and McLeay, S. J. (2011). Impression management and retrospective sense-making in corporate narratives: A social psychology perspective. *Accounting, Auditing and Accountability Journal*, 24(3), pp. 315–344.

Moreno, A. (2011). Desarrollo de una cervecera en una región poco desarrollada a la luz de sus documentos contables: El Alcázar (1928–93). *De Computis*, 15, pp. 160–204.

Moreno, A. (2013). El sector cervecero español en el Siglo XX. Una visión desde dentro: El Alcázar. *Investigaciones de Historia Económica-Economic History Research*, 9(3), pp. 165–174.

Moreno, A. and Cámara, M. (2014). Evolution of the information content from the institutional perspective: El Alcázar Brewery (1928–1993). *Accounting History*, 19(3), pp. 369–398.

Moreno, A. and Cámara, M. (2016). Stakeholders in annual reports under ownership concentration: A historical case of a Spanish Brewery Company. *Accounting History Review*, 26(2), pp. 57–81.

Moreno, A. and Casasola, A. (2016). A readability evolution of narratives in annual reports: A longitudinal study of two Spanish companies. *Journal of Business and Technical Communication*, 30(2), pp. 202–235.

Moreno, A. and Jones, M. J. (2015). President's letter textual characteristics: Impression in depression? In: *19th Annual Financial Reporting and Business Communication Conference*. University of Bristol and BAFA FARSIG.

Moreno, A., Jones, M. J. and Quinn, M. (2017). A longitudinal study of the textual characteristics in the chairman's statements of Guinness – An impression management perspective. In: *40th Annual Congress of the European Accounting Association*. European Accounting Association and University of Valencia.

Moreno Aguayo, A. (2013). *Cervezas El Alcázar (1928–1993): Un examen institucional de la información empresarial*. Jaén: Instituto de Estudios Giennenses.

Neu, D. (1991). Trust, impression management and the public accounting profession. *Critical Perspectives on Accounting*, 2(3), pp. 295–313.

Patelli, L. and Pedrini, M. (2014). Is the optimism in CEO's letters to shareholders sincere? Impression management versus communicative action during the economic crisis. *Journal of Business Ethics*, 124(1), pp. 19–34.

Pennebaker, J. W., Booth, R. J. and Francis, M. E. (2007). *LIWC: Linguistic Inquiry and Work Count*. Austin: liwc.net.

Pettigrew, A. (1990). Longitudinal field research on change: Theory and practice. *Organizational Science*, 1(3), pp. 267–292.

Solbes Mira, P. (2005). 1930–2005: 75 años de transformaciones económicas en España. *Información Comercial Española, ICE: Revista de economía*, 826, pp. 3–5.

Subramanian, R., Insley, R. G. and Blackwell, R. D. (1993). Performance and readability: A comparison of annual reports of profitable and unprofitable corporations. *Journal of Business Communication*, 30(1), pp. 49–61.

Tamames Gómez, R. (2005). La autarquía española y las rémoras para el crecimiento económico posterior. *Información Comercial Española, ICE: Revista de economía*, 826, pp. 13–24.

Trujillo García, A. (1987). La industria cervecera en España. *Cerveza y malta*, 93, pp. 30–38.

Trujillo García, A. (1989). *Dos Conferencias sobre el Sector Cervecero Español*. Jaén: Fondo de Publicaciones S.A. El Alcázar.

Twedt, B. and Rees, L. (2012). Reading between the lines: An empirical examination of qualitative attributes of financial analysts' reports. *Journal of Accounting and Public Policy*, 31(1), pp. 1–21.

3 Government proposals to acquire the liquor trade in the First World War

The case of Macardle, Moore and Company, brewers

Desmond Gibney

Introduction

At the height of the First World War (hereafter the War), the British government twice considered acquiring control of the licensed liquor trade in Britain and Ireland[1] by means of a proposed scheme to buy out the trade at a range of cost estimates prepared on different dates between £300 million and £400 million (equivalent to around £20 billion in 2017 values)[2] using a method of capitalisation of pre-War profits. These attempts coincided with a politically powerful temperance movement but, as Turner (1980) explained, the main motivations of the government were, firstly in 1915 to increase the production of munitions by reducing industrial absenteeism caused by alcohol consumption, and secondly in 1917 to increase food production by restricting the growth of barley, with a consequent impact on beer production. A key player in these moves was David Lloyd George, in his roles as Chancellor of the Exchequer from 1908 to 1915 and as Prime Minister from 1916 to 1922. This chapter concentrates on the 1917 purchase scheme and its proposals for the purchase of brewing interests by exploring the case of a family-owned Irish brewery, Macardle Moore and Company (hereafter Macardles, being the plural form of the owning family's name), which would have been valued at around £10 million in 2017 values if the purchase had proceeded. The political importance attached to State Purchase can be judged by the decision of the War Cabinet[3] on 27th March 1917:

> The case for State Purchase as a war measure – when the food, labour, and transport situation is taken into account – is so strong, that the Government ought to be prepared, if they introduced such a proposal, to face all consequences and to stand or fall by this policy.
>
> (War Cabinet and Cabinet Memoranda, file reference CAB/23/2/24)

There has been no previous research in an Irish context on these political moves to control the liquor trade. The research objective of this chapter is to assess the government's proposed scheme and, using archival records and contemporary accounting and finance principles, to apply the valuation scheme to the Macardles case and consider whether it would have been worthwhile for Macardles to accept. This involves reconstructing the information from the company's accounts to arrive at a valuation using profit multiples and comparing that result to contemporary valuation multiples. The approach of combining historical information with current accounting techniques has been used, for example, in a study of costing in American cotton mills during the early Industrial Revolution by Gervais and Quinn (2016) to 'reverse engineer', or work backwards mathematically, in order to assess the usefulness of the cost information for management decisions.

Context and literature

General context

According to Gourvish and Wilson (1994), some of the principal characteristics of the British brewing industry around the time of the War included lower levels of beer consumption; higher costs due to increased taxation and difficulties with the supply and quality of raw material; restrictions on the strength and volume of beer output; and the sale of beer mainly in public houses, most of which were contractually supplied by specific brewers and consequently became known as 'tied houses'.[4] A significant development around this time frame was the tendency of family-owned businesses to move away from partnerships and to form limited liability companies. The organisational structure of firms was studied by Gourvish (1987), who noted the importance of the general move by British firms to adopt limited liability status by around 1900. A practical guide to conversion to limited liability companies was prepared by Palmer (1890), a barrister, and listed nineteen significant examples of conversion, at least six of which were brewers, including prominent names such as Bass, Ratcliff and Gretton Limited (hereafter Bass) and Whitbread and Company Limited.

Another significant development around this timeframe was the struggle for Irish independence from Great Britain. Notwithstanding the Irish campaign for independence, the Irish Parliamentary Party (IPP) had significant influence in the British Parliament due to the balance of power in the House of Commons, up until the IPP was effectively wiped out in the December 1918 general election. The IPP, under the leadership of John Redmond (up to March 1918) and John Dillon (from March to December 1918) exerted its power in Parliament to influence budgetary and taxation measures for the United Kingdom (UK) as a whole, including those which affected the brewing industry. There were also other particular circumstances that affected the Irish brewing industry, separate from the British brewing industry, such as Irish preferences for stronger beer, the importance of brewing to Irish agriculture and the influence of one brewer, Arthur Guinness & Sons Limited (hereafter Guinness).

Background to Macardles

Gourvish and Wilson (1985, p. 147) observed that "the later Victorian brewing industry was one of rich variety. Bass was a wonder of the Victorian world", producing 1.5 million barrels annually in 1900, but "there were breweries at the other end of the scale, brewing a few hundred barrels annually in backyards with a man and a boy". By way of contrast, Macardles brewery was capable of producing 100,000 barrels annually by 1917. The northeastern Irish town of Dundalk, County Louth, had a long association with brewing. 'Macardle's Ale' was first brewed there in 1863 by the family-owned Macardles brewery. Macardles was regarded as one of Dundalk's "oldest and most progressive industries" (Ua Dubhthaigh, 1946, p. 101). The firm won a gold medal for ale and stout at the Distillers, Brewers and Allied Trades Exhibition in Dublin in 1892, and John P Macardle patented an invention for thoroughly cleansing the barrels, which was later used by Guinness and by English breweries (Ógra Dun Dealgan, 1986).

Macardles demonstrated strong family and business support for the War. The firm's letterhead described the company as 'Irish Army Brewers, Contractors to H.M. Forces'. Macardles "did a very big trade in supplying ale to the British army [. . .] and also exported to the troops in Liverpool and in the Mediterranean, and for this the brewery received wide recognition" (Ógra Dun Dealgan, 1986, p. 80). A director, Thomas Callan Macardle, was made a Knight Commander of the Order of the British Empire (KBE) "for services in connection with the War" (The London Gazette, 1920, p. 3757).[5] At a time when John Redmond, leader of the IPP, had encouraged Irish nationalists to support Britain during the War, 2nd Lieutenant Kenneth Macardle (son of Sir Thomas Callan Macardle) joined the 17th Manchester Regiment of the British Army and was killed in action in the Battle of the Somme in July 1916. After the War, Macardles adapted to the newly independent Irish Free State and played a prominent role in the brewing industry; for example, Sir Thomas Callan Macardle, chairman of Macardles, gave evidence to the Intoxicating Liquor Commission in May 1925 on behalf of the Irish Brewers' Association.

By the middle of the 20th century, Macardles had forged links with the large British brewing firm Ind Coope, whose 'Double Diamond' beer was brewed by Macardles from the 1950s until 1985. Macardles joined with Guinness and Smithwicks in 1962 to form Irish Ale Breweries. Guinness took over Irish Ale Breweries in 1988, and brewing by Macardles eventually ceased in Dundalk in 2001, but 'Macardle's Ale' continues to be produced by Diageo Ireland at the St. James's Gate brewery in Dublin.

The growing trend by British firms to adopt limited liability status by around 1900 was noted by Gourvish (1987). Features of this trend included keeping the numbers of shareholders in individual firms small, with restrictions on share transfers and control retained by families. According to Gourvish (1987), the principal reasons for the adoption of limited liability status included concerns about future viability, desire for growth and personal or family circumstances of the principal in the business. Macardles was incorporated as a limited liability company in 1895 when the business of the existing partnership was taken over, and the initial shareholders were members of the Macardle and Moore families, who were cousins. Accounts were prepared on an annual and semi-annual basis. The archival material of Macardles contains a copy of Palmer's (1890) practical guide to conversion to limited liability companies, which echoes the motivations noted by Gourvish (1987), and Palmer's guide appears to have been used by the Macardles partners when they were preparing for the move to incorporation.

Temperance movement and proposed laws

Gourvish and Wilson (1994) observed that "the consumption of alcohol was one of the great nineteenth-century social questions. On few other issues was more ink spilt" (p. 27). According to Turner (1980), drunkenness was a prominent factor in criminal proceedings, and drink accounted for a large part of working-class expenditure, and "per capita drink consumption in the thirty years before the war was the highest ever recorded" (p. 589). Lloyd George supported temperance. However, state purchase of the liquor trade "had a unique capacity to unite in opposition the licensed trade and a vociferous and influential section of the temperance movement which condemned state participation in a sinful commerce" (Turner, 1980, p. 590). In 1915, the claimed motivation for state purchase was excessive drinking in areas where munitions were being manufactured, with a consequent impact on industrial productivity, whereas in 1917, the claimed motivation was a shortage of barley due to an increased emphasis on food production (Turner, 1980). Notwithstanding the changed motivations of the government, the near-success of these proposals was primarily due to the War rather than the efforts of the temperance lobby, and state purchase "was never promoted purely as a scheme of social reform" (Turner, 1980, p. 591).

In June 1917, the government established three Liquor Trade Finance Committees (hereafter the Committees) – one for England and Wales, one for Scotland and one for Ireland – to consider the financial aspects of control of the industry. The key dates in the chronology are summarised in Table 3.1.

Sir Thomas Whittaker, MP, was one of the main spokesmen in Parliament for the temperance lobby, and Gourvish and Wilson commented that "the mere mention" of his name "could induce apoplexy in the mildest brewery director" (1994, p. 286). Whittaker was also a member of the Liquor Trade Finance Committee for England and Wales in 1917. He published an argument for the case for state purchase and control of the drink trade (Whittaker, 1917), the second paragraph of which gave a flavour of his reasoning:

> Drink is the greatest cause of inefficiency, waste, and loss of time, and consequent under-use of plant and machinery, and an output considerably less than the largest possible. Its production and sale wastes food, coal, and labour, and occupies ships, docks, and railways which are badly needed for vitally important purposes.
>
> (Whittaker, 1917, p. 1)

The brewing industry was also a powerful lobby, and Gutzke (1990) has documented the political influence of British brewers through having members of

Table 3.1 Chronology of key dates

28th July 1914	*Start of First World War*
March–April 1915	Sir William Plender prepared costings for David Lloyd George on state purchase of liquor trade
4th May 1915	Budget speech by John Redmond, MP
24th April 1916	Start of Easter Rising in Dublin
27th March 1917	War Cabinet considers state purchase and decides the government should "be prepared . . . to face all consequences and to stand or fall by this policy"
June 1917	Liquor Trade Finance Committees established
30th June 1917	Chief Secretary for Ireland tells War Cabinet that concessions are needed for Irish brewers to increase output
15th August 1917	Irish Brewers' Association agree on a precis of evidence to be given to the Irish Liquor Trade Finance Committee
16th January 1918	Irish Liquor Trade Finance Committee reports to Chief Secretary for Ireland
6th March 1918	Death of John Redmond, MP, succeeded by John Dillon, MP
April 1918	Liquor Trade Finance Committees' reports presented to War Cabinet
11th November 1918	End of First World War
14th December 1918	Irish Parliamentary Party wiped out in general election and its leader John Dillon loses his seat
21st January1919	First meeting of Dáil Eireann in Dublin

Parliament who held brewing interests and/or represented areas with a heavy concentration of breweries. However, Gutzke (1990, p. 78) noted that despite the presumed power of the brewing lobby in Parliament, "brewer MPs exhibited extraordinary disarray in Parliament – usually disorganised, often absent and sometimes even disloyal".

A prominent accountant, Sir William Plender, who was a partner in Deloitte, Plender, Griffths and a past president of the Institute of Chartered Accountants in England and Wales (ICAEW), was commissioned by Lloyd George to prepare costings for the purchase of the liquor trade in 1915 (Turner, 1980). Plender's costings in March and April 1915 contained an estimate from a trade source that the value of all property owned by breweries in England, Wales and Scotland was £250 million. Based on Plender's calculations, the trade earned a return on capital of approximately 7%, and assuming that £250 million of 4% government stock was issued, the proposed purchase scheme should be capable of earning an annual surplus of 3% of £250 million, or £7.5 million. Plender also noted the difficulties in defining purchase terms in an Act of Parliament that could be applied to all cases. One difficulty was caused by the fact that some breweries were public companies, even though there may not have been an active market in their shares. Another difficulty related to variations in profit trends between different breweries, regardless of the number of years' profits that would be averaged when arriving at the multiplier. Lloyd George took issue with some aspects of Plender's costings:

> In my opinion Sir William Plender is far too liberal both in his suggestions as to the valuation of the Brewery undertakings . . . and I am hopeful that this view would be shared by a good many taxpayers.
>
> (Lloyd George Papers, file reference LG/C/23/2/7)

A memorandum from 1915 put forward the case for far more restrictive nation-wide measures than merely reducing opening hours of public houses or introducing local prohibition on alcohol in areas where armaments were produced and noted that:

> The nation can now be asked to assent to a heavy restriction of alcohol, as a man may give up drinking when he goes into training. That is the basis for the proposal that spirits and wine and the heavier beers should be prohibited for the duration of the war and say three months afterwards . . . The real question is whether the form of prohibition thus outlined should be treated as a mere passing incident in the duration of the war, or whether the opportunity should be taken for what undeniably would amount to a fundamental revolution in the trade.
>
> (Lloyd George Papers, file reference LG/C/23/2/6, p. 2)

The memorandum also described the financial nature of the proposed purchase: the consideration would be satisfied by the issue of 4% government stock, whereby guaranteed interest would be paid during the War, but the 4% government stock would not be issued during the War – or if issued, would not be tradeable during the War. The intention behind the restriction on issuance or trading of the new stock was to avoid competition with government stock issued to pay for War costs, because "it is clearly not like the war debt, but an investment balanced by tangible and profit-earning assets" (Lloyd George Papers, file reference LG/C/23/2/6, p. 8).

Because of parliamentary arithmetic in 1915, the government felt that the proposed taxation measures on alcohol might not be approved in Parliament, so the Chancellor of the Exchequer, David Lloyd George, had to reconsider his budget proposals. However, notwithstanding Lloyd George's efforts at compromise, the IPP leader John Redmond used his speech on the budget in 1915 to make the case for the Irish liquor industry and drew attention to the fact that "the manufacture of beer in Ireland is a very large business" and that if the proposed taxes were implemented, "in England the injury, no doubt would be great, but I do not believe it would be comparable to the injury that would be done in Ireland" (Redmond, 1915). Gourvish and Wilson (1994) noted the government's dilemma in 1917 when a shortage of alcohol, particularly beer, led to industrial unrest, whereby "it had to allow brewing output to rise, but at the same time wished to stabilise or even reduce the industry's cereal consumption. The solution lay in the notorious 'Government Ale', a term applied, much to government annoyance, to the low alcohol beer established by the new regulations" (p. 321) for a maximum gravity of 1036,[6] and that "the package of government restrictions represented a considerable assault upon beer, which remained highly priced in relation to its pre-war quality and strength" (p. 323).

At the end of March 1917, there were twenty-six breweries in Ireland (War Cabinet and Cabinet Memoranda, file reference CAB/24/5/1). In March 1917, a Home Office committee reported to the Cabinet on the restrictions on output and noted that a deputation representing Irish brewing interests informed the committee that "except as to restriction in output, all Irish brewers be left to continue their business as at present" (War Cabinet and Cabinet Memoranda, file reference CAB/24/8/41, p. 6). The restrictions on beer output as they affected Ireland were also considered when Henry Duke, in his role as Chief Secretary for Ireland,[7] presented a memorandum classified as 'secret' to the War Cabinet on 30th June 1917 on concessions needed for Irish brewers in order to increase output. Duke wrote that after receiving "very urgent representations" from Ireland about the 'gravity' or strength of Irish beer being significantly higher than English or Scottish beer, he was told by a Guinness board member that if the proposed reductions in gravity for English beer were also applied to Irish beer, then the output from Guinness and "Irish Brewers generally" would not be increased beyond previous levels. The difficulty was due to the fact that Irish beer typically had an average gravity of 1066, whereas English beer typically had a gravity of 1051, so in order to meet the proposed standard gravity of 1036 for English and Irish beers, the reduction for Irish beer would be 30 points, twice the level of reduction in gravity of 15 points applied to English beer. He also added that:

> It is in the highest degree desirable that any increase in output which is allowed in the English Breweries shall be accompanied by a like increase in the Irish Breweries.
>
> (War Cabinet and Cabinet Memoranda, file reference GT1243)

Brewing in Ireland

While there is no published history of Macardles, histories have been published of other Irish breweries, including the authorised corporate histories of Guinness (Lynch and Vaizey, 1960; Dennison and MacDonagh, 1998) and histories of two Cork-based breweries, namely Murphy's (Ó Drisceoil and Ó Drisceoil, 1997) and Beamish & Crawford (Ó Drisceoil and Ó Drisceoil, 2015). There is also a small number of studies which detailed accounting practices within Irish firms in general. Clarke (1996) noted the lack of literature on Irish accounting history, even though there are many sets of archival records held on the island of Ireland (see Ó hÓgartaigh and Ó hÓgartaigh, 2004), many of which are unexplored.

There are also a small number of studies which detail internal accounting practices at Guinness. For example, Quinn (2014) explores accounting change in the cooperage at Guinness; Quinn and Jackson (2014) explore change to accounting practices at Guinness as influenced by the First World War; Hiebl et al. (2015) explore the role of the chief accountant at Guinness from 1920 to 1940; and, finally, Martinez Franco et al. (2017) detail the chief accountant role at Guinness. Quinn and Jackson (2014) outline many of the wartime restrictions that affected Guinness, including government restrictions on the supply of raw materials, the quantity and 'gravity' or strength of the beer produced and increased excise duties on beer. These restrictions, as noted, also affected Macardles. Dennison and MacDonagh (1998) noted that the profits of Guinness kept pace with inflation during the War years, in spite of the government restrictions, but suffered a decline in sales after the War. While these studies of Guinness are insightful, it should be noted that this company was one of a small number of large companies of the time, as the economy was mainly agricultural, with the government not pursuing any policy of industrialisation until the early 1930s – see for example O'Gráda (1997).

Methods and sources

This study explores the available accounting information of Macardles during the late 19th and early 20th centuries, from the incorporation of the business as a limited company in 1895 up to the period around the War, drawing on records available at the Louth County Archives and in other sites indicated later. While recognising the limitations of studying a firm's accounts, Gourvish acknowledged (2006, pp. 388–389) that the accounts "attempt to express the impact of a complex web of activities as more precise measures" and "whatever the numbers may be, there is a role for the business historian in making sense of them". There is also a gap in some of the accounting information analysed, likely due to a fire in the brewery in April 1913, when some of the important records outlining the history of the company were lost. Armstrong (1991) noted that very few companies maintained an archive, and the companies that did, tended to be large companies, which may bias any sample. In Ireland, while Ó hÓgartaigh (2008) noted many archival sources, they are rather under-utilised, with the possible exception being the Guinness archive.

The methods employed in this study were as follows. Available archival records of Macardles are in good condition, clear and readily accessible. All records were examined over the period October 2016 to July 2017. The records were photographed digitally on-site and analysed both on-site and later. In essence, the records explored are reflective of what Scott (1990, pp. 81–82) terms recurrent and special administrative records, and thus are ideal to form a picture of management at Macardles. Scott (1990) describes recurrent records as the necessary part of the daily operations, while special records are reflective of ad-hoc situations and requests. Recurrent records were the main source here, with some reference to special records – see the reference list for more detail. Copies of local and national newspapers[8] of the time period were also consulted at the National Library of Ireland (NLI). As the principal focus of this chapter is concerned with one type of regulation, namely the proposed state purchase of the liquor trade, it is worth noting Scranton and Fridenson's observation that "where there's regulation, there's also lobbying", which results in "a series of discourses often preserved in documents that merit critical analysis" (2013, p. 18). The UK's National Archives and Parliamentary Archives were consulted, and the records contained therein, including Cabinet memoranda and the papers of David Lloyd George, provide detail on the lobbying and on the process that led to the proposed state purchase scheme. Once all of these records were examined in some detail, a process of induction guided the most salient issues, which are now outlined.

Macardle Moore case

Proposals to value a brewing business

The Irish Committee appointed on 29th June 1917 to inquire into the terms for the purchase by the government of the intoxicating liquor trade in Ireland consisted of eight men, two of whom were MPs, and was chaired by a judge. Paragraph 1 of their report, dealing with the terms of reference, shows a distinction between taking control and purchasing the trade, as control might need to be taken as an urgent war measure, to be followed by purchase after the War (War Cabinet and Cabinet: Memoranda, file reference CAB/24/5/1 Report of the Liquor Trade Finance Committee for Ireland). The Committee reported to the Chief Secretary for Ireland on 16th January 1918, although two of the eight members submitted separate minority reports detailing their reservations on certain aspects. The main conclusion of the Committee in relation to Irish breweries was to decide to value Irish breweries at 13 times' annual earnings. The purchase price would be calculated by taking the average annual net profit during the five years prior to the War and multiplying that profit figure by a multiple of 13. Net profit was to be calculated after making allowance for income tax; interest on mortgages, loans and debentures; depreciation; and interest would be charged on the working capital necessary for the business. 'Tied houses' were to be valued separately. Purchase prices based on stock market valuations or balance sheet figures were not considered to be appropriate or fair:

> In any case, Stock Exchange Quotations are not a very certain means of arriving at the true value of a concern. The affairs of a company may be so presented on a Balance Sheet as to make it more attractive to an investor than its true position really warrants. Premises may not be kept in repair. Insufficient allowances may be made for depreciation. The entire available profits may be distributed in dividends without creating a reserve fund to give stability to the concern.
>
> (War Cabinet and Cabinet Memoranda, file reference CAB/24/5/1, paragraph 22 of Report of Liquor Trade Finance Committee for Ireland)

The English and Welsh, Irish and Scottish Committee reports were presented to the War Cabinet in April 1918, and a comparison of the reports noted that while the Irish Committee did not provide an estimate of the cost of purchase of the Irish trade, the "gross total, as far as calculable, appears to be somewhat more than £400 million, but substantially less than £500 million" for Great Britain and Ireland combined (War Cabinet and Cabinet: Memoranda, file reference CAB/24/5/1). Given that the cost estimates of the English and Welsh Committee and the Scottish Committee were £350 million and £61 million, respectively, it can be concluded that the Irish cost may have been significantly less than £89 million. These figures can be contrasted with earlier estimates of a cost of £250 million for England and Wales, and £50 million for Scotland and Ireland.

The Irish Committee recommended a multiple of 13 times the average profits of five pre-War years as compensation for breweries. By contrast, the English and Welsh Committee recommended a multiple of 15 times the average profits of four pre-War years as compensation for breweries. The Irish Committee did not give detailed consideration as to how the compensation would be applied because the English and Welsh Committee's report contained detailed suggestions of how the model might work. The underlying principle was that, while the average multiple of profits would be 15 (the equivalent multiple for Irish breweries is 13),

> The number of years' purchase to be applied to profits naturally depends on the security that there is for such profits. The better the security, the larger the number of years' purchase, and vice versa.
>
> (War Cabinet and Cabinet Memoranda, file reference CAB/24/5/1, Report of the Liquor Trade Finance Committee for England and Wales, p. 27)

Based on a worked example in the English and Welsh Committee's report, the calculations in Appendix 1 use a pro forma capital structure of a brewery with a profit figure of £11,000, with the average multiplier being 13 (to correspond with the number of years' profits as purchase consideration for Irish breweries) to illustrate how the purchase consideration would be divided among the providers of capital. Following the example of the English and Welsh Committee, the profits are divided into a 'range' of 11 portions, so the first eleventh (i.e. £1,000) of profits has a multiplier of 18; the second eleventh of profits has a multiplier of 17; the third eleventh of profits has a multiplier of 16 and so on until the final eleventh of profits has a multiplier of 8. The average multiplier is 13.[9] Alternatively, if the profits are divided into 13 portions, then the first thirteenth (i.e. £769) of profits has a multiplier of 19; the second thirteenth of profits would have a multiplier of 18 and so on, but the average multiplier would still be 13.[10] It is important to note that the English and Welsh Committee did not provide any guidance as to how the 'range' of portions of profits should be decided. While the total compensation would be fixed and the average multiplier would be 13, the choice of 'range' to be applied could have a significant impact on the amount paid to the owners of each category of capital. This is shown in Appendix 1, where the weighted average multiplier ranges between 9.1 and 16.5 in the worked example, with the owners of the business (the ordinary shareholders) receiving the lowest weighted average multiple. However, as Macardles only had one category of capital, namely ordinary shares, the choice of a 'range' of portions does not affect the calculations.

An important feature of the model suggested by the English and Welsh Committee is that the debenture holders and the preference shareholders would receive a share of the purchase consideration based on a capitalised value of the interest or dividends associated with their category of capital. This differs from normal practice, where, for example, debenture holders would have their capital repaid, up to but not exceeding, par value of the debentures. Another important feature is that the model ignores the time value of money. All three Committees agreed that the purchase price should be based on pre-War profits and that any favourable or adverse effects that the War may have had on profits must be excluded. The purchase consideration for the liquor trade was intended to be in the form of government stock, and the English and Welsh Committee recommended that as the financial market conditions would likely be very different post-War, with capital values significantly lower, the value of government stock issued in the future to pay the purchase consideration should be written down to reflect the financial market conditions prevailing at the time of settlement. The Scottish and Irish Committees concluded that the form of the payment should receive further study by the government.

The War Cabinet considered state purchase on 27th March 1917 and "gave particular attention to the effect on the national credit, already so heavily strained, of the addition of the estimated sum of £300 million". It also heard of the views of experts that "State Purchase should constitute a profitable transaction" but also heard that "the very fact that State Purchase might be a profitable enterprise would arouse hostilities in many sections of the Temperance Party" (War Cabinet and Cabinet Memoranda, file reference CAB/23/2/24). The valuation proposed in 1915 and 1917 was £300 million, made up of £250 million for England and Wales and £50 million for Scotland and Ireland. These 1915 and 1917 figures have been converted into current (i.e. 2017) values using Bank of England data (Bank of England, 2018) and are as follows: £50 million in 1915 would be worth approximately £4.9 billion in 2017 and £50 million in 1917 would be worth approximately £3.3 billion in 2017.

Data for Macardles

During the War years, Macardles wrote to various customers saying that orders could not be filled due to shortages of raw materials such as yeast. On 21st May 1918 the company wrote to one supplier, Marston, Thompson & Evershed in Burton-on-Trent, expressing relief that Macardles are getting a couple of hundred pounds of yeast and commented that "we are brewing considerable quantities of this Government beer for the troops". Macardles prepared a profile of their business in August 1917 and described the firm as a private limited company owned by members of the extended Macardle family, with the business consisting of a brewery capable of brewing 2,000 barrels per week, and owning a large number of licensed premises in Dundalk and surrounding areas, including Belfast, and having considerable assets in the form of loans on licensed premises. This was in response to the document dated 16th August 1917 from the Irish Brewers' Association's 'Precis of Evidence' proposed to be given before the Liquor Trade Finance Committee Ireland. The precis sets out six elements:

1) That Irish Brewers Association are absolutely opposed to purchase of Retail Licensed Trade, prior to Purchase of the Wholesale Manufacturing Producing Concerns.
2) That the Purchase of the Breweries should include the Purchase of any kindred Trade in which these Breweries are at present engaged.
3) That reasonable compensation be paid for compulsory disturbance.
4) That Directors, Officials and Employees should be adequately compensated.
5) That Stock Exchange quotations cannot be accepted as any fair indication of true value for such a purpose as Purchase.
6) That valuation of Assets is a cumbersome and slow method of arriving at value; and we consider that in the majority of cases the fairest and quickest mode would be by capitalisation of Profits; but each individual firm should have the right by appeal to be purchased on Valuation of Assets and Goodwill if it so desires.

(Macardles archive, file reference PP00240/003/012)

Accounts of Macardles

The available annual accounts for Macardles for the years ended 31st August 1909 to 1915 are summarised in Appendix 2, using the format and layout as presented in the directors' report for each year.[11] Because of the significant changes in the company's results between 1914 and 1915, an additional analysis column has been included showing the change between 1914 and 1915 for each line-item in the accounts. In addition to gaps in the annual accounts available in the archival records, a trial balance was not available for any year-end.

Using the simple accounting equation of Assets – Liabilities = Capital, it is apparent from the accounts that between 1914 and 1915 the company's capital declined from £181,071 to £136,112, a decrease of 25%. However, profits on brewing almost doubled, from £12,875 in 1914 to £24,740 in 1915, an increase of 92%. An explanation for the increase in profits is not apparent from the records. The increase in profits is matched by an increase of 104% in commission paid on profits. The directors also increased the level of dividend payout. The normal dividend policy was to pay 10% of the nominal value of the ordinary share capital. In 1912 and 1914, an additional bonus dividend of 1% was paid, and the level of bonus dividend was increased to 3% in 1915. The 3% bonus dividend in 1915 was paid in two tranches: 1% was paid with the interim dividend, 2% with the final dividend. The 1915 directors' report is also significant because it is the only year which contained a report in narrative form:

> Recognising the grave financial conditions prevailing at the present time, your Directors thought it advisable to have a complete re-valuation of the Assets of the Company, in order to ascertain as nearly as possible the exact amount of financial resources on which they might rely; in view of the future gloomy outlook for the brewing trade, due to the high cost of materials, increased working expenses, enormous Government taxation and a reduction in trade owing to the depopulation of the country as a result of the War.
>
> (Report of the Directors, as submitted to the Ordinary General Meeting held on the 11th day of November 1915)

The company appears to have carried out an exercise in 'tidying up' its balance sheet as part of the 'complete re-valuation' mentioned in the directors' report for 1915. It is not possible to re-create the movements in the general reserves (i.e. the reserves separate from retained profits), but a comparison of the 1914 and 1915 balance sheets shows that the general reserves declined by £46,323. However, it appears that the 'gross' movement in general reserves was £58,956, after taking account of the addition to the general reserve in 1915 of £9,000 from profits (compared to £2,700 in 1914) and an 'adjustment of reserve' of £3,633. An attempt at reconstructing a nominal ledger account for the general reserve is shown in Table 3.2. As the 'gross' amount of the movement on the account in 1915 is £58,956, it can be assumed (see Table 3.3) that much of this amount is accounted for by the reduction in the value of debtors, premises and investments. The accounts of earlier years show various movements in reserves as part of appropriation of profits, but no breakdown of the composition of the total figure for general reserve is available.

Table 3.2 Proforma reserve account for Macardles in 1915

Reserve Account					
		£			£
Y/E 31/8/1915	Movement for year	58,956	1/9/1914	Balance brought forward	133,323
			Y/E 31/8/1915	Appropriation of profit	9,000
31/8/1915	Balance carried down	*87,000*	Y/E 31/8/1915	Adjustment of reserve	*3,633*
		145,956			*145,956*
			31/8/1915	Balance brought down	87,000

Table 3.3 Analysis of movement in reserves for Macardles in 1915

	£
Reduction in debtors	20,249
Adjustment in investments: at value rather than at cost as previously	3,258
Reduction in book value of premises	*16,807*
Subtotal	40,314
Balancing figure: unknown	*18,642*
Movement for year 'grossed-up'	*58,956*

Table 3.4 Purchase price for Macardles expressed in 2017 values

Profit for year ended 31st August 1909	£12,098
Profit for year ended 31st August 1912	£11,462
Profit for year ended 31st August 1914	£11,414
Average of three years' profits	£11,658
Multiple of 13 times average profits	£151,554
Cost in 2017 =	Cost in 1917 multiplied by (2017 price index divided by 1917 price index):
	£151,554 multiplied by (1,074.9 divided by 16.3)
	£9,994,196 or approximately £10 million

Application of valuation to Macardles and present-day perspective

The purchase price formula provided for the averaging of five years' annual profits up to 1914 and then multiplying the average by a multiple of thirteen years for Irish breweries. Because of the incomplete data for Macardles, the formula has been modified here by taking the average of the three available years from 1909 to 1914, but this does not materially change the overall position. The detailed information available on profits is shown in Appendix 2. Multiplying the average profits of £11,658 by 13 gives a purchase price of £151,554. Using the Bank of England's inflation calculator and long-term price data from the Office for National Statistics (ONS) (Office for National Statistics, 2018),[12] the purchase price in 1917 values is the equivalent of approximately £10 million in 2017 values. The calculation is as shown in Table 3.4.

The valuation of Macardles of £10 million in 2017 terms places the brewery among the ranks of small players in the beer market. A multiple of thirteen years' profits is not uncommon in the beer industry. However, unlike the proposed state purchase where the multiple was based on an average of four or five years' profits, the more common usage of multiples is through use of a trailing twelve months' (TTM) multiple, or in other words, a historic twelve months' figure. As Peelo (2010, p. 42) explains, a principle of valuation is that it must be based on information available at the time of valuation, as outlined in the judgement of Danckwerts J. in the 1953 UK case of *Holt v. IRC*: "it is necessary to assume the prophetic vision of a prospective purchaser . . . and firmly to reject the wisdom which might be provided by the knowledge of subsequent events". An authoritative textbook on valuing companies (Koller et al., 2005) states that while discounted cash flow (DCF) is the preferred valuation tool, the use of a carefully designed multiples analysis has a role to play in improving the accuracy of DCF valuations. According to Koller et al. (2005), best practice when using multiples should take account of companies with similar growth prospects, use forward-looking rather than historic multiples and avoid flawed comparisons due to differing capital structures and non-operating gains and losses. Koller et al. (2005) noted that many financial analysts use enterprise value multiples based on earnings before interest, taxes, depreciation and amortisation (EBITDA).

In a report published by Credit Suisse on the meaning of price-earning (P/E) multiples, Mauboussin and Callahan (2014) noted the widespread use of relative or comparable multiples, where comparison with perceived peers, or comparison with past multiples for the same company, is used as the basis of judging the valuation of a company. Mauboussin and Callahan (2014, p. 11) argued that "unless the value drivers of the peer companies are very similar to those of the subject company, comparable valuations are baseless".

A recent analysis of some of the smaller British breweries showed 2015 values of £1.3 million for Delavals, £50 million for Camden Town Brewery and £305 million for BrewDog, all of which are relatively new entrants to the market and have received crowdfunding; and £32 million for Adnams, a listed company founded in 1872 (Evans, 2015). These firms had a wide range of P/E ratios, from 16.2 for Adnams to 115 for BrewDog (Evans, 2015). Camden Town Brewery has since been bought by AB InBev (Thompson, 2017). However, the use of crowdfunding for breweries has been controversial, particularly in the case of BrewDog (Williams, 2017) when crowdfunding investors have purchased debt rather than equity in a business. Further difficulties relate to the valuations based on market capitalisations or partial fundraising rather than takeover transactions and the scarcity of comparable companies that have not diversified into other areas as well as brewing.

A more concrete example of multiples paid in the brewing industry is provided by the 2015 takeover by AB InBev of SABMiller, which valued SABMiller at a multiple of 16 times EBITDA, and this compared favourably with its average multiple of 13 during the six months prior to the announcement of the takeover (Financial Times, 2015). Further analysis published on the range of multiples paid in nine recent deals in the drinks industry has shown that the SABMiller multiple of 13 was in the middle of the range of multiples, but a note of caution was sounded because "multiples on any deal are rarely clear cut", depending on whether EBITDA or adjusted EBITDA was used, as "each side can no doubt choose a number to suit themselves" (Ralph, 2015).

The modern climate for brewing suggests that if Macardles had survived as an independent brewery, it might have benefitted from a resurgence in demand for 'craft beers', notwithstanding the tendency of consolidation for the big players and the success of crowdfunding for new entrants to the market. Demand for alcoholic drinks overall has fallen, mainly driven by a decline in beer sales (Daneshkhu, 2017). The beer market has been described as a "sobering time for big brewers", and "little wonder, then, that big brewers and investors have mulled various tie-ups", involving giant brewers such as SABMiller, Heineken and Anheuser-Busch InBev (The Economist, 2015), resulting in a global beer industry that has "been shaken up beyond recognition" (Lynch, 2017). At the other end of the scale, there is a flourishing market for beers such as India pale ales (IPAs), as

> everyone can have a home-town brew and an opinion. That is bad news for the vast brewers that dominate the large but shrinking global lager market. The competition flourishes at a local level and on a modest scale that the big brewers hardly know how to understand.
>
> (The Economist, 2016)

The potential for craft brewers rooted in areas with a brewing heritage can be seen in regions of England such as Yorkshire (Tighe and Bounds, 2009). This suggests scope for a small-sized brewery in an area such as northeastern Ireland, capable of capitalising on the rich brewing heritage of Dundalk and adapting to the changing preferences of beer drinkers.

Concluding comments

The state purchase of the liquor trade in Britain and Ireland ultimately did not proceed, because by the time that the three Committees had reported to Cabinet in 1918, the War had reached a crucial stage and was the main focus of government attention. However, as Lord Milner's memorandum to the War Cabinet on 30th April 1919 noted (War Cabinet and Cabinet Memoranda, file reference CAB/24/78/63), the Cabinet decision of May 1917 to undertake state purchase of the trade was never reversed. In 1919, Milner still thought that the state purchase would be profitable and that previously identified problems caused by drink, such as crime, still remained.

This chapter has explored a topic that has not previously been researched in an Irish context, namely the political moves to control the liquor trade and the use of accounting numbers therein. In addition, although the broader topic in a UK context has been addressed by Turner (1980) and by Gourvish and Wilson (1994), the focus of previous research has not been on the accounting aspects.

The chapter offers some insights into how a small Irish brewery would have been affected by the government proposals in the historical context of the First World War and the emergence of an independent Irish Free State and compares it to contemporary accounting and finance principles. The use of a profit multiple to value a business does not find favour in financial theory but remains widely used in practice. However, elements of the government proposals appear flawed, such as the use of net profits rather than EBITDA and the use of a profit multiple for compensation of debenture holders rather than capping the payment at the par value of the debentures, thereby potentially disadvantaging the ordinary shareholders.

Appendix 1

Example of purchase consideration applied to a brewery's security-holders

Based on the *pro forma* capital structure contained in the appendix to the English and Welsh Committee's report, the purchase consideration would be allocated to the providers of capital in accordance with the security available for each class of capital, using a multiplier of 13 years' profits for Irish breweries. A brewery's profits are £11,000 and the capital structure of the brewery is as follows (Table 3.5).

The profits available to be paid as dividends to ordinary shareholders are calculated as follows (Table 3.6).

If the profits are divided into eleven portions, each eleventh (i.e. each £1,000) of profits has a different multiplier. The first eleventh (i.e. £1,000) of profits has a multiplier of 18; the second eleventh has a multiplier of 17; the third eleventh has a multiplier of 16; and so on until the final eleventh of profits has a multiplier of 8. The calculation of the average multiplier based on 11 portions is as follows: (18+17+16+15+14+13+12+11+10+9+8) / 11 = 13. However, the weighted average multiplier ranges between 9.1 and 16.5 in this example. These profit multipliers are applied to the various classes of capital as follows (Table 3.7).

Table 3.5 Capital structure of a brewery

Ordinary shares	£60,000
5% Debentures	£80,000
6.5% Preference shares with priority as to capital	*£60,000*
Total capital	*£200,000*

Table 3.6 Profits available for dividends to ordinary shareholders

Profits	£11,000
Less: Debenture interest calculated as 5% of £80,000	(£4,000)
Less: Preference dividends calculated as 6.5% of £80,000	(*£3,900*)
Profits therefore available for ordinary dividends	*£3,100*

Table 3.7 Profit multipliers applied to classes of capital

	Portion of profit	*Multiplier*	*Purchase consideration*
For debenture holders	£1,000	18	£18,000
	£1,000	17	£17,000
	£1,000	16	£16,000
	£1,000	15	*£15,000*
	£4,000	Weighted average = 16.5	*£66,000*
For preference shareholders	£1,000	14	£14,000
	£1,000	13	£13,000
	£1,000	12	£12,000
	£900	11	*£9,900*
	£3,900	Weighted average = 12.5	*£48,900*
For ordinary shareholders	£100	11	£1,100
	£1,000	10	£10,000
	£1,000	9	£9,000
	£1,000	8	*£8,000*
	£3,100	Weighted average = 9.1	*£28,100*
Total profit	£11,000	13	£143,000

Appendix 2

Macardle Moore and Company Limited annual accounts (extracts) 1909 to 1915

Table 3.8 Annual accounts extract for Macardle Moore and Company Limited for available years between 1909 and 1915

	1909		*1912*		*1914*		*1915*		*Change 1914–1915*
	£	£	£	£	£	£	£	£	£
Net profits		15,236		14,606		14,555		19,889	5,334
Less: adjustment of reserve								(3,633)	(3,633)
Carried over from last year		*3,074*		*3,143*		*3,132*		*3,133*	*1*
		18,310		17,749		17,687		19,389	1,702
Managers' salaries	(2,000)		(2,000)		(2,000)		(2,000)		0
Half year interim dividend	(1,687)		(1,687)		(1,687)		(1,687)		0
Bonus dividend 1%	*0*		*0*		*0*		*(337)*		(337)
		(3,687)		*(3,687)*		*(3,687)*		*(4,024)*	
		14,623		14,062		14,000		15,365	1,365
Appropriated as follows:									
Final dividend	(1,687)		(1,687)		(1,687)		(1,687)		0
Bonus dividend 1%			(337)		(337)		0		337
Bonus dividend 2%			0		0		(675)		(675)
Depreciation of casks, etc.	(1,138)		(1,144)		(1,141)				1,141

	1909		1912		1914		1915		Change 1914–1915
	£	£	£	£	£	£	£	£	£
Building & house property reserve	(1,024)		(1,000)		(1,000)		0		1,000
Reserve for scorage & bad debts	(2,500)		(2,000)		(2,000)		0		2,000
Reserve for depreciation of premises & plant	(1,000)		(1,000)		(1,000)		0		1,000
Reserve to meet depreciation of investments					(1,000)		0		1,000
General reserve fund	(4,500)		(4,000)		(2,700)		(9,000)		(6,300)
		(11,849)		(11,868)		(10,865)		(11,362)	
Balance to be carried forward		*2,774*		*2,894*		*3,135*		*4,003*	*868*

Table 3.9 Profit and loss accounts for Macardle Moore and Company Limited for available years between 1909 and 1915

	1909	1912	1914	1915	Change 1914–1915
	£	£	£	£	£
Profits on brewing	14,010	12,966	12,875	24,740	11,865
Interest on loans & dividends on investments	1,664	1,862	1,947	2,018	71
Balance of house rents	*624*	*821*	*787*	*936*	*149*
	16,298	*15,649*	*15,609*	*27,694*	*12,085*
Directors & auditors fees	216	222	219	233	14
Commission on profits	845	821	835	1,706	871
Bad debts written off & scorage	624	821	787	4,973	4,973
Depreciation				894	894
Balance to net revenue	*15,236*	*14,606*	*14,555*	*19,889*	*5,334*
	16,297	*15,649*	*15,609*	*27,695*	*12,086*

Table 3.10 Balance sheets for Macardle Moore and Company Limited for available years between 1909 and 1915

	1909		*1912*		*1914*		*1915*		*Change 1914–1915*
	£	£	£	£	£	£	£	£	£
Assets & Property:									
Sundry Trade Debts		44,652		43,240		48,552		28,303	(20,249)
Stocks		12,227		15,343		15,889		16,446	557
Premises		66,308		76,564		79,072		62,265	(16,807)
Investments at Cost		21,547		25,851		26,062			(26,062)
Investments as Valued								22,804	22,804
Cash on Hand & in Bank		*15,879*		*17,653*		*17,875*		*20,614*	*2,739*
		160,613		*178,651*		*187,450*		*150,432*	*37,018*
Capital & Liabilities:									
Share Capital issued		33,750		33,750		33,750		33,750	0
Reserves		105,579		125,612		133,323		87,000	(46,323)
Sundry Creditors		6,661		5,227		6,377		14,318	7,941
Net Revenue Account:									
Balance from last year	3,074		3,143		3,132		3,133		1
Net Profit for 12 months	*15,236*		*14,606*		*14,555*		*19,889*		5,334
	18,310		17,749		17,687		23,022		
Less: Adjustment of Reserve	*0*		*0*		*0*		*(3,633)*		(3,633)
	18,310		17,749		17,687		19,389		
Less:									
Managers' Salaries	(2,000)		(2,000)		(2,000)		(2,000)		0
Interim Dividend	*(1,687)*		*(1,687)*		*(1,687)*		*(2,025)*		(338)
		14,623		*14,062*		*14,000*		*15,364*	
		160,613		*178,651*		*187,450*		*150,432*	*(37,018)*

Table 3.11 Adjustments to profit figures used in applying valuation model

	1909	*1912*	*1914*	*1915*
	£	£	£	£
Net profits	15,236	14,606	14,555	19,889
Less:				
Managers' salaries	(2,000)	(2,000)	(2,000)	(2,000)
Depreciation	*(1,138)*	*(1,144)*	*(1,141)*	–
Adjusted net profits	*12,098*	*11,462*	*11,414*	*17,889*

Note: The 1915 net profit of £19,889 is *after* deduction of depreciation.

Notes

1 Ireland was ruled by Britain under the Act of Union from 1801, until the Free State was established in 1922.
2 The Bank of England Inflation Calculator calculates changes in the purchasing power of the pound sterling using a composite price index. The Inflation Calculator is located at www.bankofengland.co.uk/education/Pages/resources/inflationtools/calculator/default.aspx
3 The War Cabinet consisted of a small group of politicians to whom decision-making powers had been delegated by the Cabinet.
4 The term 'tied house' referred to a public house that was contractually obliged to purchase at least some of its beer from a particular brewery, unlike a 'free house', that was free to purchase its beer from any brewery or breweries.
5 In the official notification of his knighthood, Thomas Callan Macardle was described as "Chairman of the Louth Recruiting Committee, and pioneer of the Irish Tillage Movement" (The London Gazette, 1920, p. 3759).
6 A gravity of 1036 for beer is approximately 3.5% alcohol by volume.
7 The Chief Secretary for Ireland was responsible for governing Ireland and held a seat in the British cabinet. From 31st July 1916 until 5th May 1918, the post of Chief Secretary was filled by the Conservative MP Henry Edward Duke, who later became Sir Henry Duke and later still Lord Merrivale.
8 National newspapers studied include the *Irish Independent* and the *Irish Times*, and local newspapers studied include the *Dundalk Argus*.
9 The calculation of the average multiplier based on 11 portions is as follows: (18+17+16+15+14+13+12+11+10+9+8) / 11 = 13.
10 The calculation of the average multiplier based on 13 portions is as follows: (19+18+17+16+15+14+13+12+11+10+9+8+7) / 13 = 13.
11 Minor rounding differences occur because amounts in the original accounts are expressed in pounds, shillings and pence, whereas the spreadsheet uses numbers in pounds only.
12 An explanation of how the Bank of England's inflation calculator works can be found at www.bankofengland.co.uk/education/Pages/resources/inflationtools/calculator/how.aspx and the long-term price data provided by the Office for National Statistics can be found at www.ons.gov.uk/economy/inflationandpriceindices/timeseries/cdko/mm23.

References

Primary sources

Macardle Moore and Company Collection, Louth County Archives, Dundalk, County Louth, Ireland.

Files utilised:

PP00240/001/013
PP00240/003/012
PP00240/005/010
PP00240/007/001
PP00240/012/005/001/001
Lloyd George Papers, Parliamentary Archives, Houses of Parliament, London, United Kingdom.

Files utilised:

Chancellor of the Exchequer/Papers/Liquor Control
LG/C/23/2/6
LG/C/23/2/7
LG/C/23/2/11
The National Archives, Kew, United Kingdom.

Files utilised:

War Cabinet and Cabinet: Memoranda
CAB/23/2/24
CAB/24/5/1
CAB/24/8/41
CAB/24/78/63
GT1243
National Library of Ireland, Dublin.

Files utilised:

Newspaper archives, in microfilm holdings and in digital Irish Newspaper Archive.
Privately-held collection of a former employee of Macardle Moore and Company.

Secondary sources

Armstrong, J. (1991). An introduction to archival research in business history. *Business History*, 33(1), pp. 7–34.

Bank of England (2018). *Inflation Calculator.* [Online] Available at: www.bankofengland.co.uk/education/Pages/resources/inflationtools/calculator/default.aspx [Accessed 11th Feb. 2018].

Clarke, P. (1996). A glimpse at Irish accounting history. *Irish Accounting Review*, 3(2), pp. 23–38.

Daneshkhu, S. (2017). Beer sales slide as global alcohol consumption falls. *Financial Times*, 3rd June [Online] Available at: www.ft.com/content/5b7fab74-47a2-11e7-8d27-59b4dd6296b8 [Accessed 4th Sept. 2017].

Dennison, S. R. and MacDonagh, O. (1998). *Guinness 1886–1939: From Incorporation to the Second World War.* Cork: Cork University Press.

The Economist (2015). Beer monster; A giant drinks merger, 19th September [Online] Available at: www.economist.com/news/business/21665074-ab-inbev-may-combine-sabmiller-flat-market-big-beer-brands-beer-monster [Accessed 4th Sept. 2017].

The Economist (2016). A history of the authentically global beer, 24th December [Online] Available at: www.economist.com/news/christmas-specials/21712029-lagers-may-be-ubiquitous-india-pale-ales-are-beers-backstory-history [Accessed 4th Sept. 2017].

Evans, J. (2015). Chart that tells a story: Brewing old and new. *Financial Times*, 24th June [Online] Available at: www.ft.com/content/e6d8d8ba-15e2-11e5-be54-00144feabdc0 [Accessed 23rd Aug. 2017].

Financial Times (2015). SABMiller/AB InBev: Style and substance. *Lex Column*, 13th October [Online] Available at: www.ft.com/content/30fa92a2-717e-11e5-9b9e-690fdae72044 [Accessed 7th Dec. 2017].

Gervais, P. and Quinn, M. (2016). Costing in the early industrial revolution: Gradual change to cost calculations at US cloth mills in the 1820s. *Accounting History Review*, 26(3), pp. 191–217.

Gourvish, T. R. (1987). British business and the transition to a corporate economy: Entrepreneurship and management structures. *Business History*, 29(4), pp. 18–45.

Gourvish, T. R. (2006). What can business history tell us about business performance? *Competition & Change*, 10(4), pp. 375–392.

Gourvish, T. R. and Wilson, R. G. (1985). Profitability in the brewing industry, 1885–1914. *Business History*, 27(2), pp. 146–165.

Gourvish, T. R. and Wilson, R. G. (1994). *The British Brewing Industry 1830–1980*. Cambridge: Cambridge University Press.

Gutzke, D. W. (1990). Rhetoric and reality: The political influence of British brewers, 1832–1914. *Parliamentary History*, 9(1), pp. 78–115.

Hiebl, M. R., Quinn, M. and Martínez-Franco, C. (2015). An analysis of the role of a chief accountant at Guinness c. 1920–1940. *Accounting History Review*, 25(2), pp. 145–165.

Koller, T., Goedhart, M. and Wessels, D. (2005). *Valuation: Measuring and Managing the Value of Companies*. 4th ed. Hoboken: John Wiley & Sons, Inc.

The London Gazette (1920). Third supplement to the London Gazette of Friday the 26th March 1920, Number 31840, 30th March, pp. 3757–3870 [Online] Available at: www.thegazette.co.uk/London/issue/31840/supplement/3759 [Accessed 10th Sept. 2017].

Lynch, J. (2017). Molson's acquisition was a game changer for brewer. *Irish Independent*, 4th September [Online] Available at: www.independent.ie/business/world/molsons-acquisition-was-a-game-changer-for-brewer-36096651.html [Accessed 4th Sept. 2017].

Lynch, P. and Vaizey, J. (1960). *Guinness's Brewery in the Irish Economy 1759–1876*. Cambridge: Cambridge University Press.

Martinez Franco, C., Feeney, O., Quinn, M. and Hiebl, M. R. (2017). Position practices of the present-day CFO: A reflection on historic roles at Guinness, 1920–1945. *Revista de Contabilidad*, 20(1), pp. 55–62.

Mauboussin, M. J. and Callahan, D. (2014). What does a price-earnings multiple mean? An analytical bridge between P/Es and solid economics. *Credit Suisse*, 29th January.

Ó Drisceoil, D. and Ó Drisceoil, D. (1997). *The Murphy's Story: The History of Lady's Well Brewery, Cork*. Cork: Murphy Brewery Ireland.

Ó Drisceoil, D. and Ó Drisceoil, D. (2015). *Beamish & Crawford: The History of an Irish Brewery*. Cork: The Collins Press.

Office for National Statistics (2018). *Long-term Price Data*. [Online] Available at: www.ons.gov.uk/economy/inflationandpriceindices/timeseries/cdko/mm23 [Accessed 11th Feb. 2018].

O'Gráda, C. (1997). *Rocky Road: Irish Economy Since Independence*. Manchester: Manchester University Press.

Ógra Dun Dealgan (1986). *Dundalk: A Tradition in Industry*. Dundalk: Ógra Dun Dealgan Teamwork Project.

Ó hÓgartaigh, C. and Ó hÓgartaigh, M. (2004). Accounting and corporate governance archives in Ireland. *Irish Accounting Review*, 11(1), pp. 19–32.
Ó hÓgartaigh, M. (2008). Irish accounting, business and financial history: A bibliographical essay. *Accounting, Business & Financial History*, 18(1), pp. 7–19.
Palmer, F. B. (1890). *Private Companies: Their Formation and Advantages*. 8th ed. London: Stevens and Sons Limited.
Peelo, D. (2010). *The Valuation of Businesses and Shares: A Practitioner's Perspective*. Dublin: Chartered Accountants Ireland.
Quinn, M. (2014). Stability and change in management accounting over time: A century or so of evidence from Guinness. *Management Accounting Research*, 25(1), pp. 76–92.
Quinn, M. and Jackson, W. (2014). Accounting for war risk costs: Management accounting change at Guinness during World War 1. *Accounting History Review*, 24(2–3), pp. 191–209.
Ralph, O. (2015). AB InBev and SABMiller: Multiple multiples. *Financial Times*, 13th October [Online] Available at: www.ft.com/content/cf66a1df-25c2-3f0d-8d47-469e764f9a9e [Accessed 7th Dec. 2017].
Redmond, J. (1915). *House of Commons Debate on Income Tax*, HC Deb 4th May 1915 vol. 71 cc.1035–1045 [Online] Available at: http://hansard.millbanksystems.com/commons/1915/may/04/income-tax#S5CV0071P0_19150504_HOC_400 [Accessed 8th Aug. 2017].
Scott, J. (1990). *A Matter of Record: Documentary Sources in Social Research*. Cambridge: Polity Press.
Scranton, P. and Fridenson, P. (2013). *Reimagining Business History*. Baltimore: Johns Hopkins University Press.
Thompson, B. (2017). London celebrates international beer day with craft brewing success. *Financial Times*, 4th August [Online] Available at: www.ft.com/content/06f62050-7827-11e7-90c0-90a9d1bc9691 [Accessed 4th Sept. 2017].
Tighe, C. and Bounds, A. (2009). Family brewers sit alongside big brands. *Financial Times*, 26th October [Online] Available at: www.ft.com/content/c7b8083c-c1bc-11de-b86b-00144feab49a [Accessed 23rd Aug. 2017].
Turner, J. (September 1980). State purchase of the liquor trade in the First World War. *The Historical Journal*, 23(3), pp. 589–615.
Ua Dubhthaigh, P. (1946). *The Book of Dundalk*. Sligo, Ireland: Champion Publications.
Whittaker, T. (1917). *State Purchase and Control of the Drink Trade*. Reprinted (with additions) from The Daily Chronicle January 1917, pp. 1–10. London: The Daily Chronicle.
Williams, A. (2017). Small investors risk being lost in the crowd. *Financial Times*, 4th August [Online] Available at: www.ft.com/content/1161a174-2b68-11e7-bc4b-5528796fe35c [Accessed 4th Sept. 2017].

4 Orion Breweries Ltd.

Success, new product development and contribution to post-war reconstruction and the regional economy in Okinawa

Kazuhisa Kinoshita

Introduction

Orion Breweries, Ltd. was founded in Okinawa in 1957 and is today a representative of Okinawa. The Okinawa region consists of the Ryukyu Islands, scattered in the vast waters located southwest of Japan, and it has played an important role as a relay point for marine trade since ancient times. It has a subtropical and oceanic climate, which remains mild throughout the year and possesses an excellent natural environment.

Orion Breweries is one of the five companies that occupy the majority of the Japanese beer market. However, it has less than 1% of the market share, while the other four companies occupy 10% to 40% due to their large capital base and overwhelming sales volumes (Nikkan Keizai Tsushin, 2015, p. 147). However, by remaining close to its roots in Okinawa, Orion Breweries has succeeded in surviving such intense competition, supported by Okinawans. Orion Breweries was founded with high aspirations, as a company partially responsible for the reconstruction of Okinawa under US military rule after the Second World War. The company sought to rebuild Okinawa and the dreams of the young. Its management philosophy was to contribute to and distribute profits to society and progress together with Okinawa. Therefore, its mission was to survive and grow for the betterment of Okinawa. As Okinawa had few manufacturing industries, Orion Breweries became an important company supporting local industries.

This chapter is divided into two parts. The first part examines the foundation period of the company, based on the autobiography of its founder, the history of the company, statistical materials, etc. It includes the background of the foundation, planning and results of plant construction and production and the sales strategies for existing markets. The second part details interviews on new product development.[1] The interviews focused on manufacturing management and new product development from the viewpoint of new product strategy. Interview participants included persons in charge and responsible for each division of the head office and factory, and the total investigation time was about 12 hours. Since the 1990s, the Japanese beer market has become one of multi-product competition and thus it has become more important to develop new products according to changes in market needs and to repeatedly introduce new products to the market. Therefore, this part of the chapter examines target cost management in new product development and the response of Orion Breweries to competition.

Contributing to the reconstruction of Okinawa

On 14 August 1945, the Japanese government notified the Allies of its acceptance of the Potsdam Declaration. The Allied Forces had begun a full-scale attack against Okinawa five months previous. The Okinawa Islands are located in the Pacific Ocean in the southwest of Japan and were an important strategic base for the Allied Forces in their invasion of the Japanese mainland. The Japanese army, inferior in strength, continued fighting the Allied Forces to gain time to prepare for the battle on the mainland. The Battle of Okinawa was a long, intense, ground warfare through bombardment and mopping-up operations, which continued for more than three months, day and night. Civilian casualties were higher than military ones,[2] and buildings and production facilities were destroyed (Kinjo et al., 2005, pp. 225–227).

Immediately after landing in Okinawa, the US military placed the island under military administration and direct occupation (Kinjo et al., 2005, p. 227). Residents were put in camps, and most land was taken over for bases, such as airports and military ports. The sovereignty of Japan was restored after the signing of a peace treaty in San Francisco in 1951, and the country began its path to economic recovery. However, Okinawa remained under the rule of the United States. As the Cold War intensified, it was used as the 'keystone of the Pacific' in the Far Eastern strategy of the US military (Kinjo et al., 2005, p. 228). Okinawa returned to Japanese control in 1972; however, the US military base still remains in Okinawa and has become a major burden. After the war, Okinawa was destroyed and few manufacturing companies remained (Gushiken, 1965, p. 186). Supplies of daily necessities were only available from US camps, and wage labor was only for military work (Kinjo et al., 2005, p. 241). From 1951 to 1953, the United States allocated an enormous military budget to construct military bases in Okinawa. The Okinawan economy changed into a base economy that depended on US military bases, due to income derived from their construction and the deployment of tens of thousands of US soldiers. Between 1955 and 1966, the second post-war boom was due to the boom in Japan and strong exports of sugar (Orion Breweries, 1967, p. 71).

As living standards improved, beverages such as beer and wine were imported and a beer market developed in Okinawa. However, this boom was temporary, and the base economy was unstable. In government and business circles, the necessity of establishing an independent economy through the promotion of self-sufficient industries and export industries was understood (Orion Breweries, 1967, p. 71). Orion Breweries was founded in 1957 under such circumstances. Its founder, Mr Gushiken, felt a sense of crisis regarding the Okinawan economy, its excessive imports and dependence on the revenue of the US military base to cover shortfalls. Therefore, he aimed to develop industries to provide good-quality products to citizens at a low cost, acquire dollars through exports, prevent the outflow of dollars through self-sufficiency and the expansion of employment (Gushiken, 1965, p. 188).

Therefore, Orion Breweries aimed to develop an inexpensive beer that the public could drink every day. Its main competitor in this market was a mainland Japanese company, which was competing in a market that was more than 160 times the size of the Okinawan market.[3] Orion Breweries aimed to provide Okinawans with quality beer at a lower price than imported beer, export beer from Okinawa and support the Okinawan economy in the future. Mr Gushiken also hoped that the next generation would regain confidence and pride as Okinawans by succeeding in this difficult business and becoming a model for the reconstruction of Okinawa. Thus, he started a brewing company, a very difficult business, requiring advanced technologies (Gushiken, 1965, p. 204). He aspired to operate efficiently and use profits sensibly. He said that companies should work for, and prosper with, society. He also said, 'entrepreneurs must gain profit correctly and use it for good' (Gushiken, 1965, p. 202). Therefore, the articles of incorporation of Orion Breweries state that the company will 'return part of the profits to beneficial social projects' and 'contribution to the local community', and it continues various such activities to the present day.

Founding Orion Breweries

Business plan

One reason why Mr Gushiken began Orion Breweries was because he had tasted success operating a miso soy sauce company called Akamarusou. His brother, who was a fermentation engineer, thought that 'with refrigeration equipment, a brewing company can be established', even in Okinawa. After an intense investigation, he realized that the brewing business was a promising opportunity (Orion Breweries, 1967, p. 102). After listening to his story, Mr Gushiken conducted his own research. He realized that he could use his personal connections in the fermentation industry for this business and decided to promote the plan (Orion Breweries, 1967, p. 101, p. 103). The estimate for the construction and operation of the beer factory was $1.5 million. About $420,000 came by way of capital. The remaining $1.08 million was obtained through bank financing. The capital was about $4.17 per share, and 100,000 shares were offered publicly (Orion Breweries, 1967, p. 72, p. 74) so that as many people as possible could hold shares. As this was the first brewing business in Okinawa, the banks conducted their own investigation into the business model. Consequently, the banks decided to finance the business, subject to protection policies restricting beer imports by the government.[4] At this time, the success of Akamarusou had proven its credibility to the bank. This successful company played an important role in the foundation of Orion Breweries.

Factory production planning and import protection policy

Before foundation, a promoters' council was held in September 1956 (Orion Breweries, 1967, p. 73), which reported on the demand for beer in Okinawa and the plans of the factory to be built. At the time, beer demand was 2,900 kl for private consumption and 1,800 kl for military consumption, totalling 4,700 kl. The factory production capacity was set at 5,400 kl per year, which took into account an increase in that figure (Orion Breweries, 1967, p. 73). The amount of beer imported increased from 6,490,478 pounds in 1953 to 11,763,496 pounds in 1957; demand increased every year by 10% to 20% compared to the previous year (Statistics Agency of Planning Department, GRI, 1957, p. 115; 1958, p. 116). At this rate, the market size for private demand alone would increase to 5,400 kl in about 10 years.

The production capacity was planned in view of the government's protection policy to regulate beer imports. As mentioned, the bank requested that the Civil Administration implemented protection policies for import regulation as a necessary condition for financing Orion Breweries. The Civil Administrator approved it, and the Administration consented (Orion Breweries, 1967, pp. 102–103). As a precedent for import restrictions, a protection policy for miso soy sauce was implemented from 1953 to 1954. Akamarusou had made significant progress in selling and sharing[5] in Okinawa with this protection policy, which boosted the company's growth (Gushiken, 1965, pp. 181–182). When Orion Breweries began operations, its sales target for the 1959 financial year was 2,160 kl (Orion Breweries, 1967, p. 83). This target was 75% of the 2,900 kl of private demand[6] at the time. In September 1959, the company started petitioning the Administration to implement import restrictions (Orion Breweries, 1967, p. 113).

For Orion Breweries to compete with imported beer and export its own beer, it was essential to augment factory scale as much as possible, increase production and sales volume and raise the operation ratio of the factory. At that time, the economically viable size of a brewery factory was about 36,000 kl (Orion Breweries, 1967, p. 109, p. 111). In 1959, the brewing companies on the Japanese mainland manufactured about 896,000 kl of beer at 15 plants (manufacturing licensee) (National Tax Agency, 1960, p. 162), which averages about 60,000 kl per factory. Mainland companies achieved high-cost competitiveness through mass production at plants with large production capacities. Orion Breweries set its factory's production capacity equal to the market size of Okinawa (5,400 kl in 1959) to ensure that the production capacity was as large as possible. Despite this, it was about 15% of the size of a viable unit on the mainland, and only about 9% of the average of mainland competitors. In addition, Orion Breweries had obtained a loan from the bank of two-thirds of the total assets for the construction and operation of the factory. They had to increase sales and stabilize management as soon as possible to repay the principal and interest. To achieve this, it was necessary to build a large factory at the outset and rapidly increase sales volume to raise the operation ratio of the factory. Therefore, Orion Breweries had to acquire a high market share in Okinawa, and import regulation was necessary. Thus, we can see that during the foundation years, the business plan of the company, including sales forecasts and factory production plans, was based on import restrictions by the government. This was the lifeline of the company's management.

Budgetary control in factory construction

The promoters' council calculated the construction costs of the factory. They considered a set of used brewery facilities sold by a Japanese mainland company[7] and calculated the value based on expert evaluation (Gushiken, 1965, pp. 207–208; Orion Breweries, 1967, p. 77). Although this purchase negotiation fell through, Orion Breweries could now build a better factory by implementing budgetary control. They canceled their plans to import a used plant and equipment and decided to purchase new machines separately. As it was not possible to increase the construction budget, they began building a new factory with the original purchase budget. An engineer who was familiar with the facilities in a brewery was invited, and he developed a new factory design. This new design matched the market size of Okinawa. This was an efficient factory design that could reduce construction and operation costs by referring to facilities in various places (Orion Breweries, 1967, p. 109, p. 111). Machine makers, directors and officials of Orion Breweries negotiated directly for each machine and succeeded in purchasing new machines within the original budget. This enabled them to manage the construction costs of the factory in the original equipment import budget. The construction cost of this factory not only included the costs of additional construction and accompanying facilities, but it also was only about two-thirds of the construction costs of a new factory at that time (Orion Breweries, 1967, p. 78, p. 110). Although the initial purchase plan failed, by maintaining the factory construction budget and developing various activities, Orion Breweries built better facilities, substantially reducing construction and factory operation costs.

In 1962, Orion Breweries achieved a sales volume of 5,495 kl, equivalent to the factory's production capacity (5,400 kl). Their profit was $343,562, with a profit margin of 11.8%. Remarkably, they succeeded in making profits at a factory that was only 15% the size of the typical economically viable unit of 36,000 kl at the time. The demand for beer expanded with the economic recovery of Okinawa, and the sales volume of Orion Breweries continued to increase. Therefore, the company invested in factories to improve production capacity, reduce costs and improve quality. In 1993, the company expanded its production capacity to 72,000 kl, which is the current production capacity (Orion Breweries, 1998, p. 197). Today, Orion Breweries continues to invest in plant facilities to reduce costs and improve quality.

The success of Orion Breweries

First release

Orion Breweries released 'Orion Beer' on 17 May 1959. The beer was a German type of beer with a slightly bitter taste brewed from wheat, hops, malt and yeast from Germany (Orion Breweries, 1967, pp. 81–82, pp. 152–153; 1998, p. 33). The taste of this beer came under some criticism. Orion beer had an abundance of hops and a strong bitter taste (Orion Breweries, 1967, p. 82, p. 112). Beer importers in the Okinawan market soon strengthened their sales network and had abundant funds to advertise and protect their market share. Orion Breweries had no money to counter them and began losing out. The sales for the year were about one-third of the target – 797 kl against the target of 2,160 kl (Orion Breweries, 1967, p. 83, p. 169). Despite it having a lower price than imported beer due to the government's tax-based protection measures, sales of Orion beer did not pick up (Orion Breweries, 1967, p. 82).

The government had been taxing imported beer under the alcohol consumption tax law. The Legislature of the Government of the Ryukyu Islands (GRI) decided the tax rate through the alcohol consumption tax law. The Legislature discussed it from various viewpoints such as increasing tax revenue, protecting the industries on the islands, equivalence of liquor tax with mainland Japan, taxation on luxury goods, tax burden equality, dollar income from Americans and smuggling for tax evasion. However, the Civil Administration, which reflected the intention of the US military, would sometimes refuse the decisions of the GRI. The Legislature continued deliberation to raise the alcohol consumption tax to 200% in negotiations with the Civil Administration. In 1958, when Orion Breweries began brewing its beer, the rate of tax on all imported alcoholic beverages, including beer, reached 185%. In the following year, only the imported beer tax rate was raised to 200% to protect the industry on the islands (GRI, 1954a, pp. 41–45; 1954b, pp. 17–19; 1954c, p. 56; 1956a, pp. 18–19; 1956b, pp. 18–19; 1956c, pp. 4–5; 1956d, pp. 16–19; 1958a, pp. 1–3; 1958b, p. 1; The Legislature of GRI, 1958, p. 8; 1959, pp. 12–13). The tax rate that they had requested was thus realized only for beer.

The new tax rate for beer was $21 per 100 liters (The Legislature of GRI, 1959, pp. 10–13). The tax per larger bottle (633 ml) was 13 cents. The market price of Orion beer at the time of release was 45 cents for such a bottle (633 ml), and a price difference of about 10 cents was added to the price of imported beer (Orion Breweries, 1998, p. 25, pp. 86–87). This protection measure would result in a price difference of about 20% at retail price, due to liquor tax and alcohol consumption tax.

Tax preferential policies were implemented the year Orion Breweries began brewing; however, import restrictions such as an import ban were not implemented. Orion Breweries petitioned the Administration to implement import restrictions on foreign beer from September 1959 to April 1960 in a bid to improve sales (Orion Breweries, 1967, p. 113). As already mentioned, the import restriction was a premise for bank financing at the time of establishment, approved by the Civil Administrator and backed by the Civil Administration. Consequently, Orion Breweries faced a crisis that could result in the US military depriving them of management rights.[8] To resolve this, Orion Breweries staked their existence on their sales strategy.

Strengthening the sales structure

First, Orion Breweries reorganized their sales structure. They had insufficient finances to prepare a sales network (Falstaff Brewing Corporation, 1961, p. 22); therefore, they began granting franchises to distributors covering Okinawa. However, some franchises also sold competing imported beers, something the company could not control. Therefore, Orion Breweries established a new company to sell their beer in June 1960 (Orion Breweries, 1967, p. 86, p. 114). Next, they carried out intensive sales activities to increase the number of restaurants and bars selling Orion beer, a strategy known as 'Human Wave Tactics'. Everyone from the president to the employees of Orion Breweries went to several restaurants every day to order Orion beer. Officers and employees of affiliated companies also cooperated in this activity. They went to restaurants and bars for sales at noon and as customers at night. They reported on the previous day and made plans for the day at the morning meeting. Repeating this many times, they increased the number of restaurants and bars selling Orion beer. Employees established good relations with restaurants and bars salespeople. Consequently, salespeople began recommending Orion beer to other customers. In addition, the company conducted various sales promotion activities, including sales incentives to restaurants and salespeople (Orion Breweries, 1967, pp. 86–87, p. 116, p. 118). Through its beer and these sales activities, Orion Breweries fostered a sense of unity among Okinawans, an intimate relationship between employees and salespersons, best described by the belief 'knowing is the source of love' (Orion Breweries, 1967, p. 86, p. 119). This made the sales promotion campaign more effective. The sales promotion activities for crisis management also imposed a heavy burden on employees (Orion Breweries, 1967, p. 116), but they did help Orion Breweries to establish itself as a brewery in Okinawa.

Product strategy

Orion Breweries did not succeed purely due to promotional activities. The company declared that it would 'make beers that match everyone's taste' (Orion Breweries, 1967, p. 82) to counter criticism of the taste of its beer and improved their brew to match the tastes of the people of Okinawa.[9] They invited drinkers across Okinawa to test the quality of Orion beer through quality contests, blind tests with other beers and so on. Although the company obtained good ratings on quality, it still could not penetrate the market (Orion Breweries, 1967, p. 84).

They also implemented a product strategy that took advantage of their manufacturing capabilities. In February 1960, the company began selling bottled draft beer, an idea of the factory manager. Draft beer is not heat-sterilized[10]; as at the time, the technology for long-term storage was not yet available, and the product had to be handled with care. Initially, the company sold bottled draft beer only at restaurants and bars near the factory. While all competing imported beers were heat-sterilized beers, bottled draft beer had a 'fresh taste' and 'special image' and succeeded in increasing popularity. Focusing on this, the company started selling bottled draft beer to restaurants and bars throughout Okinawa and sales began to increase (Orion Breweries, 1967, p. 87, p. 116). In a taste test by Falstaff's examiners,[11] Orion beer was considered better than the representative beer in Japan, thanks to the passage of time after bottling (Falstaff, 1961, p. 47, p. 50). Compared to beer bottled in Japan and imported by ship, Orion beer bottled on Okinawa had a great advantage: freshness.

Draft beer is a product strategy that incorporates the perception of freshness that the Japanese associate with 'raw', such as sushi and sashimi (Fujisawa, 2009, p. 271). Regional characteristics of the small market in Okinawa made the introduction of bottled draft beer possible. Orion Breweries was able to sell this product because the area of consumption was close to the factory and they had close relationships with restaurants and bars. It became a weapon of sales promotion activities. Consequently, the sales and market share were 797 kl and 14.4% in 1959 when sales began, 1,446 kl and 24.8% in 1960 when the promotion activity started, 2,862 kl and 46.6% in 1961 and 5,495 kl and 64.5% in 1962 (Orion Breweries, 1998, p. 216). The company succeeded in increasing sales performance, and the profit and loss and profit margin on sales were ($45,070) and (10.5%) in 1959, $39,160 and 5.0% in 1960, $216,453 and 13.9% in 1961, $343,562 and 11.8% in 1962 (Orion Breweries, 1998, p. 218). From a deficit in 1959, the company entered a surplus in 1960. This is consistent with a break-even analysis in the Falstaff report conducted in March 1961. It explains that the production volume at the break-even point is 1,275 kl and contribution profit is 133.12 $/kl (Falstaff, 1961, p. 57). However, repayment of the principal and interest to banks was rescheduled until 1961, considering the business situation (Gushiken, 1965, pp. 218–219; Orion Breweries, 1967, p. 120), and the company actually began repayment in 1962 (Gushiken, 1965, p. 219). Although profits had been posted from 1960 onwards, if the company had paid loan interest as agreed, profit would have decreased into 1961.

Cooperation of banks

The banks rescheduled the repayment for several reasons. One was Akamarusou, operated by Mr Gushiken, the founder of Orion Breweries. Orion Breweries was trusted and received cooperation from banks through the difficult period after its foundation. Akamarusou inspired confidence in the bankers, who said, 'we lend money to Orion Breweries looking at Akamarusou' (Orion Breweries, 1967, p. 121). Furthermore, the banks predicted that the investment in the factory could not be recovered and they would suffer substantial losses if Orion Breweries went bankrupt. Another reason was social responsibility, as Orion

Breweries was a big project to promote industry in Okinawa. The promotion of industries in Okinawa depended on the success or failure of Orion Breweries, a reflection on the management ability of Okinawans under US military rule. If it was to fail, the management ability of Okinawans would be suspect. Therefore, the banks cooperated with Orion Breweries, considering the impact on the entire Okinawan economy (Gushiken, 1965, pp. 218–219; Orion Breweries, 1967, pp. 118–119). Orion Breweries paid its first dividend in 1961, despite the rescheduling of repayments. Okinawans knew that Orion Breweries was in a difficult business. Some invested without expectations and others predicted no dividends for 10 years (Orion Breweries, 1967, p. 104). Therefore, it was necessary to convince people that Orion Breweries was 'successful'. The dividend for 1961 was paid as sales commission (Orion Breweries, 1967, pp. 120–121) in tandem with the banks, which cooperated with the company.

Increasing share of Orion Breweries

The consumption of beer continued to increase rapidly with the development of the Okinawan economy and rising income levels. With increasing sales, brewing companies from the Japanese mainland also began to intensify sales promotion activities. However, Orion Breweries increased its sales, market share and profit (Orion Breweries, 1967, p. 90). The company cut prices in 1963 and 1964 based on the policy that profit sharing with society is to 'deliver delicious beer at a low price' above all. Consequently, sales increased but profits declined. However, inflation had become a social problem; therefore, consumers were happy with this price cut. The company's market share in Okinawa was 89.1% in 1964 when they cut prices, and 93.1% in 1965 (Orion Breweries, 1998, p. 215).

As the promise of the Civil Administration on import restrictions was not implemented, Orion Breweries landed in a management crisis. However, Orion Breweries made beer that could compete against other companies, rebuilt its sales structure and gained customer loyalty while overcoming this adversity. In addition, they gained the support of many citizens, aided by related companies, due to the company's management philosophy of supporting Okinawan society by returning its profits. Consequently, Orion Breweries achieved astonishing growth. On this management crisis, the president of the Bank of the Ryukyus opined that 'as a result, it was good for Orion Breweries' (Orion Breweries, 1967, p. 114).

Multi-product strategy and new product development

Reversion of Okinawa to Japan and multi-product competition

In 1972, Okinawa went back under Japanese control. Until then, the Okinawan economy had 'established its own economic structure under US military rule' (Orion Breweries, 1998, p. 84). Therefore, it was feared that Okinawa's economy would be unable to compete with Japanese mainland companies after the reversion without the protection policy of the island industry. Therefore, the Japanese government enacted the 'Act on Special Measures Incidental to Reversion of Okinawa'. The rate of the liquor tax was reduced as preferential treatment for alcoholic beverages produced and sold in Okinawa Prefecture.[12]

Orion Breweries was successful in taking about 90% of the beer market in Okinawa under US military rule. After the reversion of Okinawa, four Japanese mainland brewing companies competing in a market more than 100 times larger entered the beer market in Okinawa, despite transportation costs from the mainland. Distributors in Okinawa were either directly operated or grouped according to distributorship agreements (Yoshida et al., 1977, p. 222). Orion Breweries was able to increase sales volume as the beer market expanded until the 1990s; however, its market share in Okinawa decreased.[13]

Change in product line-up

Figure 4.1 shows the release and final sales of products by Orion Breweries from its foundation until 2009.[14] The main product of Orion Breweries was 'Orion beer' until the 1990s. Due to changing trends in the beer market, the company's product strategy changed from a single product line-up to a multi-product line-up. They released new products almost every year since 2000. Since 2004, the company produces and sells about seven products at the same time. The number of beer varieties manufactured relates to sales and manufacturing problems. For

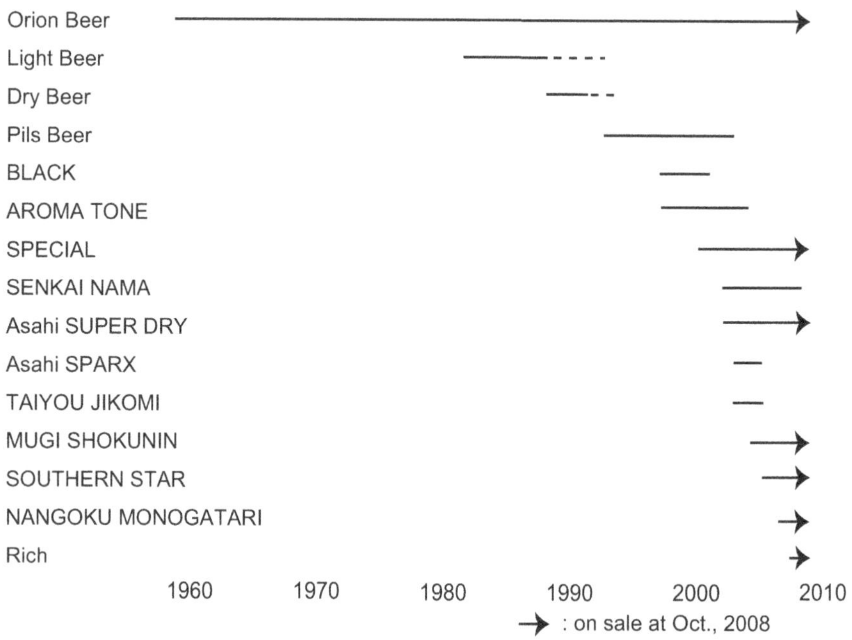

Figure 4.1 Product line-up and life cycles

Source: Orion Breweries (1998, 2008)

example, to increase sales, it is necessary to secure as much space as possible in the beer section of a retailer. However, due to limited shelf sizes, if competitors increase the variety of products, it will reduce the space for products of Orion Breweries, which decreases sales instantly. To compete with other brewing companies, Orion Breweries also needed to develop and sell as many varieties as possible. Although the sales volume of individual products will reduce, it is possible to increase the operation level of the factory, as sales volume as a whole can secure profits. As Orion Breweries needed to brew multiple beers in one factory, manufacturing costs increased due to constraints. Even in the management of quality and inventory, cost increases with more products. Since manufacturing costs are managed for each product, unprofitable products with decreasing production are sold out and new products released to meet market needs.

New product development system

While retaining Orion beer as the main product, the company researched new product development and process and quality improvement in their laboratory – both of which were necessary to survive the increased competition once mainland breweries became a more dominant feature in the market. It did not release many products, but research achievements such as recipes[15] were accumulated. Orion Breweries prepared a new product development system to deal with customer needs quickly, respond to increasing numbers of new product releases and develop a multi-product strategy. Figure 4.2 shows the process of new product development and the outline of the departments in charge. First, an operating committee composed of all directors decide long-term product plans for long- and medium-term management plans. Next, the product development review committee examines and formulates medium- and short-term product strategies and considers individual product planning. The basic members of the product development review committee are personnel belonging to the sales planning department, sales planning division, product development division, quality assurance division, quality control room and manufacturing department. In addition, members of other departments will participate as necessary. Participants from all departments of the company can consider various issues from the early stages of new product development and create better products.

As the beer market in Japan changes swiftly, if product development takes too long, the market will change before product launch. For successful new product development, it is necessary to complete the process quickly. Therefore, Orion Breweries divided new product development into two stages. In the first stage, the company develops basic recipes, irrespective of specific product development. Various developments are made according to specific themes under some free conditions. Recipes with good results are screened as recipe candidates, which become the basis of new products released in the future. In the second stage, the company develops specific individual products to release as a new product based on a definitive product concept, in a short period of about six months to one year. This is the individual product development phase and trial

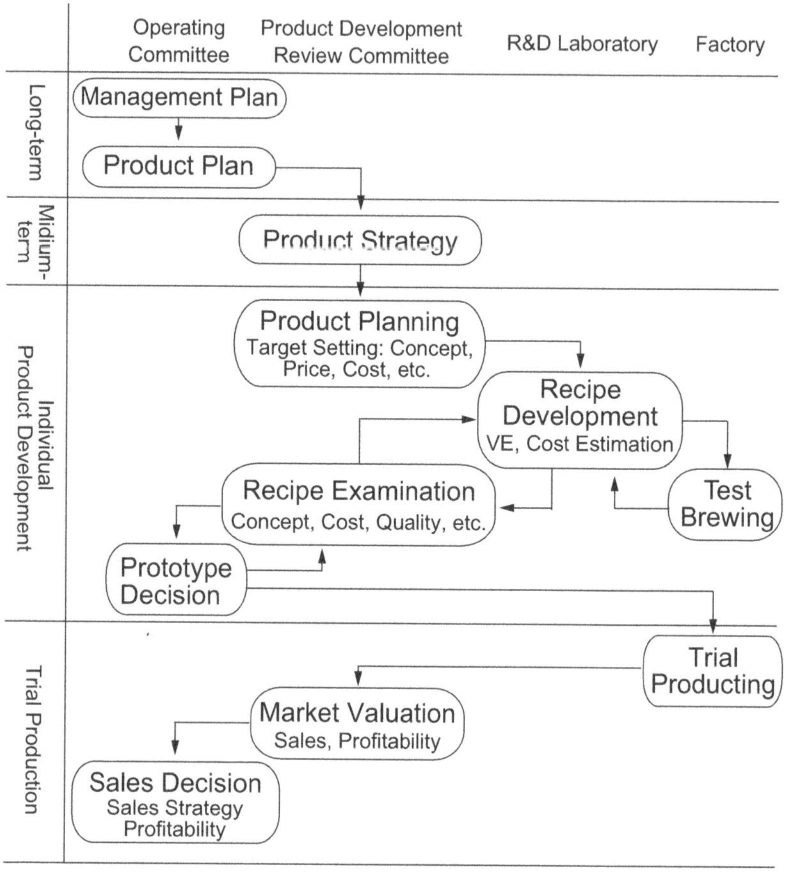

Figure 4.2 New product development process

Source: Orion Breweries materials

production in Figure 4.2. In individual product planning, the product development review committee examines the product concept, target sales price, target cost, target release date, target sales quantity, target market share, etc., of the new product, and determines the new product plan. When the operating committee approves this plan, it proceeds to recipe development.

In recipe development, several basic recipes suitable for product concepts are first selected. Product development is repeated based on these basic recipes until the new product is ready in the R&D laboratory. The development process includes the implementation of activities to achieve targets such as value engineering (VE), the use of cost tables and cooperation between departments, such as the purchasing department. The product development review committee examines recipes that have cleared strict standards from various aspects such as product concept, target cost and quality. If the committee decides that the targets are not achieved, the activities continue. The product development review committee selects one to three recipes as candidates for the new product. Furthermore, the operating committee considers whether to move the chosen recipe to the next phase. Once approved by the operating committee, prototyping at the factory and market testing are conducted. The product development review committee makes sales forecasts and profitability evaluations based on this result. If the review results are positive, the operating committee proceeds to the final review before the release of the product and makes a final judgment on whether to release it or not.

In summary, with changes in the beer market, it became necessary to sell multiple beers and release new products regularly, responding to changes in customer needs. Orion Breweries has developed its own new product development system so that new products could be quickly introduced to the market. Target cost management is implemented to simultaneously achieve a number of targets, such as product concept, selling price, manufacturing cost and release time. Therefore, Orion Breweries can sell beers that satisfy the taste buds of Okinawans and acquire a competitive advantage in the Okinawan market.

Concluding comments

In this chapter, we first examined the efforts of Orion Breweries in the historical context of the company's founding and its connection with society. The societal situation of the devastated islands and the economy in the post-war reconstruction period and US military rule became the background, playing an important role in management. At the time, the company had to change various plans, and it faced a management crisis. It implemented budget management, cost management and sales and product strategies to overcome these obstacles, leading to better performance and growth. In recent years, to respond to major changes in the beer market, the company put in place a product development system and implemented target cost management, achieving success in developing a multiproduct strategy and new competitive products.

Orion Breweries was also successful because it had the support of Okinawan society, which combined with the philosophy of Orion Breweries. The philosophy of contributing to society established the significance of companies in Okinawa and obtained empathy from society. This philosophy helped Orion Breweries continue to contribute to society. Contributing to the food culture in Okinawa helped Orion Breweries products match the needs of consumers, becoming the source of its competitiveness. Orion Breweries was born in Okinawa and grew with Okinawa. In addition, it must survive to support the Okinawan economy and contribute to Okinawan society, something they are still striving to do.

Acknowledgments

The author would like to thank Orion Breweries. Ltd., Mr Atsushi Uema, Mr Ishikawa, Mr Kina, Mr Masaki Uema, Mr Miyazato, Mr Shimabukuro, Mr Takara and especially Mr Taira.

Notes

1 These interviews were conducted in 2008 and 2009, but subsequently Orion Breweries has changed and grew as the market environment changed, and thus the content of this chapter may not be reflective of the current situation. The author alone is responsible for the content of this chapter.
2 Approximately 200,000 people were killed in the Okinawa war. Among them, 12,520 US soldiers, 65,908 Japanese soldiers outside Okinawa Prefecture, 28,228 soldiers and civilians in military service from Okinawa prefecture and about 94,000 civilians (Okinawa Prefecture Department of Welfare and Health, 1996, p. 56).
3 The total demand for beer in Okinawa was 5,533 kl (Orion Breweries, 1998, p. 215), while the production volume in Japan was 895,950 kl (National Tax Agency, 1960, p. 168) in 1959 when Orion Breweries began production.
4 As the United States Civil Administration of the Ryukyu Islands funded the banks, they thought they "lent $ 1 million to Orion Breweries" (Orion Breweries, 1967, p. 113). It was necessary to acquire the internal agreement and cooperation of the Civil Administration for the foundation and protection policy in advance (Orion Breweries, 1967, p. 72, p. 84, p. 104).
5 After a year and a half, the import ban was released in 1954 and the goods tax became 20% for soy sauce and 10% in miso after complete liberalization for about one year. Under this protection policy, in the 1960s, Akamarusou acquired Okinawa's market share of about 70% in soy sauce and about 60% in miso (Gushiken, 1965, p. 182).
6 This is approximately 40% of the demand in Okinawa (5,533 kl), which includes military demand in 1959. However, the military consumed a lot of foreign beer, and the distribution network for the military was weak. Therefore, the first sales target for Orion Breweries was private demand mainly from Japanese beer.
7 At that time, it was difficult to build production facilities in Okinawa; therefore, it was common to import equipment and plants as a set (Orion Breweries, 1967, p. 109).
8 The reason was to conserve the US funds financed by Orion Breweries through banks (Orion Breweries, 1967, pp. 113–114).
9 Orion Breweries is now an essential part of Okinawa's food culture as the beer of Okinawa. This is due to the management philosophy of "contribution to food culture" and continuing to improve their beer so that it fits the climate, food culture and market of Okinawa.
10 As the bottle was not heated for sterilization, the surface temperature of a bottle filled with beer was as low as 2 to 3 degrees Celsius, and the company could not put a label on the bottle in the beginning. Therefore, they attached a trademark seal to the bottle with rubber instead of a label. The company bought this trademark seal for 2 cents per seal. This motivated store clerks to recommend Orion beer to customers, which was an effective promotion for the company (Orion Breweries, 1998, p. 41).
11 In March 1961, the research team of Falstaff Brewing Corporation was invited to Okinawa by the High Commissioner from the United States to inspect Orion Breweries. They tested the taste of Orion beer and Kirin beer, stating that it was not fair because a taste test was for American beer. They noted problems with the taste of Orion beer and advised on manufacturing and materials.
12 This special measure was to fix liquor tax at the original 40%. It was rounded up by 10% each year, and it was equivalent to the original liquor tax in the sixth year. However, due to the oil crisis in 1973 and a depression in Okinawa's economy, it was extended and the original 80% liquor tax was applied.
13 Orion Breweries maintained 74.9% of Okinawa's market share in 1996. The subsequent market share information has not been disclosed.
14 Alcoholic beverages released as new products, except package changes, such as new labels and new designs and seasonal limited items.
15 Orion Breweries calls what is equivalent to the product's design drawing a 'recipe'. This recipe determines raw materials, procedures of manufacturing process and so on.

References

Falstaff Brewing Corporation (1961). *Report on Orion Brewing Company: Preface, Marketing, Product, Physical Plant and Financial Aspects*. Unpublished.

Fujisawa, H. (2009). *Historical Development of Brewing Equipment [Bīru jyōzō setubi hatten no keitōka tyōsa]*. Survey Reports on the Systemization of Technologies, 14, pp. 259–331.

The Government of Ryukyu Islands (1952). *Bulletin ed. extra [Kōhō gōgai]*. 6. Naha: Document Division, Chief Executive's Secretariat.

The Government of Ryukyu Islands (1954a) *Bulletin ed. extra [Kōhō gōgai]*. 17. Naha: Document Division, Chief Executive's Secretariat.

The Government of Ryukyu Islands (1954b) *Bulletin ed. extra [Kōhō gōgai]*. 21. Naha: Document Division, Chief Executive's Secretariat.

The Government of Ryukyu Islands (1954c) *Bulletin ed. extra [Kōhō gōgai]*. 22. Naha: Document Division, Chief Executive's Secretariat.

The Government of Ryukyu Islands (1956a) *Bulletin ed. extra [Kōhō gōgai]*. 20. Naha: Document Division, Chief Executive's Secretariat.

The Government of Ryukyu Islands (1956b) *Bulletin ed. extra [Kōhō gōgai]*. 21. Naha: Document Division, Chief Executive's Secretariat.

The Government of Ryukyu Islands (1956c) *Bulletin ed. extra [Kōhō gōgai]*. 29. Naha: Document Division, Chief Executive's Secretariat.

The Government of Ryukyu Islands (1956d) *Bulletin ed. extra [Kōhō gōgai]*. 30. Naha: Document Division, Chief Executive's Secretariat.

The Government of Ryukyu Islands (1958a) *Bulletin ed. extra [Kōhō gōgai]*. 35. Naha: Document Division, Chief Executive's Secretariat.

The Government of Ryukyu Islands (1958b) *Bulletin ed. extra [Kōhō gōgai]*. 63. Naha: Document Division, Chief Executive's Secretariat.

Gushiken, S. (1965). *Damn It! I Will Do It! [Nanikuso, yaruzo]*. Naha: Ryuhokai.

Kinjo, S., Uehara, K., Akiyama, M., Nakachi, T. and Oshiro, M. (2005). *100 Years in Okinawa Prefecture [Okinawa-ken no 100 nen]*. Tokyo: Yamakawa Shuppan.

The Legislature of the Government of the Ryukyu (1958). *Proceedings of the Legislature of the Government of the Ryukyu Islands. [Rippōin kaigiroku]*. 21. Naha: Report Division, Legislature Secretariat.

The Legislature of the Government of the Ryukyu (1959). *Proceedings of the Legislature of the Government of the Ryukyu Islands. [Rippōin kaigiroku]*. 21. Naha: Report Division, Legislature Secretariat.

National Tax Agency (1960). *National Tax Agency Annual Statistics Report [Kokuzeityō tōkei nenpōsho]*. ed. Tokyo: National Tax Agency.

Nikkan Keizai Tsushin (2015). *Manufacturing, Marketing Shares in the Liquor & Food Industries [Syurui syokuhin sangyō no seisan, hanbai shea]*. ed. Tokyo: Nikkan Keizai Tsushin.

Okinawa Prefecture Department of Welfare and Health (1996). *History of Okinawa's Relief Assistance; 50th Anniversary of the End of the War in Okinawa [Okinawa no engo no ayumi; Okinawa sen syūketu 50 syūnen kinen]*. Naha: Okinawa Prefecture.

Orion Breweries, Ltd. (1967). *10 Years of History [10 nen no ayumi]*. Naha: Orion Breweries, Ltd.

Orion Breweries, Ltd. (1998). *40 Years of Orion Breweries' History [Orionbīru 40 nen no ayumi]*. Urasoe: Orion Breweries, Ltd.

Orion Breweries, Ltd. (2008). *50 Years of Orion Breweries' History [Orionbīru 50 nen no ayumi]*. Urasoe: Orion Breweries, Ltd.

Statistics Agency of Planning Department, Government of the Ryukyu Islands (1957). *Ryukyus Statistical Yearbook [Ryukyu Tōkei Nenkan]*. ed. 1955–56. 1. Naha: Statistics Agency of Planning Department, Government of the Ryukyu Islands.

Statistics Agency of Planning Department, Government of the Ryukyu Islands (1958). *Ryukyus Statistical Yearbook [Ryukyu Tōkei Nenkan]*. ed. 1956–57. 2. Naha: Statistics Agency of Planning Department, Government of the Ryukyu Islands.

Yoshida, K., Toma, M., Makishi, Y., Sakihama, M. and Majikina, T. (1977). Present situation and prospect of Orion Breweries [Orionbīru no genjyou to tenbou]. *Jiryu*, 2(1), pp. 203–255.

5 What shall we do with the drunken sailor? Accounting and controls for alcohol in the Royal Navy in the time of Nelson

Karen McBride and Tony Hines

Introduction

Alcohol had been issued to seafarers as part of their staple diet from as early as 1361 (Hewitt, 1966). The reasons for this are diverse. Initially, it was a question of beer being easier than water to keep potable and to store while at sea. Later it was believed that it assisted in the prevention of scurvy (Stubbs, 2003). Even after this was found not to be the case, beer continued to be issued for health reasons (Henderson Smith, 1918). In 1796 lemon juice was finally issued to all naval ships in foreign service, for health and for the prevention of scurvy, and in 1799 this was extended to ships serving in home waters (Baron, 2009), but the beer allowance remained, even though beer was bulky to carry and required much room to store.

This chapter considers the regulations and accounting for controlling the use of beer (and other alcohol). The chapter is informed by the later works of Foucault, his ideas of 'governmentality', the distancing of control from the central power and direction being divested to the organisational level. Foucault's work observes that the unthinkable may become thinkable, where procedures and methods are put in place for one purpose but end up being utilised for another purpose that was not expected at first (Foucault, 1980). We argue that initially the accounting and control of beer was determined for cost and provision control; beer was issued for the seafarers' health and well-being, replacing often foetid water. Later it was used for the prevention of scurvy. Finally, it was used to keep the men in a controllable but mildly inebriated state, which alleviated the hardships they were under. Accounting was instrumental in this, as it provided the means by which the allocation was measured and supplemented.

This chapter considers how the administration and regulation of the Victualling Board[1] and of pursers was used to control alcohol within the Royal Navy at the time of Nelson. Archival documents have been sourced to determine these regulations and how the accounting was carried out to control the storage and allocation of beer and the purchase of wine and spirits to ensure the sailors received their daily allowances.

The chapter considers the period often referred to in naval history literature as relating to Nelson's Navy (Lavery, 1989), being broadly late 18th to early

19th century (dates for this period vary). For this chapter, we have focussed on 1793 to 1815, a period when the French Revolutionary War was followed by the Napoleonic Wars. In 1793, French troops took over Belgian land and impacted on the overland trade of the Dutch and the British, so war was declared. This was a period of huge public expenditure. Britain, focussing on possessions overseas, spent large sums of money to assist in financing their allies. Our period ends with the fall of Napoleon at the battle of Waterloo in 1815. For background we have also elucidated some material either side of these dates to provide further context.

The chapter is structured as follows. Next, there is a background section, which starts by explaining the role of beer and other alcohols in the Royal Navy during the time of Nelson. The second part of this background section, focussing on the Portsmouth Dockyard, outlines the setting up of a brewery; there were also breweries related to the dockyards at Plymouth and in London. It shows the importance of beer in the sailors' rations and consequently for the victualling yards. The following section of the chapter reflects on the regulations issued for accounting for beer and other provisions, the controls in place and the expectations for the naval officers who carried out that accounting and administered those controls and governance on the provisioning of beer and other alcohol. The next section elucidates the theoretical underpinning, exploring the later work of Foucault, his ideas on governmentality, the links between that and his previous work on power, discipline and making the unthinkable thinkable. It observes the links in time frame between the historical periods Foucault was explaining and the historical period of this chapter. The research presented is during the period acknowledged by Foucault as the commencement of governmentality (Foucault, 2009, p. 88). These theoretical ideas have been applied to previous accounting research (Armstrong, 1994 and 2015; Stewart, 1992) but not to accounting in the Navy, and the chapter builds on some seminal pieces of accounting research and their use of Foucauldian ideas. The final section of the chapter provides some analysis and discussion, followed by some conclusions.

Background

Alcohol in the Royal Navy

Royal Navy sailors had been provisioned with alcohol from as early as the 14th century (Stubbs, 2003). MacDonald (2004) explains that the main drink of the seamen in the Royal Navy was beer, not diluted rum (known as 'grog') as is often believed to be the case. The men were issued with a gallon of beer a day, in a measure known as a 'wine measure' – five-sixths of the usual gallon of the time in Britain (Table 5.1).

The beer issued was only about 2% to 3% proof. The reason for the drinking of beer is that the process of brewing required the beer to be boiled, thus killing most bacteria and preserving it for months. Water, however, unless kept sterile, would very quickly become green and undrinkable. Nonetheless, in warm

Table 5.1 Daily allowances of provisions

'THERE shall be allowed to every Man serving in His Majesty's Ships, a daily Proportion of Provisions, according as is expressed in the following Table, *viz*.

	Biscuit Pounds Averdu-poiz.	*Beer Gallons Wine Measure*	*Beef Pounds Averdu-poiz*	*Pork Pounds Averdu-poiz*	*Pease Pint Winchester Measure*	*Oatmeal Pint Winchester Measure*	*Butter Ounces*	*Cheese Ounces*
Sunday	1	1	–	1	1 half	–	–	–
Monday	1	1	–	–	–	1	2	4
Tuesday	1	1	2	–	–	–	–	–
Wednesday	1	1	–	–	1 half	1	2	4
Thursday	1	1	–	1	1 half	–	–	–
Friday	1	1	–	–	1 half	1	2	4
Saturday	1	1	2	–	–	–	–	–

Source: Regulations and Instructions relating to his Majesty's Service at Sea 1790 (p. 62). This beer allowance was first in the Regulations of 1734 (p. 62) and remained the same for the Regulations of 1808 (p. 297).

weather, beer does tend to go off, so other alcohol was allowed on ships which were employed on foreign voyages (Regulations, 1734, 1790 and 1808).

The Victualling Board brewed beer for the Navy, initially in London, at Tower Hill, subsequently at Deptford and then at Plymouth and Portsmouth; therefore, whilst some beer was purchased from contractors, most was produced by the Navy itself (MacDonald, 2004). However, beer could only be produced at certain times of the year, and not during the summer period, as noted per Knight and Wilcox (2010). They evidence this with details of an order that went out from the Victualling Board to the brewery to suspend production of beer in hot weather, use up remaining supplies and then issue wine instead (Wellcome, 6816).

Before 1753, beer was believed to be important in the constant battle to combat scurvy (Waife, 1953). In a time when the Royal Navy was constantly at war, scurvy is believed to have resulted in more deaths than all these battles (Lind, 1757, p. 1). So beer was considered a drink that could be kept on long journeys at sea and was good for the health of the seamen. Stubbs (2003) observes that beer at sea had three main uses for the seamen: it was a food, a key part of the diet at sea and a staple drink; it was a luxury, easing the hardship and inconsistency of life at sea; finally, it was also seen as an aid to health, often used as a medicine. A further suggestion is that beer and other alcohol could have been used as a sedative or to control the sailors' behaviour at sea.

Samuel Pepys, who was Secretary to the Admiralty Board (1684–1689) and the first surveyor general of the Victualling Office (from its inception in 1665), wrote in his Naval Minutes:

> Englishmen and more especially seamen, love their bellies above anything else and therefore it must always be remembered in the management of the

> victualing of the navy, that to make any abatement from them in the quality or agreeableness of the victuals is to discourage and provoke them in the tenderest point, and will sooner render them disgusted with the King's service than any other hardship that can be put upon them.
>
> (Tanner, 1926, p. 250)

Navy ships could issue wine and spirits, with half a pint of these being the substitution for a gallon of beer, or a pint of wine. Spirits were generally sourced locally: for example, brandy in the Mediterranean, brandy in the East Indies and rum in the West Indies. However, with the promotion of the merchants of the West Indies, the favoured spirit became rum (MacDonald, 2004). If provisioning was only for a month, further supplies needed to be purchased whilst at sea, in ports visited or from supply ships. The Regulations were clear on the substitutions of food and drink. Wine and rum could be substituted for beer, the Regulations clarify; a pint of wine or half a pint of brandy, rum or arrack could be substituted for the allowance of beer in foreign ports (Regulations, 1790, p. 62), although these were watered down. The Regulations and Instructions of 1808 (Regulations, 1808, p. 302) add that these substitutes can only be issued once beer was expended and that the daily allowance of beer should never be exceeded.

In 1708, Admiral Edward Vernon arrived in the Caribbean. This was the period when huge quantities of sugar were being imported into Europe from the sugar cane plantations of the West Indies, and the Navy were present to defend the merchant fleet. Rum became synonymous with the Navy at this time, but this rum was much stronger than rum today (MacDonald, 2004). Pursers would prove the strength of the rum by adding just a few grains of gunpowder and then igniting it. If it caught light it was 57% alcohol and 100 'proof', a term still used today. The definition of proof was written into law in 1818, when the scale of a hydrometer invented by Bartholomew Sikes was adopted, which measured 100 proof as 1.75 times the percentage of alcohol (Ashworth, 2001). Admiral Vernon noticed that the practice of drinking strong rum was not having a positive effect on the behaviour of the sailors and in 1740 introduced the practice of watering the rum. Vernon's nickname was 'old Grogam' on account of a favourite coat he often wore, made of 'grosgrain' or 'grogam' and so the new drink became known as 'grog'.

Brewing for the Royal Navy

Beer was a regular part of the seaman's diet, from the 14th century (Meussdoerffer, 2009). As early as 1492, Henry VII set up a brewery in Portsmouth, which produced beer for his ships (Eley, 1988). Mathias (1959) demonstrates that local brewers became rich on the demand for beer by the Navy and that naval contracts were responsible for the growth of some breweries during this period. He clarifies that these contract brewers were used to meet additional demand for beer in times of war, such as in the 18th century, when they continued to supplement the naval breweries, administered by the Victualling Office. Buchet (2013) asserts that into the 1750s there was a drive by the Navy to build and run breweries within the main dockyards in order to better monitor the quality of beer, but also to avoid the cartels' fixing of prices. The need for a brewery in Portsmouth was drawn to the Admiralty's attention in 1721 (ADM 110/8). The Portsmouth naval brewery was at Weevil in Gosport, initially leased and then purchased in 1753 (ADM 110/5). In 1756 another brewery with cooperage was constructed and started supplying beer in 1757 (ADM 110/18). The brewery, which comprised a brewery storehouse and cooperage, was within the Royal Clarence Yard in Gosport (Pearson, 2010). The example of HMS *Victory*, Nelson's flagship, a First Rate, that is, 100-gun ship, provides an illustration of the quantity of beer that could be carried on board ship. At the time of Trafalagar (1805), the *Victory* had a crew of 821 men. The men were provisioned with 1 gallon (4.5 litres) of beer each day, and the maximum capacity of beer carried on board Victory was 50 tonnes (50.8 tonnes) (Goodwin, 2004).

Supplies of beer that could be carried on board ships were limited, and beer did not keep well. The relative proportions can be seen from Richard Gibson's letter regarding the regulating of victualing from the Navy Board to the Admiralty on 7th February 1693/94: "there may be four large fly-boats lodged there, the two biggest to be stile (sic) laden with beer, a third a receptacle for beef and pork and the fourth for dry provisions" (No 114, Sergison Papers). In terms of how long these supplies would last, Beaglehole (1955) provides details of kitting out the *Endeavour* for her voyage. A year's supply of victuals was included, but only one month's supply of beer, brandy being included for the rest of the voyage. In order to reduce these storage needs, to increase the relative supply of beer, and since much of the volume of beer was water, attempts were made to produce a beer concentrate, which could be rehydrated with water in foreign ports; however, this was not hugely successful, resulting in supplies being supplemented with rum (or grog). Despite these issues, beer remained the main drink of men in the Navy, with the ration of beer finally being removed in 1831 (Pack, 1996).

Accounting and control of alcohol on board ships

In the Regulations and Instructions of 1790, the Purser's Instructions state the daily provisions of various foods and beer and specify the substitutes allowed. The Regulations and Instructions stipulate that all provisions should be acquired from agents and contractors whenever possible (Regulations, 1790, pp. 122–123, Pursers art. 22). When provisions arrived on board ship, the casks were required to identify the species, time, quantity and place packed. Beer was subject to the special requirement that the contents were to be checked by a 'sworn gauger' (Regulations, 1790, pp. 64–65, Provisions art. 10). Regular inspections of the provisions were then required by 'proper officers' (Regulations, 1790, p. 67, art. 17). If any provisions appeared unfit, these were to be surveyed by these officers and if considered unfit for consumption, returned to the agent or contractor if possible (Regulations, 1790, pp. 118–119, Pursers art.13). If the provisions had been damaged, the captain was required to charge the value against the wages of the offender (Regulations, 1790, p. 66, Provisions art. 15). Such instances had to be certified by the captain and given to the purser to enable him to claim credit the amount charged in his next accounts.

The purser received an allowance of one-eighth on most provisions, an allowance for waste and loss (McBride et al., 2016). Alcohol losses came under closer scrutiny. For beer losses an allowance was permissible after certain fairly stringent procedures:

> If any Cask of Beer shall have leaked out a Quantity, he is to apply to the Captain for a Warrant, directed to the Master, and Two or more other Officers of the Ship, (the Mate, in this Case, to be esteemed an Officer) for the surveying the same; who are to report under their Hands, on the Back of the said Warrant, the Quantity leaked out, in Words at length, according to the Form in Page (182.) and to be very particular in giving the Reasons and Occasion of the Leakage, and that no Beer was drawn or pumped out of any of the said Casks, with his knowledge, before the Time of Survey.
>
> (Regulations, 1790, p. 120)

For losses on wines and spirits, the rules were much simpler:

> He is never to expect any Allowance for Leakage of Wine, Oil, Brandy, Rum, or Arrack, but to see that the Casks be found and full at their coming on Board, and to be answerable for the Care of them afterwards, there being proper Conveniences made in the Hold for securing the said Liquors from any Abuses, which are not to be employed to any other Use whatsoever.
>
> (Regulations, 1790, pp. 120–121)

When the purser required money to pay for short allowance of provisions, likely in the case of beer as ships were provisioned with only one month's supply (Regulations, 1790, p. 64, Provisions art. VIII), he had to produce a certificate, using the specific format (Regulations, 1790, App. No.100) and signed by the captain and the master of the ship. The agent, on agreeing to the details, would initial it and forward it to the Clerk of the Cheque. The Clerk of the Cheque would verify the addition and what the sum was due for, according to the rates allowed (a table being provided in the Regulations, 1790, App. No.101); he then would pay the purser accordingly.

Accounts of provisions received, returned, lent or lost were to be made up every quarter, with details of extra expenses incurred on casks, staves and hoops. The Regulations applying to wines and spirits were again more stringent than for other provisions. These were then transmitted to the Commissioners of Victualling, who in their turn had their own instructions for their accounting and control functions (General instructions for the Victualling Establishment at Home, ADM 7/216).

A new set of Regulations and Instructions were issued in 1808. Although for the provisioning of alcohol these were substantially the same as the 1790 version, there is evidence that the Regulations became more extensive and that procedures were increasingly standardised. The number of forms accompanying the Regulations was greatly increased so that the purser was required to complete 18 forms, excluding slops/clothes (compared with 6 excluding slops under the previous edition). Some of the changes emphasised the importance of the procedures. For example, in respect of the purser:

> He is strictly required and directed to observe and abide by the following Regulations, Stipulations, and Instructions; and he is not expected that any irregularity in or omission of any part thereof, or of the Forms referred to therein for keeping accounts, will be overlooked.
>
> (Regulations, 1808, p. 318)

compared with

> "is to observe the following Instructions" in the previous edition.
>
> (Regulations, 1790, p. 115)

Some of the changes applied specifically to alcohol. Concerns about smuggling had increased, prompting the inclusion of a new article in the Regulations:

> It appearing that considerable quantities of wine and spirituous liquors have been fraudulently run-on-shore from His Majesty's Ships of War and Transports, to the great prejudice of His Majesty's Naval Service, and diminution of the Revenue; for the better preventing of such practice in future, and for punishing those who shall dare to continue or renew it, all Captains or Commanders of His Majesty's Ships or Vessels are hereby strictly required, and positively directed, not to suffer any of those species to be ever issued to the Companies, or any part of the Companies, of the Ships or Vessels respectively under their command whilst in the Home Ports, nor at Sea, until after the Beer is all expended.
>
> (Regulations, 1808, p. 302)

They were further instructed not to serve more than the daily allowance or to issue alcohol in lieu of other provisions. Captains and commanders were required to certify the number of gallons of alcohol, with descriptions, issued to their vessels. They had to ensure these amounts were recorded in the general account of provisions received and whenever any wine or spirituous liquors were taken off the ship, the officers concerned would be called to account for this (Regulations, 1808, p. 302).

Concerns about the level of alcohol consumption are likely to have prompted a new requirement that any savings made by the crew on their daily allowance of provisions were not to be paid to them in kind (i.e., in alcohol), but the purser would purchase them on behalf of the government (Regulations, 1808, p. 290). The purser was also charged with not selling or 'making undue use' of provisions (Regulations, 1808, pp. 320–321). The Regulations stipulated the price to be paid in the event of the purser being in debt for wines and spirits when not on foreign service, when these provisions would not normally be issued and any that were issued would require certification (Regulations, 1808, p. 321).

Thus, amounts of wine and spirits issued were recorded and sent every three months to the Victualling Office. A 'first in first out' system of issuing provisions was used if the ship was victualled for a length of time in port. The purser made three accounts (using Form 2, see Appendix 1) of the number of people in each mess, the quantities of provisions saved or short in each mess, the name of the person appointed to receive for each mess, the value of the savings, the signatures of the people to whom paid and the signatures of the witnesses; then, the purser and his steward signed the accounts as a true record. Of the three copies of Form 2, the purser kept one for the passing of his accounts, the captain sent one to the Commissioners of Victualling and the final one was retained by the captain for the passing of his accounts. The purser kept a separate account (Form 3, see Appendix 2) of payment for provisions saved, or short, allowed by the ships company. The bookkeeping entry was as follows: debit cash received from the agent victualler, or a bill of exchange drawn; credit payment to the ship's company by provision for a period of time at a standard price. The purser should sign an oath that the payments made to the persons specified were 'without any profit or advantage to himself' (Regulations, 1808, p. 347). The Regulations observe that no irregularity or omission in keeping the accounts will be overlooked.

Foucault governmentality

The chapter is informed by the ideas of Foucault, from his lectures as Professor of History at the College de France (1978–1984) when he enriched his earlier theories, exploring and refining his ideas and developing the concept of governmentality. The premise was that in the late 18th century there was a new discipline of individuals, making them compliant and accepting, whilst also forming something the state would be able to use (Foucault, 1979). This is the period explored in this chapter, as we consider the regulations and accounting for the allocation of alcohol and its impact.

Foucault charts a history where there are three forms of government. The first, sovereignty, was seen in the Middle Ages; the Royal Navy did not exist at this time and any equivalent was a disparate mix of the 'king's ships' gathered together as required by the sovereign. Then the rise of state-driven by administration in the 15th and 16th centuries; in this time the Royal Navy became a standing navy and subject to bureaucracy. Finally, from the late 16th century to the 19th century, it moved to a progressively governmentalised state; this move can also be tracked in the government of the Royal Navy and the formalising of many rules, for example, the issuing of the 'Regulations and Instructions relating to his Majesty's Service at Sea'.

These later thoughts of Foucault on governmentality provide an insight for empirical research and some conceptual tools to underpin research. Foucauldian theory relates to his influential earlier study of power as a discourse of discipline, and starting what has become the field of governmentality studies, concerning the analytics of government and governance discourse and recognising that government has a keen involvement in establishing agents, interests and identities.

He reworked and enhanced his ideas on power (for example, the genealogy of power) in the late 1970s (although these were not translated until more recently). These enhance and develop the study of the state and other political concerns (Lemke, 2012). Foucault (2000) (translated in Lemke, 2012) observes:

> By "government" I mean the set of institutions and practices, from administration to education, through which people's conduct is guided.
>
> (Lemke, 2012, pp. 295–296)

This study considers the Regulations and Instructions issued to naval sea officers from 1731 as such a set of practices.

Accounting studies have engaged with the discourses of Foucault to explain various aspects of the power of accounting. The idea of the governable person is where people become seen and measurable when accounting makes their actions calculable (Miller and O'Leary, 1987; Boland, 1987). Foucault's work on 'governmentality' has underpinned many seminal accounting studies in this area (for example, Miller and O'Leary, 1989; Miller and Rose, 1990; Preston, 1992; Robson, 1991; Rose, 1991), which use a Foucauldian perspective in considering the construct of power via various discourses, within organisations or populations, and these being represented in specific ways, for example, by government. Armstrong (1994) clarifies that these studies in governmentality and accounting base their concept of power not on a disciplinary system but on ideas of 'translation' and action at a distance (Callon, 1986; Latour, 1986 and 1987). The idea of action at a distance can be seen as a reworking of the agency problem (Jensen and Meckling, 1976). However, instead of control through monitoring and incentives, control is through knowledge and approaches that are administered centrally (Foucault, 1991). Our study of the Royal Navy considers these ideas of governmentality, where control of provisions aboard ship is not about monitoring and incentives, but more about knowledge and centrally administered regulations.

Analysis and discussion

This chapter focuses on the era that Foucault acknowledges as the period of history where governmentality became relevant (Foucault, 2009, p. 88). Within the Navy there is a clear move from the situation with an all-powerful monarch, with sovereign power such as in earlier eras, where all actions of the state, from the waging of wars to everyday administration, were carried out to sustain the situation of a personalised state (McKinlay and Pezet, 2010). The king had been an all-powerful monarch, for example, Henry VIII, in both financing and controlling the Navy, and Charles II, who attended more of the Admiralty Board's meetings than any other member of the Board (Rodger, 2005). This changed to a situation where the Board became self-governing, with its Regulations and Instructions to engage and control ships' officers. This perspective of governance is firmly rooted in a liberal view of the state, where differences are not seen as threatening social order, but more as a means of progress (Lemke, 2007). Foucault sees the state as "nothing more than a regime of multiple governmentalities . . . It is necessary to analyse the problem of the state by referring to the practices of government" (Foucault, 2004, p. 79) and, in the Navy and elsewhere, these practices of government were underpinned by their accounting practices. The Regulations and Instructions issued accounting procedures to impose and control this governmentality.

Relations of power are important, as they define the way in which people govern others, but for Foucault (1991, p. 102) government is not so much imposed as accepted, where power is exerted and accepted. Foucault asserts that this acceptance occurs as a function of knowledge, which in its turn is caused by discourse (Rodrigues and Craig, 2007). Institutions that further discourse should be studied in order to understand knowledge (Cowton and Dopson, 2002, p. 193). Navy regulations and knowledge of accounting create power through discourse, when the officers involved accept that governance of provisions, in particular, alcohol, will improve by use of those measures and controls. The first Regulations and Instructions in 1731 were aimed at better control of ships officers; the contents show, in a clear and organised way, the duties of these officers and can be seen as a move towards discipline for these individuals and an attempt to make them compliant and accept these rules. These rules were refined in the following years, with 13 editions being issued over the period to 1790. The 1734 Regulations and Instructions had 193 pages and the 1790 version 237 pages. These Regulations show a keen involvement in establishing agents, interests and identities for the purposes of government as identified by Foucault (2000, translated by Lemke, 2012).

This theoretical realigning can be developed with the premise of government that becomes 'guideline' (Foucault, 2007, p. 363). Foucault's governmentality acts between subjectivity and power to enable the investigation of how 'technologies of self' (Foucault, 1988) are linked with applications of self-government. The challenge of government explains the interdependent relationship between knowledge and power and clarifies Foucault's earlier ideas of the connection of 'knowledge – power' (Foucault, 1980). This inter-reaction of knowledge and power can be explained as a means of social control in institutions and highlights the role of power assisted by knowledge in the development of discourse, as understood in modernity, in society. In the governmentality methodology of Foucault, the means of power and the configurations of knowledge are interdependent. The 1808 edition of the Regulations and Instructions were redrafted and extended, the 237 pages from 1790 becoming 683 pages. Lavery (1989, p. 5) observes an improvement of accounting, but it appears to be more than just this, as the expanded Regulations attempted further uniformity in the operation of Navy vessels (Malcomson, 2016) and an increased discourse towards improved accountability and control of provisions, including alcohol. The Regulations, whilst becoming more prescriptive, become more authoritative, but also more explanatory, such as the new regulation shown above about the "wine and spirituous liquors . . . fraudulently run-on-shore" (Regulations, 1808, p. 302). With increased knowledge, increased control and power, but also self-governing.

Foucault defines governmentality as the divesting of power from the sovereign and the state to organisations to provide for the well being of and to control the people in any given population (Lemke, 2001). The idea of well-being of the populous in the Navy, related to alcohol and accounting, can be seen in two areas. Initially, the beer allowance was introduced, at least partially, because it was believed that it helped to prevent against scurvy; however, although this was proven untrue (Lind, 1757), the beer allowance remained. It can be suggested that the alcohol allowance may have alleviated suffering of their conditions on board ship for the men, and at the very least kept them inebriated, so they were less complaining of those conditions, braver and more compliant. The well-being of the broader populous was served by having a Navy that was effective and able to win battles. Accounting played its part in this in assisting in the recording and control of those supplies, the Regulations and Instructions outlining guidelines to ensure consistency between ships, limiting opportunity for seamen to consume excess alcohol, but providing them with sufficient to enhance their perceived well-being.

Conclusions

Investigating the use of regulations to govern allocation of beer in the Royal Navy during the 17th and 18th centuries has allowed reflections on the role of accounting in one of the most important roles of 'government' in the Navy, that of regular and sufficient provisioning of the seafarers.

Alcohol, and beer in particular, was a fundamental provision for sailors in Nelson's Navy. The reasons for its use, whether planned or unplanned, changed over time. Conditions were hard and the life was tough, and alcohol consumption to some extent improved that, or at least made it feel as if it did. Whilst it did not, as it transpired, protect against scurvy, it improved the well-being of the men in other ways. It was certainly a better alternative than putrid water. The Navy Board, via the Victualling Board, set allocations of rations, including alcohol, and cash accounting to measure and control that allocation and indirectly the seafarers as well. Governance and governmentality of the organisation, the Royal Navy, was both directly and indirectly carried out through accounting, measurement and recording of these provisions. The quality and cost of the beer were monitored and enforced, where possible, via the Navy's own breweries, the one we consider in this chapter, in Portsmouth, but similar methods and procedures applied in the other yards. There was thus a transfer of the use of alcohol from health reasons, where it replaced rotten water and defended against scurvy, to pseudo-health advantages or at least enhancing well-being in tough and dangerous conditions and enhancing the men's bravery at times of war.

We have focused the time period from 1793 until 1815. The accounting carried out in this period, both within the victualling yards and on board ships with the purser, is basic recording and listing of detail and creation of rudimentary cash accounts. There are clear attempts in the regulations to overcome the issue of the agency or stewardship problem, of separation of those in charge and those allocating the provisions and recording the detail of this. A rudimentary system of internal control is applied in terms of the more senior officers needing to sign the records, accounts and certificates of the purser, for example, the sealing and signing of casks and the control and certification of wastage. The victualling records contain a lot of detail, with the administration attempting to govern the individuals carrying out the roles of allocation, recording and provisioning of alcohol and other food supplies for the men.

The contribution of the chapter to accounting history is threefold. First, the chapter responds to the call for more research in the area of military accounting history (Funnell and Chwastiak, 2010) and in particular naval accounting history. Second, it develops the ideas of Foucault's governmentality and sociology of translation applying them to the accounting history literature. Third, and finally, it considers the role of alcohol in the Royal Navy. While this chapter uses the regulations to discover and assess the accounting expected and carried out within the navy, for allocation of alcohol and other provisions at the time, it does have limitations. A key limitation of the chapter is the scarcity of copies of actual accounts to show that these were actually recorded in compliance with the regulations. However, arguably the regulations were well disseminated and clarified for those expected to carry them out. In addition, controls were implemented as well to ensure the accounting was carried out correctly; for example, the purser would not receive his money if accounting records were not kept correctly, And he would also not be reemployed. Future research could be carried out to find and investigate actual accounting records of pursers.

Appendix 1

No. 2.

Forms of Vouchers for payment of Provisions, saved by or short allowed to the Ship's Company.

An Account of the Quantities of Provisions saved by or short allowed to the Company of His Majesty's Ship out of their daily allowance, between the and the with the value thereof, at the prices settled for the payment of Savings; and short Allowance, the name of the persons appointed to receive for each mess; the Signatures of the Persons to whom the amount was paid, and the Signatures of the Witness to the Payment.

No. of the Mess.	No. of Persons in the Mess	Name of the Person appointed to receive for the Mess.	No. on the Ship's Books of the Persons receiving.	Quantities of Provisions saved by or short allowed to each Mess.								Value of the Provisions due to each Mess.			When paid.	Signatures of the Persons to whom paid.	Signatures of Witnesses to the Payment.
				Bread lbs.	Wine Gallons.	Spirits Gallons.	Beef Pieces, including Flour, &c.	Pork Pieces.	Sugar lbs.	Butter lbs.	Cheese lbs.	L.	s.	d.			

Regulations and Instructions, 1808 pursers, Form 2 (National Archives, Kew)

Appendix 2

No.

Payment of Provisions saved by or short allowed to the Ship's Company.

3

Form of Account Current and Affidavit.

D. E. Purser of His Majesty's Ship in Account Current with the Commissioners for Victualling His Majesty's Navy. } Dr.

18		£.	s.	d.
March 1	To a Bill drawn in favor of Mr. John Jones at thirty days sight····	89	4	8
June 1	To Cash received of Mr. , Agent Victualler at	126	3	11½
		215	8	7½

Per Contra Cr.

18					£.	s.	d.
March 1	By paid the Ship's Company per List for Provisions due between 1st January and 28th February, viz.						
	Bread ·········· 3584 lbs. ········· at 1½d. per lb. ····	22	8	0			
	Beef including Flour 256 pieces of 8lbs. at 1s. 6d. per piece	19	4	0			
	Pork ············ 268 ditto of 4lbs. at 1s. 2d. per piece	15	12	8			
	Sugar ············ 84 lbs. ············ 4d. per lb. ···	1	8	11			
	Butter ·········· 192 lbs. ············ 4d. per lb. ···	3	4	0			
	Cheese ·········· 384 lbs. ············ 2d. per lb. ···	3	4	0			
	Spirits ·········· 130 gallons ········ 2s. per gallon	13	0	0			
	Wine ············ 224 ditto ·········· 1s. ditto ····	11	4	0			
					89	4	8
June 1	By paid the Ship's Company per List for Provisions due between 1st March and 31st May, viz.						
	Bread ·········· 5741 ·········· at 1½d. per lb. ····	35	7	7½			
	Beef including Flour 410 pieces of 8lbs. 1s. 6d. per piece	30	15	0			
	Pork ············ 219 ditto of 4lbs. ··· 1s. 2d. ditto ··	12	15	6			
	Butter ············ 307lbs. ·········· 4d. per lb. ····	5	2	4			
	Cheese ·············· 615 ·············· 2d. ditto ···	5	2	6			
	Spirits ············ 185 gallons ········ 2s. per gallon	18	10	0			
	Wine ············ 361 ditto ······ 1s. ditto ····	18	1	0			
					126	3	11½
				£	215	8	7½

2

Form

Regulations and Instructions, 1808 pursers, Form 3 (National Archives, Kew)

Note

1 The Admiralty created the Victualling Board in 1683 to replace a victualling system based on private contracts with one that gave it greater direct control. With this system, there was thought to be enhanced prospect of improving efficiency and quality control. The Board supplied food, drink and other provisions for naval ships, mostly through its victualling yards in Royal Navy dockyards and individual pursers. The purser allocated provisions to the seafarers on board the ships.

References

Primary sources

The National Archives, London, Series ADM – Records of the Admiralty, Naval Forces, Royal Marines, Coastguard, and related bodies.
ADM 110/5.
ADM 110/6 Victualling Board to Lord High Treasurer Letter 2nd December 1713.
ADM 110/8 Letter 27th June 1721.
ADM 110/18 Letter 11th April 1757.
ADM 7/216 General Instructions for the Victualling Establishment at Home, contained in the XIth report on the Board of Revision (dated 22 December 1807) Ordered to be carried into execution, by his Majesty's Order in Council of 14th September, 1808 (also App 96, 100, 101, 115, 116).
Lind, J. (1757). *A Treatise on the Scurvy: In Three Parts, Containing an Inquiry Into the Nature, Causes and Cure of that Disease*. London: A Millar.
Regulations and Instructions relating to His Majesty's Service at Sea established by His Majesty in Council, 1731.
Regulations and Instructions relating to His Majesty's Service at Sea established by His Majesty in Council, Second edition, 1734.
Regulations and Instructions relating to His Majesty's Service at Sea established by His Majesty in Council, Thirteenth edition, 1790.
Regulations and Instructions relating to His Majesty's Service at Sea established by His Majesty in Council, 1808.
The Sergison Papers 1688–1702 R D Merriman No 114.
Tanner, J. (1926). Transcription from short hand of Samuel Pepys Naval Minutes, Naval Records Society, London. One of the 'Sea – Manuscripts' Pepysian Library, Magdalene College, Cambridge.
Wellcome Library archives, 6816, 30 May 1807, Orders and letters to Samuel Lewes, Victualling Agent 1804–1815.

Secondary sources

Armstrong, P. (1994). The influence of Michel Foucault on accounting research. *Critical Perspectives on Accounting*, 5(1), pp. 25–55.
Armstrong, P. (2015). The discourse of Michel Foucault: A sociological encounter. *Critical Perspectives on Accounting*, 27, pp. 29–42.
Ashworth, W. (2001). 'Between the trader and the public': British alcohol standards and the proof of good governance. *Technology and Culture*, 42(1), pp. 27–50.
Baron, J. (2009). Sailor's scurvy before and after James Lind: A reassessment. *Nutritional Reviews*, 67(6), pp. 315–332.

Beaglehole, J., ed. (1955). *The Voyage of the Endeavour 1768–1771.* Cambridge: Cambridge University Press.

Boland, R. (1987). Discussion of 'accounting and the construction of the governable person'. *Accounting, Organizations and Society*, 12(3), pp. 267–272.

Buchet, C. (2013). *The British Navy, Economy and Society in the Seven Years War.* Woodbridge, Suffolk: The Boydell Press. Translated by A. Higgie and M. Duffy, *Marine, économie et societé – un exemple d'interaction: l'avitaillement de la Royal Navy durant la guerre de sept ans* (1999).

Callon, M. (1986). Some element of a sociology of translation: Domestication of the scallops and fishermen of St Brieuc Bay. In: J. Law, ed. *Power, Action and Belief: A New Sociology of Knowledge.* London: Routledge, pp. 196–233.

Cowton, C. and Dopson, S. (2002). Foucault's prison? Management control in an automotive distributor. *Management Accounting Research*, 13(2), pp. 191–213.

Eley, P. (1988). *Portsmouth Breweries 1492–1847.* Portsmouth Papers, No. 51.

Foucault, M. (1979). Translated by A. Sheridan, *Discipline and Punish: The Birth of a Prison.* New York: Vintage Books.

Foucault, M. (1980). Edited by C. Gordon, Translated by C. Gordon, L. Marshall, J. Mepham and K. Soper, *Power/Knowledge: Selected Interviews and Other Writings 1972–1977.* New York: Panthenon Books.

Foucault, M. (1988). Technologies of the self. In: L. Martin, H. Gutman and P. Hutton, eds. *Technologies of the Self: A Seminar With Michel Foucault.* Amherst: Massachusetts University Press, pp. 16–49.

Foucault, M. (1991). Governmentality. In: G. Burchell, C. Gorden and P. Miller, eds. *The Foucault Effect: Studies in Governmentality.* Hemel Hempstead: Harvester Wheatsheaf, pp. 87–104.

Foucault, M. (2004). Naissance de la biopolitique Cours au Collège de France 1978–79. Paris: Seuil/Galliuard. In: B. Jessop, ed. 2007. *State Power.* Cambridge: Polity Press.

Foucault, M. (2007). *Security, Territory, Population Lectures at the College de France 1977–78.* New York: Palgrave Macmillan.

Foucault, M. (2009). *Security, Territory, Population.* New York: Palgrave Macmillan.

Funnell, W. and Chwastiak, M. (2010). Editorial: Accounting and the military. *Accounting History*, 15(2), pp. 147–152.

Goodwin, P. (2004). *Nelson's Victory: 101 Questions and Answers About HMS Victory.* London: Conway Maritime Press.

Henderson Smith, A. (1918). Beer and scurvy: Some notes from history. *The Lancet*, 192(4972), pp. 813–815.

Hewitt, H. (1966). *Organisation of War Under Edward III, 1338–62.* Manchester: Manchester University Press.

Jensen, M. and Meckling, W. (1976). Theory of the firm: Managerial behaviour, agency costs and ownership structure. *Journal of Financial Economics*, 3(4), pp. 305–360.

Knight, R. and Wilcox, M. (2010). *Sustaining the Fleet 1793–1815 War, the British Navy and the Contractor State.* Woodbridge, Suffolk: The Boydell Press.

Latour, B. (1986). The powers of association. In: J. Law, ed. *Power, Action and Belief: A New Sociology of Knowledge.* London: Routledge, pp. 264–280.

Latour, B. (1987). *Science in Action: How to Follow Scientists and Engineers Through Society.* Milton Keynes: Open University Press.

Lavery, B. (1989). *Nelson's Navy: The Ships, Men and Organisation, 1793–1815.* London: Conway Maritime Press.

Lemke, T. (2001). 'The birth of biopolitics': Michel Foucault's lecture at the Collège de France on neo-liberal governmentality. *Economy and Society*, 30(2), pp. 190–207.

Lemke, T. (2007). An indigestible meal? Foucault, governmentality and state theory. *Distinktion*, 8(2), pp. 43–64.

Lemke, T. (2012). *Foucault, Governmentality and Critique*. Oxford: Routledge.

MacDonald, J. (2004). *Feeding Nelson's Navy: The True Story of Food at Sea in the Georgian Era*. Yorkshire: Chatham Publishing.

Malcomson, T. (2016). *Order and Disorder in the British Navy, 1793–1815*. London: Boydell and Brewer.

Mathias, P. (1959). *The Brewing Industry in England 1700–1830*. London: Cambridge University Press.

McBride, K., Hines, A. and Craig, R. (2016). A rum deal. The Purser's measure and accounting control of materials in the Royal Navy, 1665–1832. *Business History*, 58(6), pp. 925–946.

McKinlay, A. and Pezet, E. (2010). Accounting for Foucault. *Critical Perspectives on Accounting*, 21, pp. 486–495.

Meussdoerffer, F. G. (2009). A comprehensive history of beer brewing. In: H. M. Esslinger, ed. *Handbook of Brewing: Processes, Technology, Markets*. Weinheim: Wiley, pp. 1–42.

Miller, P. and O'Leary, T. (1987). Accounting and the construct of the governable person. *Accounting Organizations and Society*, 12(3), pp. 235–265.

Miller, P. and O'Leary, T. (1989). Hierarchies and American ideals 1900–1940. *Academy of Management Review*, 14(2), pp. 250–265.

Miller, P. and Rose, N. (1990). Governing economic life. *Economy and Society*, 19(1), pp. 1–13.

Pack, A. (1996). *Nelson's Blood: The Story of Naval Rum*. London: Naval Insitute Press.

Pearson, L. (2010). *Strategy for the Historical Industrial Environment – The Brewing Industry: A Report By the Brewery History Society for English Heritage*. Kent: Brewery History Society.

Preston, A. (1992). The birth of clinical accounting: A study of the emergence and transformation of discourses on cost and practices of accounting in US hospitals. *Accounting, Organizations and Society*, 17(1), pp. 63–100.

Robson, K. (1991). On the arenas of accounting change: The process of translation. *Accounting, Organizations and Society*, 16(5/6), pp. 547–570.

Rodger, N. (2005). *The Command of the Ocean: A Naval History of Britain 1649–1815*. London: Penguin Books, National Maritime Museum.

Rodrigues, L. and Craig, R. (2007). Assessing international accounting harmonisation using Hegelian dialectic, isomorphism and Foucault. *Critical Perspectives on Accounting*, 18, pp. 739–757.

Rose, N. (1991). Governing by numbers: Figuring out democracy. *Accounting, Organizations and Society*, 16(7), pp. 637–692.

Stewart, R. (1992). Pluralizing our past: Foucault in accounting history. *Accounting, Auditing and Accountability Journal*, 5(2), pp. 57–73.

Stubbs, B. (2003). Captain Cook's beer: The antisorbutic use of malt and beer in late 18th century sea voyages. *Asia Pacific Journal of Clinical Nutrition*, 12(2), pp. 129–137.

Waife, S. O. (1953). 1753 lind, lemons and limeys. *American Journal of Clinical Nutrition*, 1(6), pp. 471–473.

Part 2

Accounting for spirits and distilling

6 Accounting at the Watercourse Distillery

Peter Cleary

Introduction

This chapter reviews the accounting information produced between 1792 and 1864 by the Watercourse Distillery and how it was used and reported upon by the firm. The distillery was co-founded by Thomas Hewitt, John Teulon and Richard Blunt, with Hewitt (along with his cousin) eventually assuming full control of the business and re-naming it Hewitt & Co. Thomas Hewitt was the eldest son of the Reverend Francis Hewitt and Eliza Reeves and had two brothers and three step-brothers (Stewart, 2013). He qualified with an Master of Arts and a Bachelor of Law before practising as a Barrister-at-Law. Hewitt was originally a butter merchant before becoming involved in distilling (primarily whiskey) at the Watercourse distillery – the focus of this chapter.

Whiskey production in Ireland has a long history. The word "whiskey" in the Irish language translates as "uisce beatha", which in English literally means "water of life", as it is said to confer long life and good health to those who drink it. According to legend, it was Irish monks travelling to various Mediterranean countries on pilgrimages over 1,000 years ago, who on discovering the fundamentals of distilling, subsequently introduced the technique to Ireland (Townsend, 1997). This is over 500 years prior to when the distilling of whiskey is said to have begun in Scotland, now commonly perceived as the premier location for whiskey production. As remarked by Townsend (1997, p. 12), "in the annals of whiskey lore, the Irish were undoubtedly the masters and the Scots the apprentices . . . [but] . . . as the 19th century progressed, they [the Scots] . . . became the masters". There are various reasons as to why this occurred. Many Scottish distilleries began using the more efficient and cost-effective patent stills (developed by an Irishman called Aeneas Coffey) to produce their distinctive Scotch whiskey (blended using grain and malt). In addition, the amalgamation of six independent Scottish distilleries to form The Distillers Company Limited (DCL) in 1877 afforded this new entity economies of scale not previously attainable. Furthermore, the development of the United Kingdom (UK) rail network made it far easier for Scottish distilleries to transport raw materials to their production facilities and whiskey to their chosen markets (Weir, 1995). The consequent closure of many Irish distilleries due to their increasing un-competitiveness was one of the main outcomes arising from this transformation of the Scottish distilling industry (Townsend, 1997).

However, during the early part of the 19th century, the distilling of whiskey flourished in Ireland with over 30 separate operational distilleries (Townsend, 1997). This was due in part to the ready availability of key ingredients: grain, barley and water. During this time, Dublin was regarded as the primary global location for whiskey production, as its six distilleries had a combined annual production capacity of nearly 10 million gallons (Townsend, 1997). Nevertheless, the focus of this chapter is the Watercourse Distillery, which was established in 1792 on the north side of Cork, Ireland's second-largest city, situated on the south coast. The chapter continues as follows; the next section traces the British influence on whiskey production in Ireland before outlining the importance of Cork's "Merchant Princes". It then continues with a history of the Watercourse Distillery, before an analysis of the accounting information produced therein, incorporating a review of their subsequent financial performance. The chapter concludes with some final remarks.

Whiskey production in Ireland – the British influence

Before and during the existence of the Watercourse Distillery, a fractious relationship existed between Great Britain and Ireland concerning whiskey production and sale. Pre-1801, Ireland was in theory an autonomous state with its own parliament, whereas in reality, it was largely controlled by the king of Great Britain. However, the Act of Union (1801) formalised and re-enforced this relationship, with Ireland now part of the United Kingdom of Great Britain and Ireland.

Previously, due to the large volume of distillation occurring in Ireland, taxes on spirits were introduced during the reign of King Charles II (1630–1685), with tax collectors subsequently appointed. Consequently, many Irish people began distilling their own illegal alcohol (such as "poteen"), which was sold via the black market at very attractive prices. It was also reported that many "legal" distillers attempted to reduce their taxes by under-declaring their output. However, when discovered, it seems that such occurrences were "sorted" locally between the distiller and the tax collector. As a result, more restrictive legislation was passed requiring some of the bigger Irish distilleries to permanently host up to a dozen tax collectors simultaneously (Townsend, 1997).

Furthermore, in an attempt to raise income from grain used in the distilling process, the British government subsequently imposed a levy on malted barley, while the Distilling Act (1779) imposed a significant levy on the use of pot stills based upon their potential production capacity. Due to the imposition of these taxes, many legal Irish distillers did not survive, and between 1780 and 1822 their numbers decreased from a couple of hundred to just 40. In 1823, the Excise Act finally ended the tax on still capacity and replaced it with an annual £10 licence (Townsend, 1997). However, prior to this in 1817, legislation had been enacted mandating that no raw spirits could be received into the stock of any English-based spirit dealer unless they were a "rectifier". This effectively excluded Irish whiskey from being consumed in England in its "natural" state, as this law ensured that it could only be consumed in England after it had been converted into British brandy, gin or other substance (U15B/B/4/32, p. 1). Furthermore, during the 1840s and 1850s, various levies were imposed on the sale of Irish-produced spirits bound for export in an attempt to promote the interests of British distillers who were not subject to such levies. For example, Irish-distilled spirits were the only item on which taxes were payable in which leakage or loss in storage was included in the excise tax levied. By contrast, sugar (a heavily traded commodity at this time) was only liable for duty on what came out of store and not what had been deposited previously (U15/B/B/4/29).

In response, those involved in the Irish spirit trade petitioned the Irish Members of Parliament (MPs) to introduce legislation to facilitate the "enactment of a just law placing the Irish Spirit Trade on an equal footing, and under the same regulations as the spirit trade of colonial and foreign countries" (U15/B/B/4/29, p. 1). However, the legislation subsequently proposed by Lord Naas was not passed, even though it was claimed not to be just about distilling, but concerning "the employment and the consequent well-being or the idleness and resulting starvation, of thousands of the poor of Ireland" (U15/B/B/4/29, p. 2). The bill was defeated at the third stage, where it was voted upon in the early hours of the morning without many of its supporters present (U15/B/B/4/29). The British government did eventually propose that Irish-distilled whiskey could be exported without duties imposed, but only if it was declared for export by the producer when bonded. This was rejected by the Irish distillers, as it would have meant that they were unable to sell their bonded whiskey in a different market and at a potentially higher price in the future, as they had already committed to exporting it (U15/B/B/4/30). It is against this backdrop of discord and distrust that the next section examines the influence of the "Merchant Princes" of Cork – the location of the Watercourse Distillery.

Cork's Merchant Princes

During the 17th and 18th centuries, the city of Cork expanded, driven by an increase in trade via its port and in the number of buildings within its boundary. As with all cities at this time, Cork's merchants possessed most of the wealth and were therefore at the forefront of these developments, facilitating further increases in their wealth and influence. As a result, they became known locally as the "Merchant Princes". Many of Cork's merchants were active participants in local government, which was responsible for co-ordinating the city's expansion and development. The "Merchant Princes" took great pride in the city of Cork, and the businesses they established provided much-needed employment for the working classes, whilst also encouraging others to establish their own firms. Cork's merchants (Protestant and Catholic) often worked together in pursuit of common goals to further the development of the city – for example, requesting the mayor of Cork to examine the feasibility of constructing a railway between Cork and Dublin (O'Brien, 1986). Many merchant families were also involved in various local Cork-based cultural organisations. Thomas Hewitt was no exception, being involved in, for example, the Cork School of Art and the Cork Agricultural Association (U15B/P/A). Hewitt also collected antiquarian manuscripts and books, and after his death, it was reported that his vast library was auctioned in Dublin, with the process requiring eight days to complete (Foster, 1992). As their wealth increased, many merchant families moved their primary residences from the city to the suburbs. Thomas Hewitt followed suit, as he moved from Glanmire on the outskirts of Cork to Cobh in County Cork (Cork City and County Archive – Merchant Princes, 2017).

Increased investment from Cork's "Merchant Princes" invariably required additional accounting-based information to allow them to determine if, at the end of a particular time period, their commercial exploits had resulted in a financial gain (Weber, 1950) or as Edwards et al. (2009, p. 552) suggest, an increase in the value of their "Estate". Indeed, according to Gervais (2014, p. 1), "keeping accounts was a self-evident imperative in a world of rational economic agents trying to maximise their profit". However, it has also been acknowledged that during the 18th century (at the end of which the Watercourse Distillery was founded), "systematic bookkeeping was still rare . . . and that the techniques used for balancing books were often crude" (Gervais, 2014, p. 1). Where more than one investor existed (for example, within a partnership), the preparation of a set of accounts was used to divide the total reported profits/losses between them as per the terms of their prevailing partnership agreement (Gervais, 2014). As will be illustrated later, this distribution of profits/losses between partners occurred at the Watercourse Distillery.

Furthermore, as many merchants at this time bought and sold commodities of varying weights and measures in different currencies, there was a general acknowledgement of the need to possess some arithmetic skills (Clarke, 2008). This view was refined by Sombart (1916) who argued that the use of double-entry bookkeeping was inextricably linked with the growth of capitalism. Indeed, it was reported by Meagher (1994) that a Dutchman called Elias Voster established a school in Cork to which many of the city's merchants attended to learn about bookkeeping, amongst other areas. Voster (1769) subsequently wrote and published a book which contained a section on how to perform bookkeeping which, according to Meagher (1994), was still a very popular book in Cork in the mid-1860s (Clarke, 2008). Whether Thomas Hewitt (or any of his associates) attended this school or read this book is unknown, but as the accounting records from the Watercourse distillery will demonstrate, there was a considerable knowledge of this subject area held by someone employed by (or connected with) the firm.

The Watercourse Distillery – a history

The Watercourse Distillery was established in 1792 when a partnership was formed between two local butter merchants, Thomas Hewitt and John Teulon, and a London-based distiller named Richard Blunt. According to the terms of their original partnership agreement, all three partners would each invest £5,000, would share any profits/losses equally and agreed that a partner would only be permitted to leave the business upon giving one year's notice after 7, 14 or 21 years (Townsend, 1997). Having committed their capital, the construction of the Watercourse Distillery followed between 1793 and 1794 on the Watercourse Road, situated in Blackpool on the north side of Cork city. This initial partnership agreement lasted until 1799, and from the financial records available in the archive (U15/B/B/4/9), the total annual profit balance for each partner is shown in Table 6.1 (the distillery commenced trading in 1794) – see Appendix I for the annual distribution of profits (losses) between partners. As Table 6.1 illustrates, despite being equal partners, and hence being attributed the same profits, the profit balance for Richard Blunt is significantly lower than that of the others. This may be due to the fact that, as a London-based distiller, Richard Blunt could have had other business interests which required his money (i.e. capital) and hence his need to take more dividends from the Watercourse distillery than the other partners.

In 1800, the terms of the original partnership agreement were altered to facilitate the introduction of James Morrogh as an equal partner into the business. To reflect this, he invested £10,000 in the distillery with the other partners doubling their original £5,000 investments to match this amount (Townsend, 1997). As Table 6.2 shows, for Thomas Hewitt, his profit balance by the end

Table 6.1 Profit balance for each partner from 1794 to 1799 (U15/B/B/4/9)

	Thomas Hewitt	*John Teulon*	*Richard Blunt*	*Total*
1794	£3,353	£4,535	£697	£8,585
1795	£5,759	£7,613	£2,195	£15,567
1796	£8,074	£9,918	£3,838	£21,830
1797	£9,204	£10,487	£3,966	£23,657
1798	£10,907	£12,465	£5,664	£29,036
1799	£16,547	£17,539	£11,545	£45,631

Table 6.2 Profit balance for each partner from 1800 to 1805 (U15/B/B/4/9)

	Thomas Hewitt	*John Teulon*	*Richard Blunt*	*James Morrogh*	*Total*
1800	£12,000	£9,214	£7,632	£12,734	£41,580
1801	£8,066	£8,070	£7,256	£12,867	£36,259
1802	£9,000	£9,833	£8,814	£15,280	£42,927
1803	£9,790	£11,715	£11,389	£17,738	£50,632
1804	£11,633	£13,245	£12,915	£20,186	£57,979
1805	£8,682	£12,314	£12,150	£21,730	£54,876

of this particular partnership agreement (i.e., 1805) was the lowest of all of the partners. By comparison, James Morrogh increased his profit balance annually, and from an initial balance of £12,734 in 1800, this figure had risen to £21,730 by 1805, an increase of nearly 71%.

During 1806, one of the distillery's original partners, Richard Blunt, decided to leave the firm (14 years after its establishment and in keeping with the terms of the original partnership agreement). Blunt's shares were acquired by Thomas Hewitt and John Teulon, with Hewitt's cousin (Thomas Henry Hewitt) and Teulon's son also becoming partners in the same year. As per the new partnership agreement, Thomas Hewitt, John Teulon and James Morrogh were equal partners with each owning 25% of the business, while the two new partners divided Richard Blunt's shares equally between themselves (i.e. 12.5% each). It was during this time that the distillery was re-named Hewitt and Co. As Table 6.3 shows, the "new" partners both increased their profit balances significantly in the years after their introduction to the business (i.e. Thomas Henry Hewitt by 312% and Teulon's son by 650%).

By 1811, John Teulon was no longer a partner in the distillery although his son remained. As shown in Table 6.4, the profit balances of the remaining two founding partners (i.e. Thomas Hewitt and James Morrogh) continued to vary during this time. For Thomas Hewitt, his balance reached £12,937 in 1812 before falling to £1,328 in 1815. Similarly, for James Morrogh, his profit balance was recorded at £21,121 in 1814 before falling to £14,466 the following year.

Table 6.3 Profit balance for each partner from 1806 to 1810 (U15/B/B/4/9)

	Thomas Hewitt	*John Teulon*	*James Morrogh*	*Thomas Henry Hewitt*	*Teulon Son*	*Total*
1806	£17,460	£20,913	£23,215	£1,573	£1,455	£64,616
1807	£16,355	£14,338	£22,871	£1,961	£6,821	£62,346
1808	£24,971	£19,427	£22,735	£6,600	£10,799	£84,532
1809	£18,124	£18,085	£18,879	£5,716	£9,989	£70,793
1810	£19,912	£16,558	£20,545	£6,475	£10,914	£74,404

Table 6.4 Profit balance for each partner from 1811 to 1815 (U15/B/B/4/9)

	Thomas Hewitt	*James Morrogh*	*Thomas Henry Hewitt*	*Teulon Son*	*Total*
1811	£5,371	£19,169	£8,691	£13,098	£46,329
1812	£12,937	£26,873	£12,947	£18,334	£71,091
1813	£6,785	£20,450	£11,107	£15,102	£53,444
1814	£7,844	£21,121	£13,797	£16,027	£58,789
1815	£1,328	£14,466	£11,334	£14,380	£41,508

In 1816, the son of James Teulon, who had been a partner in the business since 1806, ceased to be so and was replaced by a son of James Morrogh. At this point, the ownership of the Watercourse Distillery was held solely by members of the Hewitt and Morrogh families. As illustrated in Table 6.5, the profit balance of Thomas Hewitt fluctuated during this time, falling to £452 in 1819 before recovering to £9,209 in 1825. After 1825, no further profit balances for the partners are provided in the available accounts (U15/B/B/4/9). At this point, Thomas Hewitt owned 5/16 (31.25%) of the firm while his cousin, Thomas Henry Hewitt, owned 3/16 (18.75%) of the company. Collectively, as this amounted to 50%, it may have been the case that Thomas Hewitt and his cousin opposed the publication of partner profit balances, and hence this explains why they were discontinued.

In 1827, it appears that the son of James Morrogh, who first became a partner in 1816, left the firm. After his shares were re-assigned, the ownership of the firm was as follows; Thomas Hewitt – 3/8 (37.5%), James Morrogh – 3/8 (37.5%) and Thomas Henry Hewitt – 2/8 (25%). Therefore, after this re-allocation, the Watercourse Distillery was majority-owned by members of the Hewitt family, as they now held 62.5% of the issued shares. James Morrogh eventually left the firm in 1834 and sold his shares to the remaining partners, thereby ensuring that the business was eventually owned solely by Hewitt family members.

A series of events occurred around this time which caused the distilling industry in Cork to decline. These included the temperance (i.e. abstinence) movement from the 1830s onwards (in Cork this was led by a Capuchin priest called Father Matthew, to whom a statue was erected on the main street [St. Patrick's Street] in Cork in 1864 and remains to the present day), a significant decline in the Irish population (due primarily to the Great Famine from 1845 to 1850) and a shift in drinking habits away from spirits and towards beer. Furthermore, as many of the remaining Cork distilleries continued producing their whiskey using pot stills instead of the newer and more productive patent stills, they began

Table 6.5 Profit balance for each partner from 1816 to 1825 (U15/B/B/4/9)

	Thomas Hewitt	*James Morrogh*	*Thomas Henry Hewitt*	*Morrogh Son*	*Total*
1816	£3,624	£17,935	£13,221	£17,524	£52,304
1817	£9,590	£25,263	£18,224	£18,053	£71,130
1818	£3,900	£18,589	£15,463	£15,192	£53,144
1819	£452	£14,462	£14,926	£14,347	£44,187
1820	£2,417	£14,178	£15,060	£14,948	£46,603
1821	£4,762	£16,376	£16,631	£17,352	£55,121
1822	£6,059	£18,649	£17,653	£20,035	£62,396
1823	£10,984	£24,222	£21,045	£23,101	£79,352
1824	£7,512	£20,809	£19,614	£21,362	£69,297
1825	£9,209	£23,026	£20,916	£23,435	£76,586

losing market share towards the end of the 19th century. Possible reasons for this reluctance to embrace patent stills included their perceived technological complexity, in addition to a feeling amongst Irish distillers generally that these stills produced an almost flavourless whiskey in comparison to the strong-flavoured whiskey generated from pot stills. Furthermore, the fact that the patent still concept had been developed by a former Inspector General of Excise for the whole of Ireland (Aeneas Coffey), who during his tenure in office had been repeatedly at odds with the Irish distilling industry, did little to convince them of the benefits that could potentially accrue to their businesses from adopting this new approach to distilling.

A document from the Hewitt archive, written in 1851, setting forth future working arrangements (U15B/B/4/12), reported that the non-payment of accounts by customers and the firm's accumulated debts had become major issues. Specifically, the document outlines that all future revenue should be used to pay amounts outstanding, with a special mention for their bank debt. It proposes that "small ledger" debts should immediately be requested to pay their accounts, with a threat of legal action if they failed to comply. It notes that "all due diligence be used for getting in as many of the customers' debts" but without "giving them offence to the injury of the business". If the proposals could be accomplished over the following three months, the document states that the partners should be in a position to consider "continuing the business", although it is also noted that "the bank might be induced to make a credit advance on the security of the distillery alone".

Following a period of continual decline, the Hewitt family decided to sell the distillery and all of its assets to the Cork Distillers Company (CDC) in 1864, in an amalgamation with four other Cork distilleries – Midleton, North Mall, The Green and Daly's (Townsend, 1997). Distilling whiskey finally ceased at the Watercourse Distillery from the late 1870s onwards, although their buildings were still used by the CDC (McCarthy, 2009). For example, from 1916 onwards, the CDC produced industrial spirits at the facility, which was exported primarily to Britain for use in explosives during World War I. By the end of the 1930s, the CDC was the only remaining distillery in Cork. In 1966, the CDC merged with two other Irish distillers, John Jameson and Son and John Powers and Son to form the Irish Distillers Group (IDG), whose aim was to focus on exports, whilst re-establishing Ireland as a global player in whiskey production (Townsend, 1997). In 1975, IDG consolidated all of its distilling at a new custom-built distillery in Midleton, County Cork. Following this, the Watercourse Distillery buildings lay idle for many years before they were finally demolished in the mid-1990s.

The role of accounting

Although the accounting records held for the Watercourse Distillery at the Cork City and County archives are incomplete, insofar as they do not cover the entire time period in question, an examination of the existing records reveals that the distillery did develop and maintain a comprehensive system of accounts to record both its sales and costs. This would have been in keeping with other firms that existed at the same time, for which accounting records were primarily used to determine information on creditors and debtors (Chambers, 1987). This information subsequently allowed firms to prepare annual profit and loss accounts, although Gervais (2014) has suggested that the calculation of "profit" at this time may not have been entirely consistent, and was not therefore overly relied upon by the respective merchants.

From analysing the incoming business correspondence (U15B/B/1) of the Watercourse Distillery from 1795 to the 1860s, it is possible to determine that in addition to selling to individual customers, such as public houses, the distillery employed a number of travelling salesmen/agents charged with promoting/selling its spirits. For example, correspondence received from J. J. Clarke in 1853 (U15B/B/1/1/4/1) outlines details of sales made (i.e. products, quantities and prices) to various customers and from different towns, including Clonmel, Waterford and Limerick. This correspondence also contains details of cheques from customers and bank drafts with instructions to, for example, "place it to the credit of James Cleary". The Watercourse Distillery also engaged a firm of merchants based in Dublin, namely Connolly, Maxwell and Fortescue, to sell its produce in Dublin and surrounding areas. A selection of the firm's accounts have survived (U15B/B/1/8/3), with each one generally covering a period of approximately one year (e.g. 9th June 1807 to 1st June 1808). In this context, the archives contain records of two main accounts: (1) a sales account outlining how much of each type of whiskey was sold by Connolly, Maxwell and Fortescue on its behalf on a particular day; and (2) an account providing details of daily customer payments, in either cash or bank drafts, in addition to amounts outstanding. As well as selling its output in Ireland, the Watercourse Distillery sold its whiskey in Britain via a number of different agents (for example, Peter Lunell in Bristol, Jordaine and Shaw in London). Indeed, it was noted that the Watercourse Distillery "catered to quite a sophisticated and discerning clientele" (Cullen, 1998, p. 30). The same two accounts as those outlined earlier were also used here (U15B/B/1/8/3).

The archive also contains letters from customers, many of which contain orders for various types of whiskey, in addition to paying some/all of the balance due on their accounts. For example, a letter posted in 1855 from John Hannigan, based in Dungarvan, Co. Waterford (U15B/B/1/1/2/1/25), makes reference to an enclosed letter of credit which "pays my account in full up to this date". Other customer correspondence from, for example, Catherine Healy in Kenmare, Co. Kerry (U15B/B/1/1/2/1/48), refers to partial payment of her debts with the promise that the "balance shall be paid very soon". Each letter received from a customer was dated by the Watercourse Distillery on the rear and the relevant customer's name was also added. In terms of customer payments, the archive also contains a letter sent to James McCall and Co. in 1812 (U15B/B/1/6/2) confirming that the distillery would agree to its request to deliver 800 puncheons of spirits in eight equal weekly instalments but that in terms of payment "you are to pay us in Bank of Ireland notes for each weekly delivery of spirits on or before Thursday in the week succeeding the delivery".

Correspondence from the distillery's many suppliers (for example, brass, timber, blacksmith, rope and candles) are present in the archival material, and collectively it allows for an analysis of how the firm made payments and carried out its business more generally. For example, there is a letter sent to the distillery from a barley supplier (U15B/B/1/6/1) acknowledging the receipt of a payment outstanding whilst also complimenting them for their "promptness as always in closing accounts". Other letters remind the distillery of bills outstanding, for example, in 1852 a letter from Mallow, Co. Cork remarks that "oblige by your kindly remitting at your convenience the balance of £11.18.8". A review of the account of John and Isaac Carroll (timber merchants) reveals great detail with each delivery of timber recorded by date, quantity and price (U15B/B/1/25/1). Each supplier account held by the Watercourse Distillery appears to have been for an average of one year and, once paid, the word "Settled" was physically written on it.

In Thomas Hewitt's letter-book containing outgoing correspondence (i.e. U15/B/B/3), there are copies of letters confirming the fulfilment of orders for whiskey, rum, etc., for the period from 1794 to 1802. It also includes copies of circular letters sent to some of his customers outlining what each of them owed the distillery on closing their "books" at the end of a given month. As an example, "we beg to state the balance on your account due us this day [September 30th, 1802], on closing our books is". Also, from this letter-book, it can be seen that many of their regular customers had credit terms of up to a number of months in which to settle their outstanding debts. In a letter to Mary Holland from Bandon, Co. Cork, it is stated that for her recent order "the usual credit" is "2 months. I beg to remind of its being due on 21st Aug therefore request you will please order payment of the same". If a customer did not comply with their credit terms, they were sent a letter by the distillery requesting them to do so. For example, in a letter sent to Eliza Holland from Bandon, Co. Cork it is stated that "we beg to advise that the time of credit on a [delivery] of whiskey sent you in April last amount £18.2.8 is elapsed [and we] request you will make provision for the same which will oblige". A number of customers appeared to have pre-paid their accounts, meaning that the value of any subsequent orders were simply deducted from their remaining credit balance to determine whether or not they owed the distillery any money at that time. For example, in a letter sent to John Flyn from Castlelyons, Co. Cork, confirming that his order for whiskey had been dispatched, it is stated that "the difference being 5p is placed to your credit". As with most firms even today, cash flow was also an issue for the distillery, as in a letter to a customer (Mr. Somerville) on 25th November 1799, a request is made for prompt payment stating that as "this is the season in which we most need the use of all our funds, we request your particular attention thereto".

A copy of a letter from 1794 vividly illustrates how well the Watercourse Distillery performed in its early years. In it, a customer is informed that "our demand is so great that we must beg of you in future to write to us two or three days before you want saying exactly the time your courier will be here". Similarly, on 22nd September 1797, a potential customer, Mr. Murphy from Killarney, Co. Kerry, is informed that his request for spirits cannot be satisfied as "at present we have not a gallon of spirits to spare from a customer". The letter-book also contains copies of letters sent to customers informing them of increases/decreases in the price of certain proofs of whiskey. For example, in a letter dated 28th December 1795, it is stated that "we have the pleasure to inform you that the price of whiskey proof [. . .] is reduced per gallon".

This section of the archival records is extremely interesting as it provides evidence that the majority of the distillery's customers were local, that is, in towns in Cork (for example, Youghal, Fermoy, Mallow), the neighbouring county of Kerry (for example, Dingle, Tralee and Killarney) and various other towns primarily throughout Munster. Towards the end of the existence of the Watercourse Distillery, it was estimated that between 500 and 600 licenced premises served the approximate 80,000 population of Cork (Murphy, 1986). This local orientation is also demonstrated when, writing in 1800 to Mr. John Purcell, a customer based in Killarney, Co. Kerry, it is stated that "when you were last in Cork we were not a little surprised at having you left town without calling to discharge your account", before being requested to pay the balance on his account "by the very first opportunity". Although the distillery did have some customers in Dublin, the archive reveals details of a number of letters sent from the Secretary of the Distillers Committee in 1812 reminding Hewitt & Co. of a resolution which had been passed which no longer permitted Cork-based distillers from selling their produce in Dublin (U15B/B/1/6/2). In one of these letters, it is remarked that, as per the resolution, "the Distillers of Cork will make no sales for this market", and that if they find themselves in the position of having excess stock, "they will in the first place make an offer of it to the Distillers here". It further states that on the day that this letter was written (17th July, 1812), there "arrived two hundred and twenty puncheons from your market" whose repeated occurrence has precluded "the Distillers here fixing any general prices". The letter concludes by claiming that this "is equally against the interests of both Cork and Dublin".

This emphasis on financial accounting-type information is in contrast to the experiences of some firms operating in Britain around the same time. For example, the study of the evolution of the accounting practices of Ransomes of Ipswich (a manufacturer of agricultural implements) by Boyns and Edwards (2016) for the period between 1856 and 1863 revealed an emphasis on direct material and direct labour costs, in addition to the recovery of overheads. This finding is in keeping with the content of accounting textbooks published in Britain at this time, as by the 1840s there appears to have been an increasing interest in how to satisfy the information requirements of manufacturers for performance measurement and decision-making purposes (see, for example, Henderson, 1841; Krepp, 1858). Furthermore, research conducted by Jones (1985) found evidence that from the 1820s onwards, there was an acknowledgement that the opportunity cost of capital should be recognised prior to the determination of partners' profits. No evidence of any of these accounting practices from the information available for the Watercourse Distillery was found.

Edwards and Boyns (2013) also summarise the use of cost calculation techniques between 1870 and 1914. Although this time frame excludes the Watercourse Distillery, their findings suggest that the scale of use of such techniques is not accurately known. This is supported by Vent and Milne (2000), who reported that many firms were operating with extremely limited costing practices. Furthermore, research conducted by Talbot (2008) on the malt costing practices between 1700 and 1939 found that the costing systems in situ were extremely basic and did not provide management with much useful information about how much the process of malting actually cost to engage in. Nevertheless, other studies have shown that accounting within certain industries from approximately 1886 to 1940 appeared to have become quite sophisticated. For example, using Guinness as their case study, papers by Hiebl et al. (2015), Quinn (2014) and Quinn and Jackson (2014) have been able to highlight the development and use of cost and management accounting. Ultimately, it appears that during the existence of the Watercourse Distillery, developments such as those mentioned earlier had not been implemented in this company.

Another component of the business correspondence section of the Thomas Hewitt archive (U15/B/B/4) is the "Hewitt Managerial Correspondence File", primarily covering the period from 1810 to the 1860s. This includes correspondence from suppliers, from other distilleries and copies of annual profit and loss accounts for particular periods of time. From reviewing the annual total profit/loss figures provided (U15/B/B/4/9 – these accounts are for the period 1794 to 1833 only – see Figure 6.1 for a graphical summary), it can be determined that they generated a profit of £2,528 in their first year of trading. In the subsequent five years, reported profitability increased, although with some volatility, up to a 1799 record of £19,109. Over this initial six-year trading period (the accounts are summarised according to various different number of year groupings in the Thomas Hewitt archive [U15/B/B/4/9]), the distillery reported total net profits of £42,202 (an average of £7,034 per annum), with no reported losses. During the next reported phase (from 1800 to 1812), it had its best financial performance, with total net profits amounting to £148,720 (an average of £11,440 per annum). By 1808, along with its biggest trading rival in Cork, Saint Dominick's distillery, they were collectively producing approximately a million gallons of whiskey annually, representing 59% (Watercourse Distillery – 24%; Saint Dominick's – 35%) of the city's distilling capacity (Townsend, 1997). During this period, the Watercourse Distillery also reported losses of £1,325 in 1801 and £5,339 in 1809. In the subsequent reporting period (between 1813 and 1820), it reported a total net profit of £25,247 (an average of £3,156 per annum). During this eight-year time horizon, it reported both profits and losses in equal measure – illustrating the volatility of the distilling sector at this time. Finally, between 1821 and 1833, total net profits amounted to £41,467 (an average of £3,190 per annum). This included losses for four years, including three consecutive years from 1827 to 1829.

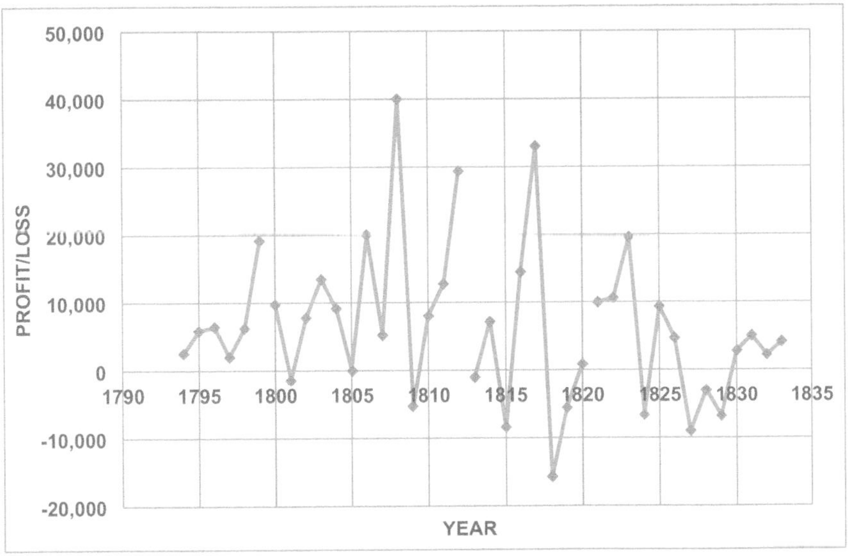

Figure 6.1 Summary profits/losses between 1794 and 1833 (U15/B/B/4/9)

Concluding comments

This chapter has traced the existence of the Watercourse Distillery from its establishment in 1792 until its eventual amalgamation with a number of other distilleries in 1868. Based upon the limited archival information available and secondary sources, it seems that the distillery maintained comprehensive financial accounting–type records for the main elements of its operations. However, it appears that no management accounting–type information was produced as an aid to managerial decisions. This is in contrast to other countries and industries where this type of information had begun to be produced (see, for example, Boyns and Edwards, 2016)). Nevertheless, the accounting records that do exist for the Watercourse Distillery allow us to better consider how business and society operated at this particular time in Irish history, thereby further enriching our knowledge and understanding of this era.

Appendix I

Table 6.6 Distribution of profits/losses per partner per annum – 1794 to 1833

Year	*Thomas Hewitt*	*John Teulon*	*Richard Blunt*	*James Morrogh*	*Thomas Henry Hewitt*	*Teulon Son*	*Morrogh Son*
	£	£	£	£	£	£	£
1794	842	842	842				
1795	1,950	1,950	1,950				
1796	2,150	2,150	2,150				
1797	670	670	670				
1798	2,084	2,084	2,084				
1799	6,369	6,369	6,369				
1800	2,434	2,434	2,434	2,434			
1801	(331)	(331)	(331)	(311)			
1802	1,941	1,941	1,941	1,941			
1803	3,356	3,356	3,356	3,356			
1804	2,280	2,280	2,280	2,280			
1805	32	32	32	32			
1806	5,000	5,000		5,000	2,500	2,500	
1807	1,294	1,294		1,294	647	647	
1808	10,000	10,000		10,000	5,000	5,000	
1809	(1,334)	(1,334)		(1,334)	(667)	(667)	
1810	2,004	2,004		2,004	1,002	1,002	
1811	3,971			3,971	2,382	2,382	
1812	9,156			9,156	5,494	5,494	
1813	(325)			(325)	(195)	(195)	
1814	2,291			2,291	1,374	1,374	
1815	(2,680)			(2,680)	(1,608)	(1,608)	
1816	4,649			4,649	2,789		2,789
1817	10,348			10,348	6,209		6,209
1818	(4,917)			(4,917)	(2,950)		(2,950)
1819	(1,731)			(1,731)	(1,039)		(1,039)
1820	255			255	153		153

Year	*Thomas Hewitt*	*John Teulon*	*Richard Blunt*	*James Morrogh*	*Thomas Henry Hewitt*	*Teulon Son*	*Morrogh Son*
	£	£	£	£	£	£	£
1821	3,111			3,111	1,867		1,867
1822	3,317			3,317	1,990		1,990
1823	6,120			6,120	3,672		3,672
1824	(2,086)			(2,086)	(1,251)		(1,251)
1825	2,904			2,904	1,742		1,742
1826	1,458			1,458	875		875
1827	(3,408)			(3,408)	(2,272)		
1828	(1,138)			(1,138)	(759)		
1829	(2,566)			(2,566)	(1,711)		
1830	1,036			1,036	691		
1831	1,876			1,876	1,251		
1832	814			814	542		
1833	1,518			1,518	1,012		
Total	74,714	40,741	23,777	60,669	28,740	15,929	14,057

Source: Thomas Hewitt File, Cork City and County Archives (U15B/B/4/9)

References

Primary sources

Archive of Thomas Hewitt, Cork City and County Archives, Blackpool, Cork (IE CCCA/U15B)
Files series utilised
U15B/P/A Memorabilia, societies, associations, committees, 1840s – 1870
U15B/B/1 Incoming business correspondence, 1795–1860s
U15B/B/1/1/2/1/25 Handwritten correspondence to Thomas Hewitt & Co. from customers, 1850–1858
U15B/B/1/1/2/1/48 Handwritten correspondence to Thomas Hewitt & Co. from customers, 1850–1858
U15B/B/1/1/4/1 Correspondence from J. J. Clarke, a travelling salesman, employed by Hewitt & Co., 1851–1854
U15B/B/1/6/1 Bills and correspondence from suppliers of Hewitt & Co., 1849–1856
U15B/B/1/6/2 Correspondence from Joseph Miller, Secretary of the Committee of Distillers, 17th July, 1812
U15B/B/1/8/3 Customer accounts, sales accounts, etc . . ., 1797–1808
U15B/B/1/25/1 Accounts with various suppliers and businesses, 1793–1800
U15B/B/3 Hewitt & Co., letterbook, outgoing correspondence, 1794–1802
U15B/B/4 Managerial correspondence file, 1810–1860s
U15B/B/4/9 1798–1833 Balances, P & L Account, T. Hewitt & Co.
15B/B/4/12 Jan 1851 – Covenants for company partnership deed and proposed arrangements
U15/B/B/4/29 Pamphlet, 'The Spirit Trade of Ireland'
U15/B/B/4/30 Notice, 'Irish Spirit Trade'
U15B/B/4/32 Pamphlet, 'A Statement of the Means adopted for excluding Irish Whiskey from English Consumption'

Secondary sources

Boyns, T. and Edwards, J. R. (2016). The advent of double-entry-based costing practices in the British engineering industry: Ransomes of Ipswich, 1856–1863. *Accounting History Review*, 26(3), pp. 171–190.

Chambers, R. (1987). Accounting education for the twenty-first century. *Abacus*, 23(2), pp. 97–106.

Clarke, P. (2008). The teaching of bookkeeping in nineteenth-century Ireland. *Accounting, Business and Financial History*, 18(1), pp. 21–33.

Cork City and County Archives (2017). *Merchant Princes.* Available at: www.corkarchives.ie/merchantcity/home/merchantprinces [Accessed 4th Aug. 2017].

Cullen, L. M. (1998). *The Brandy Trade Under the Ancien Regime.* Cambridge: Cambridge University Press.

Edwards, R. and Boyns, T. (2013). *A History of Management Accounting: The British Experience.* London: Routledge.

Edwards, R., Dean, G. and Clarke, F. (2009). Merchants' accounts, performance assessment and decision making in mercantilist Britain. *Accounting, Organizations and Society*, 34(5), pp. 551–570.

Foster, M. (1992). *Inside their World: An Archival Exhibition Focusing on the Lives of Three Nineteenth Century Cork Gentlemen: Richard Dowden, Thomas Hewitt and William Coppinger.* Cork: Cork Archives Institute.

Gervais, P. (2014). Why profit and loss didn't matter: The historicized rationality of early modern merchant accounting. In: P. Gervais, Y. Lemarchand and D. Margairaz, eds. *Merchants and Profit in the Age of Commerce, 1680–1830*. London: Pickering & Chatto, pp. 33–52.

Henderson, A. (1841). *Book-Keeping by Single and Double Entry: The Theory and Practice Familiarly Explained and Illustrated by Examples of Modern Business*. London: Simpkin, Marshall.

Hiebl, M. R., Quinn, M. and Martinez Franco, C. (2015). An analysis of the role of a Chief Accountant at Guinness c. 1920–1940. *Accounting History Review*, 25(2), pp. 145–165.

Jones, H. (1985). *Accounting, Costing and Cost Estimation, Welsh Industry, 1700–1830*. Cardiff: University of Wales Press.

Krepp, F. C. (1858). *Statistical Book-Keeping: Being a Simplification and Abbreviation of the Common System by Double Entry, For the Use of Merchants, Bankers, Tradesmen Manufacturers*. London: Longman, Brown, Green, Longmans and Roberts.

McCarthy, K. (2009). *Northside Narratives: Shandon Street Heritage Trail*. Available at: http://corkheritage.ie/?page_id=434 [Accessed 27th June 2017].

Meagher, J. (1994). Elias Voster: The father of Irish accountancy. *Journal of the Cork Historical and Archaeological Society*, 99, pp. 111–119.

Murphy, M. (1986). Cork commercial society 1850–1899: Politics and problems. In: P. Butel and L. M. Cullen, eds. *Cities and Merchants: French and Irish Perspectives on Urban Development, 1500–1900*. Dublin: Trinity College, pp. 233–244.

O'Brien, J. B. (1986). Merchants in Cork before the famine. In: P. Butel and L. M. Cullen, eds. *Cities and Merchants: French and Irish Perspectives on Urban Development, 1500–1900*. Dublin: Trinity College, pp. 221–230.

Quinn, M. (2014). Stability and change in management accounting over time: A century or so of evidence from Guinness. *Management Accounting Research*, 25(1), pp. 76–92.

Quinn, M. and Jackson, W. J. (2014). Accounting for war risk costs: Management accounting change at Guinness during the First World War. *Accounting History Review*, 24(2/3), pp. 191–209.

Sombart, W. (1916). Der Modern Kapitalismus. Quoted in Chiapello, E. (2007). Accounting and the birth of the notion of capitalism. *Critical Perspectives in Accounting*, 18(30), pp. 263–296.

Stewart, M. (2013). *Rectors and Curates of St. Paul's With Biographical Notes*. Available at: www.corkrecords.com/StPauls/Rectors.htm [Accessed 27th June 2017].

Talbot, P. A. (2008). Sir John Barleycorn, Miss Hop and their only child. Master Beer: Accounting for malt 1700–1939. *The Journal of the Brewery History Society*, 129, pp. 2–30.

Townsend, B. (1997). *The Lost Distilleries of Ireland*. Glasgow: Neil Wilson Publishing.

Vent, G. and Milne, R. A. (2000). Accounting practices of the St. Joseph Lead Company: 1864–1900. *Accounting, Business and Financial History*, 10(2), pp. 97–128.

Voster, E. (1769). *Arithmetic in Whole and Broken Numbers*. 12th ed., revised by Daniel Voster. Cork. Dublin, Ireland: R Cross.

Weber, M. (1950). *The Protestant Ethic and the Spirit of Capitalism*. New York: Charles Scribner's Sons.

Weir, R. (1995). *The History of the Distillers Company, 1877–1939*. Oxford: Clarendon Press.

7 Accounting for vodka in Russia

Viatcheslav I. Sokolov, Svetlana N. Karelskaia and Ekaterina I. Zuga

Introduction

Russian literature on the history of accounting lacks papers on the evolution of accounting for alcoholic beverages, although Russia has been considered a global leader in terms of alcohol consumption per capita for a rather long time (according to, for example, the World Health Organisation). Its traditional beverage, vodka, is known all over the world. In the current sense of the term, vodka appeared at the end of the 19th century after a government monopoly was established causing changes in the production technology, regulatory framework and accounting treatment of alcoholic products. This was preceded by a long evolution of alcohol production and accounting since Ancient Russia, with kvass,[1] mead and wine, for example, being produced since the 10th century.

Regardless of the time period, alcohol levies have been one of the main sources for raising funds to the Russian budget. The first known levies in cash or in kind charged on raw materials used for the production of alcoholic beverages (hops, malt and grain) were registered in the 11th century. The registers of alcohol at that time were birch bark manuscripts,[2] which were used until the 16th century, when they were replaced by paper books. The 16th century was also the beginning of a new stage in the evolution of production, distribution and accounting for alcohol in Russia. It involved not only changes in the forms of registers, but also the introduction of regulatory documents and of restrictions and control of alcohol production and distribution on behalf of the state. Thus, we chose the 16th century as the starting point for this research. The period under our review extends until the start of the First World War (1914), which was followed by ten years of prohibition. This prohibition introduced a complete ban on production and distribution of alcoholic beverages, including vodka, in Russia.

The purpose of this research is to systematise the description of alcohol accounting practice in Russia and include it in the accounting literature as an essential backdrop to the history of accounting in a state-regulated industry, which is a typical subject matter in Russia. This is the first research that offers a full description of the evolution of accounting treatment and control of production and circulation of alcohol in Russia from the 16th to early 20th centuries, and it will primarily analyse the bookkeeping process.

This chapter proceeds as follows. Next, we briefly set out the methods used in the study. The next section is dedicated to the origin and subsequent evolution of the term "vodka". Then we describe bread wine as the predecessor of vodka, the collection of income from its production and distribution and some accounting procedures. We then describe the introduction of double-entry accounting, followed by the disclosure of the circumstances and conditions in which vodka appeared in Russia, containing a detailed description of its production stages, accounting treatment and documents flow, among other aspects. The final section summarises the key findings of the research, which includes an overview of the evolution of documents flow and registers used to keep records of vodka production and distribution in Russia in the 16th to early 20th centuries, a review of the calculation of profits in *kabak* books[3] in the early 17th century, an identification of the first regulation on the accounting treatment of alcohol dated 1703, an analysis of its main provisions and an indication of potential areas of further research.

Method

This chapter is based both on primary and secondary sources. Primary sources include the Olonets[4] *kabak* book for the period from 4 May through 2 August 1609 as one of the earliest *kabak* books preserved to date (translated by A. I. Razdorsky); the receipts/expenses books of Moscow *prikazes* (public offices) for 1619–1621 (translated by S. B. Veselovsky (1876–1952), prepared for publication by L. G. Dubinskaya, A. L. Stanislavsky and published in 1983); regulatory documents included in the Complete Compilation of Laws of the Russian Empire ("Compilation") as the fullest collection of regulating documents adopted in 1649–1913, including those concerning accounting and tax treatment of alcoholic products; and the Corpus Juris of the Russian Empire ("Corpus") as a collection of laws effective in the Russian Empire arranged by disciplines. The Corpus was first printed in 1832 and contained a Corpus of Accounting Rules concerning accounting, reporting and review. Our secondary sources can be classified into three groups. First, we draw on papers on legal aspects of the state wine monopoly (Larina, 2011; Rusakov et al., 2016), history of finance (Ilovaisky, 1904) and tax systems (Tolkushkin, 2001; Kucher and Gulina, 2006; Tersky, 2012), organisation of wineries (Lvov, 1887; Borodin, 1910; Pryzhov, 1914) and vodka distilleries (Pokhlyobkin, 2005; Rodionov, 2012; Akinfiev, 2016) in Russia. Second, we draw on publications by foreign authors on the economics of alcohol in the world (Blake et al., 1998; Phillips, 2014; Viana and Rodrigues, 2006). And third, we draw on papers on production, accounting and tax treatment of alcohol and its impact on such countries as England, France and the United States (Herlihy, 2002; Himelstein, 2009; Krom and Krom, 2013; Loo and McKerchar, 2014; Passant, 2016; Pennock and Kerr, 2005; Schrad, 2014; Stanziani, 2009; Tracy, 2016).

This chapter takes into account that Russian accounting rules developed within the continental legal framework, which sets rigid standards on accounting rules in order to serve the interests of the state. This was particularly true in respect of alcohol, as in Russia it was state-controlled at all stages of national development.

As a result, by the 17th century there was a comprehensive regulatory framework consisting of detailed statutory instructions on a broad range of subject matters, from the selling price of alcoholic beverages to accounting rules.

Vodka: evolution of the term and production process

The term "vodka" is currently used to describe a type of strong liquor with a distinctive aroma, popular in the Eastern and Northern Europe. Russia and Poland compete as the country where vodka was first invented (Pokhlyobkin, 2005, pp. 2–5). This is still an open question, the reason for discussion being the lack of a unified approach to the term "vodka". Modern vodka is an alcoholic beverage produced by mixing ethyl alcohol made from agricultural products with water. According to European Union regulations, it should be manufactured from grains, potatoes or other primary agricultural products and contain at least 37.5% alcohol by volume ("% vol.").[5] Ethyl alcohol used to make vodka should contain at least 96% vol. of alcohol (Wiśniewska et al., 2015, p. 2000). The only process that yields 96% ethyl alcohol is called rectification. *Rectification* (from Latin *rectus*, direct and *facio*, make) is a process of separating liquid mixtures into practically pure components that have different boiling temperatures through repeated evaporation of liquids and condensation of vapour. As a method, it became popular in the 19th century.

The first document in the Russian legal framework that used the word "vodka" was the *ukase* (edict) "On charging import duties on various types of wine and vodka", approved on 4 August 1683 during the co-reign of Ivan V[6] and Peter the Great (Peter I) (Compilation I No. 1037, 1683, pp. 558–559). At that time, vodka was the term used to refer to alcoholic beverages imported into Russia. Bread vodka in the meaning of bread wine is first mentioned in a document of 1 September 1696, regulating the government levy on sold alcohol (Compilation I No. 1548, 1696, pp. 258–262).

This varying opinion of researchers is caused by the evolution of the meaning of the term "vodka" over time. In the 16th century, it meant a medicine (an alcoholic infusion of herbs); in the 17th, a flavoured beverage (bread wine) produced by means of distillation; in the 18th, any strong liquor; and starting from the second quarter of the 20th century, vodka as we understand it today (Rodionov, 2012, p. 257). This chapter follows the recipe and process-based perspective of the origin of vodka, so it considers the accounting rules that took shape towards the end of the 19th century. However, to explain the specific features of these rules, we will describe the accounting rules applied earlier to bread wine as the predecessor of vodka.

Accounting treatment of distilled vodka – bread wine

Before vodka appeared in Russia, another popular alcoholic beverage was bread wine. It was produced by distilling fermentation products (based on grain, normally rye) (Rodionov, 2012, p. 15). In terms of production process, it was similar to the production of cognac, whisky, tequila and grappa (Rodionov, 2012, p. 10). In the 16th century, Russia gradually introduced a state monopoly over the production and distribution of alcoholic beverages, achieved by restricting private manufacturers' rights in individual regions. For example, in 1547 Ivan the Terrible[7] banned the free sale of strong liquor in Moscow (Borodin, 1910, p. 34). It could be sold only in special drinking establishments owned by the state, known as *kabaks*.[8] Later, this ban was expanded to other regions of Russia, and a chain of state-owned *kabaks* was created. Profit generated by *kabaks* was public income received by the state. Its calculations were made in *kabak* books, a special type of accounting register. Requirements as to the form of these *kabak* books were set in the instructions issued by regional fiscal bodies (*Zemstvo* houses)[9] directly to the *kabak* heads. Surviving fragments of *kabak* books from various regions allow us to conclude that they are generally similar (Razdorsky, 2015).

Accounting in kabaks

As noted earlier, *kabak* books were the accounting registers of *kabaks* in the early 17th century. Since *kabaks* were places not only for the distribution but also the production of bread wine and beer, the books recorded the procurement and consumption of raw materials (malt, hops, grain) and other production costs (transportation, pre-processing, workers' salaries), product yields and information about its distribution and cash proceeds. The records were measured in kind and in cash. Their content is demonstrated by a *kabak* book from the town of Olonets, containing records from 4 May until 2 August 1609 (Kabak books of the reign of Vasily Shuisky . . . 2014, pp. 5–15).

Records in the Olonets book are a descriptive text using old Slavic symbols for numbers. The records were made in the form of straight text without splitting into columns (not formalised) and were divided into sections only based on separate production cycles. The book contains information about three months, during which *kabak* heads completed six full production cycles, two each month. Olonets *kabak* produced beer and bread wine. Information on each production cycle covers everything from procurement of raw materials to the sale of finished product. Each record ends with the indication of product yield in kind (measured in "state buckets")[10] and the total production costs in cash. Then, the book indicates the amount of cash proceeds from selling the entire batch and price per volumetric unit. The last part of the record was the amount of profit per production cycle, calculated by deducting costs from revenues. At the end of the *kabak* book, there is a summary of total profit from all production cycles and its split into the amount forwarded to a *prikaz*[11] and the amount kept by the *kabak* to buy raw materials for the next production cycle. The *kabak* book was at the same time a register for record-keeping purposes and a reporting tool. Upon the end of reporting period, it was submitted to the *prikaz* together with the cash. It was a report on the work of *kabak* heads and at the same time it was the document recording the sources of public income and respective calculation methods through comparison of revenue and costs required to generate such revenue. Whenever a *kabak* head was replaced, they made a detailed inventory of *kabak* property known as an *rospisnoy* (inventory) list. These *kabak* documents were part of a complex document flow system supporting the collection of public income (see Figure 7.1 for more detail).

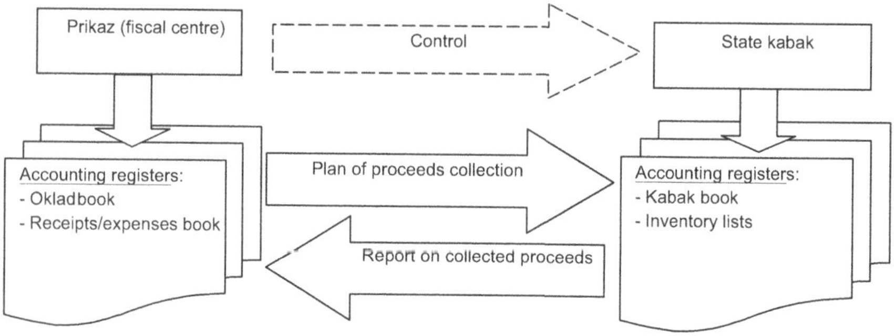

Figure 7.1 Collection of public income from production and distribution of alcoholic beverages and their accounting treatment in Russia in the 16th to 17th centuries

State accounting in the prikaz

In *prikazes*, records were kept in two types of accounting registers, *oklad* (plan) books and receipts/expenses books. Like in *kabak* books, records in these books were not formalised, and they consisted of straight text without splitting into columns. *Prikaz* accounting registers were opened for a reporting period equal to one year starting from 1 September (Sokolov, 1996, p. 223). *Oklad* books were drawn up at the beginning of each year or at the end of the current year. They contained estimated amounts of state levies by municipality (Medvedev, 2011, p. 283). The amounts of estimated *kabak* income were also recorded in the *oklad* books. Minimal target income from the sale of alcoholic products was annually set for each town (Razdorsky, 2015, p. 44). The figures from *oklad* books and *kabak* books received by *prikazes* as reporting documents were reconciled and entered in the receipts/expenses books. If arrears were identified, the decision about collecting the outstanding amount from the responsible person was recorded in the book. For example, the receipts book of Novgorod *prikaz* from 1619/20 contains information about the receipt of servage, customs and *kabak* money from 22 towns, arranged by town and by type of receipts (The receipts/expenses books, 1983, p. 4, pp. 7–141).

Beginning of state accounting regulation

The procedure described earlier for collecting *kabak* profits to state treasury in the middle of the 17th century was applied across the country, as the monopoly for wine distribution covered the whole territory of Russia. Exclusive rights to sell wine were recorded in the Council Code adopted in 1649 (Compilation I No. 1, 1649, p. 161). This document became the first regulation in Russia that indicated the cancellation of the practice of issuing local regulations for *prikazes*, which had caused lack of coordination. It marked the transition to a standardised legal framework from 1649, that is, to a unified interpretation of legal requirements. It remained in effect for almost 200 years, until 1832. The Council Code became the first Russian printed legal document. Previously, publication of laws had consisted in their reading at market squares and in churches, which was specifically mentioned in the documents. This was the beginning of a period when regulations on alcohol production and distribution were issued annually. On September 9, 1652 it became legally prohibited to open private *kabaks* (Compilation I No. 82, 1652, p. 271).

State *kabaks* could be organised in two ways: based on trust and farmed out. The accounting system described earlier was applied to running a *kabak* based on trust. In that case, a *kabak* was run by a public supervisor – *kabak* head – who was responsible for producing and selling bread wine and other permitted alcoholic beverages and at the same time controlled compliance with the ban on private alcohol distillation and trade. For *kabaks* based on trust, state income equalled the profits made by the *kabak*. This form was legalised at national level on 30 December 1651 in the Order "On having one drinking establishment in each town and big village" (Compilation I No. 72, 1651, p. 262). The second form of *kabaks* was a kind of outsourcing, and essentially resembled a lease. Farmers bought the rights to produce and sell wine at *kabaks* in a market place. The relations between a farmer and *prikaz* were recorded in a contract which set the rules for selling alcoholic beverages and the farmer's obligations. In this form, the state received a fixed amount that the farmer paid prior to commencement of the lease term (Kucher and Gulina, 2006, p. 74; Tolkushkin, 2001, p. 28).

Reforms by Peter the Great

The regulatory framework for accounting rules in Russia dates back to the reign of Peter the Great, continuing the legal reform replacing local regulations with national ones that started in 1649. The word "accountant" and the first regulation of accounting appeared in Russia under his rule (Sokolov, 1996, p. 226). This regulation was a document "On preparing bound books . . . for drinking enterprises" approved on 1 January 1703 (Compilation I No. 1922, 1703, pp. 201–209). It presented national accounting rules for *kabaks* based on trust. It introduced fundamental changes to how *kabak* books were filled out and when they were submitted. Since 1703, *kabak* heads were required to 1) prior to making entries in *kabak* books, to bind and seal them off at the local government office; 2) to make entries in the book on a daily basis; and 3) to present the accounting books to the controlling authority on a monthly basis. Moreover, it introduced a strict ban against making any entries in any books other than *kabak* books.

Accounting and reporting rules for farmers were set in a law of 1711, which required that registers showing receipts and expenses of drinking establishments be submitted to the country's highest governmental body, the Senate. This information was accounted for in special notebooks (Compilation I No. 2369, 1711, p. 690). They were filled with straight text without columns, like the register described earlier (see Figure 7.2).

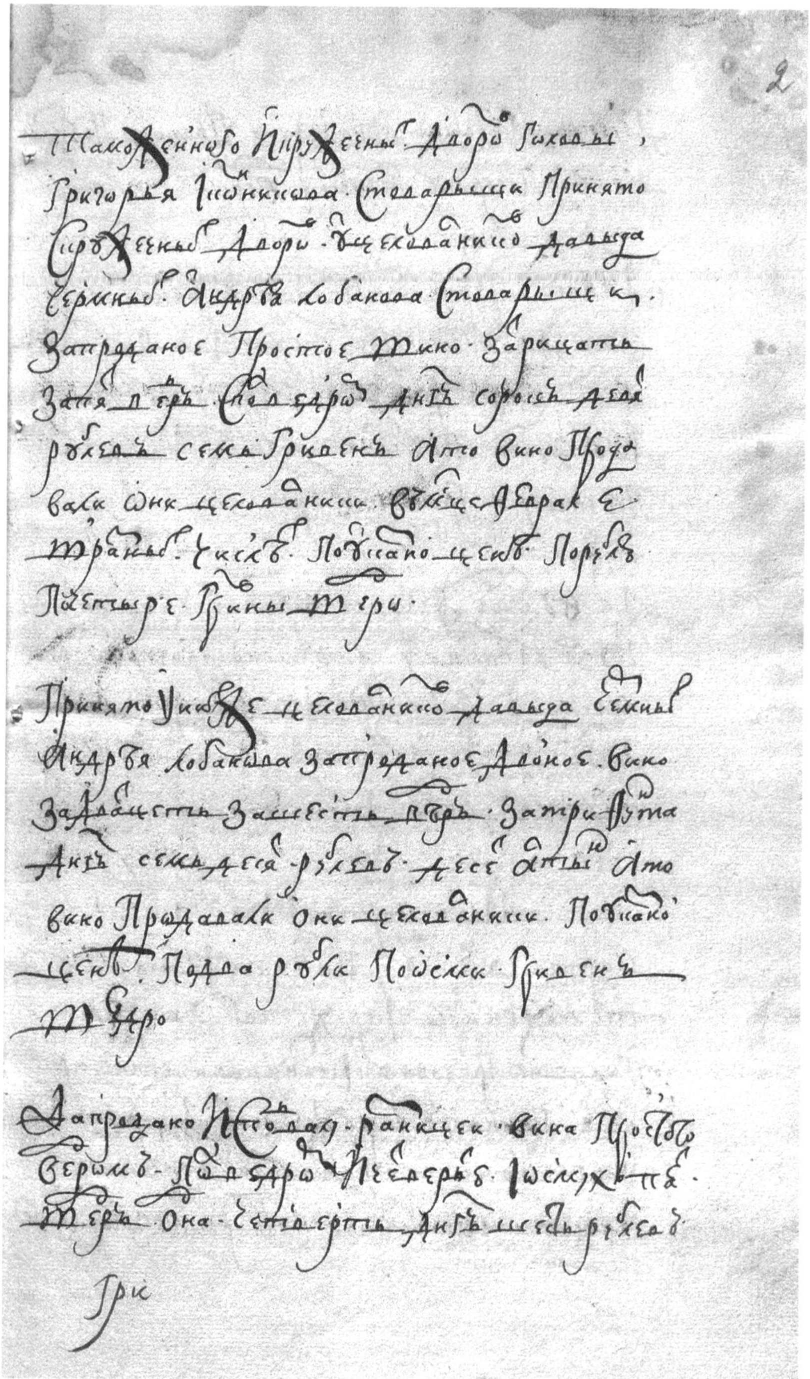

Figure 7.2 Notebook of wine sales and duties from the Tyumen Region, 1712

At the time of Peter the Great, numerous private and public distilleries were built, which eventually transformed the traditional system of *kabaks* into a more complex structure, comprising individual production and storage facilities and wholesale and retail businesses (Pronina, 2011, p. 172). Warehouse management was delegated to farmers, just as with *kabaks* under the state wine monopoly. However, the farming rules changed. Farmers bought bread wine from public or private distilleries at fixed state-controlled prices (Rodionov, 2012, p. 93). Its selling price was also supposed to be fixed. The reforms of Peter the Great influenced multiple aspects of accounting. The accounting books took on the format of tables with a breakdown into months and entries for debit and credit (Kuter and Sokolov, 2012, p. 81). However, these rules did not reach the distilleries until much later.

Introduction of the double-entry accounting and the excise system

The first tabular form for registering public income from the alcohol business appeared in 1782, in a document introducing a template for Treasury Chamber[12] income reports to the Expedition for Public Income.[13] It presented a summary of drinking establishments' proceeds and expenses by *okrugs* (districts), separating those farmed out and those based on trust. It also included volume, prices and total procurement amounts and product consumption of private and public distilleries (Compilation I No. 15560, 1782, p. 717). Later, in 1800, a Statute on Bankrupts was introduced for private enterprises. It contained a separate section on accounting registers (Compilation I No. 19692, 1800, pp. 456–457), amended in 1807 by an annex containing templates of accounting registers (Compilation I No. 22522, 1807, pp. 1175–1179). These documents introduced double-entry accounting with annual balance sheets drawn up based on the records in the ledger. This rule did not apply to public wine enterprises, which continued to use single-entry accounting.

Accounting under an excise system

In 1817, excise taxes were imposed on private alcohol manufacturers. The tax was calculated not based on actual alcohol output, but on the total output permitted by a certificate acquired by the producer. Producers as well as farmers were required to record different types of beverages in a special book, where they registered the volume of product output, its bottling and delivery from the plant with the addresses of customers (Compilation I No. 26764, 1817, pp. 136–137). Significant transformations in the alcohol business were made after the Decree on Alcohol Tax was published in 1861 (Compilation II No. 37197, 1861, pp. 39–70), which introduced the excise system in Russia in 1863. This document cancelled the state wine monopoly, following which private alcohol production and distribution enterprises appeared and operated in parallel to public ones (Compilation II No. 37197, 1861, p. 39). State income from alcohol was levied in two forms, namely excise and patent fees. Excise was paid by the producers of primary products (ethyl alcohol and bread wine), that is, distilleries (Rodionov, 2012, pp. 94–95). It was calculated based on alcohol content and product output (Compilation II No. 37197, 1861, p. 60). Patent fees were paid by the distributors of alcoholic beverages (stores and drinking establishments) and producers of secondary products based on ethyl alcohol and bread wine (wineries and alcohol refineries at wholesale warehouses where ethyl alcohol was refined to increase alcohol content, and where flavoured wines were produced) (Compilation II No. 37197, 1861, pp. 256–257; Rodionov, 2012, p. 98). The charge was calculated based on enterprise type and location.

Collection of alcohol income to the treasury was supervised by the Department of Various Levies and Taxes within the Ministry of Finance. Excise taxes and patent fees were collected and recorded by special structures – excise offices (at the province and *okrug* level), and payments were made to *uyezd* treasuries. The list of accounting registers and types of reports required by the Decree on Alcohol Tax are shown in Figure 7.3.

Producers of primary products (ethyl alcohol and bread wine) kept plant (distillery) and cellar books. A distillery book was kept to record daily materials consumption and product output (Compilation II No. 37197, 1861, p. 55). It contained a summary of materials consumption, calculations of expected product output and actual output volumes. The payable amount of excise tax was calculated based on these figures. It was required to summarise the distillery books and to make a copy of these books for submission to the *Okrug* Excise Office. At the year-end the original books were submitted to the same

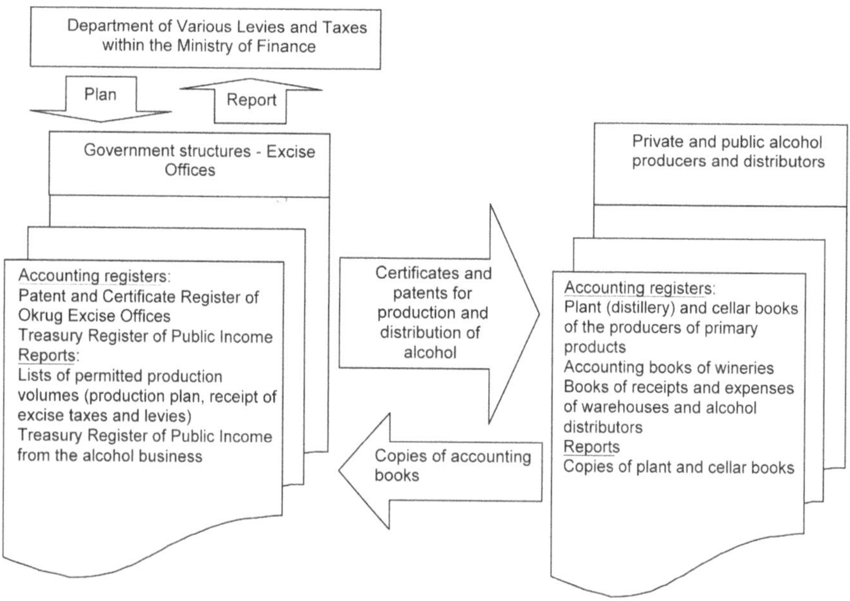

Figure 7.3 Communications and document flow of the excise period

Excise Office, and new books were issued (with numbered pages, bound and sealed off). Balances from the previous accounting registers were copied to the new books and verified by an excise officer. Cellar books were accounting registers of finished product warehouses that recorded the movements of finished product and the amounts of excise taxes paid on such products (Compilation II No. 37197, 1861, p. 55) Producers of secondary products (refined ethyl alcohol and flavoured wine) – wineries and alcohol refineries at wholesale warehouses – kept their accounts in the books where they recorded the quantities and alcohol levels of acquired bread wine and ethyl alcohol, and the quantities of their own product and its consumption. Alcohol retailers (stores) and drinking establishments kept accounting books where they recorded receipt and consumption of alcoholic beverages (Compilation II No. 37197, 1861, p. 68).

Excises paid by the producers of primary products and patent fees paid by distributors, wineries and refineries were received by the *uyezd* treasury that kept special books to record cash receipts, based on which they prepared monthly reports for the Provincial Excise Office on public income received from alcohol operations. *Okrug* Excise Offices kept records of issued patents for production and distribution of alcoholic beverages. *Okrug* Excise Offices also prepared and submitted to Provincial Excise Offices standardised reports on permitted volumes of primary product output (ethyl alcohol and bread wine) based on certificates issued. Distillation of alcohol was not permitted without such certificates (Compilation II No. 37197, 1861, p. 54). The reports showed estimated output of primary products and excise tax that had to be paid to the state budget, a plan for product distribution to other enterprises and estimated remaining stock (Compilation II No. 37197, 1861, p. 49). Provincial Excise Offices verified and summarised the information received from *Okrug* Excise Offices and treasuries, based on which it prepared the annual report on income from alcohol on a standard form for the Department of Various Levies and Taxes (Compilation II No. 37197, 1861, p. 46). Therefore, in summary, the excise system gave rise to a complex structure of public income collection, accounting and reporting system.

The appearance of rectified vodka – accounting treatment of alcohol production and distribution under a monopoly

The appearance of vodka as defined in terms of the modern recipe and production process coincided with the introduction of double-entry accounting within Russian public vodka producers and distributors. These two events were a result of a long evolution of statutory regulation in the sphere of bread wine production and distribution. In 1895, Russia reinstated a state alcohol monopoly, which eventually caused complete substitution of bread wine with vodka in the market (Rodionov, 2012, p. 22). After the monopoly was introduced, ethyl alcohol and alcoholic beverages could be produced both by private and public enterprises, but their distribution (sale) became once again the exclusive right of the state. This helped the Russian government reach a new level in market regulation and set unified requirements on the quality of product bought by public wine and alcohol distributors. Such requirements were mandatory for all players of the alcohol market. Another important factor that contributed to the appearance of vodka in Russia was the introduction of rectifiers in the last 20 years of the 19th century (Rodionov, 2012, p. 9). This technical novelty in alcohol production made it possible to produce pure ethyl alcohol with over 95% vol. at low cost. Lower production cost allowed the use of any raw materials that contained starch, so rye and wheat previously used to make bread wine were replaced with alternatives like potatoes and sugar beet (Rodionov, 2012, p. 9, pp. 11–12).

Accounting under a state monopoly

In 1895, the government passed a regulation requiring that "monopoly wine" be produced only from rectified ethyl alcohol with mandatory carbon treatment. This document became the first government "standard" on vodka, describing it as a product of mixing rectified 95% ethyl alcohol with water resulting in 40% vol., which was called "government wine" (Corpus, 1912, No. 568). Private manufacturers of ethyl alcohol still had to pay excise tax, so the whole state income collection system remained the same (see Figure 7.4).

State-owned production and distribution of alcoholic beverages was organised by the Main Office of Unassessed Taxes and State Sales of Alcohol within the

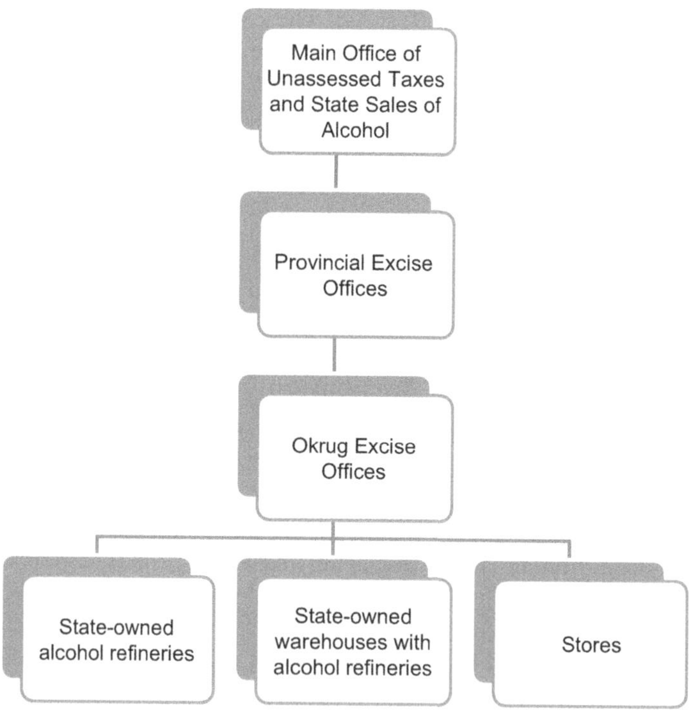

Figure 7.4 Organisational structure of alcohol production and distribution in 1895–1914

Ministry of Finance, which supervised Provincial Excise Offices that managed public enterprises. Locally, these functions were performed by Provincial Excise Offices that controlled the operations of public warehouses, alcohol refineries and stores under their supervision. The accounting rules for this complex organisational structure were enacted in 1896 (Rules and forms of accounting and reporting on state sale of alcohol beverages, 1897). This document introduced the requirement to keep a double-entry accounting system. Provincial Excise Offices, together with all the structures under their supervision, were regarded as one enterprise that conducted accounting for all its components. Accounting rules were revised several times and were finalised by 1911 (Rules and forms of accounting and reporting on state wine operations, 1911). The Provincial Excise Offices played a key role in the accounting process. They kept the ledger containing a system of accounts to track cash flows, assets and settlements with the manufacturers, distributors and financial institutions relating to production and distribution of alcoholic beverages (Figure 7.5).

The accounting system was based on documents that accompanied business transactions and on the reports from *Okrug* Excise Offices and production and distribution locations. Figures from these documents were entered in the journal, which contained a correspondence of accounts, and were allocated to additional books according to the accounts in the main ledger and additional analytical books. Then the information was summarised in the ledger, based on which the closing balance sheet was calculated. Structural subdivisions kept auxiliary books where they calculated monthly results and prepared reports to be submitted to

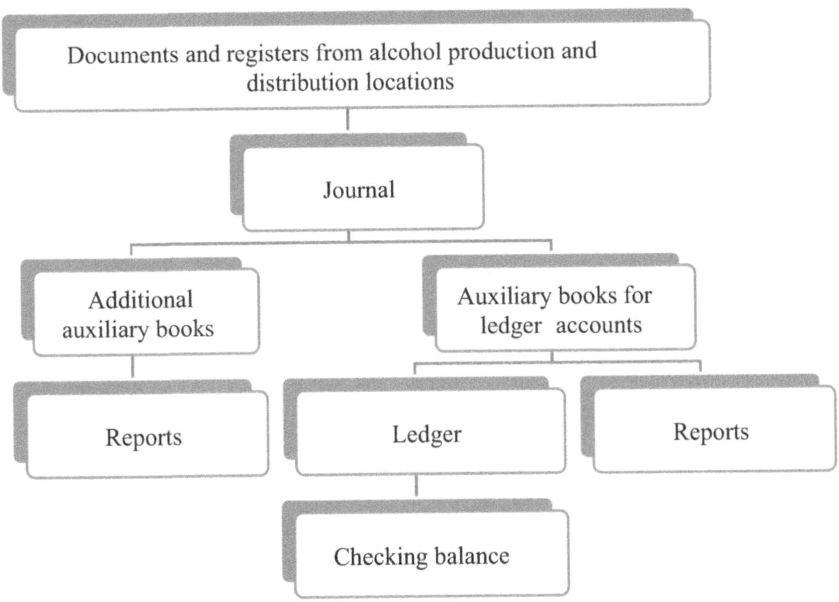

Figure 7.5 Accounting system at a Provincial Excise Office

the Provincial Excise Office, where these figures were entered in a journal similar to the registers of documents. All auxiliary books of structural subdivisions (*Okrug* Excise Offices, plants, warehouses and stores) and the books of the Provincial Excise Office were reconciled with its ledger, which contained 33 accounts, on a monthly basis. The main account in the ledger was the account of the Main Office for Unassessed Taxes and State Sales of Alcohol, which was equivalent to the capital account for a business entity. The profit and loss account was opened only when the ledger's accounts were closed at the end of the reporting year. Its balance represented net profit and was transferred to the account of the Main Office for Unassessed Taxes and State Sales of Alcohol. This balance represented the final result of the Provincial Excise Office over the reporting year. A procurement account contained information for calculating the actual value of assets. During the month, discharge of stock was recorded at standard price (Ivanov, 1898, p. 10). The standard price of ethyl alcohol was based on average production cost for vessels at the selling rate (Rules and forms of accounting and reporting on state wine operations, 1911, p. 6). At the year-end and/or at the closure of the reporting period, the difference between standard price and actual costs was recognised within expenses. Accounts were kept not only in cash, but also by quantity (% vol. alcohol), for which there was an additional column in each account (Rules and forms of accounting and reporting on state wine operations, 1911, p. 48).

Concluding comments

This chapter examines the evolution of the accounting treatment of vodka in the period from the 16th through early 20th centuries. This evolution passed three stages: 1) accounting of distilled vodka – the period when accounting practices were formed; 2) the appearance of the double-entry system and excise system, when detailed regulations on accounting rules were introduced; and 3) accounting for vodka under the state wine monopoly at the end of the 19th century, when the accounting treatment of vodka became considerably more complex due to the introduction of the chart of accounts in the ledger and auxiliary accounting registers.

The introduction of Prohibition in 1914, followed by the Revolution, destroyed this accounting treatment system for alcohol. As production of vodka at public enterprises was resumed in 1924, it was encompassed by the newly introduced Soviet accounting system. Its peculiarities, including those relating to alcohol circulation, could be the subject of future research. Our analysis of the evolution of the accounting treatment of vodka showed that production of alcohol was the first industry where state regulation of private enterprises was introduced (referring to specific public enterprises). This was due to the high profitability and financial appeal of the industry. Taxation always requires strictly regulated accounting and control. Apart from reports, regulation influenced the form and contents of accounting registers and the procedure of register maintenance. Meanwhile, the strictness of regulations tended to increase with time.

Russia went through a number of various approaches to levying public income from alcohol. Individual elements of Russian systems applied in various periods were similar to those applied in other countries. For example, in the 19th century, both Russia and Europe imposed excise taxes on alcoholic products (Gredinger, 1897, pp. 14–24). Like England, Russia additionally charged a patent fee on the right to trade in alcoholic beverages (Gredinger, 1897, p. 12). In future research, the comparison of the accounting treatment of alcohol in Russia with relevant rules in other countries could serve as an excellent basis for a comparative analysis of accounting systems, since they would relate to an equivalent item in a regulated market. From such an analysis, conclusions could be drawn on the roots of similarities and differences between various accounting systems, and their mutual influences.

Notes

1 *Kvass* is a traditional fermented beverage made from rye bread. It is common in many Eastern European countries and Russia.
2 Samples of birch bark manuscripts can be found on the site http://gramoty.ru.
3 A *kabak* book is an accounting book that was kept in *kabaks,* a place where alcohol was served (similar to a tavern).
4 Olonets is a town and the administrative centre of the Olonetsky District in the Republic of Karelia, Russia. It is the oldest documented settlement in Karelia, mentioned by Novgorodian sources as early as 1137.
5 The strength of alcoholic beverages is expressed in "degrees" – percentage of alcohol by volume, i.e. the volume of diluted anhydrous alcohol divided by the total volume of the beverage and multiplied by 100%. International standards allow to measure alcohol content in percentage by weight.
6 Ivan V (1666–1696) jointly ruled with his younger half-brother Peter I, from 1682 to 1696.
7 Ivan IV Vasilievich, also known as Ivan the Terrible (1530–1584), was the sovereign, the Grand Prince of Moscow and all Russia since 1533, the first Tsar of All the Russia since 1547.
8 The word "kabak" was borrowed from the Plattdeutsch dialect word *kabacke*, *kaback* meaning "an old tattered house".
9 *Zemstvo* House is an elected municipal body consisting of *Zemstvo* Head, *Zemstvo* Clerk and a Sworn Man that were elected by the town tenants for one to two years. *Zemstvo* House was financed by the local folk and existed until the reforms of Peter the Great, in 1721–1724.
10 State bucket is a Russian pre-metric measurement unit of the volume of alcoholic beverages. In the 17th century, there was no unified unit of measurement. Each region used their local vessels, ranging from 21.8 to 48.5 pounds of liquid (Special Historical Disciplines, 2003, p. 496).
11 *Prikaz* is a public office. Its main functions included collection of duties and public income from monopolies (Central State Archive, 1991; Platonova, 2009, p. 442). Each *prikaz* collected duties from the region to which it was allocated to cover its costs.
12 The Treasury Chamber was a provincial office of the Finance Ministry of Russia, founded in 1775. Its functions included accounting and reporting of amounts received and spent by provincial and *uyezd* (district) treasuries reporting to the Treasury Chamber. It monitored the receipt of public income, but neither introduced nor collected any levies, nor could it cancel statutory charges. It controlled all the expenses within the province (governorate), but with the Finance Ministry's permission. (A governorate, or a *guberniya*, was a major and principal administrative subdivision of the Russian Empire; *Uyezd*, the district, was a lower administrative subdivision of the Russian Empire (since 1775) and consisted of a city and the area subordinated to it).

13 Expedition for Public Income was a financial institution established in 1773 under the Senate. Its functions included ensuring that public income was collected, kept safe and used in accordance with its intended usage. In 1780, it was split into four expeditions, the first of which received information about proceeds, the second about expenses, the third verified the calculations and the fourth recovered arrears and shortages.

References

Archival and regulatory documents

Central State Archive of the Ancient Acts of the USSR (1991). Guide in four volumes. Moscow: Glavarkhiv USSR. Vol. 1. Центральный государственный архив древних актов СССР. Путеводитель в четырех томах/ ЦГАДА СССР. М.: Главархив СССР.

Compilation of the laws of Russian Empire. Digest the first (I) (1649–1825). Полное собрание законов Российской Империи.

Compilation of the laws of Russian Empire. Digest the third (II) (1825–1881). Полное собрание законов Российской Империи.

Corpus Juris of the Russian Empire (1912). Свод законов Российской империи.

Kabak books of the reign of Vasily Shuisky in the archives of the St. Petersburg Institute of History of the RAS (2014). Translation by A. I. Razdorsky, *Saint-Petersburg Historical Journal*, 1, pp. 5–15. Кабацкие книги времени царствования Василия Шуйского в архиве С.-Петербургского института истории РАН/перевод А.И. Раздорского.

Note Book of Wine Sales Wine Duties and Distillery Expenses (1712). State archive of Tyumen region. Fund I-47. List 1. File 1191. Available at: www.prlib.ru/item/336440?mode=rusmarc [Accessed 15th Jan. 2018]. Книга записная винной продажи и винных сборов и расходов на винокурение // Гос. архив Тюменской области. Ф. И-47. Оп. 1. Д. 1191. URL: www.prlib.ru/item/336440?mode=rusmarc (датаобращения: 15.01.2018).

The Receipts/Expenses Books of the Moscow Orders During 1619–1621 (1983). Comp. by academician S. B. Veselovsky. Prepared for publication by L. G. Dubinskaya, A. L. Stanislavsky. Moscow: Publishing House Science. Приходно-расходные книги московских приказов 1619–1621 гг. Сост. Академик С.Б. Веселовский. Москва: Издательство 'Наука'.

Rules and Forms of Accounting and Reporting on State Sale of Alcohol Beverages [Approved by Ministry of Finance on April 4, 1896] (1897). St. Petersburg: Publishing house of M. Stasyulevich. Правила и формы счетоводства и отчетности по казенной продаже питей. Санкт-Петербург: тип. М. Стасюлевича.

Rules and Forms of Accounting and Reporting on State Wine Operations [Approved March 23, 1911] (1911). St. Petersburg: Publishing house of Headquarters of Otd. corp. border. guardians. Правила и формы счетоводства и отчетности по казенной винной операции. Санкт-Петербург: тип. Штаба Отд. корп. погран. стражи.

Secondary sources

Akinfiev, A. V. (2016). The problems of production and consumption of vodka and beer in Russia XIX: Early XX century (history review). *Bulletin of the Nizhny Novgorod University After N.I. Lobachevsky*, 5, pp. 9–17. Акинфьев А.В. Проблемы производства и потребления водки и пива в России XIX- начала XX века (историографический обзор). Вестник Нижегородского университета им. Н.И. Лобачевского.

Blake, J., Amat, O. and Dowds, J. (1998). The drive for quality: The impact on accounting in the wine industry. *Journal of Wine Research*, 9(2), pp. 75–85.

Borodin, D. N. (1910). *Kabak and Its Past.* St. Petersburg: St. Petersburg Commercial Publishing House Wilenchik. Бородин Д.Н. Кабак и его прошлое. СПб.: С-Петербургская Коммерч. Типо-Литография Виленчик.

Gredinger, M. (1897). *Foundations of a Drinking Monopoly in Russia.* 2nd ed. Pernov: Publication of the bookstore of Emil Treifeldt. Гредингер М. Основы питейной монополии в России. Пернов: Издание книжного магазина Эмиля Трейфельдта.

Herlihy, P. (2002). *The Alcoholic Empire: Vodka and Politics in Late Imperial Russia.* New York: Oxford University Press.

Himelstein, L. (2009). *The King of Vodka: The Story of Pyotr Smirnov and the Upheaval of an Empire.* New York: HarperCollins.

Ilovaisky, S. I. (1904). *A Textbook of Financial Law.* 4th ed. Odessa: Tipo-Chromo-lithography of AF Sokolovsky. Иловайский С.И. Учебник финансового права. Одесса: типо-хромо-литография А.Ф. Соколовского.

Ivanov, S. F. (1898). *Accounting for Public Sale of Alcohol Beverages.* Novgorod: Provincial Printing House. Иванов С.Ф. Счетоводство по казенной продаже питей. Новгород: Губернская типография.

Krom, C. L. and Krom, S. (2013). The whiskey tax of 1791 and the consequent insurrection: 'A wicked and happy tumult'. *Accounting Historians Journal*, 40(2), pp. 91–114.

Kucher, V. V. and Gulina, N. S. (2006). State, finances and the alcohol market in the history of Russia. *Siberian Financial School*, 2, pp. 73–78. Кучер В.В., Гулина Н.С. Государство, финансы и алкогольный рынок в истории России. Сибирская финансовая школа.

Kuter, M. and Sokolov, V. (2012). Russia. In: *A Global History of Accounting, Financial Reporting and Public Policy: Eurasia, the Middle East and Africa.* Bingley: Emerald Group Publishing Limited, pp. 75–107.

Larina, O. G. (2011). Stages of the development of legislation on drinking legality in Russia. *News of South-Western State University*, 2(35), pp. 117–122. Ларина О.Г. Этапы развития законодательства о питейной регалии в России. Известия Юго-Западного государственного университета.

Loo, E. C. and McKerchar, M. (2014). The impact of British colonial rule on the Malaysian income tax system. *eJournal of Tax Research*, 12(1), pp. 238–252.

Lvov, D. (1887). *Course of Financial Law.* Kazan: Printing House of the Imperial University. Львов Д. Курс Финансового права. Казань: типография Императорского университета.

Medvedev, M. (2011). *Accounting Academic Dictionary.* Moscow: Moscow Financial and Industrial Academy. Медведев М.Ю. Бухгалтерский академический словарь. Москва: Московская финансово-промышленная академия.

Passant, J. (2016). Historical note: The history of taxation is written in letters of blood and fire. *Australasian Accounting Business and Finance Journal*, 10(2), pp. 93–100.

Pennock, P. E. and Kerr, K. A. (2005). In the shadow of prohibition: Domestic American alcohol policy since 1933. *Business History*, 47(3), pp. 383–400.

Phillips, R. (2014). *Alcohol: A History.* Chapel Hill: University of North Carolina Press.

Platonova, N. V. (2009). Peter the Great's government reforms and accounting practice in Russia. *Accounting History*, 14(4), pp. 437–464.

Pokhlyobkin, V. V. (2005). *The History of Vodka.* Moscow: Tsentrpoligraf. Похлебкин В.В. История водки. Москва: Центрполиграф.

Pronina, N. V. (2011). Accounting for the turnover of alcohol products in pre-revolutionary and modern Russia: Historical and legal analysis. *Bulletin of the Vladimir Law Institute*, 2(39), pp. 169–176. Пронина Н.В. Учет оборота алкогольной продукции в дореволюционной и современной России: историко-правовой анализ. Вестник Владимирского юридического института.

Pryzhov, I. G. (1914). *History of Kabaks in Russia in Connection With the History of the Russian Nation.* 2nd ed. Kazan: Young Forces. Прыжов И.Г. История кабаков в России в связи с историей русского народа. Казань: Молодые силы.

Razdorsky, A. I. (2015). Customs and kabak salaries and collections in the cities of the south and west of European Russia in 17th century (Based on the materials of the income-expenditure books of the Moscow orders). In: *Trade, Merchants and Customs in Russia in the 16th–19th Centuries: Coll. Materials of the Third International Scientific Conference*, Kolomna, Russia, 24–26 September 2013, Vol. 1: XVI–XVIII centuries. Kolomna, pp. 44–61. Раздорский А.И. Таможенные и кабацкие оклады и сборы в городах юга и запада Европейской России в XVII в. (по материалам приходо-расходных книг московских приказов). Торговля, купечество и таможенное дело в России в XVI-XIX вв.: Сб. материалов Третьей международной научной конференции.

Rodionov, B. (2012). *The History of Russian Vodka From Polugar to the Present Days.* Moscow: Eksmo. Родионов Б. История русской водки от полугара до наших дней. Москва: Эксмо.

Rusakov, I. B., Larina, O. G. and Dolzhenkova, E. V. (2016). 'State sale of food' in the system of Russian monopolies during 15–18 centuries (historical and legal study). *News of South-Western State University*, 4(21), pp. 10–14. Русаков И.Б., Ларина О.Г., Долженкова Е.В. 'Казенная продажа питей' в системе российских монополий в XV-XVIII веках (историко-правовое исследование). Известия Юго-Западного государственного университета.

Schrad, M. (2014). *Vodka Politics: Alcohol, Autocracy, and the Secret History of the Russian State.* New York: Oxford University Press.

Sokolov, Ya. V. (1996). *Accounting: From the Sources to Our Days.* Moscow: Audit, UNITI. Соколов Я.В. Бухгалтерский учет: от истоков до наших дней. Москва: Аудит, ЮНИТИ.

Special Historical Disciplines (2003). S. V. Beletsky, I. V. Vorontsova, Z. V. Dmitrieva and et al. Edited by M. M. Crom. 2nd ed. St. Petersburg: Dmitry Bulanin. Специальные исторические дисциплины/С.В. Белецкий, И.В. Воронцова, З.В. Дмитриева и др.; сост. М.М. Кром. 2-е изд. Санкт-Петербург: Дмитрий Буланин.

Stanziani, A. (2009). Information, quality and legal rules: Wine adulteration in nineteenth century France. *Business History*, 51(2), pp. 268–291.

Tersky, N. S. (2012). *Drinking Fees and Excise Tax System in Russia: Experience of Comparative Study of the Main Results of the Excise Tax System and Its Significance for the State, Treasury and the Population.* 2nd ed. Moscow: Librokom Book House. Терский Н.С. Питейные сборы и акцизная система в России: Опыт сравнительного исследования главнейших результатов акцизной системы и ее значения для государства, казны и населения. Москва: Книжный дом Либроком.

Tolkushkin, A. V. (2001). *History of Taxes in Russia.* Moscow: Lawyer. Толкушкин А.В. История налогов в России. Москва: Юристъ.

Tracy, S. W. (2016). Vodka politics: Alcohol, autocracy, and the secret history of the Russian State. *Historian*, 78(3), pp. 590–592.

Viana, R. C. and Rodrigues, L. L. (2006). A special accounting treatment for regulated industries? The case of the Port wine industry. *Journal of Wine Research*, 17(1), pp. 11–34.

Wiśniewska, P., Śliwińska, M., Dymerski, T., Wardencki, W. and Namieśnik, J. (2015). The analysis of vodka: A review paper. *Food Analytical Methods*, 8, pp. 2000–2010.

8 Accounting history of the Scotch whisky industry

Managing consumption, production and maturation

Julie Bower

Introduction

Alfred Chandler (1990) identified the significance of the consumer goods industry in the United Kingdom (UK) pre–World War II industrial prowess. Four firms were instrumental in creating the platform of wealth and influence: Lever Brothers, Imperial Tobacco, Distillers Company Limited (DCL)[1] and Guinness. Notwithstanding the constraints to trade that emerged in the early 20th century, specifically the anti-alcohol Temperance movement and the resulting Prohibition era, Scotch whisky extended its position in the global spirits market. Adaptation to an evolving and increasingly obtrusive institutional environment, particularly at the level of regulatory intervention, was a necessary capability to master. The post-Prohibition recovery was augmented by the formal assistance of the UK government in negotiating reduced import tariffs compared to that of the post–World War II era, and this was supported by the UK's requirement for foreign exchange to balance the books. The special political status reinforced the internationalisation that cemented the industry's growth prospects for the remainder of the 20th century.

Over and above the geopolitical and socio-economic constraints to trade, the Scotch whisky industry faces a multitude of other complexities in the ordinary course of managing an international consumption profile, specifically in financial and tax management. These consumption-based risk factors are compounded by the intricacies of the production process and nature of stock management. The legal designation of 'Scotch whisky' defines production and maturation in Scotland for a minimum of three years, leading to an array of temporal managerial risks. Firm and industry viability, at its most fundamental level, is highly dependent on the accuracy of forecasting future demand and matching production accordingly. The industry's record of achieving this through the course of history is poor, with observable patterns of over-production and under-production, particularly in the modern era (since the 1970s), leading to what is known as the 'whisky cycle' (Bower, 2016).

This chapter proceeds as follows. After first outlining a relevant approach that frames the evolution of the Scotch whisky market, specifically internationalisation and the impact of taxation, the socio-political environment is set out in historical context. The narrative then addresses the structure and operation of the industry in terms of its sales and production profile. The complex rules and regulations that accompany overseas sales, with an extensive international supply chain that incorporates multi-jurisdictional tax treatments as well as shipment and depletion asymmetries, are highlighted. Finally, in discussing the heavy financial commitment the industry makes to the maturation of whisky stocks, the optimisation opportunities presented by financial innovation in the capital market in areas such as securitisation and portfolio investment are explored. The narrative therefore traces the evolution of the industry, from its origins as an international branded category at the turn of the 20th century, through its consolidation of global leadership in the post–World War II era, to its engagement in innovative financial and tax management in the 1990s and 2000s.

Background

Firms have two broad ways to optimise profitability – growing revenues and/or managing the production process to increase margins. While there is considerable mainstream management scholarship that addresses firm performance at both levels, encompassing the core theoretical principles of marketing, international business, operations and production research and accounting and finance, there are residual performance attributes that have been relatively under-investigated. These fall largely under the general guise of balance sheet manipulation (Haslam et al., 2013); a response to the evolving globalisation of the capital markets that encourages and supports financialisation and securitisation (Girón and Chapoy, 2012; Stockhammer, 2004) and the exploitation of differential taxation practices that accrue to firms with multi-jurisdictional sales and production profiles.

Multinational corporations are characterised by a high degree of managerial efficiency arising from resources and competences they have captured, modified and embedded over time. This renders them capable of thinking strategically on a global scale to organise complex integrated production networks (Buckley, 2009). Since cost allocation mechanisms are highly subjective, firms have considerable discretion in allocations to product and service lines, as well as geographical jurisdictions (Sikka and Willmott, 2010). As part of this process, multinational corporations engage in complex and dynamic relationships with their institutional environment and are far from passive as they interpret, manipulate, negotiate and partially construct these relationships to their advantage (Kostova et al., 2008).

One of the key institutional relationships firms must manage is with tax authorities. There is ample anecdotal evidence that taxation influences corporate decision making (Killian, 2006), playing a key role in foreign direct investment (FDI) and location-specific siting of overseas subsidiaries (Mollan and Tennent, 2015). As taxation is largely source-based, firms are presented with two legal ways to minimise taxation: shifting profit-generating activities to low-tax countries through FDI, or through intra-firm transfer pricing activity whereby deductible expenses are allocated to subsidiaries in high-tax countries, with profits being generated in subsidiaries in low-tax countries. While the basic tenets of tax arbitrage are simple, they have the effect of creating highly complex and non-transparent organisational structures (Genschel and Schwarz, 2011).[2] Where a multinational firm has subsidiaries overseas, the complex interaction of the tax systems of the home and host countries is difficult, if not impossible, to model using publicly available accounting data (Killian, 2006). As rational economic actors, firms exploit these opportunities to maximise their after-tax global income, not all of which are sustainable, as governments, notably those of the United States, Canada and the UK have sought retrospective recompense through the courts.[3] A key legal dispute in the US Supreme Court in 1994 involving Barclays highlights the highly politicised nature of transfer pricing, a feature that continues in contemporary debates concerning perceived aggressive tax planning by major multinational firms. As clarified in the Court's decision, "the image of a politically impotent foreign transactor is surely belied by the battalion of foreign governments that has marched to Barclays' aid, deploring worldwide combined reporting in diplomatic notes, amicus briefs, and even retaliatory legislation" (Justice Ginsburg, SC 92–1384, 92–1839, 20 June 1994).

In addition to the potential for bolstering profitability through exploitation of differential tax treatments, firms aggressively take advantage of the increasingly sophisticated financial instruments that emanate from the deregulation and globalisation of the financial services industry. The term 'financialisation' refers to the trend of the past thirty years where the capital markets have come to directly and indirectly determine the structure and behaviour of firms in important areas such as setting capital structure and fixed asset investment strategies (Orhangazi, 2008; Stockhammer, 2004). Although financialisation is often considered from the investment perspective of the returns secured by financial intermediaries such as private equity funds (Wood and Wright, 2010), several notable studies of major firms illustrate how such firms benefit from the arrangements. For example, in the case of Enron, researchers noted it gained more from the capital markets than from operating productively in its industry, although this was a temporal and contributing factor to its ultimate demise (Froud et al., 2004; Haslam et al., 2013). During the 1990s, vocal protagonists of principle-agent theory considered that high leverage was the optimal disciplinary mechanism in the divorced ownership models typical of liberal economies (Jensen and Meckling, 1976; Shleifer and Vishny, 1997), where the accounting and finance-based criteria that supported value-based control systems aligned managers' interests to those of shareholders (Fiss and Zajac, 2004). More recently, the downside of the influence of the financial system in promoting a permanent restructuring of economic activity has come to light in the aftermath of the 2008 financial crisis (Lazonick, 2010). Much of this relates to the phenomenon of 'securitisation' (Girón and Chapoy, 2012),[4] which allowed firms to raise capital from sources which would not normally engage in funding such economic activities and it does not utilise existing funding lines or limits (PricewaterhouseCoopers, 2011).

Securitisation encouraged different ways through which participants, many of whom either had no prior expertise as managers of the underlying assets or were new entrants to the capital markets, could monetise the benefits of financialisation (Jacobides and Winter, 2012), highlighting that financialisation does not work in simple, predictable, cause–effect ways to produce changes in corporate behaviour and performance (Froud et al., 2014).

This study of Scotch whisky, an industry that has evolved over more than a century to become one of the UK's major export earners (Facts and Figures, Scotch Whisky Association, 2017), adopts a longitudinal narrative approach, consonant with the general theme of 'history as evaluating' to stimulate thinking in important areas of organisation, such as institutional interaction, that might otherwise remain under-appreciated (Maclean et al., 2016). In keeping with the historic case-study approach, the chapter engages with a wide set of historic accounts incorporating official and legal archive information and other contemporaneous data (Mordhorst, 2014). The data utilised here were extracted from the industry's trade association, the Scotch Whisky Association (SWA), which provides comprehensive annual statistics reports and other periodic publications, firm reports and accounts, relevant firm merger filings, US Securities and Exchange Commission and UK legal documentation and UK Parliamentary records. This information, in addition to contemporaneous press commentary, are available to view directly online and are referenced in either the main text or in the endnotes to this chapter.

The socio-political context

In his famous treatise, *Scale and Scope*, Chandler (1990) documented the history of the managerial business system from a ten-year research study of patterns of growth and competitiveness of US, UK and German enterprise. In considering the structure and performance of UK firms relative to their US counterparts, Chandler noted that the smaller scale of the domestic market meant that UK firms were incentivised to promote their goods overseas. Consequently, the ratio of British foreign trade to national income was around 30% in the years from 1860 to 1913, largely comprising sales of traditional industries such as textiles, and iron and steel products (Chandler, 1990). The rapid internal migration from country to city and from agriculture to industry resulted in a large, concentrated and increasingly sophisticated consumer market, with firms developing expertise in the production of branded, packaged goods.[5]

Of the UK's foreign direct investments before 1929, those in the consumer goods sector were among the longest lasting, with brands recognised today as global then in the early stages of internationalisation (Da Silva Lopes and Casson, 2012). Many were Scotch whisky brands, given the strong position established by the owners of blended Scotch whiskies such as Dewar's and Johnnie Walker. Challenges to their corporate survival emerged as the Temperance movement of the late 19th century gradually took hold (Da Silva Lopes, 2007; McGahan, 1991),[6] with the Great War of 1914–1918 providing the Temperance movement with an 'emergency' in which highly controversial policies became acceptable under the guise of military discipline, industrial efficiency and the need to preserve grain and other raw materials to be deployed elsewhere (Weir, 1988; see also, Gibney, Chapter 3). The passing of the Eighteenth Amendment to the US Constitution, the National Prohibition Act of 1919, was potentially a major restraint to trade for alcohol producers, although in practice consumption continued largely because the laws instituting it did not provide for sufficient enforcement (McGahan, 1991; see also Gaytán, Chapter 9). That Prohibition served to merely punctuate the growth of Scotch whisky in the United States owed much to collaborative industry-led 'controlled bootlegging', introduced and operated with the implicit support of the UK government (Weir, 1988).[7]

Political support for the Scotch whisky industry was as important in countering Prohibition as it was in the more formal trade agreements agreed between the UK and United States in the War years, for example, in securing import licences as part of the 1937 Anglo-American Trade Treaty (Weir, 1995). The lobbying efforts of the industry's trade association, the SWA, were instrumental: the SWA not only orchestrated the attack on Prohibition but also played a key role in ensuring distillers could access scarce cereals during the rationing of World War II and thereafter. Export sales for dollars were deemed in the wider national interest, and annual export targets were agreed with the UK government.[8] The Ministry of Food assumed control over the Scotch whisky production process on 1 March 1940 (Glen, 1963). By the end of 1940, the UK was close to bankruptcy, with most of industry turned over to war efforts at the expense of exports of manufactured goods, and with the import of basic foodstuffs having depleted both gold and dollar reserves (Dobson, 1986). Against this backdrop, the United States and UK formed the Lend-Lease programme of 1941 for vital basic supplies. However, the US position was that the UK should focus its non-war industrial capacity towards exports of 'traditional' British products, such as woollen goods, rather than products that would compete directly with US firms.[9]

Although the US dollar was the major reserve currency and medium of exchange after World War II, the US foreign trade financing market lacked both the depth and sophistication of the pre-war London market, with no commercial banking system to finance longer-term import activity (Wasserman, 1951). Most import business was conducted by recourse to irrevocable letters of credit, often imposed on European exporters by their own governments as part of post-war foreign exchange controls. In the UK, for example, there were stringent policy tools, orchestrated through the Treasury, the Capital Issues Committee and the Exchange Control Authorities, that were designed to promote British exports at the expense of supressing domestic consumer demand (Plous, 1958). As trade expanded in the post-war recovery, firms were additionally challenged by the complexity of the evolving tax system. The UK government was committed to maintaining tax levels after World War II, imposing legislation to restrict the latitude of firms to relocate their domicile. The 1947 Exchange Control Act gave the Treasury powers to block a change of domicile, reinforced by Section 36 of the 1951 Finance Act. The Overseas Trade Corporation (OTC) was established in the UK in 1957 to offer companies relief from international taxation. By 1958, the UK had concluded 63 tax treaties, though only ten were with countries that were not former British colonies. However, when the OTC disbanded in 1965, there was a significant increase in the complexity of corporate international taxation arrangements (Mollan and Tennent, 2015).

Managing international sales

Data for 2015 show that over 90% of Scotch whisky sales are derived from overseas markets, the largest of which are France, the United States and several newly emergent markets, including India, Brazil and South Africa, as shown in Figures 8.1a and 8.1b. This is the outcome of exploiting successfully the rapid internationalisation that occurred after World War II. Other important markets for Scotch whisky have emerged, matured and in some cases gone into rapid decline driven by factors largely outside the control of the industry. Venezuela, once a leading export market for Scotch in the 1970s and 1990s, illustrates this trajectory most acutely (Bower, 2016). However, as quickly as one market opportunity dissipates, another has filled the shortfall, meaning there has been a steady trend of volume growth over many decades, punctuated for only short periods by economic recession.

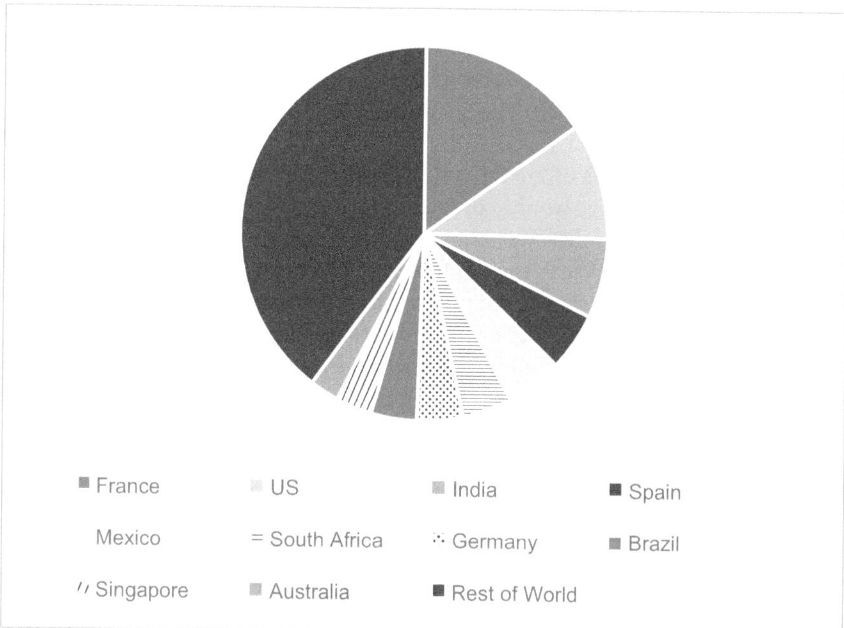

Figure 8.1a Major export markets (volume)

Source: Derived from SWA Statistical Report, 2015

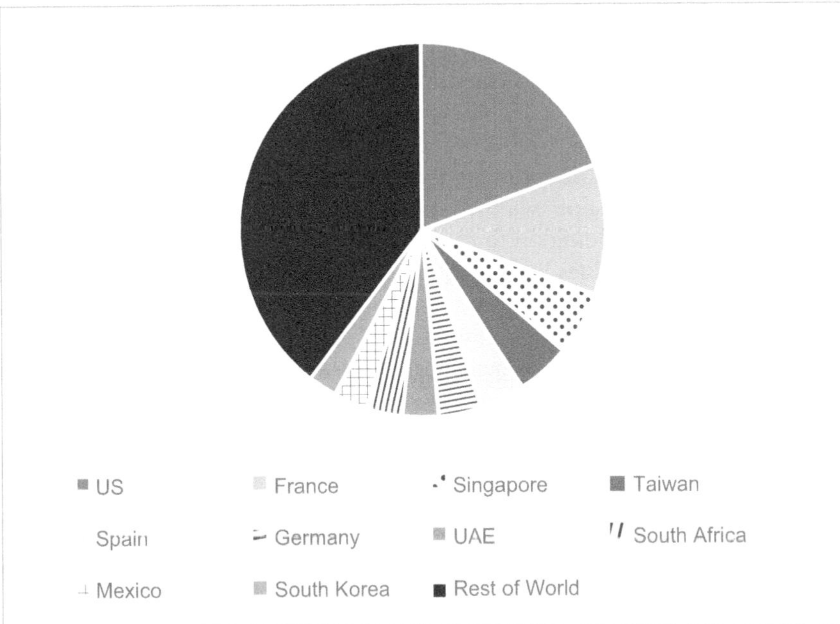

Figure 8.1b Major export markets (value)

Source: Derived from SWA Statistical Report, 2015

Traditionally, the producers of spirits brands have shipped their products from their own, or shared, home market bonded warehouses to overseas distributors on fixed terms, splitting the profit between them on an 'arm's-length' buyer–seller transaction basis. However, the alcoholic beverages industry was an active participant in aggressive tax planning initiatives at a very early stage, seeking to exploit the differentials between their domicile and the multitude of export markets they sold to. The example of Bailey's Irish Cream, a liqueur based on Irish whiskey – an e is used when referred to Irish whiskey is a case in point. Established in the early 1970s, it was arguably the most successful new product introduction in the international spirits industry. Its success to the ultimate brand owner, Grand Metropolitan Plc, extended beyond the cachet of an international brand. Bailey's utilised the inherent tax advantage of a production base in Ireland aligned to a consumer base in the highly taxed US market. Further advantage accrued from registering the brand name in the Netherlands,[10] a practice that still forms part of topical political debate, notably Starbucks' tax profile in the UK.[11] For Scotch whisky, this type of tax planning is constrained more generally by Scotland's and the UK's less attractive tax regime, although there have been two specific instances where Diageo, the successor company of Grand Metropolitan, has been subject to US regulatory inquiry for accounting practices with regard to brand valuation and its associated tax treatment,[12] and payments to other jurisdictions in lieu of favourable tax status on Scotch whisky imported brands such as Johnnie Walker.[13]

Historically, there were only minor tax-related disputes relating to sales in the United States. The leading US blend, J&B Rare, was the subject of a legal claim at the office of the US Commissioner for Taxes in 1990.[14] The litigation concerned the amount of tax payable by the owner of J&B for the years 1971–1973, before the UK's Grand Metropolitan acquired the brand from the Liggett Group, Inc. Liggett was contesting whether sales of Scotch whisky by petitioner's (fully owned) subsidiary Paddington to third-party US customers via "Direct Import in Bond FOB British Isles" produces income from sources without the United States.[15] In concluding the case in favour of the petitioner, the Commissioner stated that it was satisfied Paddington both acquired and transmitted title to the goods at issue in the UK, with 'beneficial ownership and risk of loss passed to its customers outside the United States'. Consequently, Liggett Group was entitled to utilise the foreign tax credit of $799k for the tax year 1973.

The details in this litigation inform the nature of Scotch whisky sales more generally, and the relationship between brand owners and the distribution network.[16] As a fully owned subsidiary and the exclusive distributor for the brand, Paddington sold J&B Rare to customers by two types of procedures: FOB United States Warehouse sales, whereby Paddington sold to third-party customers from its own inventory, and Direct Import in Bond FOB British Isles, whereby the customer acquired the Scotch from Paddington in the British Isles on terms FOB United Kingdom. In the latter situation, customers incurred the subsequent liability and costs of transportation, insurance, tax, duty and storage. This was the preferred shipment method for large customers, and some 80% of Paddington's $80m total sales of J&B Rare were made by the Direct Import method. The Commissioner acknowledged that the arrangement was not a tax avoidance mechanism: The fact that the brand owner, J&B, did not deal with Paddington's customers underscored the understanding of all involved that Paddington obtained title from J&B and passed such title *immediately* to its customers.

Historically, it was normal for brand owners to rely on third parties for distribution, including those as large as industry leader DCL. Agencies oversaw pre-specified pricing policies, advertising and marketing initiatives and all other brand support processes. So, for example, the New York firm Schenley Industries, which was licenced by the US authorities to produce 'medicinal whisky' in the post-Prohibition era, developed alliances with foreign firms to import and distribute their liquors, most notably the 1936 agreement with DCL for the distribution of Dewar's Scotch whisky (Da Silva Lopes, 2007). A consolidated and independent distribution network evolved in the United States around a state-level three-tier distribution system aimed at barring alcohol producers from owning and controlling retailers.[17] Following the acquisition of DCL in 1986, Guinness acquired Schenley Industries for $480m "to strengthen the British company's control over its brands in the United States".[18] This was part of a dominant strategy that emerged in the international spirits industry of the

1980s, where formerly independent distributors were either acquired outright or were subject to intra-industry joint ventures and strategic alliances to wrest control of marketing in key geographic markets for specified, and usually non-overlapping, portfolios of brands. Guinness' spirits subsidiary, United Distillers (UD), controlled over 75% of its distribution network by 1988, compared to 25% when it acquired DCL (Jones, 2003). When Guinness and Grand Metropolitan merged in 1997 to form Diageo, UD had full ownership of distribution and/or joint venture arrangements in place for approximately 85% of its overseas distribution.[19]

Notwithstanding the strategic initiatives that delivered greater control of the distribution network, problems in accounting for the exact whereabouts of stock-in-trade at any point in time continued, most notably at Allied Domecq. Having suffered various high-profile mishaps, including losses in its foreign exchange hedging programme in the early 1990s (discussed later), Allied Domecq garnered a reputation for 'serial destocking'. A failure to match accurately the profile of shipments and depletions continued up to the point at which it was acquired by Pernod Ricard in the mid-2000s. During 2003, in addition to announcing that the weaker US dollar would cost it £40m, European operations 'fell short of plan' due to destocking by Spanish wholesalers, costing an additional £25m.[20] In the same accounting year, the US-filed accounts noted additional destocking in the US supply chain with a £10m impact on trading profits, following the prior year's 'planned destock' that had an adverse impact of £19m, although this was related to the non-Scotch portfolio.[21]

Production planning and maturation

The Scotch whisky industry is governed by strict locational production and maturation criteria with heavily prescribed legal constraints. Notwithstanding the industry's long duration and prosperity, managing the operating and financial risks inherent in the production process has been far from a smooth ride (Bower, 2016).[22] The legally supported geographic designation that protects the legitimacy and status of Scotch as a discrete premium spirits category has evolved over more than a century under the auspices of UK and latterly European legislation. In the early years of the industry's evolution, defining what constituted Scotch, with the implications for productive capacity, was the subject of several high-profile legal and political interventions. The depth of the industry's lobbying efforts, manifest in various key Parliamentary debates, is summarised in Table 8.1.

Innovation in blending, whereby mass-produced Scottish grain spirit was mixed with a number of batch-produced single-malt whiskies, was crucial in the development of an international market for Scotch whisky. The bankruptcy of whisky broker Pattison's Limited in 1898 was an important catalyst in the fortunes of blended Scotch whisky, triggering the collapse of a series of malt distillers and their associated creditors (Moss and Hume, 2000, pp. 149–153). The largest grain distillers, DCL,[23] and the independent North British Distillery

Table 8.1 Key parliamentary debates in the evolution of the Scotch whisky industry

Debate	*Reference*	*Comments*
Increase in the excise duty charged on spirits	*HC Deb 08 September 1909* *vol 10 cc1303–4*	Concerns increase on responsibility for release of 'new' and 'inferior' grain spirit. Reminder that Royal Commission found new and grain spirit not deemed inferior. Suggestions for graduated tax to reflect age of spirit.
Effect of 1915 Immature Spirits Act	*HC Deb 08 December 1919* *vol 122 cc916–7W*	Discussion whether shortage of whisky related to the Act or deliberate manipulation of stocks by a 'whisky trust' of three distillery combines.
Barley release for manufacture of Scotch whisky	*HC Deb 23 February 1949* *vol 461 cc1864–5S*	Allocation increased on condition the entirety of the whisky was directed to export. Concerns about lobbying by the SWA and the extent of profits made by firms, with calls for the industry to be nationalised.
Proposal for legislation to require Scotch whisky labelling to state the percentages of malt whisky and grain whisky in the blend	*HC Deb 08 February 1972* *vol 830 cc1118–9*	Government refusal by reference to the 1909 Royal Commission. View that the quality of a blend reflected the quality and character of the single whiskies used and the skill of the blender. Referenced high rate of duty and need to communicate the 'unique contribution' of Scottish malt whisky.
Highland Distilleries	*HC Deb 14 December 1979* *vol 975 c805W*	Request for referral of hostile bid by Hiram Walker-Gooderham and Worts to the Monopolies and Mergers Commission.
Scotch Whisky industry	*HC Deb 03 February 1986* *vol 91 cc120–6*	Prompted by Guinness' acquisition of Distillers Company Limited. Impact of Mergers and Acquisitions more generally on industry of 'strategic national interest'.
Scotch Whisky Bill	*HC Deb 11 December 1987* *vol 124 cc681–735*	Provisions sought by SWA, trade unions, management and employees of firms to counter proposals for 'Euro-whisky' definition in impending European-wide legislation. Reference to champagne's protection under French law since 1934. Calls to ban export of bulk malt whisky (to mix with local grain, such as in Japanese whisky).

Source: Hansard, UK House of Commons

Limited (NB)[24] were both better capitalised and supported by their blending clients, and this augmented their defence against a challenge from the remaining malt distillers to restrict the use of the term 'whisky' to their production alone (Weir, 1995). A 1905 complaint, filed at the North London magistrates' court under the Sale of Food and Drugs Act 1875, alleged that blended Scotch whisky contravened the nature, substance and quality of the liquor legally defined as 'whisky'. The malt distillers were successful in the complaint, threatening the viability of the burgeoning blending trade. A Royal Commission was appointed subsequently to investigate the industry. It concluded, however, there was no evidence that the product of grain distillation was injurious, and in 1909 the blenders were exonerated from the charge of offering bogus Scotch for public consumption under the 1875 Act. This had the effect of defining Scotch whisky in UK law.

The origins of the bonded warehouse system are in the 1915 UK budget of Liberal Chancellor of the Exchequer, David Lloyd George. His proposal for a doubling in spirits duty was heavily opposed by Scottish and Irish Members of Parliament (MP), and a compromise deal brokered by James Stevenson of John Walker & Sons saw the introduction of compulsory bonding of whisky to prevent immature spirits coming to market at a time of war. Facing defeat of his budget, Lloyd George accepted the bonding proposal, which came into law on 19 May 1915 as the Immature Spirits (Restriction) Act 1915, for a minimum of two years, extending to three years in 1916. This three-year bonding (maturation) rule has remained in place for Scotch whisky ever since. The reality is that the industry's stock maturity profile is significantly longer than this, with an average maturity of some eight years, reflecting the fact that some of the best-known brands in the blend and single-malt categories contain whiskies that are at least 10 years old (Bower, 2016).

Profit optimisation and the investment market

The international profile of consumption brings with it two key risks that require substantial expertise to navigate successfully: 1) the ability to understand and manage a multitude of currency exposures, and 2) accounting and control systems to manage the production and maturation process from 'cradle to grave'. The spirits industry and its major firms are no strangers to the implications of failing to instigate sufficient oversight to prevent currency-related financial risk as well as the mismatch in shipments, depletions and the maturation process more generally. The former was seen most prominently in a scandal at the UK's Allied Domecq (formerly known as Allied-Lyons) in 1991, where the firm's disclosure of a $285m loss from 'unusual exposures in unspecified currencies and instruments' forced the immediate resignation of the finance director and that of the firm's chairman and chief executive officer two months later.[25] Following this event, the major firms tightened their treasury functions with the aim of hedging transaction exposure as closely as possible. Consequently, Diageo's stated policy is to 'hedge up to 24 months forecast transactional foreign currency risk on the net US dollar exposure of the group targeting 75% coverage for the current financial year and up to 18 months for other currency pairs'.[26] Although failure to balance shipments and depletions remained an issue, as discussed earlier, it was largely considered to be reflecting management failure. More recently, however, Diageo has been the subject of an inquiry by the US Securities and Exchange Commission (SEC) for 'channel-stuffing': a deliberate action whereby brand owners over-ship product into their distribution network to flatter short-term sales figures.[27]

The accounting treatment of stocks and the associated tax liability has always presented problems for industry observers, if not the firms and the tax authorities. This was highlighted in the case of *HMRC v. William Grant & Sons Distillers Ltd*, which was settled in the UK House of Lords in 2007. The case centred on the requirement to provide for depreciation that reduces the carrying cost of an asset over its useful economic life and whether that write-off must go directly to the profit and loss account. There was a dissenting opinion in the HMRC's successful appeal to the Court of Session that found favour ultimately at the House of Lords. The correct treatment of depreciation included in the year-end stock valuation should be the net amount for the purposes of computing the firm's corporation tax liability and not the full depreciation charge reflected in non-current assets in the balance sheet: "This fundamental principle is given effect by taking the revenue which has arisen in the relevant year and deducting from it only those costs which are attributable to those sales".[28] Using the following in his dissent, Lord Reed elaborated:

> when a pack of "Glenfiddich 12 year old" is sold, the "pack cost" will include the cost of producing the whisky twelve years ago (including the depreciation of the relevant non-current assets during the year, divided by each litre produced), and the first three years' warehousing costs (including the depreciation of the buildings and casks during those years, divided by each litre produced).[29]

The maturation of stocks also brings the associated issues of financing. Diageo's balance sheet shows maturing stocks of £3.8bn, comprising Scotch, rum, tequila and Chinese white spirits. The figure excludes an allocation of financing costs.[30] To indicate the scale of finance required, albeit in an era when interest rates were considerably higher than today, the former Guinness, prior to the merger with Grand Metropolitan in 1997, held maturing whisky stocks of £1.5bn, of which £563m was accumulated financing costs.[31] The scale of the financing required explains why the Scotch whisky industry, following on the heels of a successful securitisation of champagne inventory,[32] at least explored securitisation as a means of capitalising the implicit value of maturing whisky stock, with Whyte & Mackay exploring options to release value in this manner. The prominent German financial institution, WestLB, backed the £208m management buyout of Whyte & Mackay from US multinational drinks firm, Fortune Brands.[33] The management buyout firm planned to raise £188m from a bond issue, backed by the collateral of the Whyte & Mackay maturing whisky portfolio, as a means of repaying the purchase loan from WestLB.[34] However, the securitisation was abandoned due to difficult market conditions,[35] with WestLB withdrawing from the business completely by 2005.[36] The reason why there is relatively less interest in this type of innovation in the Scotch whisky industry likely owes much to its highly consolidated ownership, with the two major firms, Diageo and Pernod Ricard, being large multinationals with deep pockets and access to the global capital markets on already favourable terms.

Investors continue to show interest in whisky as an alternative investment. This interest continued to advance following the launch of an online platform, called *WhiskyInvestDirect*,[37] that evolved from the first stand-alone whisky sales in Glasgow some 15 years ago of small units of whisky maturing in barrel. The online platform gives smaller investors access to the whisky market with a limited and flexible investment in barrels stored in bonded warehouses, promising a "low correlation to other asset classes, such as bonds or property, and because 93% of Scotch whisky is exported, it provides a hedge against weak sterling".[38] The investment case for Scotch whisky is that, after deducting storage costs, the profits for stockholders of blending spirit have averaged 8% to 9% per annum over the decade to 2015.[39] In the past, many providers of whisky investment schemes have gone bust, mirroring the industry's supply and demand fluctuations, and their liquidators have taken the investors' whisky and sold it for the general benefit of creditors, usually the banks that have financed maturation. This new investment scheme is structured as a 'bailment', meaning the whisky bought through *WhiskyInvestDirect* is a property in the care of another; if *WhiskyInvestDirect* or the bonded warehouse were to fail, no liquidator could claim the whisky as an asset of the failing company.[40] A disadvantage for investors, however, is that investments are not covered by the Financial Services Compensation Scheme.

Concluding comments

A long history of internationalisation and the requirements of managing a complex profile of consumption, production and maturation make the Scotch whisky industry a valuable theatre for empirical inquiry with the objective of informing academic studies in several business management areas. Chandler (1990) was one of the first authors to draw attention to the prowess of the UK's consumer goods industry, and specifically the Scotch whisky leader, DCL, in the UK's pre–World War II industrial development. Weir (1988, 1989, 1995) and Da Silva Lopes (2007) have made important contributions to understanding the evolution of the industry in the 20th century, most notably as it addressed the constraints of Prohibition and the impact of the war years. These works have established the industry, centred on market leader DCL, and with the support of its trade association, the SWA, as particularly adept at marshalling political influence as it charted the course to international dominance.

Securing and extending international growth opportunities brings with it the necessity to manage an array of institutional interactions, incentivising multinational firms to go beyond merely interpreting the rules of the game (Kostova et al., 2008). One of the key institutional relationships is through taxation, with the centrality of taxation in influencing corporate decision making (Killian, 2006). There is a long and colourful history of multinational corporations featuring in complaints brought by the US regulatory and tax agencies, and the spirits industry has not been immune to such oversight. Scotch whisky does not possess the inherent attraction of a manufacturing base in a low-taxation domicile, and this constrains opportunities for legitimate tax management, such as shifting profit-generating activities to low-tax countries through FDI, or through intra-firm transfer pricing (Genschel and Schwarz, 2011; Mollan and Tennent, 2015), given the long-established legal requirements of the production and maturation process. The industry seeks to exploit, as far as possible, accounting treatments that allow it to defer payments for tax purposes through the lengthy maturation process, or in optimising transit through the multi-layer distribution network. There has been prominent litigation in both the UK and United States, where the authorities have considered whether firms may have stepped over the mark into areas such as 'channel-stuffing' or through gaming shipments from bond to fully owned versus third-party distributors.

The heavy financial commitment required to support Scotch whisky brands through the extended production and maturation process has always presented a key risk, and the industry's record in managing it has been chequered at best (Bower, 2016). The advent of financialisation and securitisation offered opportunities for smaller independent firms particularly to source alternative capital provision (PricewaterhouseCoopers, 2011). The limited engagement in this financial innovation prior to the 2008 financial crisis may owe more to the highly consolidated ownership structure around two firms, Diageo and Pernod Ricard, that emerged in the 1990s and 2000s, than the failure of Whyte & Mackay to cement transactions comparable to those seen in the champagne sector. It is clear, however, that investor appetite remains for more esoteric investments, notably in the establishment of the online platform *WhiskyInvestDirect*, as well as more widely for shares in international spirits firms, with a recently launched Exchange Traded Fund, listed in the US market.

Notes

1 Guinness acquired DCL in 1986.

2 Genschel and Schwarz (2011) provide an in-depth review of the international tax literature, illustrating with the example of Swedish furniture retailer, IKEA, and its use of subsidiaries and holding companies domiciled in the Netherlands, Luxembourg and the Dutch Antilles (Genschel and Schwarz, 2011, pp. 346–347).

3 For example, the transfer pricing policies of UK pharmaceutical giant GlaxoSmithKline (GSK) were scrutinised by the US tax authorities, who claimed that the rate the company charged for marketing services supplied by its US affiliate from 1989 to 1996 led to the avoidance of $5.2 billion of US taxes. After some 17 years of litigation and negotiations, GSK settled the dispute by making a payment of US$3.4 billion (Sikka and Willmott, 2010, p. 350).

4 This is a financial innovation whereby contractual debt obligations, such as mortgages and car loans, are pooled and packaged into capital market stocks and shares.

5 Chandler noted how the UK had an extensive rail network by the 1860s, that in conjunction with steamship travel assisted access to an expanding market for branded, packaged goods such as chocolate, tobacco, jams and sauces, beer and whisky. The role of salesmen employed either directly or on commission was significant in that the owners of the brands could access wholesalers and distributors both at home and overseas without having to invest capital in production and distribution infrastructure, relying instead on branch operations staffed by salaried managers to facilitate the trade in markets such as the UK's colonies, the United States and Europe (Chandler, 1990, pp. 262–267).

6 The starting point for the Prohibition era is usually traced to the creation of the Women's Christian Temperance Union in 1874 (Da Silva Lopes, 2007, p. 36), although McGahan (1991, p. 252) notes the movement was firmly established in the United States in the 1840s.

7 Whisky runners collected Scotch in Scotland and shipped it to 'scheduled areas' – locations immediately adjacent to the US mainland, including Mexico, Cuba, the Bahamas and islands in the Gulf of St. Lawrence. The brand Haig & Haig, sold by Robertson & Baxter in 1922, was bought specifically to facilitate this trade and retain the 'Bottled in Scotland' cachet. This regulation of the trade by the industry "minimised the number of unsavoury incidents which got bootlegging a bad name in the early 1920s", with the additional consequence of diverting political pressure from the UK government in its dealings with its US counterparts (Weir, 1988, p. 1294).

8 For a full history of the SWA and the role it fulfils for its members, see www.scotch-whisky.org.uk/what-we-do/history-of-swa/.

9 Concern was expressed by the Congress that the Lend-Lease programme should not act as a subsidy for the UK commercial export trade. Although there may have been gaming from the British, it is also clear the United States was seeking to gain competitive advantage for its firms in third-party export markets, and Scotch whisky was significant in this export trade (Dobson, 1986, pp. 64–65).

10 The tax planning initiatives of Bailey's Irish Cream were highlighted in a report for the Adam Smith Institute by former Grand Metropolitan insider, Tim Ambler ('Multinational Taxes: What do politicians know', 16 April 2015, available at www.adamsmith.org/blog/tax-spending/multinational-taxes-what-do-politicians-know/).

11 'Corporate tax posturing should stop' (*Financial Times*, 30 January 2013).

12 In a letter of 14 March 2007, Diageo responded to SEC queries about moving its brand rights from the UK to the Netherlands (www.sec.gov/Archives/edgar/data/835403/000110465907018941/filename1.htm). This led to a tax credit of £315m, reflecting the tax deduction obtained for the amortisation of the tax value, an amount agreed with the Dutch fiscal authority. Further, a provision of £294m was made in the accounts for potential tax exposures, the largest being in respect of a non-specified transfer pricing enquiry.

13 'Diageo to pay $16m in "illicit payments" case' (*Drinks International*, 28 July 2011). Diageo agreed to "cease and desist" from further violations, though it neither admitted nor denied the findings. The full terms of the US case can be found at www.sec.gov/litigation/admin/2011/34-64978.pdf.

14 *Liggett Group Inc. v. Commissioner*, Docket No 28427–84, 11 January 1990.

15 *Liggett Group Inc. v. Commissioner*, Docket No 28427–84, 11 January 1990, p. 3 states "the use of the term FOB raises the presumption that title passes to the buyer on the seller's delivery of goods to the indicated place".

16 *Liggett Group Inc. v. Commissioner*, Docket No 28427–84, 11 January 1990, pp. 2–3 gives extensive details of the nature of bonding and shipping for the brand.

17 Williams (2017) provides a comprehensive summary of the origin of the three-tier system that was introduced after the repeal of Prohibition, considering in detail its impact on the evolution of the craft beer market in North Carolina.

18 *The New York Times* (18 September 1987).
19 Proposed Merger of Guinness Plc and Grand Metropolitan Plc, '*Listing Particulars*', p. 15.
20 *The Telegraph* (5 February 2003).
21 Allied Domecq Plc [1100427] SEC filing 20-F for the fiscal year ending 31 August 2003.
22 A pattern of over-production in an environment of positive demand growth, and under-production in times of less favourable economic conditions, particularly in the 1970s and 1980s, defines the 'whisky cycle', as shown graphically in Figure 4 in Bower (2016, p. 8).
23 DCL was created from the merger of six Lowland grain distillers in 1877, after several unsuccessful attempts to establish what amounted to a price-fixing cartel. The merchants were adept at playing one distiller versus another, meaning that profit margins on grain distillation varied from a high of 15% to a low of negative 5% in the 1853–1867 period (Weir, 1995, pp. 27–29).
24 The North British Distillery Limited was formed in 1885 as an industry co-operative by a group of Edinburgh merchants and blenders to counter the dominance of DCL as a supplier of grain spirit to the blending trade (Bower, 2016, p. 10).
25 *The New York Times* (4 May 1991).
26 Diageo Annual Report 2017, p. 130.
27 'SEC investigating Smirnoff maker Diageo' (*The Wall Street Journal*, 23 July 2015).
28 Lord Hoffmann, Session 2006–07, UKHL 15, para 8 (*Taxation*, 29 June 2011).
29 Dissenting view of Lord Reed at the Court of Session (*Taxation*, 27 October 2005).
30 Diageo annual report 2017, Note 14, p. 127.
31 Proposed Merger of Guinness Plc and Grand Metropolitan Plc, '*Listing Particulars*' (Note 16, p. 37).
32 'Securitisation – after the credit crunch: Is it right for your business' *PricewaterhouseCoopers*, 2011.
33 'West B may securitise whisky stocks' (*Morning Advertiser*, 6 November 2001), trailing the possibility of the securitisation of whisky stocks detailed the new ownership of Whyte & Mackay. Prior to its acquisition by Fortune Brands (formerly known as American Brands) in 1990, Whyte & Mackay had been owned by several other conglomerates, including Lonrho and Brent Walker.
34 '"Scotch bond" to spirit up £188m' (*This Is Money*, 26 February 2002).
35 'Whyte & Mackay poised to buy out WestLB stake for £50m' (*The Scotsman*, 23 January 2005).
36 'WestLB poised to sell Scots distiller' (*The Telegraph*, 18 January 2005).
37 For the background and details of this business venture see 'Investing in Scotch whisky maturation' WhiskyInvestDirect Ltd, February 2016, available at www.whiskyinvestdirect.com/.
38 Mr Rupert Patrick, founder and chief executive officer of WhiskyInvestDirect Ltd., quoted in *Financial Times* (25 September 2015). The article chronicled the evolution of the auction market for Scotch whisky and Japanese whisky and how this has led to the dedicated online selling platform. It gives examples of auction prices for especially rare whiskies, such as a 64-year-old Macallan single malt which was bought at auction in the United States for $460k.
39 WhiskyInvestDirect Ltd, February 2016, p. 8.
40 WhiskyInvestDirect Ltd, February 2016, pp. 19–20.

References

Bower, J. (2016). Scotch Whisky: History, heritage and the stock cycle. *Beverages*, 2(11), pp. 1–14.

Buckley, P. J. (2009). Business history and international business. *Business History*, 51(3), pp. 307–333.

Chandler, A. D. (1990). *Scale and Scope: The Dynamics of Industrial Capitalism.* Cambridge, MA: The Belknap Press of Harvard University.

Da Silva Lopes, T. (2007). *Global Brands: The Evolution of Multinationals in Alcoholic Beverages.* Cambridge: Cambridge University Press.

Da Silva Lopes, T. and Casson, M. (Summer 2012). Brand protection and the globalization of british business. *Business History Review*, 86, pp. 287–310.

Dobson, A. P. (1986). The Export White Paper, 10 September 1941. *Economic History Review*, 39(1), pp. 59–76.

Fiss, P. C. and Zajac, E. J. (2004). The diffusion of ideas over contested domain: The (non) adoption of a shareholder value orientation among German firms. *Administrative Science Quarterly*, 49(4), pp. 501–534.

Froud, J., Johal, S., Leaver, A. and Williams, K. (2014). Financialisation across the pacific: Manufacturing cost ratios, supply chains and power. *Critical Perspectives on Accounting*, 25, pp. 46–57.

Froud, J., Johal, S., Papazian, V. and Williams, K. (2004). The temptation of houston: A case study of financialisation. *Critical Perspectives on Accounting*, 15, pp. 885–909.

Genschel, P. and Schwarz, P. (2011). Tax competition: A literature review. *Socio-Economic Review*, 9, pp. 339–370.

Girón, A. and Chapoy, A. (2012). Securitisation and financialisation. *Journal of Post Keynesian Economics*, 35(2), pp. 171–188.

Glen, I. A. (1963). *The Scotch Whisky Industry (1939–1961): An Economic Study.* Unpublished Bachelor of Letters Thesis, The University of Glasgow.

Haslam, C., Andersson, T., Tsitsianis, N. and Yin, Y. P. (2013). *Redefining Business Models: Strategies for a Financialized World.* New York and London: Routledge.

Jacobides, M. G. and Winter, S. G. (2012). Capabilities: Structure, agency and evolution. *Organization Science*, 23(5), pp. 1365–1381.

Jensen, M. C. and Meckling, W. H. (1976). Theory of the firm: Managerial behaviour, agency costs and ownership structure. *Journal of Financial Economics*, 3, pp. 305–360.

Jones, S. R. H. (2003). Brand building and structural change in the Scotch whisky industry since 1975. *Business History*, 45(3), pp. 72–89.

Killian, S. (2006). Where's the harm in tax competition? Lessons from US multinationals in Ireland. *Critical Perspectives on Accounting*, 17, pp. 1067–1087.

Kostova, T., Roth, K. and Dacin, M. T. (2008). Institutional theory in the study of multinational corporations: A critique and new directions. *Academy of Management Review*, 33(4), pp. 994–1006.

Lazonick, W. (Winter 2010). Innovative business models and varieties of capitalism: Financialisation of the US corporation. *Business History Review*, 84, pp. 675–702.

Maclean, M., Harvey, C. and Clegg, S. R. (2016). Conceptualizing historical organization studies. *Academy of Management Review*, 41(4), pp. 609–632.

McGahan, A. M. (Summer 1991). The emergence of the national brewing oligopoly: Competition in the American market, 1933–1958. *Business History Review*, 65, pp. 229–284.

Mollan, S. and Tennent, K. D. (2015). International taxation and corporate strategy: Evidence from British overseas business, circa 1900–1965. *Business History*, 57(7), pp. 1054–1081.

Mordhorst, M. (2014). Arla and Danish national history: Business history as cultural history. *Business History*, 56(1), pp. 116–133.

Moss, M. and Hume, J. (2000). *The Making of Scotch Whisky.* Edinburgh: Canongate Books.

Orhangazi, O. (2008). Financialisation and capital accumulation in the non-financial corporate sector: A theoretical and empirical investigation on the US economy, 1973–2003. *Cambridge Journal of Economics*, 32, pp. 863–886.

Plous, H. J. (1958). Control of capital issues in the United Kingdom. *The Journal of Finance*, 13(3), pp. 357–369.PricewaterhouseCoopers (2011). Securitisation – after the credit crunch Is it right for your business? Available at www.pwc.com/gx/en/structured-finance/pdf/pwc-publications-securitisation-after-the-crunch.pdf [Accessed 01 April 2018].

Scotch Whisky Association (2017). Facts & figures. Available at www.scotch-whisky.org.uk/what-we-do/facts-figures [Accessed 01 December 2017].

Shleifer, A. and Vishny, R. W. (1997). A survey of corporate governance. *The Journal of Finance*, 52(2), pp. 737–783.

Sikka, P. and Willmott, H. (2010). The dark side of transfer pricing: Its role in tax avoidance and wealth retentiveness. *Critical Perspectives on Accounting*, 21, pp. 342–356.

Stockhammer, E. (2004). Financialisation and the slowdown of accumulation. *Cambridge Journal of Economics*, 28, pp. 719–741.

Wasserman, M. J. (1951). United States import financing methods. *The Journal of Finance*, 6(3), pp. 325–328.

Weir, R. B. (1988). Alcohol controls and Scotch whisky exports (1870–1939). *British Journal of Addiction*, 83, pp. 1289–1297.

Weir, R. B. (1989). Rationalization and diversification in the Scotch whisky industry, 1900–1939: Another look at 'old' and 'new' industries. *Economic History Review*, 42(3), pp. 375–395.

Weir, R. B. (1995). *The History of the Distillers Company, 1877–1939*. Oxford: Clarendon Press.

Williams, A. (2017). Exploring the impact of legislation on the development of craft beer. *Beverages*, 3(18), pp. 1–16.

Wood, G. and Wright, M. (2010). Wayward agents, dominant elite or reflection of internal diversity? A critique of Folkman, Froud, Johal and Williams on financialisation and financial intermediaries. *Business History*, 52(7), pp. 1048–1067.

9 Life of the party

Tequila in the American marketplace

Marie Sarita Gaytán

Every *Cinco de Mayo* (May 5th) in bars across the United States, *fiesta*-seekers consume copious amounts of tequila, Mexico's national spirit. Enticed with two-for-one margarita specials and all-you-can-eat guacamole and chips, revelers drink, dine and dance the night away. Although most of these consumers are Anglo, there is a significant amount of Mexican American and Mexican immigrants who also raise a glass to celebrate the Mexican army's 1862 defeat of French forces in Puebla. At first glance, it seems unlikely that a regional Mexican holiday would evolve into one of the United States' most raucous drinking days of the year. However, Mexican culture – its influences, attributes and flavors, especially Mexican food and drink – has profoundly shaped American tastes (Arellano, 2012; Gaytán, 2008). Indeed, by the early 1990s salsa outsold ketchup, becoming the nation's top-selling condiment (Vila, 1997). By the mid-2000s, another unexpected change took place: more tequila was consumed by volume in the United States than in Mexico (Simon, 2007). Yet tequila has not always been associated with lighthearted pleasure or celebration; for much of its history in the United States, it was seen as a symbol of Mexican danger and depravity.

In this chapter, I trace tequila's reputation as it shifted from feared to fun in the American marketplace. What does the history of a product's social and economic life tell us about the development of identity and taste? How did tequila become permissible, pleasurable and profitable? I argue that the case of tequila illustrates how, far from an individual endeavor, taste distinctions are mired in political and cultural contingencies that intersect with racial ideologies. Although scholars have written a great deal about social classes' significance in the creation of lowbrow and highbrow categories (Baumann, 2007; Levine, 1988), less is known about the role that race plays in forging status designations in the marketplace. A focus on tequila's evolving identities is a pertinent and important undertaking. Very little, if any, scholarship considers the critical connections between its commercial travels and accounting histories – which is thwarted to some extent due to a scarcity of accounting-related documents in archives. This is nonetheless surprising given the burgeoning international interest in alcohol studies and tequila's ranking as the world's fastest-growing sprit category. Drawing on the content of government reports, print ads and newspaper articles from the 19th and 20th centuries, I examine how and why tequila's significance evolved – from dreaded to delightful – by considering the various connotations it signified for different groups of people. Tequila's progression into one of the United States' most popular party drinks was far from an inevitable process; instead it was mired in conflict related to colonial aspirations, ideas of racial inferiority and the evolution of United States–Mexico relations. I begin by providing an overview of tequila's history and development.

Background: tequila

Tequila is a distilled alcoholic drink made from the juices of the *Agave tequilana* Weber, also known as the blue agave plant. The name "tequila" comes from the Náhautl word, *tequitl*, which means "work" or "job" and *tlan*, which means "place" (Muría, 1995); it is also the name of the small town in the western state of Jalisco where its production first flourished. Despite its indigenous nomenclature, tequila was not the first or the most important drink in pre-colonial communities. Long before the 15th-century arrival of the Spanish, native people consumed the fermented drink known as *pulque*. Made from the nectar of a variety of agave species, *pulque* was a ritual intoxicant and medicinal beverage that provided much-needed calories and nutrients for populations throughout most of Mexico.

Accustomed to drinking imported wine, cognac and sherry, the Spanish colonial elite found *pulque*'s sour flavor, foul smell and milky texture unpalatable (Viqueira, 1987). More importantly, they saw *pulque* as instigating disorder and inciting uprisings among the indigenous populations. Not surprising, during the 16th century, the crown outlawed its sale across Nueva España (New Spain) (Nemser, 2012). Thus, initially it seemed unlikely that colonizers would express interest in the production, let alone the consumption of *pulque*. However, despite prohibition, the market expanded and the Spanish eventually instituted a system of taxation. This in turn required accounting records to determine the basis for such taxation. As a "calculative practice", the incorporation of new tax policies (and the underlying accounting records) helped transform a product despised by elites into a "commercially viable" commodity (Mikes and Morhart, 2017, p. 66). By the 17th century, the manufacture of *pulque* had evolved into a commercial enterprise. At the peak of its popularity, there were several hundred *pulque* haciendas in operation in the central highlands surrounding Mexico City (Kicza, 1980).

In his research on research on accountability arrangements and settler–indigenous relations in Canada, Neu (2000) argues that accounting techniques rationalized the terms of colonial governmentality. Applying a broad definition to accounting, one that considers the myriad power relations between individuals, groups and institutions (Tinker, 1980), Neu addresses the ideological and historically contingent functions of accounting (Lehman and Tinker, 1987). In colonial arrangements, as he and others note, the exercise of governmentality (Foucault, 1991) was successfully mobilized from a distance. Neu (2000, p. 270), drawing on Miller and Rose's (1990) notion of "technologies of government" writes how, when it came to exploiting fish, timber and other resources in North America, European colonial authorities were able to "shape, normalize and instrumentalize the conduct, thought, decisions and aspirations of others in order to achieve the objectives they considered desirable" (Miller and Rose, 1990, p. 8). Although many of these goals evolved over time (e.g., the containment, annihilation, and assimilation of indigenous people), accounting techniques were central features of these accumulation-driven endeavors.

Much like the colonial administration of Canada, in Mexico accounting practices were actuated for the purposes of domination and profit, serving as methods that legitimized "the annexation and exploitation of colonial lands" (Thornburg and Roberts, 2012, p. 205). Central to the perpetuation of Spanish domination was their ability to exploit available natural resources and indigenous knowledge. Together with vast supplies of agave and technological advancements in the process of distillation, the drive for new markets eventually led to the commercial production of mezcal, a generic name for all distilled agave spirits. In the early 18th century, Pedro Sánchez de Tagle, a member of the Spanish elite, reportedly opened the first mezcal distillery in Tequila, Jalisco (Luna, 1991). In 1758, Tequila Cuervo was established on the Cuervo-Montaño hacienda in the town of Tequila. Other smaller distilleries were operating at this time, producing what was then known as "*vino mezcal de Tequila*" (mezcal wine from Tequila). Demand for mezcal from Tequila increased when Mexico gained independence from Spain in 1821 and Spanish imports were suspended. The rising reputation of nearby Guadalajara, as a city ripe for investment (Lindley, 1983), attracted new capital into the region, while infrastructural improvements, such as the development of the port of Acapulco, facilitated the transport of the spirit to other parts of the country (Muría, 1995). By the early 20th century, mezcal from Tequila was beginning to acquire its own unique status and was soon known as "tequila" (Gaytán, 2014a).

Although tequila's reputation continued to spread, by the late 19th century *pulque* remained Mexico's most popular drink. No longer considered a strictly religious intoxicant, *pulque* continued to serve as a readily available source of sustenance for the poor and working classes. The consumption of *pulque* began to gradually decline in the early decades of the 20th century, when European-owned beer companies initiated operations in the northern part of the country (Hibino, 1992). Beer was marketed by business owners and politicians as a European and enlightened product – an association that stood in contrast to *pulque*'s deep ties to antiquated methods of production and its primitive association with indigenous populations. What is more, beer entrepreneurs were among the earliest adopters of glass bottle technology, a strategy that further accentuated its modern appearance and reputation (Beatty, 2009). By 1907, an unprecedented 100 million pints of bottled beer had been sold in Mexico. In the words of Beatty (2009, p. 325), "changing tastes reflected changing attitudes [. . .] it was beer, not pulque, that brought men 'comfort and happiness, and open[ed] the way to a higher civilization'".

More political and cultural shifts were brewing as the Mexican Revolution (c.1910–1920) ushered in vast social changes and altered how Mexicans related to each other. From novels to songs, authors and musicians regularly honored the working-class heroes associated with the revolution. Folk ballads known as *corridos* recounted the sacrifice and struggle of the decade-long war, oftentimes referencing revolutionary icons, such as Pancho Villa, drinking tequila in cantinas or on the battlefield (Gaytán, 2010). Artists such as Manuel Manilla and José Guadalupe Posada, whose political cartoons and lithographs reflected the lives of ordinary people, depicted tequila in scenes with their famous *calaveras* (Day of the Dead skeleton icons) (Gaytán, 2016). Tequila began gaining favor among the "popular" classes and was steadily becoming associated with an emergent post-war national identity. This evolving reputation was solidified during the period of Mexican Golden Age Cinema (c.1935–1959), an era that played a crucial role in shaping the contours of Mexican national identity, or what is better known as *lo mexicano* (Mexicanness) (Gaytán, 2014a).

The period's most popular genre, the *comedia ranchera* (Western melodrama), frequently featured the adventures of male tequila-drinking heroes in the idealized world of Mexican ranches, *haciendas* and villages. In seeking to recapture many of the traditions associated with the revolutionary period, directors made films with patriotic motifs in bucolic settings. On the big screen, nationalistic symbols were created and, importantly, repeated within the genre. *Comedia rancheras* were steeped in pastoral nostalgia, with themes spotlighting life in the Mexican countryside. Famous actors sang *ranchera* songs, played the guitar, protected the less fortunate and imbibed tequila in cantinas in what eventually became well-loved, classic films (Gaytán and Bowen, 2015). For instance, as the movie poster for *Muchacho Alegre* (The Happy Young Man) illustrates, dashing protagonists were commonly dressed in traditional *charro* (Mexican cowboy) outfits, proudly reflecting their rural Mexican background. In Figure 9.1, *comedia ranchera* star, Luis Aguilar, confidently strums his guitar accompanied by his drink of choice, a bottle of tequila, which enhances his likability and relatability to Mexican audiences.

Tequila's ties to various forms of media played a vital role in elevating its place in the national consciousness and cementing its association as an authentic drink that Mexicans with limited resources could afford. This reputation would take on a life of its own, and in the decades that followed tequila would become perceived as a drink for "common", working-class people. As a result, tequila's consumption represented "an act of interpretation" that closely aligned with the nation's shifting collective consciousness (Lawrence and Phillips, 2002, p. 431).

Figure 9.1 Movie poster for *El Muchacho Alegre* (1948)

Although considered a popular drink in Mexico, across the border in the United States, a different, yet equally complicated set of meanings was simultaneously unfolding with regard to tequila and its ties to Mexican identity.

Tequila travels

As a result of the Mexican-American War and the signing of the Treaty of Guadalupe Hidalgo, in 1848, Mexico ceded 1.35 million square kilometers (525,000 square miles) to the United States. In the years following the conflict, thousands of residents were repatriated to Mexico, but many remained and continued to reside in their former homeland. Ethnic Mexicans' desire to continue with their daily routines and cultural traditions did not simply end when they were incorporated into the United States. One custom that endured was the pastime of communicating through print media. Though the earliest publications date back to 1808 (Kanellos, 2000), US Spanish-language newspapers started to grow in popularity and in numbers in the 1840s (Rodríguez, 1999). Journalists reported on stories from Latin America but also "informed the community about current affairs and politics and advertised local businesses and products" (Kanellos, 2000, p. 5). The flourishing press defended ethnic Mexican populations against discrimination and helped forge allegiances and shape identities as new "Latino" communities formed throughout the country.

In addition to covering local and international news stories, the publications included poems, commentaries, letters, jokes, political cartoons, song lyrics and advertisements. Tequila ads began appearing in the later part of the 19th century. Newspapers in cities such as Los Angeles and Chicago announced the arrival of shipments of tequila along with other sought-after Mexican products. Most often, ads, such as the one for Garcia's Grocery, listed *mezcal de Tequila* as one of the many alcohol and household products they offered (*Clamor Público*, 1857). By 1868, retailers started to include more descriptive information about the array of Mexican products they carried. For example, ads like those for shops owned by J. M. Fuentes (*Cronica*, 1874) listed the availability of "legitimate" mezcal from Tequila, suggesting that some stores were selling fake or poor-quality tequila. The origins of unlawful tequila – whether it was manufactured in the United States or if it came from Mexico – remain uncertain. What is clear, however, is that customers preferred and sought out authentic tequila.

Other locales began to highlight *mezcal de Tequila* as one of the specialty goods they carried. Bars and cantinas, like *La Plaza* in Los Angeles, California, described having "a complete assortment of wines and spirits imported from the country [Mexico] and the famous mezcal from Tequila" (*Dos Repúblicas*, 1892, p. 17). Given the variety of locales that offered tequila, shops and cantinas, it is likely that it appealed to a broad spectrum of consumers – those who preferred to drink it at home and those who drank it while out in the public. Although not explicitly stating so, these ads were primarily directed at men. According to the gender norms of the time, "good" women did not imbibe hard alcohol or drink in public in the presence of men who were not their husbands (Vargas, 2012). Because cantinas were places where single and married men could drink with friends, let off steam and "release tensions, feelings, and passions", "respectable" women were not welcome (Palafox, 2001, p. 169). Some women, however, were present, including prostitutes, singers, food vendors and *ficheras* (women who were paid to accompany or dance with men) (Gaytán, 2016). Tequila's traditional gendered associations catalyzed rather than compromised its growing popularity in the United States.

At the same time that ethnic Mexican consumers and other Latin Americans were seeing an increasing number of ads for tequila in Spanish-language newspapers, Anglo readers were being introduced to tequila via the accounts of government officials, American entrepreneurs and travel writers who began publishing formal documents and informal stories detailing 19th-century life in Mexico. Early English-language representations primarily focused on tequila's ties to nature and well-being. For instance, many writers addressed the diverse attributes of the agave (or maguey) plant. One article described the plant as having an "infinite variety of uses", a plant with "special virtues" from which *pulque* and tequila were produced (*Springfield Republican*, 1884, p. 2).

By the end of the 19th century, portrayals of tequila evolved as Anglo Americans, once curious readers, became potential drinkers. However, unlike Spanish-language ads that focused on tequila as an alcoholic spirit, in English-language publications it was initially lauded for its medicinal qualities. For example, Tequila Tonic Export boasted that their product provided "strength and vigor to the digestive organs" (*Topeka Weekly Capital*, 1889, p. 8). Described as a natural product, tequila was pitched as healing and preventing dizziness, sleeplessness and muscular weakness. In addition to having a pleasant taste, "physicians throughout all Mexico prescribe it with the best results in the treatment of all general diseases" (ibid.). Another ad (see Figure 9.2) from California Wine Co. describes tequila as a "great and beneficial treat to your kidneys" (*Tucson Citizen*, 1906, p. 8). According to these retailers, tequila is an impressive remedy for a range of ailments.

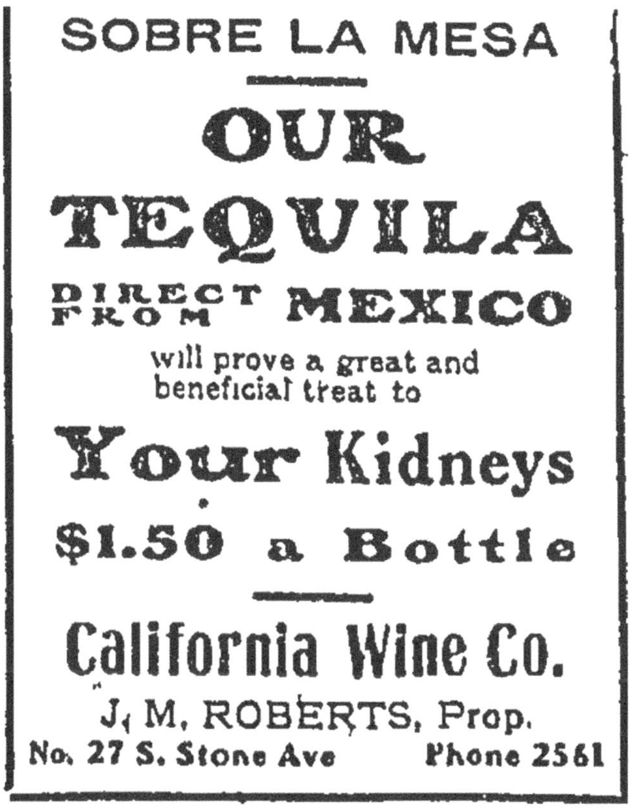

Figure 9.2 Tequila ad, *Tucson Citizen* (1906)

The heightened focus on the agave and tequila's bountiful and virtuous properties builds on a long history of travel writing that dates back to the 16th century, when Europeans began venturing to Latin America to catalog the flora and fauna. Pratt (1992, p. 26) argues that travelers' early reports focused on the democratic dimensions of exploration and served as a type of "planetary consciousness" that allowed writers and readers alike to understand themselves as engaging in "non-exploitative relations to nature". Authors' reliance on seemingly secular depictions of nature "interrupted existing networks of historical and material relations among people, plants, and animals" (p. 30). Much like the stories relayed by their European forefathers, 19th-century journalistic interpretations of tequila failed to recognize the broader exploitative context in which their accounts were embedded, such as increasing capitalist interest and expansion into Mexico – aspirations that echoed earlier colonial endeavors.

Tequila's introduction into the American marketplace coincided with changes taking place between urban and rural relations, especially those difficulties associated with adjusting to the effects of industrialization. The focus on tequila (and agave's) therapeutic qualities introduced medical paradigms of progress that had the potential to soothe rising anxieties regarding the "effects of overwork", as it helped rationalize the need to intensify exploration into the Mexican countryside. In addition to serving this purpose, the focus on tequila's curative properties perpetuated another common framework used by financially savvy investors: the urgency to dominate nature for the benefit of humanity. The necessity for order and discipline was linked to the desire to control and profit from all that was exotic and primitive. In prevailing over the wilderness through the language of scientific discovery, entrepreneurs, writers and readers were able to understand their own superiority to those foreign inhabitants – and their plants, drinks and foods – that existed among them.

U.S. government representatives and scientific journalists also started to write about the agave plant and document its drinks (for example, types of *pulque*), including tequila. Though many interpretations were impartial, some of the work produced by these influential authors took on a decidedly discriminatory tone when describing Mexican life in general and tequila in particular. For example, an 1896 newspaper article described a local labor delegation's tour of Mexico. The average Mexican worker, the author explained, was more content with sleeping on the floor rather than a bed. The article later cautioned Americans from seeking employment in Mexico, because, in addition to not having many of the luxuries from home, they would likely "be obliged to subsist on cactus and the sap of the tequila plant" (*The Free Lance*, 1896, p. 1). Mexicans were portrayed as content with living in squalor and comfortable surviving on alcohol for nourishment (Gaytán, 2016).

American journalists and other writers frequently used the term "greaser" to exemplify Mexicans' (that is, ethnic Mexicans in the United States and Mexicans in Mexico) penchant for pleasure, danger and over-indulgence. Although its true origins are lost to history, "greaser" primarily referred to Mexicans' skin color – suggesting that it was similar to grease. "Greaser" likewise signaled the darkness associated with physical appearance and inner character. In an article published in the *Chicago Herald* (1890, p. 13), tequila is described as a drink that is "good" for greasers, "but for a white man, whose throat and stomach are built on ordinary lines . . . it is equivalent to a big dose of prussic acid". As a "fearful liquid", tequila was regularly depicted in relation to the moral "peculiarities" of greasers (*Kansas City Star*, 1887, p. 2). Mexican men were represented as not only having a higher tolerance for alcohol, but as enjoying tequila, a drink that was understood to be dangerous to white men. As one US travel writer in Mexico put it, "It is difficult to determine what a man will not use as a stimulant, but certainly tequila is not a beverage for which anyone, whose taste is not perverted, would 'hanker' after" (ibid.). Tequila, a Mexican-origin product, symbolically allowed Anglo writers the opportunity to make ethical comparisons and affirm prejudiced assertions based on Mexicans' affinity for instability and lawlessness. This journalistic trend continued for several decades, evolving in both tone and momentum, as broader socio-political changes started taking place within and between Mexico and the United States.

Shifting policies and politics

In the early years of the 20th century, Mexico was regularly portrayed as a site of potential danger to upright Americans who could be tempted to travel across the border in search of alcohol and other vices. Hazardous or not, the tequila industry continued to expand. By 1907, there were ninety-six distilleries, producing upwards of 800,000 gallons a year that yielded a state tax of between 25 and 29 cents per each ten liters sold (*Dallas Morning News*, 1907). Newspapers started to report on individuals, in states like California, who were filing for permission to open plants to manufacture tequila in the United States, where it was fetching $2.35 a gallon (*San Francisco Chronicle*, 1907).

From an accounting perspective, this growth is likely to be driven by the perceived demand and profitability of tequila distilling at that time. However, despite robust growth and the potential for profit, tequila's negative reputation continued to spread with the initiation of the Mexican Revolution in 1910. In particular, American print media depicted tequila as a central aspect of the revolution that underscored the barbaric nature of Mexicans and highlighted their tendency towards lawlessness. Mexican soldiers were frequently described as violent, erratic and unable to control their fondness for alcohol in general and tequila specifically (Gaytán, 2014b). As the war in Mexico came to a close, another major political change was afoot. In 1919, with the support of temperance advocates, the Volstead Act was passed, outlawing the sale and manufacture of alcohol in the United States. Although not everyone agreed with the new federal regulations, the formal shift in governing policy drew increased attention to the moral and health hazards associated with drinking. As breweries and bars closed, alcohol drinkers turned to the underground economy to satiate their thirst for booze. To the dismay of powerful temperance advocates, bootlegging thrived in both big cities and small towns. Further, Prohibition increased the price of alcohol (and associated profitability) and created a new international smuggling enterprise along the US-Mexican border. Historian Gabriela Recio (2002, p. 27) explains, "[t]otal prohibition created black markets worth millions of dollars, and the long border shared with the United States encouraged the expansion of liquor [. . .] markets on the Mexican side". The manufacture and distribution of drinks like tequila were important sources of employment for poor and working-class Mexicans in both countries. Tequila bootleggers participated in contraband rings, helping transport illegal products into the United States; they crisscrossed the border with skilled packers fitting "about fifty protectively wrapped bottles on a mature mule or donkey" (Díaz, 2011, p. 65).

From the late 19th century until the early 1930s, tequila embodied a range of meanings, but for Anglo audiences in particular, it was regularly portrayed by the media as an index of Mexican inferiority. Yet the personification of Mexico and Mexicans as primitive and dangerous would gradually undergo a transformation, as American "political pilgrims" (for example, artists and intellectuals) started to travel to Mexico in greater numbers. According to Delpar (1992), left-leaning adventurers were drawn to Mexico because of their interest in learning about the social impact of the revolution. These educated, liberal and financially resourceful Americans felt alienated within the United States and sought out alternative examples (of countries and cultures) that aligned with their values. In Mexico, political pilgrims found a symbolic means to escape "the materialism, inequality, and conflict they associated with capitalism" (p. 15).

Prompted by the desire to experience what they saw as a more authentic way of life, they turned their admiration to Mexican traditions and crafts. In the United States, they sponsored art exhibitions, attended academic lectures and founded US-Mexican educational associations. Mexican officials encouraged political pilgrims' newfound fondness for Mexican culture. In particular, they were eager to cultivate the bases for the political pilgrims' budding appreciation, not only because they were wealthy but also because their affection was compatible with the reigning government-backed discourse of the time, *indigenismo* (indigenism). Adopted during the post-revolutionary period, *indigenismo* exalted the importance of indigenous populations as central to the national consciousness (Dawson, 1998). The Mexican government's focus on tourism likewise coincided with the predilections of political pilgrims and the effort to industrialize in the post-revolutionary period. Together, these circumstances created a new context for greater acceptance and appreciation of Mexico, its people and its products, by middle-class and upper-class American consumers.

From primitive to popular and profitable

Shifting cultural attitudes in the United States contributed to evolving international relations. Specifically, public opinion about Prohibition started to waver during the onset of the Great Depression in 1929. During this time, politicians began lobbying for the need to tax rather than police alcohol. There was also growing concern over the proliferation of organized crime as mafia groups gained greater control over bootlegging. Initially heralded by proponents as a sure-fire remedy for a range of social ills, by the 1930s it was becoming clear that Prohibition was not solving the nation's problems. In 1933, the 21st Amendment was passed, repealing Prohibition throughout the country.

No longer criminalized, alcohol's immoral and hazardous associations started to diminish (although they were never completely eliminated). Similarly, Mexico's standing – especially its threatening image publicized by the US media – started to lessen. Together with the growing interest in tourism, Mexico's nascent reputation as a welcoming and pristine holiday destination continued to gain traction. Mexican leaders sought to nourish positive impressions among this fresh group of middle-class tourists, who, like the political pilgrims before them, were affluent. In addition to no longer requiring Americans to have a passport to enter Mexico, officials created new agencies, including the National Commission of Tourism, and published English-language tourism magazines (Berger, 2006). Mexico's lure relied on descriptions and imagery that simultaneously captured its quaintness and sophistication, a destination that was just exotic enough for middle-class tourists. Guadalajara and the town of Tequila were often listed as must-see stops for visitors.

The popularity of Mexican culture marked a major turn in mainstream American attitudes and interests. Within the United States, all things Mexican reached new trendy heights, which created opportunities for business, including the sale of tequila. By 1940, Mexican-themed bars and lounges, such as La Conga Club in Cleveland Ohio, featured live performances with "south of the border songs", a "Mexican menu" and tequila flowing from the bar (*Cleveland Plain Dealer*, 1940, p. 13B). In San Francisco, bartenders served mixed drinks like the Tequila Sunrise, while restaurants like Sinaloa enticed customers to "Dine in Old Mexico" and drink their "tequila cocktails". Americans flocked to the movies to see films like *Sing, Dance, Plenty Hot* (1940) and *Ice-Capades Revue* (1942) that featured musical scenes with songs simply called "Tequila" (*Seattle Daily Times*, 1942). Even a brand of lounging pajamas was named "Tequila", with imprinted images of "palm trees, girls dancing to the twang of a guitar, all Mexican motifs. Gay Mexican sombreros are the buttons" (*Idaho Statesman*, 1944, p. 10). To be sure, tequila was becoming synonymous with merrymaking, comfort and leisure.

Favorable diplomatic relations between the two countries would become even more important – for the United States especially – with the onset of World War II. Mexico became the United States' most prized "good neighbor" as official foreign policy focused on reciprocity with Latin America. This new cooperative climate was reflected in travel and tourism advertising. An article from *The New York Times* titled "Fun and Adventure under Mexican Skies" boasted that "Mexican hands are out-stretched toward the Good Neighbors from the North in a hearty welcome" (Goodfriend, 1942, p. XX1). Newspaper headlines declared "Life in Mexico Little Changed by Global War, Food Is Abundant, Theaters Prosperous, Gasoline Plentiful" (Vinson, 1943, p. 10). Magazines praised Mexico as a society "more authentic and soul-satisfying than the highly industrialized United States" (Delpar, 1992, p. 62). Portrayed as a carefree holiday haven, the splendors of Mexico were fetishized as a destination that was picturesque, cheerful and affordable. The exaltations heralded by the US media portraying Mexico as a pleasurable getaway created a new, consumption-driven context that depicted Americans as entitled to indulging in the "fun" and "abundant" offerings of Mexico.

Mexican politicians and entrepreneurs participated in efforts to profit from the nation's representation. Holding that tourism "ensured progress and strengthened nationalism", public- and private-sector representatives supported the building of new airports and elegant resorts (Berger, 2006, p. 34). Mexican officials published commentaries in newspapers, inviting Americans "to enjoy with us this summer . . . the white beaches of our coasts, the countless resorts and attractions . . . because of our common purpose the Mexican government itself is concerned in making your visit comfortable and enjoyable" (*Milwaukee Journal-Sentinel*, 1942, p. 23). Investment in the Pan-American Highway made traveling to Mexico much easier and more affordable for middle-class Americans. Not having to cross the Atlantic, which was unadvisable during World War II, and without breaking their budget, "American tourists got more for their money and time south of the border" (Berger, 2006, p. 108). Pitched as an easy escape from the challenges associated with wartime troubles, Mexico was lauded by both US and Mexican representatives as an inexpensive retreat for those who could afford "recreation" during conflict-ridden times.

Cooperation between the two countries continued to grow as American soldiers went to war. Approximately 200,000 Mexican *braceros* (seasonal agricultural worker) were welcomed by American agribusiness to fill the need for manual labor in fields across the country. Good neighbors supplied a steady workforce during difficult socio-economic periods. They also provided difficult-to-obtain merchandise: when shipments of European spirits came to a standstill as the global conflict expanded, US consumers looked to Mexico to help fill some of this void. In 1943, *La Prensa* reported that as much as $250,000 worth of tequila was being imported into the United States per month. By the end of the same year, the Office of Price Administration established price controls because of the war-induced whiskey shortage (*Daily Herald*, 1943). This strategy changed in 1944 when the rationing board reduced taxes on tequila and vodka imports by 5 percent, which cut costs from $4.99 per fifth to $4.45 per fifth (*San Luis Obispo Telegram-Tribune*, 1944). Lower prices and new demand subsequently led to the first tequila "boom" or unexpected increase in sales: between 1940 and 1945, the production of tequila increased nearly 400 percent (Luna, 1991). Making the most of these circumstances, Mexican distillers increased production in order to quench the thirst of American consumers (*Wall Street Journal*, 1943) and benefited from increased sales and profits. Brands such as Jose Cuervo capitalized on the mounting interest and started to invest heavily in magazine and newspaper ads. By the mid-1950s, US-based distributors were spending upwards of $100,000 to promote the "Mexican beverage in cocktails and mixed drinks", which marketers saw as contributing to a one-year jump of 36 percent in US tequila sales (*Vogue*, 1956, p. 125). Liquor distributors, like Vernon Underwood of Los Angeles, California, signed a ten-year contract to bottle bulk tequila in the United States (*State*, 1956).

Conclusion

Tequila's reputation as a go-to party drink among tourists continued to grow over the next several decades to the present day. The Mexican spirit's new place in the American imaginary was reflected widely throughout popular culture. Notably, in 1958, *The Champs* released the one-word song "Tequila" – a track that not only reached number one on the US Billboard charts but also became an international hit and a global cultural phenomenon in its own right. The tequila-based drink, the margarita, today regarded as the world's most popular cocktail, likewise became a staple of American bars and restaurants (Gaytán, 2017). Over the course of a century, tequila's image went from feared to fun – a striking but complicated, consumption-based transformation.

Revenue-generating holidays like *Cinco de Mayo* provided new opportunities for companies to profit from the growing numbers of ethnic Mexicans who celebrated the Battle of Puebla. Although festivals and reenactments honoring the event (primarily in the American Southwest) date to the 1930s, today there are hundreds, if not thousands, of cultural celebrations throughout the country that feature Mexican food, dance and music. José Alamillo (2003, p. 59) reports that Mexican Americans, especially those born to Mexican immigrant parents, celebrate *Cinco de Mayo* both as a means of honoring national pride but also as a way of commemorating their "new-found American identit[ies]". In other words, over the years, Mexican Americans have transformed the festivity's meaning on their own terms to reflect their lived experiences.

The growing popularity of the holiday, however, has also caught the attention of large corporations, eager to capitalize on and profit from the emergent invented traditions associated with its merriment (Hobsbawm and Ranger, 1983). Tequila companies such as Jose Cuervo were quick to appeal to new consumers by drawing on cultural memories – as in the case of their campaign, "*Si Se Party, Si Se Cuervo*", which was reminiscent of the late Mexican American labor activist César Chávez's social justice slogan, "*Si se puede*" (Alamillo, 2004, p. 343). Alcohol advertisers, along with bars/restaurants, such as 101 Cantina in Tallahassee, Florida, were keen to tap into the new and lucrative "Cinco de Drinko" market. As Figure 9.3 shows, revelers can enjoy drink specials and receive "free tequila on the hour". Perhaps offered as a loss leader, by providing free tequila along with free "swag bags" and an all-you-can drink two-hour draft beer deal, this bar creatively incorporated popular interpretations about Mexican culture that aligned with their branding and the growing significance of *Cinco de Mayo* as a drinking holiday.

This capturing of market and profits by Mexican tequila producers is in contrast to the events recounted by Jackson et al. (2012), who reported how

Figure 9.3 Cinco de Mayo advertisement for 101 Cantina

some Scottish whiskey distilleries collapsed despite the presence of an opportune market, with accounting failures (namely accounting fraud) contributing to such fate. Thus, while this chapter does explore accounting archives, we can only conclude that such information must have played a role as the tequila export market grew – distilleries were unlikely to have invested in expanded plant and advertising unless some form of accounting records were showing a positive monetary return, which in turn contributed to a positive image of tequila. The policy move, from prohibiting to regulating and, in particular, taxing the tequila trade also certainly required the development of accounting techniques to support the calculation of taxes to be handed to the government, and the associated reporting. Therefore, the development of some form of accounting records can be described as having been a requirement for tequila companies to become a legitimate actor within the United States, for their product to be traded within the mainstream, legal distribution system and for tequila to become more widely consumed and accepted. Further research into this development and role of accounting is worthy of further research.

By examining tequila's shift from feared to fun in the American marketplace, I illustrate how attitudes about tequila evolved from a cross-border context. At first, it seemed unlikely that tequila would become a staple of American party culture, as it embodied racial anxieties through which Anglos narrated Mexicans' supposed penchant for danger and debauchery. Despite the early 20th-century representations promoted by journalists, scientists and government officials, ethnic Mexicans consumed tequila as part of their continuing cultural rituals. Tequila's connotations further evolved when alcohol Prohibition ended and World War II began to unfold. As the war concluded, increased tourism to Mexico likewise created a context in which tequila's associations would change once more. Broader geo-political circumstances played an important role in elevating its shifting economic and symbolic capital in both nations, and it may be argued that accounting may have had a role in legitimating and enabling its insertion within the US economy and society.

References

Abarrotes Los Garcia. *Clamor Público*, 6 June 1857, p. 4.

The Agave of Mexico, Joaquin Miller writs of the Maguey Plant and its universal usefulness. *Bismarck Tribune*, 24 April 1886, p. 4.

Alamillo, J. (2003). More than a fiesta: Ethnic identity, cultural politics, and Cinco de Mayo festivals in Corona, California, 1930–1950. *Aztlan: A Journal of Chicano Studies*, 28(2), pp. 57–85.

Alamillo, J. (2004). Parading ethnic identities. *Journal of American Ethnic History*, 23(3), pp. 102–105.

Arellano, G. (2012). *Taco USA: How Mexican Food Conquered America*. New York: Scribner.

Baumann, S. (2007). *Hollywood Highbrow: From Entertainment to Art*. Princeton: Princeton University Press.

Beatty, E. (2009). Bottles for beer: The business of technological innovation in Mexico, 1890–1920. *Business History Review*, 82(2), pp. 317–348.

Berger, D. (2006). *The Development of Mexico's Tourism Industry: Pyramids by Day, Martinis by Night*. New York: Palgrave Macmillan.

Cave dwellers feast. *Chicago Herald*, 23 February 1890, p. 13.

Colorful ice review at palomar tomorrow. *Seattle Daily Times*, 27 December 1942, p. 29.

Dawson, A. (1998). From models for the nation to model citizens: Indigenismo and the revindication of the Mexican Indian, 1920–1940. *Journal of Latin American Studies*, 30(2), pp. 279–308.

Delpar, H. (1992). *The Enormous Vogue of Things Mexican: Cultural Relations Between the United States and Mexico, 1920–1935*. Tuscaloosa: University of Alabama Press.

Díaz, G. (2011). Twilight of the Tequileros: Prohibition era smuggling in the South Texas borderlands 1919–1933. In: E. Carey and A. Marak, eds. *Smugglers, Brothels, and Twine: Historical Perspectives on Contraband and Vice in North America's Borderlands*. Tucson: University of Arizona Press, pp. 59–79.

Foucault, M. (1991). Governmentality. In: G. Burchell, C. Gordon and P. Miller, eds. *The Foucault Effect*. Chicago: University of Chicago Press, pp. 87–104.

Gaytán, M. (2008). From Sombreros to Sincronizadas: Authenticity, ethnicity and the Mexican restaurant industry. *Journal of Contemporary Ethnography*, 37(3), pp. 314–341.

Gaytán, M. (2010). Drinking the nation and making masculinity: Tequila, Pancho Villa, and the U.S. Media. In: H. Gray and M. Gómez-Barris, eds. *Toward a Sociology of the Trace*. Minneapolis: University of Minnesota Press, pp. 207–233.

Gaytán, M. (2014a). *¡Tequila! Distilling the Spirit of Mexico*. Stanford: Stanford University Press.

Gaytán, M. (2014b). Drinking difference: Race, consumption, and alcohol prohibition in Mexico and the United States. *Ethnicities*, 14(3), pp. 437–458.

Gaytán, M. (2016). 'Una Copita Amigo': Ethnic Mexicans, consumer culture, and the American marketplace. *Latino Studies*, 14(4), pp. 458–481.

Gaytán, M. (2017). The transformation of Tequila: From hangover to highbrow. *Journal Consumer Culture*, 17(1), pp. 62–84.

Gaytán, M. and Bowen, S. (2015). Naturalizing neoliberalism and the de-mexicanization of the Tequila Industry. *Environment and Planning A*, 47(2), pp. 267–283.

Goodfriend, A. (1942). Fun and adventure under Mexican Skies. *New York Times*, 15 March 1942, p. XX1.

Hibino, B. (1992). Cervecería Cuauhtémoc: A cast study of technologial and industrial development in Mexico. *Mexican Studies*, 8(1), pp. 23–43.

Hobsbawm, E. and Ranger, T., eds. (1983). *The Invention of Tradition*. Cambridge: Cambridge University Press.

Jackson, W. J., Paterson, A. S., Pong, C. K. and Scarparo, S. (2012). 'How easy can the barley brie': drinking culture and accounting failure at the end of the nineteenth century in Britain. *Accounting, Auditing & Accountability Journal*, 25(4), pp. 635–658.

Kanellos, N. (2000). A brief history of hispanic periodicals in the United States. In: N. Kanellos and H. Martell, eds. *Hispanic Periodicals in the United States, Origins to 1960: A Brief and Comprehensive Bibliography*. Houston: Arte Público Press, pp. 3–8.

Kicza, J. (1980). The Pulque Trade of late colonial Mexico City. *The Americas*, 37(2), pp. 193–221.

La Plaza. *Dos Repúblicas*, 17 May 1892, p. 4.

La Sonorense. *Cronica*, 12 September 1871, p. 1.

Lawrence, T. B. and Phillips, N. (2002). Understanding cultural industries. *Journal of Management Inquiry*, 11(4), pp. 430–441.

Lehman, C. and Tinker, T. (1987). The 'real' cultural significance of accounts. *Accounting, Organizations and Society*, 12, pp. 503–522.

Levine, L. (1988). *Highbrow/Lowbrow: The Emergence of Cultural Hierarchy in America*. Cambridge, MA: Harvard University Press.

Lindley, R. (1983) *Haciendas and Economic Development: Guadalajara, Mexico at Independence*. Austin: University of Texas Press.

Low wages in Mexico, labor committee submits its report, pitiful conditions of peons. *The Free Lance*, 15 October 1896, p. 1.

Luna, R. (1991). *La Historia del Tequila, de sus Regiones y sus Hombres*. México: Conaculta.

Mexican Peculiarities: Something about the manners and morals of our Southern Neighbors: 'Gringos' and 'Greasers'. *Kansas City Star*, 28 March 1887, p. 2.

Mexi-Conga. *Cleveland Plain Dealer*, 11 August 1940, pp. 13–B.

Mikes, A. and Morhart, F. (2017). Bringing back Charlie Chaplin: Accounting as catalyst in the creation of an authentic product of popular culture. *Management Accounting Research*, 35, pp. 66–82.

Miller, P. and Rose, N. (1990). Governing economic life. *Economy and Society*, 19(1), pp. 1–31.

Muría, J. M. (1995). Momentos del tequila. In Alberto Ruy Sánchez Lacy, ed, *El Tequila: Arte Tradicional de México*. Mexico City: Artes de Mexico, pp. 17–25.

Nemser, D. (2012). 'To avoid this mixture': Rethinking pulque in colonial Mexico City. *Food and Foodways*, 19(1), pp. 98–121.

Neu, D. (2000). Accounting and accountability relations: Colonization, genocide, and Canada's first nations. *Accounting, Auditing & Accountability Journal*, 13(3), pp. 268–288.

[No headline]. *San Francisco Chronicle*, 11 November 1907, p. 4.

OPA Establishes Price Controls for Tequila. *Daily Herald*, 13 October 1943, p. 3.

Palafox, R. (2001). Cantinas and drinkers in Mexico. In I. de Garine and V. de Garine, ed., *Drinking: Anthropological Approaches*. New York: Berghahn Books, pp. 169–180.

People Are Talking About. *Vogue*, 1 January 1956, p. 125.

Pratt, M. L. (1992). *Imperial Eyes: Travel Writing and Transculturation*. New York and London: Routledge.

Products of Jalisco. *Dallas Morning News*, 17 August 1907, p. 3.

Tequila Lounging Pajamas. *Idaho Statesman*, 28 April 1944, p. 10.

The prosperity of Mexico. *Boston Daily Advertiser*, 26 July 1873, p. 1.

Recio, G. (2002). Drugs and alcohol: US prohibition and the origins of the drug trade in Mexico, 1910–1930. *Journal of Latin American Studies*, 34(1), pp. 21–42.

Reynolds, L. (1943). Made in Mexico: U.S. imports: Tequila, pottery, glass, limes, huaraches and spiders. *Wall Street Journal*, 24 November 1943, p. 1.

Rodríguez, A. (1999). *Making Latino News: Race, Language, Class*. Thousand Oaks: Sage Press.
Simon, K. (2007). *Almost Famous: How Tequila Will Claim Its Place Among the World's Great Spirits*. Available at: www.imbibemagazine.com/almost-famous [Accessed 19th Feb. 2016].
Sobre la Mesa. *Tucson Citizen*, 18 January 1906, p. 8.
Tequila popular in US. *State*, 19 January 1956, p. 25.
Tequila tonic. *Topeka Weekly Capital*, 11 April 1889, p. 8.
Thornburg, S. and Roberts, R. (2012). 'Incorporating' American colonialism: Accounting and the Alaska native claims settlement act. *Behavioral Research in Accounting*, 24(1), pp. 203–214.
Tinker, T. (1980). Toward a political economy of accounting. *Accounting, Organizations and Society*, 5(1), pp. 147–160.
Vargas, D. (2012). *Dissonant Divas in Chicana Music: The Limits of La Onda*. Minneapolis: University of Minnesota Press.
Vila, P. (1997). The employment of the Mexican on the U.S.-Mexican border. *Sociological Quarterly*, 38(1), pp. 147–183.
Vinson, C. (1943). Life in Mexico little changed by Global War. *Dallas Morning News*, 24 January, p. 10.
Viqueira, A. (1987). *Propriety and Permissiveness in Bourbon Mexico*. Wilmington: Scholarly Resources Inc.
Vodka, tequila prices slashed. *San Luis Obispo Telegram-Tribune*, 26 May 1944, p. 4.
A wonder of the vegetable world, maguey and its cultivation. *Springfield Republican*, 28 July 1884, p. 2.
A wonderful plant: Marvels of the Mexican maguey, or century plant. *Wisconsin Weekly Advocate*, 28 December 1905, p. 6.
You're invited to old Mexico. *Milwaukee Journal-Sentinel*, 14 June 1942, p. 23.

10 Spirited accountants

The rise of the Distillers Company

William J. Jackson, Audrey S. Paterson and Darren Jubb

Introduction

Scotch whisky, like many alcoholic drinks, has a public persona that is so powerfully linked to its marketing that it can be difficult to detect the immense business presence that underlies it. Whisky is portrayed as a traditional craft product, made in the Highlands from pure water and simple fine ingredients in a process that has remained unchanged for centuries. Images of its origin show beautiful remote places, while images of its consumption display it as a sophisticated lifestyle choice, offered in crystal glasses and clubrooms. Through this, it is difficult to detect the multinational nature and vast scale of many of the businesses behind the product. Even less is it possible to detect the importance of accounting to the industry. The casual observer of the marketing around whisky could easily be misled into thinking that the individual businesses are so small and craft-orientated that sophisticated accounting practice would be out of place.

Of course, the reality is far different. Certainly, historical examination would suggest that two centuries ago the vast majority of distilling operations were small and individually owned, but now the industry is dominated by huge companies like Diageo, Pernod Ricard and Louis Vuitton Moet Hennessy (LVMH). These companies have arisen out of aggressive competition in an intense business environment that is characterised by extreme periodic cycles. This chapter will examine some of the roles that accounting has played in the transformation of the whisky industry from its simple roots to its current complexity, with particular reference to the development of the Distillers Company Limited (DCL). To achieve this, we have drawn upon a range of sources that discuss the 1850–1925 period, but particular weight has been given to Barnard's (1887) *Whisky Distilleries of the United Kingdom* for the background to the distilleries, Jackson et al. (2012) for the Pattison's crash and Weir (1995) for the development of DCL.

Accounting in the whisky industry: a calculative environment

A cursory examination of the modern whisky industry quickly reveals the intensity of its focus on numbers, including accounting numbers. The website of the Scotch Whisky Association, for example, gleefully talks about £4bn of exports, 10,000 directly employed and 40,000 jobs supported, £1bn in taxes that annually goes to the UK exchequer and 115 licensed distilleries responsible for producing the 20 million casks currently maturing in warehouses across Scotland, amongst a host of other often quirkily presented statistics (Scotch Whisky Association, 2015). But an examination of reliable sources quickly reveals an equal enthusiasm for figures even in the early days of the industry. One such source is the encyclopaedic *The Whisky Distilleries of the United Kingdom*, produced by Alfred Barnard in 1887.

Barnard was the secretary of the wine trade journal *Harpers Weekly Gazette* and around 1885 he conceived the idea of visiting every active distillery in the United Kingdom, which at that time included the island of Ireland. The ambition of this plan becomes apparent when we consider that he and his companions ultimately visited 161 distilleries in Scotland, England and Ireland over the course of two years. The resultant volume is an extraordinary compendium of information on distilleries and distilling practice in the late 19th century, with a wonderful level of detail shown throughout. It might have been expected that Barnard would have adopted a colourful prose style for the magazine, but despite occasional digressions into descriptions of Highland scenery the work was clearly aimed at a specialist readership.

Each distillery receives its own section, and its assets and processes are described in detail, although on some occasions, when it is clear that the distillery was the second one visited in a day, the descriptions are briefer and the details less fulsome. We can only speculate on the reasons for this.[1] However, the entries are typically two pages in length, but sometimes much longer, as in the case of Dail-Uaine, which received a full six pages of text and two full-page engravings.[2] The quantification in the entries is extensive, with details of the lengths and breadths of buildings (including the materials of construction); the capacities of the plant, such as the mash tun, washbacks and stills; quantities of raw materials used; and volumes of spirits produced and stored.

No doubt, some of this measurement could have been done by Barnard on site by pacing out the distances, but the fine details of capacities and quantities clearly indicates data derived from distilleries' records. The ability to do this without fail at each distillery is notable and demonstrates a high level of record keeping at each site. We might speculate that this is evidence of the increasing sophistication of Victorian business practice, were it not for an entry earlier in the book, in a section on the history of the industry, where he reproduces a detailed statement of the cost and potential profit of a batch of distillation from Smith's (1725) work *The Compleat Body of Distilling*. This statement suggests a long association between distilling and record keeping, and it is not necessary to read Barnard's book in any great detail to understand why, for regularly throughout the text we find the presence of the exciseman. At the vast Port Dundas distillery in Glasgow, for example, he observes that 'the collection of the Inland Revenue necessitates a staff of 21 officers, including two supervisors' (Barnard, 1887, p. 23), to oversee the production of a workforce of 250. Indeed, it was normal for any distillery, even one of moderate scale, to have an in-house exciseman, and obviously this was an important driver of meticulous accounting.

At Dundashill distillery, Barnard witnessed the excisemen in action:

> [T]he vats have ample capacity for reducing five thousand gallons at a time, and from them, the Whisky is filled off into puncheons, hogsheads or quarter-casks as may be required. The contents of the casks are ascertained by weight and by means of the indication or specific gravity of the spirit, which is taken by the Inland Revenue Officers and checked by one of Messrs. Harvey's clerks. After being filled off the Whisky is generally allowed to remain in the spirit-store for forty-eight hours; the strength is then carefully tested by the excise officers, checked again by the clerk, and thereafter the casks are filled full to the bung, and removed to the bonded Warehouses.
>
> (Barnard, 1887, p. 23)

This process was obviously highly labour intensive, and no doubt the employment of such a large army of staff by the Inland Revenue was an extremely costly undertaking. But the reason for their presence is entirely clear. As Barnard observed early in the book:

> [S]o vast has this industry grown, that for the financial year 1884–5, the duty on British Spirits realised no less than £13,987,422, being a sum nearly one-sixth of the entire Revenue of the Nation, and being more than sufficient to entirely provide for the expenses of the Navy; and its importance can only be fully realised by a careful consideration of these vast figures of revenue.
>
> (Barnard, 1887, p. 6)

Given the scale and importance of this to the British government, it is easy to understand why excise/revenue men were swarming around the distilleries. Under these conditions it can be no surprise that the quality and completeness of accounting data would be of the very highest standard.[3] Indeed, the administration of distilleries was taking place in a highly calculative environment, which seems to have affected the industry overall. Perhaps it is unlikely that Barnard appreciated the impact that the tax collectors were having, but we suspect he must have noticed the facility with which distillery managers were able to produce the figures that he requested.

In every distillery the bookkeepers and clerks must have been constantly busy checking and recording production data as the business of whisky making went on. It also seems clear that the tools of their craft must have been in plentiful supply. Burns (2009, pp. 149–152) quotes in full the contents of a pamphlet entitled *Doings of a Notorious Glasgow Shebeener*, from the 1870s, which is an extraordinary exposition on the costs and profitability of producing and selling bad whisky. Daiches (1969, p. 99) tells of William Sanderson, the founder of the firm that made the 'Vat 69' blend, experimenting with blending and noting the results of his experiments 'in a cash book headed "Adventures in Aqua"'. Other distillers showed great facility with numbers in the furtherance of their business. The legendary Thomas Robert (Tommy) Dewar, who regularly travelled the world on sales missions, found himself confronted upon his arrival in Québec by a commission considering the possibility of applying prohibition to the sale of alcohol. Undaunted, Dewar did not seek to make wordy arguments on the rights and freedoms of man, rather, he sent to the commissioners:

> some statistics showing the average life of various classes of drinkers; amongst them being the total abstainers, who had the shortest average, and the habitual drunkard, whose average was two years longer!
>
> (Quoted in Andrews, 2002, p. 41)

As some of these examples illustrate, any reading of the history of whisky will quickly reveal a constant struggle, at least until the 20th century, between whisky producers and the law. The traditional issues were illegal production and smuggling, but by the late 19th century these problems were waning. First, changes to taxation and the introduction of a new licensing system in 1823 meant that good profits could be made through legitimate operations, with a resultant decline in illegal activity. Second, the issue of bad whisky as described by Burns (2009)[4] began to reduce as reputable manufacturers moved towards the production of sealed bottles, rather than delivering their whisky in casks which could be tampered with. Also in the second half of the 19th century, a row broke out about the exact nature of whisky and whether or not Scotch whisky included all of the categories of malt, blended and grain whiskies, or, as the purists would have it, only malt whisky qualified. The outcome of the struggle over identity was largely determined by those companies that by then were the key players in the industry, as we explore next.

The development of the industry

At this point, we will provide a little context. By the second half of the 19th century, whisky was being produced in two basic forms: malt whisky and grain whisky. Malt whisky is made via the traditional form of production in pot stills using entirely malted barley, which is a relatively expensive base ingredient. Grain whisky, on the other hand, can be made from a variety of ingredients such as unmalted barley, wheat, rye and maize. These can be mixed and are typically cheaper than malted barley. In addition, the process of making grain whisky uses the patent or column still, a much more efficient continuous distillation process that again reduces cost. However, the output of a grain distillery is typically much less flavoursome than that of a malt distillery, due in part to the ingredients used, but mainly due to the very high alcohol strength of the output, which means that only a small amount of flavor-bearing compounds are left in the distillate. This led to accusations from malt distillers that the output of grain distilleries was not true whisky. The dispute was ultimately resolved after a series of cases brought by the Islington Borough Council in London, which took it upon itself to defend the rights of its consumers against what it saw as fraudulent trading practices.[5] The real crux of the matter, however, was the competition that the malt distillers felt from the cheaper and more efficient industrialised process employed by the grain distilleries.

In the seeds of this industrialisation, we can detect hints of sophisticated capital investment decision making. Before the introduction of the patent (or Coffey) still, distilling equipment had changed little for hundreds of years, and anyone entering the industry was faced with a similar level of investment as the competition. The patent still, however, was a much more expensive piece of plant than a traditional pot still, by a factor of around five. By what process then did the manufacturers of the patent stills (mainly Coffey) manage to convince the distillers that this much larger-scale investment was worthwhile? Weir (1995) points to the evidence presented before the *Royal Commission on Whiskey* of 1908, in which a distillery owner, who operated both pot and patent stills, gave evidence based upon the differing capital:output ratios of the two approaches. In all instances the patent still provided a much higher level of output for capital employed. While this evidence was being presented several decades after patent stills were first used, it is indicative of the kind of thinking that distillers were using to transform processes towards a more industrial style of production.

Prospective investors in the industry may also have been persuaded that there was less risk of ending up with an unusable product after the adoption of a patent still. Malt whiskies are famously variable. McDowall (1975) discusses the possible reasons for variations in malt whisky, ranging from the water source, type of barley, source of barley, type of peat, shape of still, size of still, method of heating and speed of heating (pp. 114–117).[6] The extent to which these factors affect the finished product was then, as now, very poorly understood. However, the danger for the distiller was that the peculiar combination of factors of any particular malt distillery might produce a product that was unpalatable, with the resultant disastrous effects on profit. The patent still virtually removed this risk by producing output that was so close to pure alcohol, with very little flavor-bearing compound left in, that it was highly unlikely to taste bad since it did not taste of anything much at all. In addition, and because of the reasons noted earlier, the patent still distilleries could be located almost anywhere that had a good water supply, so distilleries could be located close to the main markets, thereby reducing transportation and distribution costs (Weir, 1995, p. 25). Thus, it seems likely that the calculations involved in capital investment decision making over the industrialisation of the process hinged not only on production efficiencies but also on risk reduction and distribution costs.

While patent still distillers were able to mitigate some risks of production mentioned earlier, there were a number of others that were harder to deal with. Regular rises in duty on alcohol was a constant threat to the industry as a whole, with each rise bringing a reduction in UK consumption of whisky. Exacerbating this problem were the longer lead times associated with whisky, as there was increasing expectation of cask ageing, especially in those expressions that were being marketed as high quality. As the number of patent stills in use rose, so did the output of the Scottish distilleries, giving rise to the danger of serious oversupply. Because of the enormous capacity of each additional patent still, the volume of whisky produced stepped up dramatically in the middle of the 19th century. This danger was recognised by many of the patent still producers, which made initial attempts to cooperate in 1856 and 1865. Although the first attempt was short lived, the second had more duration, and six of the larger grain whisky producers formally combined into the Distillers Company Limited (DCL) in 1877, in one action creating a giant of the industry that would ultimately become the largest alcoholic drinks company in the world.

The malt distilleries were relatively disparate voices against the might of DCL, but there was a counterweight in the form of the great blending houses. In the second half of the 19th century, experimentation had begun with the mixing of malt and grain whiskies, a practice that was to become known as blending. The merit of blending was that it reduced the potency of malt whisky while giving flavour to the grain, resulting in a product which had a much wider market appeal. This happened shortly before the French vines were decimated by an American aphid called phylloxera, resulting in a shortage of grapes for wine and brandy. In 1877, Barnard observed:

> French brandy is, as an article of general consumption, hopelessly discredited, the phylloxera and other diseases of the vine have destroyed the material for the production of a spirit which will suit the ordinary purse. For some occult reason, nobody that is anybody drinks, except for the treatment of a cold. Gin, with all its many merits, fails to gain new drinkers, while the old consumers seem to be dying out. The opportunity of whisky is, therefore, overwhelming.
>
> (Barnard, 1887, p. 11)

The new blended Scotch whiskies moved swiftly into the gap in the market, and a number of blenders quickly became exceedingly wealthy.[7] The big five brands were Haig, Buchanan's, Dewar's, Johnny Walker and White Horse, and they became ubiquitous throughout the British Empire, North America and beyond, and it was their influence that stopped DCL from immediately dominating the whisky business.

The business environment generally was intensely competitive and it was no different in the spirit trade; in fact, many of the practices employed were extremely risky, anti-competitive or downright fraudulent. Financiers in general seemed willing to take significant risks in the whisky business. One example of this was the overdraft held by Dewar's, which at one point exceeded £300,000, twice the authorised capital of the original business. Such risk taking was indicative of both the confidence of the players in the industry and their financial backers. However, such confidence was not necessarily justified by the accounting practices being employed at the time. DCL was formed out of what was effectively a cartel called the Scottish Distillers Association (SDA) formed in 1865 and held much the same aims as its predecessor. Its anti-competitive aims were to 'regulate prices, sales, and "conditions of sale", such things as discounts, warehouse rents, and credit' (Weir, 1995, p. 33). Ironically, perhaps, the amalgamation of six of the largest grain distillers into DCL occurred due to repeated breakdowns and infringements of the rules of the SDA. Clearly, to operate such an arrangement indefinitely, there needed to be reasonably open and honest sharing of information, but Weir points to secret deals and discounts that were happening between members and external parties and amongst the members themselves (Weir, 1995, pp. 32–41). The accounting between the members of the SDA was, therefore, clearly not always as open and honest as the founders of the body had intended. Nevertheless, the SDA was successful enough to persuade the majority of its members that there was merit in amalgamation, which would eliminate the competition between them. In other instances, however, questionable accounting practices were less successful, and in one particularly catastrophic case, fraudulent accounting was responsible for terrible damage to the entire industry.

Accounting and the Pattison's crash

As the 1890s opened, the whisky industry was in an enviable position, with a major boom in sales and exceptional profits being realised. Wilson (1970) gives the annual growth in UK spirits sales as 3.9% throughout the decade, and whisky was taking a growing share of that market. Furthermore, global demand was rapidly increasing as the image of whisky shifted from that of a poor man's drink to the drink of choice for the middle and upper classes. The profits of DCL more than doubled across the decade (Wilson, 1970), but it was the blenders that made the biggest profits. The big companies opened offices in major English cities and began to expand across the British Empire, which was then at its zenith. Stable trading networks, safe passage for British vessels (guaranteed by the dominance of the Royal Navy) and access to new and growing economies seemed to offer limitless potential for expansion – a prospect seized by both the blenders and their financiers alike (Jackson et al., 2012). The primary problem that the industry faced was a lack of capacity to meet the demand and so huge expansion ensued, with production volumes rising by 43% between 1893 and 1898 alone. The boom drove confidence in the trade and the companies increasingly sought stock market listings, the proceeds of which further enriched their founders and drew even more attention to their success. Some of the players realised the potential of the publicity surrounding the boom and deliberately sought to draw attention to their success with a view to further promoting the industry and, of course, their own wealth.

Tommy Dewar and James Buchanan employed the tactics of publicity seeking extensively and perfected the art of placing their brands in the public eye, and in doing so they became famous public figures and celebrities in their own right. These tactics were observed by others and copied to greater or lesser effect. For a while, in the 1890s, the Pattison brothers, Walter and Robert, adopted these tactics and their antics were regularly reported in the news media. Alongside large volumes of dramatic advertising, the brothers engaged in publicity stunts, such as training parrots to say 'Drink Pattison's Whisky!' before placing them in bars. No doubt the newspaper reporting of the campaign had far more impact than the unfortunate birds did. Other reports spoke of Robert missing the last train to his Borders estate so that he could order a private train to take him home at phenomenal expense (Daiches, 1969). This form of conspicuous consumption fuelled both publicity and the boom and led to investors throwing money at the industry with the inevitable formation of a speculative bubble. We can surmise that the undue inflation of asset values was an objective promoted by some industry participants, and certainly in the case of the Pattison brothers it had the desired effect, at least initially. What the public did not know was that in some cases the inflation of asset values was affected by much more than just publicity seeking.

To this day it remains unclear how prevalent questionable accounting practices were in the whisky industry in the late 19th century, but what is clear is that the Pattison brothers worked hard at generating cash flow from what was, in reality, a fairly limited asset base. The boom itself was undoubtedly partly to blame, as it created an unwarranted confidence among suppliers and financiers alike. DCL was caught in the Pattison's web as it offered extraordinarily generous terms to the company. Weir (1995) recounts how the mighty grain whisky producer gave Pattison's loans substantial discounts and ultimately a business agreement that, in retrospect, was eye-watering in its generosity. The essence of the deal centred around the practice of holding whisky in bond until it was required for sale. Bonds are secure warehousing units that allow the spirit to be stored without paying duty on it. This was, and remains, extremely important for the financing of the industry. If duty was to be paid at the point of production, then clearly it would create an onerous funding requirement for producers to the point of being a major barrier to entry and drag on competition. By holding whisky in bond until the point of sale, at which point the duty is applied, producers defer this substantial cost. However, DCL offered Pattison's a deal that went much further. The agreement was that DCL would transfer stock from their bond to one owned by Pattison's without any payment, either for the duty or the spirit. Further, when Pattison's sold the spirit they were not immediately required to pay DCL. Instead, DCL recognised the sale and the potential future cash flow and wrote Pattison's a cheque for the duty, which was immediately payable to the tax authorities, thus supporting Pattison's cash flow until three months after the sale to the final customer, at which point they were required to repay DCL with interest. There can be little doubt that these terms were generous, but no accusation can be laid at the door of DCL beyond that of a supportive (although perhaps slightly naïve in this case) attitude towards its customers.

As stated earlier, such deals were reflective of the prevailing confidence in the industry at the time, a confidence that was also held and acted upon by the finance industry; a confidence that might have suffered a gentle cyclical decline if all the players had acted in good faith. However, by the late 1890s the

Pattisons were up to their necks in such deals. Fuelled by easy credit and cheap loans, they had built a personal lifestyle and public persona that demanded large amounts of cash flow to support country estates, 'palatial' new headquarters in Leith and extravagant marketing campaigns. As a result, they began to perpetrate a series of accounting frauds in a range of forms. In relation to their arrangements with DCL, they were required to show excise certificates to their supplier to establish the stocks that they retained in bond. This was acceptable, but they were also using these same certificates as evidence of assets to obtain bank loans (Weir, 1995). In addition, they were selling these same assets multiple times to different customers who sought to secure future stocks in a market where prices were rising but who did not seek to take possession of the stocks at the point of sale in order to avoid paying the duty before they needed the whisky. Thus, the ownership of any particular barrel of whisky in Pattison's bond was extremely obscure. As Jackson et al. (2012) recount, the brothers were able to:

> generate huge amounts of cash by exchanging bills drawn on overvalued whisky that had often been sold to more than one customer, used as an asset for borrowing from the bank and which had probably been supplied by DCL and not yet paid for.
>
> (p. 651)

In the light of this fraud, Pattison's other fraudulent practice of blending grain and malt and selling it as pure malt, which carried a higher price, seems relatively trivial. In 1896 the brothers floated the company and offered £150,000 of preference shares, which were massively over-subscribed and clearly, in retrospect, based on fictitious asset values. Ultimately, the fraudulent practices adopted by the Pattisons led to their company's collapse,[8] which in turn led to the collapse of a number of supplier companies[9] along with investor and consumer confidence in the industry (Jackson et al., 2012). The extent of the accounting fraud, alongside the failure of the auditors, shocked investors, and it became clear under the ensuing scrutiny that accounting practice across the industry left much to be desired.

What followed was a period of lost confidence, retrenchment, falling sales, a recognition of overvalued stocks throughout the industry and a need to reduce the production of spirit. It was at this time that DCL began to adopt a pattern of activity that would see them attempt to rescue the industry from its woes. Recognising the overcapacity in the industry and the weakness of many of its players, DCL began to acquire distilleries, often at very low prices, and take them out of production in order to protect the future values of existing whisky stocks. As a result, a number of distilleries were closed, including some of those that had been newly built in the boom of the 1890s. With this approach, DCL stabilised its asset values and consolidated its position as the giant at the heart of the industry, until the outbreak of World War I, when nearly all distilleries were either closed or diverted to the production of war materials.[10]

The rise of the Distillers Company

In the meantime, the blenders began to have increasing concerns about the power of DCL and the level of competition in the market, which was requiring them all to spend increasingly inflated sums on advertising. In 1909, Buchanan's, Dewar's and Walker attempted merger talks, but according to Weir (1995) failed on the rock of distrust, as each of the parties was unwilling to open their accounts to the others. In particular, they each offered balances of their assets, but little further information. John Dewar observed in a letter that Walker's 'do not wish us to see how the balances have been arrived at . . . and they have little hope that we will be fools enough to go eight years back' (Weir, 1995, p. 168). Each of them was most likely trying to inflate the asset values by including their best years and excluding the worst. The problem was worse for Walker's, as their policy was to buy new and store to maturity, which had cost them heavily as the price of aged stock fell during the first decade of the century. The others had profited by holding much less stock and buying mature whisky increasingly cheaply from the market. There was a proposal that the adoption of uniform accounting methods would promote sharing of information and progress towards agreement (Weir, 1995), but this plan also failed. In the end the attempt failed on the ambiguity of asset values and an inability to agree on the earning power of the constituents. Soon, however, another scheme raised its head and this time it included DCL. Discussions around a possible merger with DCL were broadly seen in a positive light by these three big blending companies, but once again foundered on their own inability to reach agreement amongst themselves. Nevertheless, Buchanan's and Dewar's did finally amalgamate without Walker's in 1915 (Daiches, 1969), the similarity of their operations in the previous few years allowing them to have confidence in the valuations.

World War I created many challenges for the industry and production was hit hard as the UK government sought to discourage drinking and at the same time looked for other outputs, more supportive to the war effort, from the distilleries. During this time the big blenders and DCL learned to cooperate more effectively, but William Ross of DCL continued to seek amalgamation and consolidation of the industry. By 1922, DCL had effective control over the production of grain whisky, having subsumed its major competition and made trade agreements to control production and pricing with the majority of the remaining small producers (Wilson, 1970). In addition, DCL had begun to make acquisitions in the UK blending trade, a move that was ostensibly forced by a wartime ruling that they needed to continue to supply the customers of a firm that they had acquired in 1917 for the stocks it held. This looked less convincing as an excuse when, in 1919, DCL also amalgamated with Haig and other blending companies. As the 1920s ensued, cooperation over production, pricing, marketing and consolidation continued to grow; however, an argument between the big three and DCL over the use of a brand threatened initially to derail friendly relations, but ultimately led to recognition that the only way to secure their common interests was to reconsider amalgamation (Weir, 1995).

Inevitably, the primary challenge, once again, was to agree on valuations. Ross for DCL sought to simplify matters by asking for stock exchange values to be used, but Gilbert Garnsey, Buchanan-Dewar's accountant was opposed on the grounds that they were not disclosing full profits and were therefore undervalued on the exchange. What Garnsey failed to appreciate was that the limited disclosure practiced by Buchanan-Dewar was also a fact for DCL. Ross pressed the negotiations to the point of near fracture, pushing his position until it looked as if failure was inevitable and then, at the eleventh hour, he revealed the true financial position of DCL (Weir, 1995). The company's profits were three times what was reported and reserves, mostly private, amounted to around £4m, with evidence of trading arrangements that guaranteed its future profitability (Weir, 1995). After Price-Waterhouse confirmed the truth of Ross's figures, opposition amongst the blenders collapsed as they realised the advantages to be gained by combination with the DCL juggernaut and all of Ross's main conditions were accepted, with completion in 1925.

Conclusion

The merger of 1925 between DCL and Buchanan-Dewar completed the horizontal and vertical integration of the whisky industry into an effective monopoly, with DCL becoming the UK's sixth-largest manufacturing company by 1930. There can be little doubt as to the importance of accounting practices to this development. The high tax scrutiny environment of the distilleries inevitably made them a highly calculative environment, and a facility with numbers would have been a prerequisite for success. It is clear from the aftermath of the Pattisons' crash that the boundary between creative accounting and fraud was rather fuzzy and resulted in problems that extended far beyond the crash alone. The tendency towards partial disclosure and extremely selective valuation practices arguably delayed the consolidation of the big firms for about 15 years. Of course, it is hard to argue that the creation of a monopoly was advantageous to any individual consumer, but it did allow for the creation of a world-bestriding giant company that to this day retains the admiration and respect of its competitors at home and abroad. It is also notable that despite all the obfuscation practiced by the players, it was ultimately a move towards transparency that allowed this feat to happen.

Notes

1 One interesting example of this is the now world-famous Macallan distillery. In the morning, Barnard and his team had visited the Glen Spey distillery and may have received exceptional hospitality. The entry for the afternoon visit to Macallan runs to a cursory seven lines and is almost embarrassing in its brevity, referring to it as an 'old-fashioned establishment'.

2 While the entry on Dail-Uaine is indeed very detailed on the workings of the distillery, it is also one of the places where Barnard breaks into floral language, observing that 'never was there such a soft, bright landscape of luxuriant green, of clustering foliage, and verdant banks of wildflowers, ferns and grasses. The whole scene is dainty enough for a Fairy's palace' (Barnard, 1887, p. 201).

3 Where records survive, distillery archives are likely to be an important source for the accounting historian, due to the detailed and accurate nature of the records kept.
4 This largely related to the production of drinks using cheap and often dangerous materials and passing them off as the real thing. Profits from this were substantial, but the danger to the public was great. Attempts by the authorities to clamp down on the illicit trade met with limited success, and it was eventually changes in the distribution methods that had the greatest impact.
5 The first 61 pages of Wilson (1970) provide an excellent, detailed account of these events, which clearly reveals the tensions that existed variously between the malt and grain distillers and the blenders
6 It is almost certainly the case that this variability discouraged experimentation in malt distilleries. Distillers that were happy with the quality of their spirit were very reluctant to make changes, especially to the stills, for fear it may be detrimental to their product (Weir, 1995, p. 25).
7 For an excellent account of the rise of the whisky blenders, see Andrews (2002).
8 Ironically this happened only 13 days after the Pattison's auditor had given them a clean bill of health.
9 There is no clarity on the extent to which Pattisons were defrauding other suppliers. The court case was long and complicated, and ten of Pattison's suppliers had collapsed long before it was concluded and the brothers convicted and jailed.
10 During the war many distilleries produced acetone for munitions, an effort that arguably helped the industry to survive the duration of the conflict. This effort was led by William Ross, then managing director of DCL.

References

Andrews, A. (2002). *The Whisky Barons*. Glasgow: The Angels Share, Neil Wilson Publishing.

Barnard, A. (1887). *The Whisky Distilleries of the United Kingdom*. London: The Proprietors of Harper's Weekly Gazette.

Burns, E. (2009). *Bad Whisky: The Scandal that Created the World's Most Successful Spirit*. Glasgow: Neil Wilson Publishing.

Daiches, D. (1969). *Scotch Whisky: Its Past and Present*. Norwich: Jarrold & Sons Ltd.

Jackson, W. J., Paterson, A. S., Pong, C. K. M. and Scarparo, S. (2012). 'How easy can the barley brie': Drinking culture and accounting failure at the end of the 19th century in Britain. *Accounting, Auditing and Accountability Journal*, 25(4), pp. 635–658.

McDowall, R. J. S. (1975). *The Whiskies of Scotland*. Throwbridge: Redwood Burn Ltd.

The Scotch Whisky Association (2015). *Facts and Figures*. Available at: www.scotch-whisky.org.uk/what-we-do/facts-figures/ [Accessed 25th Sept. 2017].

Smith, G. (1725). *A Compleat Body of Distilling, Explaining the Mysteries of that Science: In a Most Easy and Familiar Manner: Containing an Exact and Accurate Method of Making All the Compound Cordial-Waters Now in Use, With a Particular Account of their Several Virtues: As Also a Directory Consisting of all the Instructions Necessary for Learning the Distillers Art: With a Computation of the Original Cost of the Several Ingredients, and the Profits Arising in Sale: Adapted No Less to the Use of Private Families, than of Apothecaries and Distillers: In Two Parts*. London: Printed for Bernard Lintot.

Weir, R. (1995). *The History of the Distillers Company 1877–1939: Diversification and Growth in Whisky and Chemicals*. Oxford: Clarendon Press.

Wilson, R. (1970). *Scotch: The Formative Years*. London: Constable.

Part 3

Accounting for wine and viniculture

11 Accounting and wine in Anjou (Maine et Loire) during the 19th century

Valentin Taveau and Béatrice Touchelay

Introduction

In Anjou, as elsewhere in France, viniculture was practised during the 19th century on numerous smallholdings and with two or more different grape varieties being fermented in the same vat. The sale of wine brought in an income which, although meagre and uncertain, provided for the producer's subsistence. Except in the Bordeaux and Champagne regions (Perron, 2016, p. 118), where it had been established for longer, specialisation in grape cultivation in regions such as the Anjou Valley and the organisation of the wine market (Fontaine, 2014) were in the hands of more or less specialised intermediaries, the so-called *négociants*. At the mercy of the uncertainties of the climate and the quality of the grapes, these *négociants* sought to diversify their suppliers and to safeguard their outlets. Since transactions were seldom immediately settled in cash, their success depended on the trust their partners accorded them, on the worth of their signature and on their ability to repay the sums required for their activities. Legal rules, such as those contained in the edict of 1673 and the Code of Commerce 1807, obliged them to keep accounts books in order to record their operations. Each of these books – *Brouillard, Journal* (Lemarchand, 2016a, p. 389), *Grand livre* (Lemarchand, 2016b, pp. 388–389), *Inventaire*, general ledgers and sub-ledgers (Degos, 2016, p. 386) – had a specific function; they were complementary and hierarchised. They shed light on *négociants'* day-to-day commercial activities, providing information on the location of clients and suppliers, the volume of business, the costs incurred and the capital committed. Yardsticks for a company's influence and reputation (Gervais, 1996), they shaped its good name and renown.

The archives of the *département* of Maine et Loire (ADML) contain the accounts books of two *Maisons de vin*, that of René-Jean Goubault-Lambert at Rochefort sur Loire and that of Jean-Baptiste Ackerman-Laurance, a Belgian *négociant* who introduced the production of wine in the *façon de champagne* in 1831, after settling in Saumur since 1811 as *négociant*. These documents bear witness to the changes in accounting practices and make it possible to follow the development of these businesses. The small number of books from the first *Maison* provide information on a small business that operated on a regional basis, failed to make a name for itself in the wine market and collapsed (1810–1848).

The books kept by Ackerman-Laurance, *négociant* and producer of sparkling wines for England and Belgium mainly, traditional markets for Anjou wine producers, testify to the foundation of a new economy in Saumur. The Ackerman-Laurance collection is remarkable in its size, the length of the period covered (1831–1984) and the business expansion recorded in the documents, despite the company's difficult beginnings.[1]

The first part of this chapter is given over to an examination of the oldest books, kept by the *négociants* themselves in order to meet their legal obligations. It finishes with the closure of business of Goubault Lambert in 1848 and the bankruptcy of the Ackerman-Laurance business in 1842. The downward spiral leading to collapse is evident in the accounts. While the first *Maison* ceased to exist altogether, Ackerman-Laurance enjoyed renewed prosperity from the mid-19th century onwards, as the *Grand livre* examined in the second part shows. The increase in the volume of business, diversification of partners, technical innovation, a boom in orders from abroad, the support provided by creditors and the improved bookkeeping all help to explain the successes of the 1860s. After the founder's death in 1866, the family business was taken over by his son, Louis Ferdinand Ackerman-Laurance, who modernised it, started the specialisation in sparkling wines and laid the foundations for its conversion into a limited liability company, thereby launching the company into its third period. The *Compagnie générale des vins mousseux – Société Ackerman-Laurance* with capital of 3 million Francs was founded in 1894. The accounts, already meticulous, became positively pointillist, and the books proliferated in size and number. Their purpose now was to provide accounts for members and to produce a balance sheet and a profit and loss account (Labardin, 2016, pp. 228–229). Accounting was no longer simply descriptive and for the sole use of the *négociant*; it became forward-looking and was intended to convince members of the managers' good practices. It was no longer confined to a description of operations but also placed profits, profitability and cost control among its priorities. What did these changes indicate and what was their nature? Were they specific to the trade in alcohol? The accounting documents and analysis of the purposes, techniques and practices of their compilers will provide a basis for answering these questions. The history of the wine-producing area of the Anjou Valley, where the *Maison* Ackerman-Laurance played a role, will be now be briefly presented.

The history of vineyards and winemaking in Anjou

The development of viniculture in the French countryside has always supplied a supplement of cash essential to the farmers, but the phylloxera (or Great French Wine Blight) of the 19th century decimated vineyards. The cost of the restoration of vineyards condemned the smallest wine growers and led to the specialisation of wine-producing regions. Anjou benefits from its closeness of the Parisian market and of the episodic demand of champagne production. The region benefited by specialising (Moulin, 1988). This demands a network of intermediaries, suppliers and regular financing and careful management because neither orders nor production is certain. Only *Maisons* with family capital and robust financial networks can prosper. The rigour of bookkeeping and a precise inventory of customer accounts and suppliers are essential conditions of a durable success.

There is evidence that grapes have been cultivated in the Anjou Valley since the final years of the Roman Empire. In the Early Middle Ages, the cultivation of grapes was undertaken and administered by monasteries and churches in the towns and cities of the province, and notably in the city of Angers. The rule of the House of Plantagenet brought the wines of Anjou to the tables of the English aristocracy. They enjoyed the protection of the kings of England (John Lackland and Henry II), who issued edicts and safe conducts. Wines were exported to the kingdom's northwestern provinces and to England by river (Dion, 2010). The multiple crises of the Late Middle Ages put an end to the expansion of the vineyards, which became concentrated again around the towns of Angers and Saumur and were subjected to stricter control by the ecclesiastical and seigniorial authorities for commercial and fiscal purposes. Administered by the towns and oriented more to serving the far-flung parts of the province, the vineyards and wines of Anjou relied on the Loire as a trading route, which ensured their continued existence (Matz, 2010).

The French Revolution and the Napoleonic Wars cut the Anjou vineyards off from their foreign markets. Winemakers redirected their output to the domestic market, which absorbed wines of mediocre quality (*vins de Paris*). It was only the hope of finding outlets in Northern Europe that kept a small amount of good-quality winemaking alive (*les vins de mer*).[2] The presence of the Loire and then the arrival of the railways, the keys to opening up the region, are two of the reasons why winemaking survived in the Anjou region in the 19th century (Dion, 1978). Another crucial factor was the introduction of *façon de champagne* vinification for Touraine and Anjou wines by a far-sighted *négociant* named Jean-Baptiste Ackerman-Laurance (Taveau, 2017).

Perfunctory accounts books: termination of business and bankruptcy

Jean-Baptiste Ackerman-Laurance was a contemporary of René-Jean Goubault-Lambert, a wine merchant at Rochefort sur Loire, who also sold *eau de vie*, vinegar and building materials and, according to his accounts books, established his business in 1810 and ceased trading in 1848. The Ackerman-Laurance summary accounts (1831–1842) and several of Goubault-Lambert's books shed light on accounting practices that were still in their infancy. Compiled by the *négociants*, the first was completed in haste to satisfy the requirements of the official assignee and the second is too muddled to sound an alarm on increasing debt. These books are evidence of the poor management of both businesses which, despite a certain degree of expansion, lost the confidence of their creditors.

The accounts books of the négociant Goubault-Lambert, or the chronicle of a bankruptcy foretold[3]

These documents are the only remaining traces of this business. They are handwritten notebooks, bound, with hardback covers. Some of them are in a poor state, but they are legible. They are all written in the same hand, undoubtedly that of Goubault-Lambert. The collection is part of the J series (private collections) and consists of three classification marks (108 J 1 to 3), which will be presented here in chronological order. The first (108 J 3) is entitled *Comptabilité de René-Jean Goubault-Lambert.* It consists of two notebooks similar to *Grands livres* covering the periods from 1 January 1801 to 9 May 1816 and from 13 April 1818 to 13 November 1820, respectively. A third document is a list of the *négociant*'s contacts, in alphabetical order and with an indication of their status ('owner at', etc.); each entry has a number referring back to the *Grand livre.*

The *Grand livre* records the transactions between the *négociant* and partners classified by accounts. In its most polished version (see later), a distinction is made between two categories of transactions listed on two pages of the notebook: on the left-hand side the *Doit* (debit) and on the right the *Avoir* (credit), listed in chronological order and by the accounts to be debited or credited. Consistency with the *Journal* is ensured by a transaction number (see later). Using the double-entry accounting system (Lemarchand, 2016c, pp. 390–393) and with numbered pages, this *Grand livre* was intended both as a record of the transactions and their originators and as a means of ensuring that the debit/credit balance remained in equilibrium.

In Goubault-Lambert's books, the *Doit* (X owes such and such a sum to Goubault-Lambert for such a transaction on such a date) and the *Avoir* (Goubault-Lambert received such a sum from Y for such a transaction on such a date) are recorded one after the other on the same page and in chronological order (day, month and year), with the name, in many cases the occupation and, as a matter of course, the account holder's place of residence and then the total amount of the transaction in francs. A line separates each account. On the left-hand side of each page there is a column headed *soldé* (paid or settled). Some of Goubault-Lambert's *Grands livres* are not available, as there are no figures for the period between 9 May 1816 and 13 April 1818. The way they were kept sometimes reveals a degree of disorganisation. The chronological limits heralded in their titles are not always adhered to. Thus, for example, although the stated end date was 13 November 1820, transactions up until 10 April 1821 were entered on a loose sheet inserted at the end of the second *Grand livre*. This *Grand livre* does not take up the whole notebook. Its final pages contain a series of tables added after 1821 that list the freight brought in by boat, the names of the vessels, the consignees and the shippers. There are also a number of omissions. On 29 February 1820, for example, in the case of a transaction settled on 3 June 1820 and involving an "*Avoir* from M Aubeux of Angers relating to 14 batons delivered on the *Soquié*", there is the following note: "owes me delivered at 3 *th* a pound, received on the 26th of the aforementioned but forgot to enter in accounts". Another omission was noted on 12 June 1820: "Brayé failed to turn up for work on the 3rd, 4th, 5th and 6th of the month last May and forgot to note it down". These early registers also display certain vagueness as to the unit of measurement used for the payments, with "*th*" and francs being used indiscriminately. This book also indicates that this was a family business: "1 July 1820, delivery of a barrel of lees to the widow Fouriat, hatter at Segré, 24 June by my mother at Samet".

The next classification mark 108 J 1 relates to a *Journal* of 497 pages intended to record the business affairs of René-Jean Goubault-Lambert starting on 1 January 1820 and finishing on 30 January 1830. The *Journal* is presented in the same way as a *Grand livre*. It overlaps with the previous one, which finished on 13 November, but does not refer to the same transactions. In all likelihood, this *Journal-Grand livre* relates to a new business, but there is no evidence to confirm this. The first entry dated 1 January 1820 is an *Avoir* from "Madame Vve Goubault Moreau, my mother, of Angers" concerning "the sum of one thousand francs that she lent to me and which is to be repaid when one or other party so wishes or by giving six months' notice in advance at a rate of interest of 5% per year from this day onwards". Goubault-Lambert used this loan to finance his *Maison*. It was not until 1 January 1821 that the next *Avoir* was entered, resulting from "two invoices addressed to M Chantelou at Les Rairies close to Durtal and another delivery to the commissioning company in Angers, settled for the total amount of 625 francs". This was an exceptional sum, since most of the recorded transactions were less than two decimals.

The occupations of the business's suppliers and customers were diverse. They included landowners (farmers no doubt), tavern keepers and coopers, as well as a notary and a locksmith. The scope of its operations was regional and it had one employee ("*Doit* to M Huet, my assistant, to pay him as much as previously and today in cash"). The business seemed to prosper from 1821 onwards. It sold in Mayenne on "22 May 1821 *Doit* Ecaril Barbutte brothers, hat makers in Courson, department of la Mayenne, two flagons of press wine shipped by Charbon, boatman at Angers, to the address of M Colet Corbinière, master of the port at Laval at the price of 18 francs each". A third *Avoir* was recorded in June 1821, in consideration of "the delivery of a barrel of vinegar", a commodity that could be used to build up customer loyalty ("*Doit* 13 July 1821 M Cormice, bursar at the royal college in Angers, 2 barrels of vinegar delivered to the courtyard of the said college", then "delivery to the royal college at La Flèche"). The cash flows inward thus improved as the clientele started to expand. Butchers rubbed shoulders with a baker, a priest at Behuard, a hat maker in Laval and another at Château-Gontier. The director of Hayon et Loire mines became a loyal customer. The scope of the *négociant*'s operations expanded as far as Cholet. He recorded *Avoirs* more regularly, often at the end of the calendar year, and for greater amounts. On 7 June 1825, for example, the accounts book records "the *Avoir* from Mr Giscqueau, grocer at Cholet, in the sum of 305 francs plus 280 francs drawn on Davillier et Cie of Paris transferred to my account on 10 July this year". Entries ceased on 26 January 1830 with no total or summary statement. Another document entitled *Journal des Avoirs 1820–1822* details the operations concluded with customers. The pages are numbered, on the left the *Doit* and on the right the *Avoir.* They are presented in columns headed, respectively: date, commodity, payment, number (a number referring to the *repertoire* and to the *Journal*) and *Doit* in francs; and: date, payment, number and *Avoir* in francs.

The final classification mark in the collection (108 J 2) is entitled *Grand livre. Journal destiné à établir les affaires de commerce de René-Jean Goubault-Lambert né à Rochefort sur Loire, commencé le 25 janvier 1830 et terminé le 19 décembre 1848.* It is evident from this that the business was in a state of collapse. Vinegar became its main commodity with some pressed lees but no wine. The book is less detailed. From 1833 onwards, the nature of the transactions is no longer specified in the *Avoir*, with only the sum in question being listed and the indication *pour solde* – for settlement – which denotes the end of the commercial relationship. The *négociant* was finding it difficult to get his clients to pay: "4 January 1839, *Avoir* M Jahon, mason in Rochefort 1.10 francs now just a memory" or: "30 November 1839, *Avoir* Widow, address at Duretal 24, Emile her brother has not paid back the money" or again "6 August 1841, the Rogeron and Chaux *Avoir* adds up to 52 francs to be credited against my warrant served on Guitton, the butcher still without payment". The *Avoir* increasingly reflected settling of debts incurred with bankers in Angers, including Descherers, who advanced a loan of 2,129 francs in 1841, and then Rogeron and Chaux. For example, on "13 April 1841, an *Avoir* of 46 francs from M Lamoureux, grocer at Chollet, paid in settlement transferred to M Rogeron on 30 April to cover the debt of 349 francs incurred with Rogeron and Chaux, bankers in Angers". The amount of loans exceeded the cash obtained from commercial transactions and was increasing. The *négociant* was becoming a tightrope walker. On 27 August 1848, 2195.37 francs were paid "in exchange for discounts on 30 June this year, from which the payment of 500 francs on 6 July has be deducted". On 2 September, the payment was "370 francs in exchange for a payable on presentation from Landais Delessard", while on 10 September it was "447 francs in exchange for a bill of exchange from Gastineau and a cash advance of 887 francs". Having already slowed down, the *négociant*'s activities were eventually to cease altogether. There were only six sales in 1843 and just a single one in 1846 and 1848, all for modest sums. The competition, the specialisation in vinegar, a little prized commodity, and the indebtedness to local bankers had got the better of the business.

Ackerman-Laurance the wine merchant and the Livre journal compiled for the bankruptcy

Jean-Baptiste Ackerman-Laurance's *Livre journal*, a handwritten document maintained between June 1831 and August 1842, is another exceptional document and the oldest one in the collection.[4] It brings together the information contained in the *Grand livre* and *Journal* and presents all the Ackerman-Laurance company's general accounts, purchases and sales. This substantial bound volume is not entirely complete: only the first 464 pages of the 600 that were available have been used. The entries stopped in 1842 when the company went bankrupt and an official assignee was appointed (Dequidt, 2016, p. 232). The book's final pages, which relate to operations between 1841 and 1842, were compiled hastily so that it could be submitted in good time. The headings of these pages, which specify the account for which each *Doit* and *Avoir* is intended, are simply jotted down with a lead pencil, in contrast to the preceding pages, where they are carefully inscribed in pen and ink. Thus, documents were not compiled day by day but in several stages, with the chronological information being transcribed and classified by account and the nature of the operation. An amalgam of the *Journal* and the *Grand livre* existed but is unavailable. It is constantly referred to, and this book would have given the history of the operations and the state of Ackerman-Laurance's finances. The company's bankruptcy occurred in the absence of any calculation of the debit/credit balance, which was also missing from Goubault-Lambert's accounts.

Nevertheless, this book represents an original source that sheds light on the *négociant*'s practices. It provides information on the development of his network of partners (creditors, suppliers, customers) and on the flows of merchandise, capital and cash that it generated. It also reveals the limits of a *Maison* that does not attract the capital required for expansion. However, the book is the demonstration of a management of the *Maison* which was not based on organisational rules and rational accounting practices, but on the daily decisions taken by Jean-Baptiste Ackerman-Laurance to meet the demands of suppliers and customers. Unfortunately, the work and traits of the *négociant* may not have been totally adapted to managing the industrial activity of sparkling wine production at this time.

This book records the *Doits* and *Avoirs* in columns, with a note made of the date (year, month, day), the reason for the operation, its number in the *Journal* and the *Grand livre* and the total value of each operation in francs. It includes all operations (bills of exchange, discounts, sales), classified by customer and type. "Bills of exchange and discounts" are recorded on the first 10 pages, then "interest and deals" on the following pages and "household expenses" spread over four pages (this heading suggests a degree of overlap between private and business life). The "client and supplier accounts" are then set out, their length depending on the volume of transactions; they are followed by two pages under the heading "overheads". Next come "private accounts", arranged more or less in alphabetical order, which list Ackerman-Laurance's main collaborators and business partners. Bourdon Constant, for example, "a young person from the Champagne region", worked for Ackerman from 1840 to 1842, having been posted to Saint Hilaire Saint Florent (where the *négociant*'s cellars were located) in 1838. And there was Noël Douzillé, "a middleman who purchases wines in the area of Tours". It would be tedious to list all the document's headings, so only the most noteworthy will be mentioned here. They include the "profit and loss" account (two pages), in which partial totals are recorded; accounts for individual towns and cities (Antwerp, Brest, Bruges, Brussels, Frankfurt on Main, Ostend, Leuven, London, Nantes, Rennes, Marseille and Saumur); and a two-page account with Belgium that attests to the extent of Ackerman's network. The operations are classified by type ("colonial commodities accounts" or "travel account", which records the costs incurred in visiting clients in Belgium, for example) and by product, attesting to the diversity of the commodities traded ("Wheat, broad bean, haricot bean, oil, rye, leather and wax account"), while the classification of the wines according to their provenance ("Bordeaux wines") and container ("wine in bottles") also helps to sustain the image of an active *Maison*.

The document also indicates that the *négociant* had savings and had diversified his investments ("Belgian loan", "Spanish bond at 3%" and "shares in the omnibus company 1835–1839", for example). Nevertheless, neither the family's involvement in the business (as evidenced by a number of references, such as those to "credits for the widow Laurance Olivier", Ackerman-Laurance's mother-in-law), nor the prominence of bankers in the "client accounts" prevented the bankruptcy. Having said that, the next section details documents which attest to the trading company's renaissance.

The *Grand livre:* a testament to Ackerman-Laurance's expansion

The first in a long series, the *Grand livre* in the Ackerman-Laurance's collection records the company's transactions between November 1863 and January 1868.[5] It was well maintained and it is in good condition. A number of pages bear witness to the presence of an accountant and others show evidence of the trust that was established with a local bank.

The Grand livre

The qualifier *Grand* is justified by the book's volume and weight, both of which are considerable. The paper is thick, the volume is bound in boards and covered in skin and the stiffeners are metal in order to prevent wear. Like all the notebooks in the collection, this one was purchased from a printer in Saumur. It is pre-printed with columns and lines, a heading on each page with *Doit* on the left and *Avoir* on the right, separated by a triple vertical blue line in the middle and a space in the centre to write the name of the account holder. This book is dedicated to the systematic recording of the company's commercial operations, which are entered in the *Doit* and *Avoir* columns in chronological order for each named account by descending order of size. The pages are numbered from 1 to 798 and its cover bears the title: *Grand livre A-L*, initials for Ackerman-Laurance.

All the company's collaborators are listed in this book: commercial partners, suppliers (wines and dry goods), private clients (hotels, restaurants, wealthy individuals), *négociants* both in France and abroad, cellar workers, company employees, banks, transport companies, etc. It records monetary flows, whether anticipated (bills of exchange) or completed (transfers, payments). Most of the accounts remained open only for a few months, at most two or three years, which means that most of the partnerships lasted only a short time. Each page can contain up to five accounts of different operations. The account holder's title – *monsieur, messieurs* or *madame* – sometimes appears at the top of each account, but each one has the account holder's name, whether it is a person or a separate legal entity. In 65% of cases, the occupation is also given. The address is sometimes reduced simply to the town or city (Saumur, Brussels, London) or even the country (France, Belgium, England), but on occasion was also precise (street name and house number). The *Grand livre* contains a total of 1,987 transaction accounts. Some names appear several times, having carried out transactions on several occasions and the previous account having been closed. In this case, there is a reference back to the number of the preceding folio.

The content of the *Doit* and *Avoir* columns is well ordered. Starting from the left-hand side of the page, the month, year and day of the transaction or transactions are entered first, followed by details of their purpose (nature of the merchandise, bills of exchange, etc.) and, in the right-hand column, the corresponding number in the *Journal*. The amount of the transaction is listed in francs in the last column. At the bottom of each column is the amount the account holder owes Ackerman-Laurance (*Doit*) or the amount of credit with Ackerman-Laurance (*Avoir*). Like most accounts of the period, each account uses the double-entry accounting system (Lemarchand, 2016c). In comparison to the *livre journal* from 1842, *le Grand Livre* is a proof of a new management of the business, and them being more conscientious and formal. There are differing accounting methods for production, sales, stock and bills. It is highly likely that the *Grand Livre* is an innovation from the management and leadership of Louis Ferdinand Ackerman-Laurance, the son of Jean-Baptiste, who took over from his father in 1866.

The first 200 pages list the largest accounts, the 133 with the largest number of transactions, probably classified by order of appearance in the ledgers (more than 37% of the operations began in October 1863). From page 201 onwards, the transactions for each account are recorded in roughly chronological order. The first 133 accounts take up 1½ pages, compared with about a third of a page for the others, spread over the remaining 598 pages. The occupations of the holders of these large accounts are indicated in 61% of cases, with 33% being described as *négociant*, 9% as commercial travellers and the same proportion as commercial representatives. Outside the world of trade, basket makers hold three accounts, the same as glass makers, one sugar refiner and four Ackerman-Laurance employees (three cellar workers and a household employee). The Ackerman family has accounts in this *Grand livre*: three for "Ackerman *père*" (the founder) and 1 for "Madame Ackerman *mère*" (born Emilie Laurance). The detail of the account held by Louvet, Trouillard & Cie, the local bank, which appears on the first 10 pages of the book, attests to the intensity of its relations with the *négociant*, and we will explore this now in more detail.

The relations between the wine merchant and the Louvet, Trouillard & Cie bank

Louvet, Trouillard & Cie was a *Maison de banque* founded in May 1835 by three growers and *négociants* from Saumur.[6] Its connections with Ackerman-Laurance were long-standing, back to 1842 at least, the period of the bankruptcy; another bank (Defos Lethuelle) had been its main financier before that. In 1863, Louvet, Trouillard & Cie took the leading role. Its account was opened in October 1863 and was closed on 1 January 1868. It comprises 12 handwritten pages, with the account from July 1867 to 1 January 1868 being laid out on two further pages. Statistical analysis of the number of operations recorded for this account for the whole of the period shows that a greater number of transactions were recorded in the *Avoir* column (67% of the total) than in the *Doit* column. The rate at which the transactions took place was twice as high in the *Avoir* column, with an average of ten transactions per month between November 1863 and October 1867, a period of almost four years. This imbalance between *Avoir* and *Doit* is due to differences in the nature of the two parties' activities, like Figure 11.1 illustrates. Figure 11.1 is an extract of the Louvet, Trouillard & Cie account pages 2 and 3 of the *Grand Livre* and reveals the main activities of the account. The *Doit* column records the discounts, bills of exchange, rebates and interest that were transferred to the bank for negotiation. Large sums of money were involved here. Ackerman-Laurance made deposits "in Paris, London, Brussels, Bordeaux, Antwerp, etc." at longer intervals. On the other hand, the transactions recorded in the *Avoir* column manifest the costs incurred in the course of Ackerman-Laurance's day-to-day operations (purchases and settlements). A high proportion of the transactions are listed under the heading of *caisse*, a generic term meaning "cash". However, the *Avoir* also includes travel costs, postage and cash payments to "Ackerman *père*" and "Madame Ackerman *mère*". Ackerman *père* received a regular cash remittance of 1000 francs, which equates to the life annuity fixed at the notary's office on 17 June 1863 in exchange for the transfer of his rights to the *Maison*;[7] a cash remittance recorded in the account is shown in Figure 11.1, highlighted by the rectangle on the left.

The account also records the debit or credit balances in each *Doit* and *Avoir* column. Examination of the rate at which the credit/debit balances appear shows that the balance with the bank followed a three-phase cycle over the course of the year: one balance was recorded in the summer in June, after the wine was shipped; another in the autumn in October, after the wines were purchased by clients; a final balance is listed at the end of the year or the beginning of the next. The evolution of the balance amount attests to both the regularity of the deposits and withdrawals of cash and the increase in the bank's confidence in the *négociant*. The presence of an accountant at Ackerman-Laurance, a Monsieur Bougrier, and the responsible way in which the accounts were maintained certainly helped in this regard.

Uses of the Grand livre

The Ackerman-Laurance *Grand livre* is a register of flows (of remittances and merchandise) maintained in francs for each of the transaction accounts, and it traces the history of the balances carried forward from one date to the next. It is not a general accounting document that records all the company's activities. Consequently, it cannot be used to judge whether the company was in good or bad health. However, it does show, account by account, partner by partner,

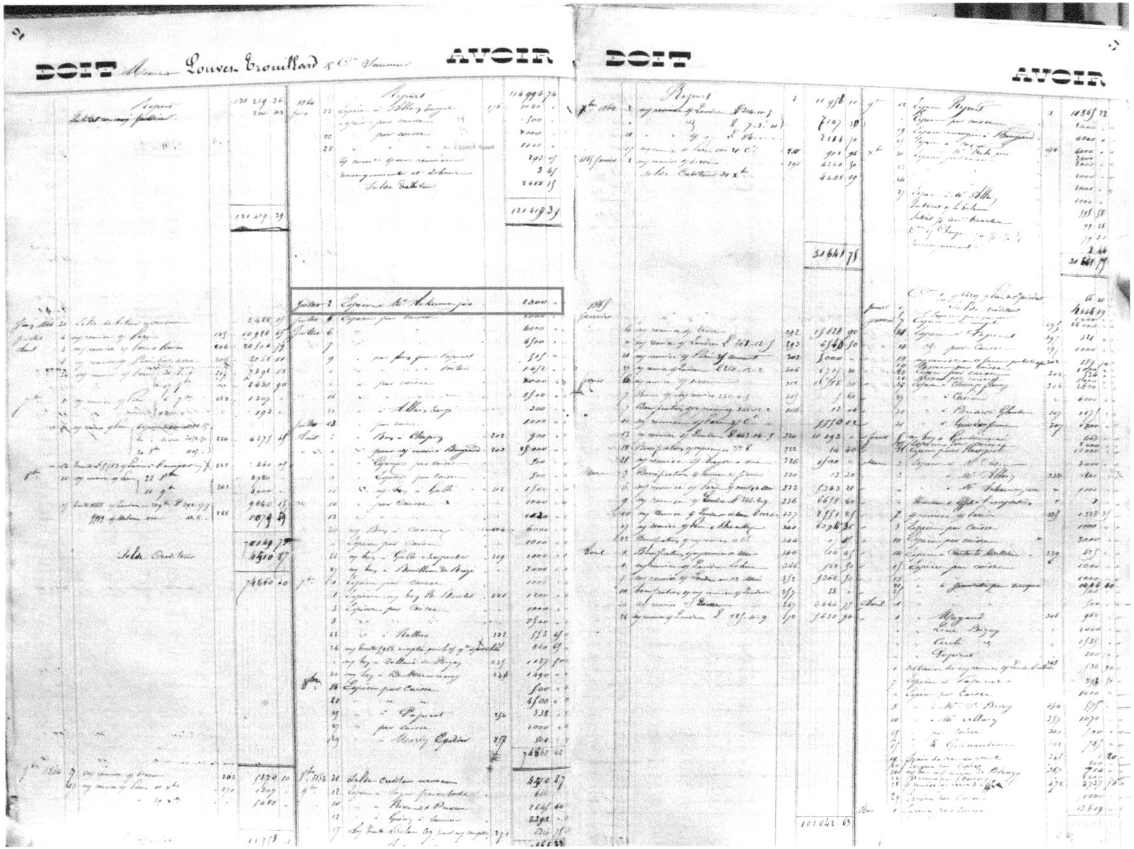

Figure 11.1 Extract of the account of Louvet, Trouillard & Cie from the Ledger of Ackerman-Laurance – from Fonds Ackerman-Laurance, 222 J 1047

© Ackerman.

the state of the company's commercial balance and of the credit/debit balance between Ackerman-Laurance and a given actor. Therefore, it provides information on its network of relationships that can be used to map that network (Gervais, 2012, p. 16). It also reveals how rare cash payments were, how routine the use of credit and advances was and how inventive the *négociants* were when it came to obtaining credit. It is a record of trading activity and an account of flows, but it cannot be used to analyse the profit mechanisms (Gervais, 2012, p. 36). The company's development in the last third of the 19th century was driven by the introduction of new practices, to which we now turn.

Pyramidal accounting to inform members and measure profitability

The number of accounts books, detailed inventories, day books, sales charts, notebooks and so on began to proliferate after the founder's son arrived alone on the scene in 1866. His advent paved the way for the establishment of the limited company in 1894. This obliged it to meet legal obligations to render its accounts, and particularly its profit and loss account and balance sheet.[8] This proliferation of documents also supported the sharp growth in sales. The accounts books, which summarised a diverse range of transactions and were the result of a round of data gathering, were also a means of making sure that the business was being well managed. They were no longer intended simply to record the company's commercial activities but to justify the use of resources and to ensure that the strategy adopted by the company was well founded.

Change of scale

The nature and content of the main accounts books, the *Journal* and *Grand livre*, for the years 1881–1885 were no different from the preceding one, but the books became ever more voluminous.

Maintained on a daily basis, the *Journal*, in its left-hand column, listed numbers corresponding to the nature of the transaction. For example, an entry for 30 November 1881 reads: "6 sundry income – current accounts with number 10 bills receivable; 24 sundries and short accounts (by client; 58 overheads; profits and losses 73 and by client presented successively)".[9] There was also an expenditure column (e.g., general merchandise or overheads) that specifies the recipient (workers paid for October, for example). Each account was allocated a number that enables it to be carried forward to the *Grand livre*. The right-hand column in the *Journal* lists total expenditure and income and the sub-totals. The transactions balances were noted at the bottom of each page and carried forward to the top of the following page. The headings in the *Journal* were sometimes allusive ("petty expenses for the month" or "Boucard treatment for workers"). Other books supplemented it. There was, for example, a list of bills receivable, which, from 1901 onwards, specified the date of the entries, the name of the signatory, the value of the transaction and a register number that linked each transaction with the withdrawal register for bills receivable that was started in 1902.[10] The additional books also played a major role in establishing links between the accounts. Those in the *Grand livre* classify partners in alphabetical order and by location.[11] Besides these books, a whole series of extremely meticulous secondary and supplementary accounts books provide detailed descriptions of the company's fixed assets, transactions and stocks of merchandise.

The importance of the British outlets resulted in a number of *Grands livres* and their notebooks being given over to the English market from 1893 onwards.[12] The pages of the notebook are divided into two columns, one specifying the town and the other the classification of clients by alphabetical order and register number for carrying the information forward to the *Grand livre*. Each name appears as many times as there are transactions, generally once, twice more rarely and three in exceptional cases. They denote either physical persons or institutions, such as the *County Hotel* or the *Great Western Railway*. This notebook attests to the scale of the company's commercial era. The diversification of entries and the proliferation of books made it necessary to recruit specialist staff and to establish a dedicated department, on which unfortunately the archives have little detail. As the end of the 19th century drew closer and closer, the books became ever more meticulous. This is true of the inventories and the *carnets noirs* (or black notebooks, detailed next), wrongly classified in the register of bills receivable, which enable us to track, year by year, the company's policy and results.[13]

The black notebooks

These notebooks, which are extremely comprehensive, are supplementary accounting documents, handwritten and with numbered pages, which comprise several headings. The first contains the company's annual balance sheet, drawn up when the accounts were closed in April. It attained its definitive form from 1904 onwards, with the reserve fund differentiating between the extraordinary reserve and the legal reserve and the contingency fund differentiating between preference and ordinary shares (see Table 11.1).

Table 11.1 Examples of headings in black notebooks

Assets heading	*Liabilities heading*
Goods purchased for resale and stock	Share capital
Furniture and equipment	Special reserve
Establishment	Statutory reserve
Goodwill, brand, clientele	Contingency fund: preference shares and ordinary shares
Cash	Current accounts in credit
Bills receivable	Profits and losses
Current accounts in debit	Share capital

To give some examples of the detail in these notebooks, a table summarises the consignments of wine dispatched in every half-year. The rows provide information on the destinations of the consignments; the entries include "England" and "retail", as well as "characteristics" such as "b quality", "A2 quality", brand ("Carte noire", "Royal", "Carte d'or", "Dry Royal") or, more generally, "red", "sparkling", "ordinary champagne", "superior champagne" and "various". The total number of bottles dispatched during the period is entered under the rows. The columns of the table relate to the containers ("bottles", "half bottles", "quarter bottles" and "Imperial Pints"). Another example is inventory on a given date. Denominated in francs, it first lists the goods purchased for resale ("wines", "cooperage", "empty bottles", "corks", "packaging including capsules") and then the stock ("office supplies classified as overheads", "candles", "lamp wicks and chimneys", "labels", etc.); the totals are carried forward to the "goods purchased for resale and stock" column of the balance sheet. The inventory reflects the modernisation of the *Maison* Ackerman-Laurance. The "Otto" engine appears in 1905, under the heading "electrical device". The inventory also provides information on work organisation. The list of furniture tells us that the "workers" had a "large table", that there were several offices, including a "large", lavishly furnished one with "four padded armchairs", "a bull's eye wall clock" and "a mahogany desk" and another occupied by the directors and furnished with "6 small armchairs, 13 pictures (13) and a mirror". The office of M. De Luze (commercial director and future managing director of Ackerman-Laurance) was the most luxurious, with its "porcelain vase", "2 armchairs", "bronze mantle clock with Cupid" and "dining room sideboard". One office was occupied by the "typists", who had a "large table" and four "assorted tables", five "straw-bottomed chairs" (for five typists?) and a "stool", no doubt for the office boy. There was also a "duplicating machine", two "Remington typewriters, one nº 7 and one nº 10" and a "Bar Loch No 12" machine. Also recorded in the inventory are a "dining room", a "kitchen" and a "Fichet safe", which comes under the heading of "miscellaneous".

Finally, the *cahier noir* itemises the "overheads" for each financial year. "Advertising" costs are listed separately for each market (England, America and France), along with those for shipping, labour, rent of the premises and "wear and tear" (10%). The cost of the vintages in the inventory is then calculated using the following formula: "The proportion for each bottle shall be: Overheads/bottles shipped, let that be X, which we shall apply as usual to the bottle, let X – the cost of the bottle = average unit cost price". Costs are also calculated for half bottles and wines of different qualities and vintages, since the costs ("cork", "cork wire", "label", "loss on decanting") vary considerably from one wine to another. The detail of these documents is worthy of an international trading company.

A response to members

The presence in the company of British shareholders, even though they were in a minority, is undoubtedly not unconnected with the meticulousness of its accounting. Used to having at their disposal an organised accountancy profession (Chartered Accountants) and to monitoring costs, these shareholders demanded rigorous accounts. From the accounts described, we can only conclude the company was managed in an extremely prudent manner. Priority was given to the reserves and the interests of majority shareholders. A focus on keeping overheads down promoted regular dividends for members. The minutes of the annual general meetings show that it adapted successfully to the principles of capitalism, making profits, rather than the renewal of credit, a priority objective.[14] Nevertheless, the company was refused entry to the Paris stock exchange on the pretext that the market for its shares was too restricted.[15] Neither the extent of its market nor the existence of a real accounting system, which was fairly rare in 19th century France (Touchelay, 2011) – and was doubtless fostered by the experience of bankruptcy and the need to manage foreign business – was sufficient to ensure its entry to the exchange.

Concluding comments

A close parallel to the moral contract – the relationship of trust between supplier and client – accounting can provide a measure of the solidity of the network established by commercial relationships. In the two cases revealed here, accounts books were initially conceived as personal files, kept as a sort of logbook or record that was not to be made public unless there was a problem (bankruptcy). They subsequently became the medium through which the companies' activities could be presented to their partners, or shareholders, first of all. They conveyed an image of the companies' activities and reveal the differences in management styles between Goubault-Lambert, Ackerman-Laurance *père* and his son. While the first two ran their businesses as *négociants*, Ackerman-Laurance *fils* (son) was a veritable captain of industry who contributed to the expansion of sparkling winemaking in Anjou. Ackerman-Laurance's accounts books attest to the changes in accounting practices that accompanied the development of winemaking and the growing fame of the Anjou vineyards in the 19th century.

These two brief stories of *négociants* show the necessity of good books of accounts. The first ended up in bankruptcy, with difficulties in converting his assets into cash and knowing exactly who his creditors or debtors were. His account books became incomplete when he stopped keeping them, and bankruptcy followed. The second example is a success story based on rigorous bookkeeping. Development of accounting accompanied the development of the volume of the business and the geographical extension of customers and suppliers. Bookkeeping was not only a way to be accountable to the partners but also was an essential condition to build a *Maison*. These characteristics were not specific to the *Maisons* unless they had dealings with numerous partners and had a wide geographical scope.

Notes

1 The archives of the *Maison* Ackerman were deposited in three instalments between 2000 and 2010: it is the Ackerman-Laurance, De Neuville, Rémy Pannier collection, 209 J and 222J. The most voluminous items in the *Maison* Ackerman collection (222J) are the accounts books and these include general ledgers (including balance sheets, journals, day books and inventory), client accounts and materials accounts.

2 ADML 7 M 72 Renseignements sur la viticulture en Maine et Loire: correspondance et rapports, lettre du préfet de Maine et Loire à la commission d'enquête sur les boissons, 11 mai 1850.
3 ADML 108 J 1–3 Comptabilité de René-Jean Goubault-Lambert.
4 ADML 222 J 1289 Comptabilité Ackerman-Laurance, *Livre Journal.*
5 ADML, Ackerman-Laurance collection, 222 J 1047, *Livre journal.*
6 ADML 6U4 143 *Tribunal de commerce de Saumur, société et procès verbaux des dépôts des actes de sociétés, 2 mai 1835*; Charles Louvet was an important political figure, and he was mayor of Saumur since 1844, president of the General Council of Maine et Loire since 1856, and a member of parliament since 1848. Later, he was Minister of Agriculture for a brief period from January to August 1870.
7 ADML, 5 E 42, article 261, *Étude de Saumur,* Emile Leroux, acte No 3942, 17 juin 1863.
8 A statement of the company's assets, liabilities and capital, the balance sheet summarised the debit and credit balances from the *Grand livre.* The annual balance sheet was prepared by the accountant and presented at the annual general meetings by the management.
9 ADML 222 J 1099, Livres journaux (1881–1888).
10 ADML 222 J 1178 Effets à recevoir 1901-. . . et 222 J 1196 Sortie des effets à recevoir.
11 ADML 222 J 1073 Répertoires du grand livre. N° 10 (1883–1885).
12 ADML 22 J 1092 *Grands livres* (Grande-Bretagne) 1893–1908
13 ADML 222 J 1199 Registre de sortie des effets à recevoir – *Les Carnets noirs.*
14 ADML 22 J 1359 Registre des procès verbaux des AG (1894–1924).
15 *Id.*, Assemblée générale du 3 février 1902, p. 72.

References

Primary sources

Maine et Loire Departmental Archives (ADML). The archives of the *Maison* Ackerman were deposited in three instalments between 2000 and 2010: Ackerman-Laurance, De Neuville, Rémy-Pannier collection, 209J; 222J. The most voluminous items in the Ackerman collection (222J) are the accounts books.

The following were used in this chapter:

ADML 7 M 72 Renseignements sur la viticulture en Maine et Loire: correspondance et rapports, lettre du préfet de Maine et Loire à la commission d'enquête sur les boissons, 11 mai 1850.

ADML 108 J 1–3 Comptabilité de René-Jean Goubault-Lambert, 7 registers.

ADML 222 J 1289 Comptabilité Ackerman-Laurance, *Livre Journal.*

ADML, Ackerman-Laurance collection, 222 J 1047 *Livre Journal.*

ADML 6U4 143 *Tribunal de commerce de Saumur, société et procès verbaux des dépôts des actes de sociétés, 2 mai 1835.*

ADML, 5 E 42, article 261, *Etude de Saumur,* Emile Leroux, acte n°3942, 17 juin 1863.

ADML 222 J 1099 Livres journaux (1881–1888).

ADML 222 J 1178 Effets à recevoir 1901- . . . et 222 J 1196 Sortie des effets à recevoir.

ADML 222 J 1073 Répertoires du grand livre. N° 10 (1883–1885).

ADML 22 J 1092 *Grands livres* (Grande-Bretagne) 1893–1908

ADML 222 J 1199 Registre de sortie des effets à recevoir – *Les Carnets noirs.*

ADML 22 J 1359 Registre des procès verbaux des AG (1894–1924). *Id.*, Assemblée générale du 3 février 1902, p. 72.

Secondary sources

Degos, J.-G. (2016). Livre d'inventaire et inventaire. In: D. Bensadon, N. Praquin and B. Touchelay, eds. *Dictionnaire historique de comptabilité des entreprises*. Villeneuve d'Ascq: Septentrion, pp. 386–387.

Dequidt, M.-A. (2016). La réglementation des faillites 17–19e. In: D. Bensadon, N. Praquin and B. Touchelay, eds. *Dictionnaire historique de comptabilité des entreprises*. Villeneuve d'Ascq: Septentrion, pp. 232–235.

Dion, R. (1978). *Le Val de Loire, étude de géographie régionale*. 2nd ed. Marseille: Laffitte reprints.

Dion, R. (2010). *Histoire de la vigne et du vin en France des Origines au XIXe siècle*. 2nd ed. Paris: CNRS Editions.

Fontaine, L. (2014). *Le Marché: Histoire et usages d'une conquête sociale*. Paris: Gallimard.

Gervais, P. (1996). Gestion et profit marchands avant la "Révolution industrielle": l'exemple d'une route privée entre New York et Philadelphie, 1815–1828. *Le Mouvement Social*, 176(3), pp. 47–67.

Gervais, P. (2012). Crédit et filières marchandes au XVIIIe siècle. *Annales, Histoire, Sciences sociales* 2012/4, 67e année, pp. 1011–1048.

Labardin, P. (2016). Comptabilité et faillites 18–19e. In: D. Bensadon, N. Praquin and B. Touchelay, eds. *Dictionnaire historique de comptabilité des entreprises*. Villeneuve d'Ascq: Septentrion, pp. 228–229.

Lemarchand, Y. (2016a). Journal – livre journal 18e. In: D. Bensadon, N. Praquin and B. Touchelay, eds. *Dictionnaire historique de comptabilité des entreprises*. Villeneuve d'Ascq: Septentrion, pp. 389–390.

Lemarchand, Y. (2016b). Grand livre. In: D. Bensadon, N. Praquin and B. Touchelay, eds. *Dictionnaire historique de comptabilité des entreprises*. Villeneuve d'Ascq: Septentrion, pp. 388–389.

Lemarchand, Y. (2016c). Partie double. In: D. Bensadon, N. Praquin and B. Touchelay, eds. *Dictionnaire historique de comptabilité des entreprises*. Villeneuve d'Ascq: Septentrion, pp. 390–393.

Matz, J.-M. (2010). Viticulture, vin et société en Anjou à la fin du Moyen âge. *Archives d'Anjou, mélanges d'histoire et d'archéologie angevine*, Hors-série, 14, pp. 7–22.

Moulin, A. (1988). *Les paysans dans la société française. De la révolution à nos jours*. Paris: Le Seuil.

Perron, F. (2016). La comptabilité des négociants en vins de champagne (1789–1807). In: D. Bensadon, N. Praquin and B. Touchelay, eds. *Dictionnaire historique de comptabilité des entreprises*. Villeneuve d'Ascq: Septentrion, pp. 118–120.

Taveau, V. (2017). Ackerman and the sparkling wine from Saumur: A local winemaking innovation and his consequences on the industrial development of a rural territory around the middle of the XIXth century. In: *The European Rural History Conference*, Leuven, 11–14 September.

Touchelay, B. (2011). *L'État et l'entreprise, une histoire de la normalisation comptable à la francaise*. Rennes: PUR.

12 The Bordeaux classified growth system

A strong legacy

Stéphane Ouvrard, Hervé Remaud and Ian Taplin

In memory of Jean-Guy Degos

Introduction

Bordeaux for many people is synonymous with wine. For some, it represents the apex of fine wine, the quintessential beverage that complements a memorable gastronomic event. But for much of Bordeaux's history, wine from the area was of dubious quality, with grapes picked unripe, overripe or even spoiled (Philips, 2016). Furthermore, there was no proper way of storing wine once it was made, and if there was, the wine would not have improved with age – quite the opposite in fact. We start this chapter with a discussion of the early commercial developments facilitated by trade with the English and their demand for a low alcohol wine (*claret*) that can be drunk soon after production. The English were replaced in the 17th century by the Dutch and other Northern Europeans who brought technical skills to reclaim more agricultural land, as well as a preference for more robust wines that could improve with age if stored appropriately. This set in place further improvements in viticulture and the realization that quality wines could be made in the region if there were significant investment in appropriate techniques. In turn, this led to regulations by local authorities designed to impose a framework for basic production that could guarantee the requisite output. When the French introduced a formal classification system in 1855, this was the culmination of decades of effort to rank wines based on price and quality recognition from wine professionals of the '*Place*'.

The so-called Bordeaux Place remains the organizing principal by which much fine wine from the region is sold. This is a marketplace with key actors (winery owners, brokers, *négociants* [merchants] and the officials within the city) interacting both contractually and on trust, to guarantee the delivery of a product of high standard. Of long-standing relevance, its role has assumed the greatest importance in the 20th century as the arbiter behind the Bordeaux brand. This is especially the case with wine sold through the *en primeur* system, which started as a way of ensuring supply of quality wine for the merchants and improving the financial stability of wineries and has recently become a grand marketing exercise designed to cultivate demand for high-priced wines. This chapter will discuss this process in detail, drawing on several renowned textbooks[1] and analyzing the cash management involved at the Château level by the *en primeur* sales system. From this analysis, it will become clear that the role of accounting in the price setting of Bordeaux top fine wine is, and possibly has always been, minimal. For this type of luxury product, a fundamental issue is how to manage cash efficiently.

Building of the Bordeaux Place market over time (Middle Ages to 18th century)

Based near the mouth of the Gironde estuary and with a direct access to the Atlantic Ocean, Bordeaux has benefited from a privileged location to facilitate the trade of wine with England. The famous marriage in 1152 of Eleanor, Duchess of Aquitaine, to Henry of Plantagenet, Duke of Normandy, of Anjou, Maine and heir to the throne of England, marked the start of three centuries of English rule over Bordeaux. However, that came to an end at the battle of Castillon on July 17, 1453, with the defeat of the English army. Two months later, against its will, Bordeaux returned to the kingdom of France.

Whilst Bordeaux was under English rule, trade between the two areas was a crucial component in the development of business. The English Court became accustomed to drinking Bordeaux wine, a pattern that largely persists to the present day and explains the importance of major distributors and the wine market based in London. Furthermore, at this time half of the wine of Bordeaux was destined for the English market. This leads Chastenet (1980, p. 57) to conclude that "as early as the 13th Century it becomes impossible to celebrate, in aristocratic circles of England, one any solemnity without Bordeaux wine". He further notes: "at the turn of the 13th Century, Bordeaux wines will be shipped to England and Ireland . . . wines the Islanders were the most fond of" (Chastenet, 1980, p. 53). As a result of this trade, by the beginning of the 13th century, the port of Bordeaux took on considerable importance.

The wine trade rapidly became institutionalized, and the collection of taxes proved lucrative both for the city and for England. In his article entitled *Customs and tariff seen in Bordeaux wines and goods by the English administration*, Trabut-Cussac (1950) notes revenue sharing between England and the city of Bordeaux. Significant tax revenues were also levied by the *Jurade* and benefited the city of Bordeaux. In simple terms, the *Jurade* was the municipal organization of the city of Bordeaux, whose legal existence was recognized in 1224 by the King John – Duke of Normandy. It was responsible for the routine administrative activities that govern economic and social life. At the end of the 13th century, the *Jurade* counted 24 *jurats*. These were administrators, magistrates, military leaders and tax collectors for the commune of Bordeaux. This organization continued in existence until the French Revolution and it ensured the independence of the city. From an early date, the *Jurade* was aware of the importance of the wine trade and took responsibility for organizing much of the wine production. It fixed the date of the harvest, required 'business citizenship' and implemented favorable measures for the Bordeaux wines. In the Middle Ages, the *jurats* also performed an advocacy role, promoting the wines of the region within the province but also across the kingdom, including in Paris and Versailles (Meyzie, 2012, p. 166). The registers of the *Jurade* listed the existence of different taxes like the '*trademark*', which stipulates that wines of the upper lands must be marked and taxed 5 cents per barrel at entrance to the city. Another tax, the '*small Yssac*', regarded as the most important source of money for the city, was applied to wines sold in taverns by the unit or in bulk. Whilst revenue generating, these taxes were also designed to regulate and restrict competition in the embryonic wine market. It is during this period of extensive trade in wine with England that one begins to see the emergence of institutional structures that shape not just external relationships but also the internal market in Bordeaux. Aside from the fiscal initiatives listed, powerful social forces were also imposing their own imprint on the industry. It is these groups that shaped the evolution of the wine market, manipulating as well as reinforcing extant structures, and making a significant contribution to the subsequent construction of Bordeaux's wine reputation.

Following the growing trade with the English, Aquitaine's economy prospered and there was a dramatic increase of cultivable land in the Bordeaux region. In 1279, the King Edward I – Duke of Aquitaine cleared land to plant vines. This experience was a success, and the stony soil of the region allowed the rapid development of vineyards. Similar clearing and cultivating land for vines was undertaken by many '*burghers*' (or *bourgeois*) from the city. At the beginning of the 14th century, the size of the Bordeaux vineyards was estimated at 18,000 hectares – 50 years later, this reached around 30,000 hectares. With this growth in vineyards came a corresponding increase in individuals who played a key role in the industry (winemakers and Gascon merchants who arranged for the distributions of the product) and institutions (*Jurade*) which facilitated such market activity.

Winemakers inevitably played a leading role since production requires know-how and an almost daily presence in the vineyards. At this stage, knowledge was not formalized and was tacit. As conservation techniques remained rudimentary (the most common being topping) (Philip and Lacarce, 2015, p. 53), most wine was consumed shortly after production. A wine that was designated a good wine was probably a result of favorable climatic conditions, and since this varied from year to year, so did quality. The English favored a low-alcohol, pale-colored wine to be drunk shortly after delivery.[2] These so-called *Claret* wines were probably quite ordinary with 7% to 8% alcohol, but by the 14th century the English had a virtual monopoly on the supply of these wines (Markham, 1997, p. 56).

Another key player in the burgeoning wine trade with England was the *Gascon* Merchant. These merchants were in charge of marketing and represented intermediaries between producers and consumers. They arranged for wine to be bought, stored and then sold. According to Lavaud (2003, p. 93), they were the "main actors of the wine trade" since they had developed the requisite trust between producers and buyers. These relationships were crucial in harmonizing activities that effectively institutionalized the wine trade between Bordeaux and England.[3] The Anglo-Gascon trade depended on inter-merchant agreements, who were quick to realize the business opportunities of foreign markets, particularly in England. Their ability to prosper, however, was dependent upon the growth of a formal market structure that would provide legitimacy to their actions and guarantee financial transactions. Without such a framework, market exchange is fraught with uncertainty. Aggregate transactions when reaching a critical mass require some forms of structure to sustain their vitality. The structure that emerged to fulfill this essential regulatory role was the *Jurade*. This proved to be the piece that finally organized and institutionalized the wine trade.

The Bordeaux burghers (*bourgeois*)[4] were required to comply with trade rules set by the *Jurade*. For instance, in 1414 and 1420, the *Jurade* prohibited the purchase of wine from the upper lands in order to protect production of Bordeaux wine. The *Jurade* also fixed a ban on wines from upper regions to access the port of Bordeaux before Saint Martin's Day (November 11). This measure allowed Bordeaux to have a *de facto* monopoly of the trade in wine especially during the great fair of November. Such early protectionism was crucial in limiting lower-priced competitors from threatening Bordeaux's market control. During the 'best years' of the 13th century, about 80,000 barrels of Bordeaux wines were shipped to England (Philip and Lacarce, 2015, p. 52).

Since the Middle Ages, local government continued to play an active role in the wine trade (Meyzie, 2012, p. 166). However, that trade dissipated somewhat in the 15th and 16th centuries after England was forced to relinquish control over Aquitaine. The commercial vacuum left by the English was eventually filled by the Dutch, who increased their imports of wine from Bordeaux in the 17th century. The Dutch were also instrumental in draining much of the land adjacent to the rivers in the Bordeaux area, thus creating additional quality land for vineyard development. After this 'golden age' of the Netherlands (Markham, 1997, p. 56), the English wine trade resumed in the 18th century, but this time the notion of quality became a central part of the wine market. At the beginning of the 16th century, Henri IV had begun to dry out unused and unsuitable swampy areas and appealed to experienced Dutch engineers who had mastered these techniques in their *polders*[5] (Philip and Lacarce, 2015, p. 80). In the 17th century, these engineers became new business partners with the *Bordelais*, and together they significantly expanded wine production. By the 18th century this increased volume is notable since it marked not only the return of wine sales to England, but also those from another wine region – the Medoc.

In contrast to the English who bought wine for resale in their own country, Dutch merchants bought it to resell throughout the world. Very large quantities of wines loaded at Bordeaux on Dutch ships were carried not only to their ports of origin but also to German and Baltic ports (Chastenet, 1980, p. 86). The Dutch had a preference for medium-sweet or dry white wines intended to produce *eaux-de-vie* after distillation. Apart from the traditional *claret*, the '*Bordeaux bourgeois*' redirected their production to sweet white or even syrupy wines, in particular those from the Barsac and Sauternes regions. In 1700–1701, export sales reached 95,000 barrels (Chastenet, 1980, p. 87). According to Markham (1997, p. 57) Dutch merchants were also interested in dark red wines, referred to as 'black wines', wines from the edges of the Gironde and Dordogne which kept better and were able to resist longer voyages to distant destinations. For this reason, these wines were designated 'cargo wines' (*vins de cargaisons*).

New areas were opening vineyards, particularly in the Haut-Médoc on the left bank of the Garonne River downstream of Bordeaux (Chastenet, 1980, p. 85). Moreover, changes in the tastes and expectations of consumers pushed owners to improve the quality of their wine. The gradual realization that the new land could produce better-quality wine if tended and harvested with improved techniques led to further experimentation. New vineyard practices such as sulphating, racking, topping, pasting and yield management were introduced, and this led to dramatic improvements in wine quality. One of the first to realize this was a local large landowner, Arnaud de Pontac, who had an area of about 40 hectares in Pessac outside Bordeaux, called Château Haut-Brion (Birlouez, 2015, p. 101). He managed to produce a premium wine that improved with time in new oak barrels. Shortly after the great fire of London in 1666, he opened a tavern in London – the 'Pontac's Head' – where he introduced his famous nectar *Ho Bryan* (Haut-Brion). His success was immediate, and English guests, including Samuel Pepys, the Secretary of the English Admiralty (Birlouez, 2015, p. 102), began to appreciate the qualities of this exceptional wine sold at very high prices – which was served at the king's table. Pontac's gamble had paid off, namely make a high-quality wine and charge a high price (Philip and Lacarce, 2015, p. 79). This also highlighted that developing an international reputation via brand image means understanding what consumers want (in this case, quality) and being able to deliver it in a reliable and fairly consistent way following increased technical knowledge and improved winemaking skills.

After the rapid growth of plantings and the reorganization of the land by the Dutch in the 17th century, many traditional Medoc owners resisted further change. At that time, operations limited yields to about 15 hectoliters per hectare, and harvesting was delayed to encourage further ripeness of the grapes to increase quality (Birlouez, 2015, p. 104). Wines were now matured in new oak barrels of 225 liters, whereas in the past only the wines of the year "pure, natural and new" (Chastenet, 1980, p. 91) had a real market value. In 1725, there were about 15 Châteaux producers of fine wines, the most famous being those of Haut-Brion in the Graves, and Lafite, Margaux and Latour in the Médoc. Already at that time a selling price hierarchy was noticeable between the different vintages of Bordeaux (Chastenet, 1980, p. 95). In 1740 for example, Pessac, Pauillac and Margaux wines reached considerable prices for the time: 1,500 to 1,800 pounds per barrel of 900 liters, or 10 to 12 times the price of the 'ordinary' wines of the region (Birlouez, 2015, p. 106).

In the 18th century, trust between the different actors of the wine economy continued to be a necessary and integral part for the proper functioning of the market. This continues to this day as an underlying structuring principle of the Bordeaux Place whereby wine growers, brokers and wine merchants negotiate within a subtle *de jure* market framework. This ensures a reputational interdependency that can lead to informal sanctions for those who fail to live up to expectations. Since the notion of quality became a central part of the wine market, reputation was increasingly crucial to avoid undermining the market's credibility. For according to Meyzie (2012, p. 166), "the sale of quality wines is based in large part on their reputation". In this context, owners and dealers took care to adapt their wines to the evolution of the market and paid close attention to customer trends and preferences. Consideration of this increasing demand by the different actors of the Aquitaine wine market led to an improved value of the product.

Bordeaux wine classifications

A multitude of individual classifications have existed over time, resulting from the knowledge and experience of merchants, brokers, producers' associations or the *Jurade*. Most of these classifications were introduced to provide some form of evaluation and legitimacy for wines from a particular property or region. The most important one, the 1855 classification, is briefly summarized next.

The 1855 Paris classification

In contrast with earlier exhibitions organized in France since 1797, the 1855 exhibition welcomed for the first time manufactured products and global exhibitors. The key objective of these exhibitions was to promote French industry, but as wine was not considered a manufactured product, it had not been given much emphasis (Markham, 1997). The exhibition committee desired to have regional best (manufactured) products represented and invited Bordeaux wine producers to take part (Markham, 1997).

The first classifications to be used by the wine merchants of Bordeaux dates back to 1745, 1776 and 1786, and indicated the greater reputation (and price) of four estates – Haut-Brion, Margaux, Latour and Lafite. In each case, high price was used as a signifier of quality in the reputational rankings. These four estates were identified as first *crus*, allowing all other wines to establish their price on a graded scale below them (Markham, 1997). For example, when first growths (*crus*) were sold at 2,400 francs (a barrel), the best second growths were sold at 2,100 francs, the best third growth wines at 1,700 francs, and the best fourth growth wines (also called '*Bourgeois Supérieurs*') sold at 1,500 francs. Since about 1810, multiple books were written, each delivering a wine classification. When the 1855 classification was established, it was in many respects systematizing and formalizing previous evaluations of wine. However, in introducing a *de facto* hierarchy, it conferred status (and pricing power) to those at the top and left those below clamoring for prestige. Established by the brokers' association, the list includes 57 classified red wines and 21 classified white (sweet) wines, split into five different classes of growths (*crus*): first-growth wines sold at 3,000 francs, second growths at 2,500 to 2,700 francs, third growths at 2,100 to 2,400 francs, fourth growths at 1,800 to 2,100 francs and fifth growths at 1,400 to 1,600 francs. When the exhibition ended in 1855, medals were given to classified wines in line with their 'growth' level. The classification was updated later in 1855, with Château Cantemerle gaining its request to be part of the fifth growth category. Since then, the 1855 classification remained the benchmark, although the criterion for selection has slightly changed depending of the price evolution of specific estates. Nonetheless, it has been consistently used as a tool by chateaux to promote their wine – the ultimate seal of legitimacy and high status. However, it was not until 1949 that the 1855 classification gained a legal position in the French law, indicating the legal requirements for an estate to have the right to use 'classified growth', linking these requirements to the 1855 classification. Starting their battle in the 1850s, the owners of Château Mouton Rothschild fought for about 120 years before being moved to the first-growth circle, in 1973. This change was the last one that has occurred since the 1855 classification.

The '*en primeur*' trading system and the Bordeaux Place

In essence, what is called Bordeaux Place includes four key players trading wine and based in Bordeaux (and its surrounding areas) – producers (*châteaux* or *Crus*), brokers (*courtiers*), merchants (*négociants*) and institutions (mostly the Bordeaux Wine Council, CIVB). Most Bordeaux fine wines are sold using the 'Place', while many smaller châteaux, cooperatives and other wine growers have their own sales force. They could work with brokers and merchants of the Place but do not engage with the *en primeur* sales system. In this Place, many players have been trading and dealing with each other for generations under implicit and *intuitu personæ* rules. In brokers Tastet & Lawton's accounting books dating back to the 18th century, there are familiar names of wine businesses – Schröder and Schÿler, Barton et Guestier, Cruse, Brane Cantenac, Pontet Canet, Lafitte, etc. – who still work in the industry today. The key principle for the Bordeaux Place players is its 'usage' (contracts, negotiation, etc., are made almost the same way today as 150 years ago) and discretion (trust between players and confidential relationships) (Remaud et al., 2015). In simple terms, it enables producers to access thousands of points of sale around the world, although they only deal with around two to five brokers or intermediaries to sell their wines (see Figure 12.1).

Role of key players

We now examine the role of each of the key players in the Bordeaux Place, starting with producers. The fine wine producers' key role is simple at first glance – producing wine of the best quality possible. However, producers tend to promote their brand today much more than they did a few decades ago. For the 50 to 350 wine producers who partake, dealing with brokers and merchants of the Bordeaux Place is critical. However, for the 7,000 to 8,000 other châteaux estates and growers of the Bordeaux region, the demand for their wines is not

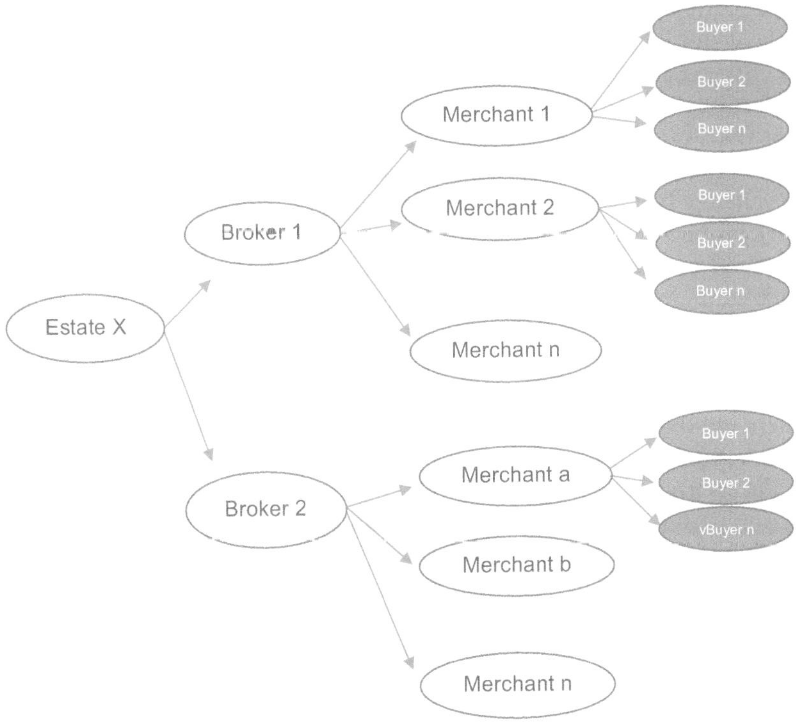

Figure 12.1 The Bordeaux Place

strong enough to get attention of the brokers and merchants of the Bordeaux Place, at least to have merchants paying for the wine before its release and delivery.

The brokers are well-established intermediaries whose mission is to connect, match and secure a deal between producers and merchants. They are independent third parties, who assist from the initiation of a transaction to completion (Baritaux et al., 2006). They are paid a commission by merchants on the basis of 2% of transaction value. Being at the interface of multiple producers and multiple merchants, brokers are the voice of both, but especially the voice of the merchants, as one broker can convey a similar message to many merchants (Remaud et al., 2015). In older times, a broker could spend a few days visiting estates in the Medoc region, often by horse (until the railway was constructed). At this time, it was not unusual for the broker to take an order from merchants and bring back samples to Bordeaux (Remaud et al., 2015). The fact that brokers were the messengers at that time explains the expertise they gained over time and the critical part they played in the 1855 classification. Brokers' trust is key, and is transferred from one generation to the other. One producer will not work with one single broker, and most estates would have around three to four brokers. Today, the five largest broker offices endorse the biggest proportion of deals of Bordeaux fine wines. With new technologies, the role of the broker has changed and information asymmetry has been reduced. They have created platforms where producers and merchants can have real-time quotations of the wine they want to sell or buy, on delivery or on the secondary market. From this perspective, it is closer to a traditional marketplace where demand and supply generate the best possible price for each party. For the *en primeur* campaign (see later), brokers help the producers they work with to establish the best possible price and fine-tune the allocations to the merchants that the producer should work with.

The wine merchants of the Bordeaux Place had a price-making power until the 1980s. Having access to the market and selling the wines produced in the Bordeaux region gave them the information they needed to drive wine style, orders and the relationship with the producers. Succinctly put, producers were good at producing wines and merchants were good at selling wines, but with producers having no access to the final consumers, the merchants had the price-making power in their hands. The total number of merchants depends on the definition adopted. Around 800 entities are presently stocking wine, and more than 300 merchants are registered at the Union des Maisons de Bordeaux (the merchants' association); and while about 250 really trade and sell wines, about 50 make the majority of the sales of Bordeaux fine wines. Some well-known merchants have established offices in other countries to facilitate local distributors. Some have a greater expertise working with the on-trade, while others do work exclusively with retailers and the off-trade. Some are as old as well-known brokers and Châteaux, while others are more recent. Becoming a Bordeaux merchant is not easy and is financially risky. When a vintage is of great quality, the demand for Bordeaux fine wine is strong enough to generate easy sales (assuming the price is right), but with more difficult vintages it is harder for merchants to generate sales. For an average merchant, a campaign could cost up to €15 million (Remaud et al., 2015). If there is enough demand to finance the campaign (orders from clients/customers), the extra cost is easily self-funded and/or funded by bank loans. But when there are multiple vintages with low demand, it is more and more difficult for merchants to have the cash to buy the wines, and for banks to follow. In that case, merchants have to decline allocations from the producers, with the risk that they might not get them back for the following vintages.

In terms of institutions, the largest institution of the Bordeaux Place is the CIVB, the Bordeaux wine council, formed by representatives of the wine producers, brokers and merchants. The CIVB has three key missions: technical, economical and marketing. It operates advertising and communication campaigns, but also tasting with key importers and retailers in specific cities, organization of major events in Bordeaux and abroad, etc. From an economic perspective, the CIVB collects data from producers (yields, harvest, cost of production, sales destination, etc.), merchants (prices, sales destination, etc.) and the market (consumers' preferences, on-trade trends, etc.). From a technical perspective, the council investigates the climate change impact on Bordeaux vines and wine, the implementation of sustainable practices, etc. Other key institutions that have an impact on the image and reputation of Bordeaux fine wines include the *Union des Grands Crus* (UGC), the 1855 Club and the Appellation wine councils (Saint Emilion, Pessac-Leognan, etc.). The 1855 Club is a more selective club, as it includes only Châteaux which were part of the 1855 classification. The key mission of this association is to represent the interest of their members wherever such promotion is required.

The 'allocations' mechanism

An allocation is a specific number of cases allocated by a château to a merchant per campaign (i.e., for each new vintage). This simple mechanism hides a very complex 'game', the objective of which is for the château to secure full sales of the total number of cases put on the market, at the price they want, and for the merchants to access the number of cases they believe they could sell (and/ or speculate on). To spread and minimize the risk of selling all cases put on the market at a specific price, château owners have some options. First, for the first classified growth estates, they could release all their allocations in two to three 'slices'. For example, Château X will release a first 'slice' of allocations corresponding to 30% of all cases they want to offer on the market at €2,400/case. The first slice being 'cheaper' compared to the second (and third), there is (in theory) a stronger demand from the merchants to buy quickly (as soon as it is announced). If the market (the merchants, and then the importers, distributors, etc.) react well, Château X will release a second slice of 30% (or more in the case of two slices) at a slightly higher price, say €3,000/case, etc. If the idea to get a greater return per case slice after slice for the château is well known, the idea is also for the most prestigious châteaux (first growth, super seconds, etc.) to remain in the same range of price amongst peers. Most fine wine producers work with various merchants. For estates that are acknowledged brands and where merchants believe that the value of the wine will increase over time, they will buy cases of the wine to hold in stock before releasing them later for a higher return. Also, some merchants specialize in markets that the historical merchants do not cover (or cover poorly), including emerging markets or specific channels such as airlines and duty-free. Most châteaux would or could request 'exclusivities', giving them more opportunities for more merchants to work their brand and reduce the competition between merchants of the Bordeaux place on a specific zone.

One important aspect of the allocation is its implicit rule shared within the Bordeaux Place – when a vintage is very good or exceptional, wine merchants are mostly sure that they can generate a good return. Over the years, one can observe that the average price of fine Bordeaux wines increases when the vintage is considered exceptional (in recent years such as 2005, 2009, 2010, 2015, 2016), and decreases when the vintage is not that great (see Figure 12.2 for an example).

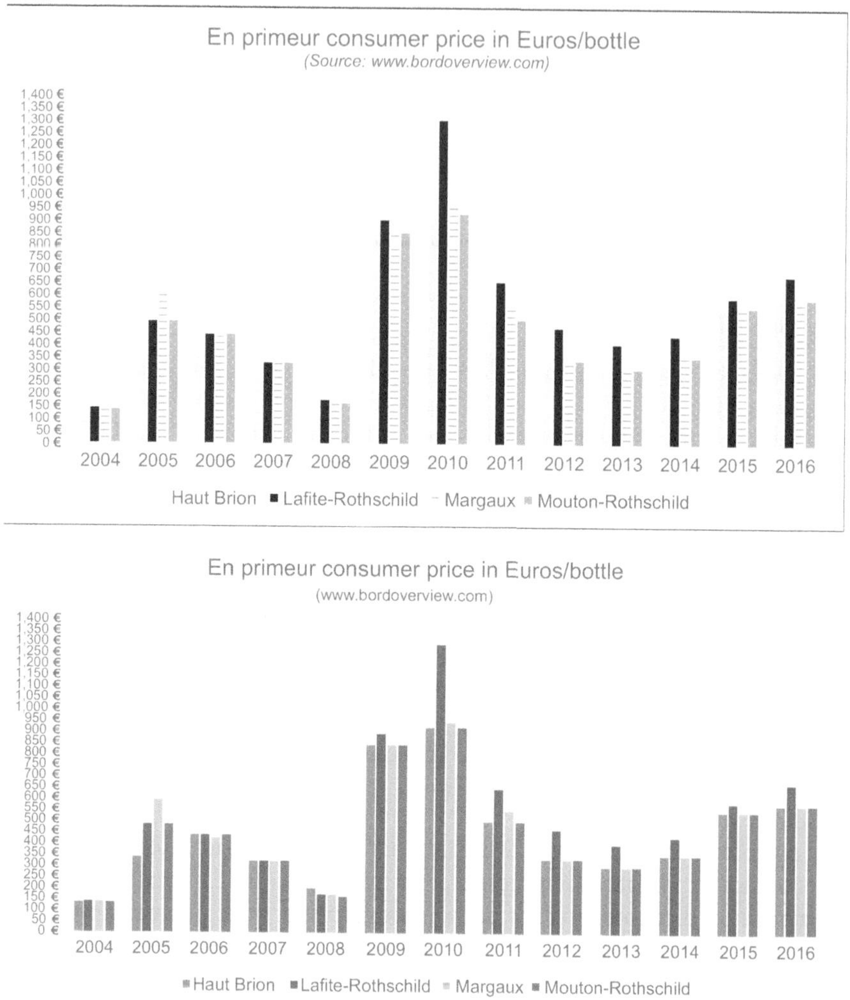

Figure 12.2 Evolution of the *en primeur* consumer price

Source: www.bordoverview.com

The en primeur *system*

The *en primeur* system is a futures system whereby customers (wine merchants of Bordeaux, distributors, final buyers) buy (and pay for) wine today, to be delivered about 18 months later. When buying *en primeur*, final buyers are paying in full at that specific date for the wine. For the wine merchants of the Bordeaux Place, the payment process is negotiated with the estate – one third can be paid when the wine is proposed on allocation, one third after six months and one third on delivery time. Three key *en primeur* prices can be distinguished:

- Ex-château – the price of one bottle (or a case) that a producer will offer to the merchants of the Bordeaux place.
- Ex-négociant – the price of one bottle (or a case) that merchant will offer to its customers (distributors or importers). It includes 2% commission paid to the broker to endorse the transaction (between the merchant and the estate) and a 10% to 20% margin that the merchant will apply to the ex-château price.
- Ex-distributor – the price of one bottle (or a case) that a distributor (for example based in the UK, United States, China) will offer to its customers (who could be final consumers/buyers). It does include the distributor's margin and taxes.

The *en primeur* campaign starts early in the estate year. As weather contributes to the quality of the wine, the final four weeks before harvest time determine the overall quality of the wine and its price. During the following weeks, producers send 'signals' through various channels about the quality of the vintage. Producers are in fact preparing the market that the price of the vintage may be high this current year due to good quality. At the same time, distributors around the world counteract, suggesting the market is not willing to pay that much for the vintage. By the end of March, wine producers officially present their wine to the brokers and merchants of the Bordeaux Place. Following this presentation, the wine is officially unveiled to journalists, wine critics, distributors and all other wine professionals during the *en primeur* week, usually the first week of April. The *en primeur* tasting week is a critical moment of the Bordeaux wine industry. Depending on the year, more than 4,000 people from around the world come to Bordeaux to taste the new vintage. The *en primeur* week is organized by the *Union des Grands Crus* association, and tastings are organized per key appellation. During and following the *en primeur* week, wine journalists and critics release their scores and comments related to all wines tasted. For the more famous brands (first growth, 'super' seconds) the wine is not tasted blind, and each estate invites journalists to a tasting. It gives them the opportunity to discuss the vintage and deliver the story they want the journalists to remember – as a first growth, they do not want to take a risk of being scored lower than a second-, third- or fourth-growth wine, as they are 10 to 30 times more expensive. If many estates release their *en primeur* price after the scores of the journalists are released, some will announce their price very early in the campaign to gain attention from the merchants.

Deciding the **en primeur** *price*

Making the decision for a specific price is not an easy one. Obviously, the price has to cover the cost of producing a classified growth wine, but for a substantial number of estates, marketing (at large) does play a more critical role in price setting. Wine producers can get help from brokers, obtaining indications about the price the market is willing to pay. But this is partial and somewhat biased, as merchants and the market prefer cheaper prices. In essence, wine producers base their decision on six main aspects (Remaud et al., 2015): vintage quality (the greater the quality, the more expensive the wine); how prices of similar quality wine have evolved over time; the level of stock (of their brand on the market); the global economy at large, including interest rates, stock exchange prices and confidence in the economy; the status of the brand; and the extent to which an estate has been able to build a brand and not just a (high-quality) wine. The price paid for a classified wine in 2017 (or any recent date) may not respect the original 1855 classification price at all. Whilst some estates have been able to improve the quality and image of their wine, others are traded below their original category. However, there is always a temptation for an estate to price its wine at levels reflecting its classification more than its quality. When such a situation occurs, the total amount of wine allocated to the market may not be sold. In addition to the price, deciding a date to release its price is a difficult choice. If an estate starts too early, most merchants will wait for other estates before making their decisions. On the other hand, waiting too long may place the estate in a situation where merchants have spent their entire budget on other brands, and therefore cannot buy more.

Most of the wine produced by Bordeaux classified growth estates is sold *en primeur*. The prices these estates will charge for their wines rely mostly on the reputation these estates experience, linked to the relative rarity of these famous wines. The first growth–classified estates as well as the 'super seconds' play the luxury game, as they are seen as luxury goods. As with many luxury goods, the prices charged for the product do not reflect its cost. In brief, history, rarity, reputation and marketing are playing a key role in creating and delivering value on the market. Such wines are expensive, are difficult to access and are perceived as the pinnacle of excellence in oenological terms. They have become the quintessential 'experience' product – that rare item whose cost and limited availability enhances their apparent objective quality and desirability. For this type of wine, accounting does not play a key role (if any) in the price setting. The *en primeur* system and the 'noise' created around it all year round sustain the reputation of these wines and have become a crucial marketing exercise.

Since the 1980s, the *en primeur* system has remained mostly unchanged – wine producers gradually became price makers and make most decisions affecting the way the *en primeur* and Bordeaux place work. They have built brands strong enough to be in high demand worldwide and generate greater interest than volume offered on the market. The key point here is that merchants take the risk between the date of the transaction and the time when the wine is delivered.

For customers, and especially for final buyers, one would buy wine *en primeur* for two major reasons: for speculation purposes and to secure the supply of a specific wine/brand they prefer. The decision to invest in one brand compared to another is based on the reputation of that brand. The critical variable to include in the decision to buy a brand for speculation is time. Depending on the vintage and the economy, some brands generate high return in the early years of release, while others deliver a return in the long run. For example, Château Cheval Blanc, 2006 is a famous brand giving good returns in the early months of release. Less known vintages such as 1998 offer greater return in the longer term, as can be seen in Figure 12.3.

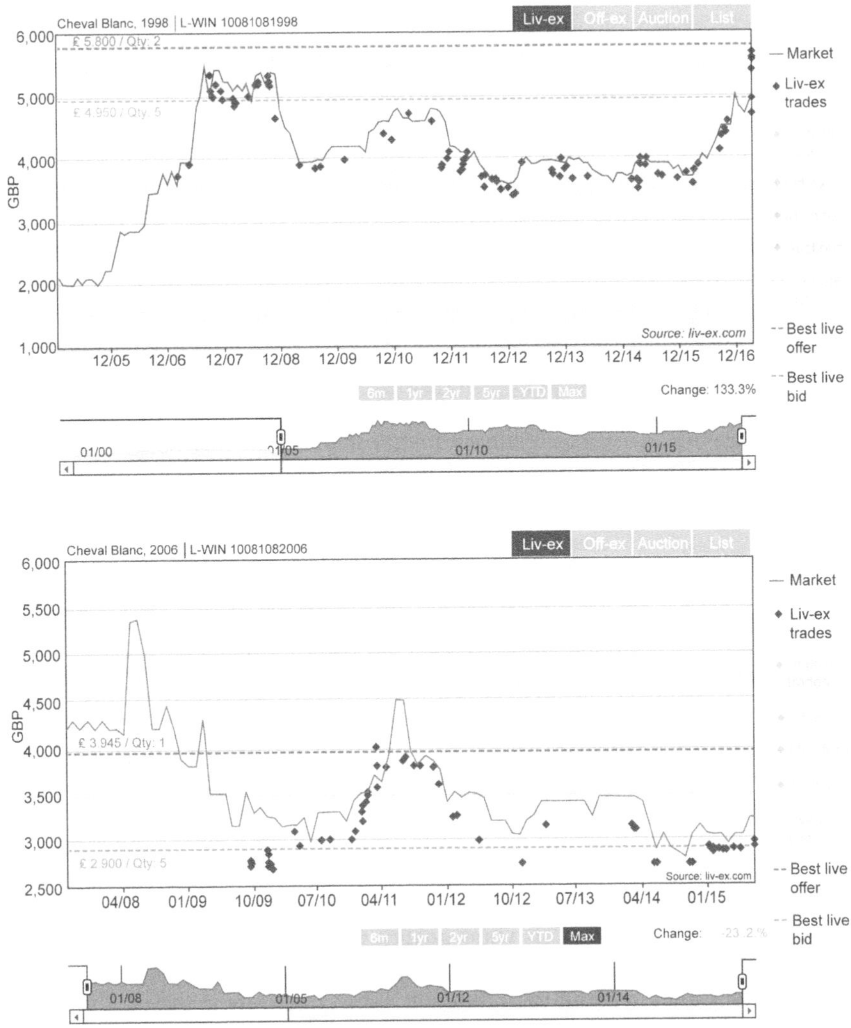

Figure 12.3 Evolution of the market price of *Château Cheval Blanc* (1998 and 2006) vintages

Source: liv-ex.com.

Cash management in the en primeur *sales system*

For each wine estate owner, cash management remains a key concern. In the case of traditional wine estates (excluding top wines), the main question is how to finance inventories. For top wine producers, the question addressed is different because of the *en primeur* sales system. Originating from extant Bordeaux wine practices for fine wines, this original sale system alleviates the need for short-term financing. As mentioned earlier, *en primeur* allocations result in prepayments made in one to three installments before the end of the current financial year. At an accounting level, these prepayments are recorded in 'Down payments received' accounts in the books of the wine estate. Each prepayment has to be accurately identified and followed through as per vintage 'Down payments received' account. The monitoring of the payments received must be very rigorous. Until the delivery date, the 'Down payment received' accounts are aggregated and reported in the 'current liabilities' item of the balance sheet. The volume of wines reserved through the allocations system remains recognized at its production cost in the inventories on the asset side of the balance sheet. This accounting scheme may appear a bit surprising in as much as the parties have already agreed on the goods and the price. In a different domain from that of wine, title would be transferred at this stage. In the case of wine, it is necessary that it should be of 'fair marketable quality'.[6] It is only at the delivery date (minimum two years after the harvest of each vintage) that the revenue related to the wines reserved through the allocations system has to be recorded in the income statement and the gross profit margin recognized. This mismatch between the growing of vine, harvests, *en primeur* prepayments and delivery date leads to a sensitive cash management.

Concluding comments

In this chapter, we have endeavored to analyze different historical periods of the Bordeaux wine trade since the Middle Ages by focusing upon a sociocultural framework that shaped market activities, mainly price setting. Key to our analysis has been the important role of reputation and trust, embedded in an evolving institutional structure that provided growing legitimacy for the wine market in the region. We also note the serendipitous nature of political circumstances in facilitating the requisite international trade that sustained the industry in its early years. In addition to significant local and state institutions that have provided a regulatory framework since the Middle Ages, we note the importance of increased knowledge and technical innovations that resulted in dramatic improvements in wine quality. From the 17th century onwards, improved quality was at the heart of subsequent industry growth. By the 18th century, consumer demand for a different, more robust wine played a vital role in the expansion of Bordeaux red wines in England and Holland. Finally, local authorities and institutions, such as the *Jurade*, played a key role in promoting Bordeaux wines.

Throughout all these changes, the product itself – the actual wine – was acquiring a cultural dimension. The evolving market was predicated upon trust and power relationships that acknowledged implicit normative operational rules and governed transactions. This was further substantiated by opinion leaders and wine professionals who conferred respectability upon the product, legitimizing its status. Thus, what we see is a nuanced synthesis of price, status, reputation, history, quality and quantity that all come together in a marketplace designed to protect incumbents and enforce transactional behavior. In other words, tradition and history remain significant symbolic markers that structure market transactions.

Although we are in effect on the outside looking in, it would seem reasonable to conclude that accounting has had little role to play in the price-setting process that brings fine Bordeaux to the market. The vine harvest is of course affected by factors such as the weather and vintage (see Figure 12.2), which cannot easily be accounted for. Having said that, it is reasonable to assume that any wine estate will keep good records of production and of associated costs of production. However, the price of the end product has been – and is – influenced by the socio-cultural factors mentioned earlier, and thus we can assume that accounting tasks have little or no role to play with regard to price setting. Of course, once a price has been agreed – through the *en primeur* system, for example – then accounting can easily calculate the profit (or loss) made. Nevertheless, accounting plays a key role in effectively managing the cash generated through this original sales system.

Notes

1 Unfortunately, access to archival data – such as accounting records – of Bordeaux wine estates is difficult, as they are mainly privately owned and do not make detailed records available to the public.
2 *Claret* was a young and light wine; at that time, older wines were not appreciated.
3 It is at this time that the inter-merchants credit developed. It was based on the use of variable-rate loans and on a garnishment system in case of unpaid bills.
4 Given by the *Jurade*, the '*bourgeois*' status granted some privileges. This status was passed down within families.
5 Lowlands.
6 This double condition implies respect for the technical specifications of the Registered Designation of Origin (AOC) that notably defines the duration of the aging process to be respected before the wine should be bottled and delivered.

References

Baritaux, V., Aubert, M., Montaigne, E. and Remaud, H. (2006). Matchmakers in wine marketing channels: The case of French wine brokers. *Agribusiness*, 22(3), pp. 375–390.

Birlouez, E. (2015). *Histoire du vin en France de l'antiquité à la révolution.* Éditions Rennes, France: Ouest-France.

Chastenet, J. (1980). *L'Epopée des vins de Bordeaux.* Paris: Perrin.

Lavaud, S. (2003). *Bordeaux et le vin au Moyen Age: Essor d'une civilisation.* Bordeaux: Éditions Sud-Ouest.

Markham, D., Jr. (1997). *1855 Histoire d'un classement des vins de Bordeaux*. Bordeaux: Éditions Féret.

Meyzie, P. (2012). Du négoce aux journaux d'annonces: les mécanismes de diffusion des vins aquitains au XVIIIème siècle, article extrait du livre. In: *Vendre le vin de l'Antiquité à nos jours, Cervin*. Bordeaux: Éditions Féret, pp. 159–176.

Philip, M. and Lacarce, X. (2015). *Petite Histoire de Bordeaux*. Pau: Éditions Cairn.

Philips, R. (2016). *French Wine: A History*. Berkley: University of California Press.

Remaud, H., Jaillette, M. and Villain, C. (2015). *The en primeur Wine Sales of Bordeaux Classified Growths*. JAREDOC Distribution (www.filmenprimeur.com).

Trabut-Cussac, J. P. (1950). Les coutumes et droit de douane perçus à Bordeaux sur les vins et les marchandises par l'administration anglaise. *Annales du Midi: revue archéologique, historique et philosophique de la France méridionale*, 62(10), pp. 135–150.

13 Accounting in Spanish co-operative wineries during the 20th century

Francisco J. Medina-Albaladejo[1]

Introduction

Historically, the food sector has dominated the Spanish economy, and viticulture has played a leading role within this sector. Internationally, Spain is one of the leading wine producers and exporters, alongside France and Italy. Co-operative wineries emerged in the late 19th century and have played an increasingly important role in the sector ever since – their importance is especially notable from the second half of the 20th century onwards. As a result of the expansion by co-operative wineries during that period, by 2008 co-operative wineries accounted for 70% of overall production in Spain (General Committee for Agricultural Cooperation in the European Union, 2010). In a wider context, however, Spanish literature on accounting has paid little attention to this type of organisation. The only studies to examine co-operative wineries have done so from the perspective of economic history, agrarian history or business history. The main aim of this chapter is to show the evolution of accounting practices in the Spanish co-operative wineries throughout the 20th century and how they helped members and managers of these companies in the decision-making process to operate in markets with increasing competition. The chapter analyses the main organisational changes undergone by co-operative wineries in the mentioned period, and also describes how the wineries' accounting practices adapted to these changes and to external pressure posed by the state and the market.

The theoretical framework adopted for this analysis is worthy of brief elaboration. This study uses elements of institutional theory, which is aligned with Cook's (1995) model of the co-operative life cycle. The key idea is that, in organisational terms, from a starting point characterised by diversity, institutions tend to move towards the adoption of homogeneous models because of pressure posed by environmental factors. Isomorphism can be either competitive or institutional. Competitive isomorphism is the result of economic pressures posed by competitive markets, whereas institutional isomorphism is a consequence of the normalisation and routinisation of given practices (Quinn, 2014). The transformation of the organisational and formal structure of firms responds to technological, political and legal changes – that is, to internal and external factors which trigger organisational changes. Di Maggio and Powell (1983) divided these changes into three categories of institutional isomorphism: coercive, mimetic and normative. Coercive isomorphism is chiefly related to political pressure and legal rules; normative isomorphism is associated with organisational maturity and the professionalisation of firms' management; mimetic isomorphism involves responding to uncertainty by adopting existing models that are believed to be successful (Di Maggio, 1983; Di Maggio and Powell, 1983; Powell, 1988, 1991; Powell and Di Maggio, 1991). Cook (1995) divided the life cycle of the agrarian co-operative firm into five stages: economic justification, organisational design, growth and consequences, crisis and identification of conflict and restructuration. The present chapter focuses on changes or stability in institutionalised organisational and accounting practices in Spanish co-operative wineries, using this model as a point of reference.

The sources used for this study consist mainly of the accounting records of three Spanish co-operative wineries – Rosario (Murcia), San Isidro (Murcia)[2] and Pinoso (Alicante). San Isidro was one of the largest Spanish co-operative wineries in terms of production and turnover during the second half of the 20th century (Medina-Albaladejo, 2011). The records span the period between the early 1930s and the 1980s. Accounting records dating to the late 1960s and 1970s, which belong to another 75 co-operative wineries located in the main wine-producing regions, have also been consulted; these records are stored in the archives of the Spanish Ministry of Labour and the General Administrative Archive (Madrid).

This chapter is organised chronologically, following the different stages of co-operative wineries, concentrating on their organisational and accounting practices. After the introduction, the first section deals with the emergence of these organisations between the late 19th century and the beginning of the Spanish Civil War, in the late 1930s. The second section addresses evolution during Francoism, which was a period of expansion for co-operative wineries in Spain. The third section discusses the changes brought about by the end of Francoism and the arrival of democracy, including the modernisation of accounting systems. Lastly, some concluding comments are given.

Initial steps (late 19th century to 1936)

The origin of co-operative wineries in Spain dates back to the late 19th century. During the first third of the 20th century, these entities expanded into several regions of the country and by 1935 there were 116 such societies, 70% of which were concentrated in a single region, namely Catalonia. The dissemination of the co-operative model throughout Spanish wine-producing regions was slow compared to France, which was the leading wine-producing country of the time. The widespread adoption of the model occurred after the Spanish Civil War (1936–1939), during Francoism (1939–1975). This expansion was supported by legal and financial support of the state in a context of falling prices for grapes and wine (Fernández and Simpson, 2017; Planas and Medina-Albaladejo, 2017).

By and large, Spanish historiographers have not regarded these first co-operative wineries as a successful model. Problems caused by poor cohesion and a conflict-ridden social and political environment in the Spanish countryside support this negative perspective. Agrarian co-operatives were an inter-class phenomenon, and within this phenomenon, two trends may be noted. First, an earlier model was secular and reformist in character, whereas the other, which crystallised at a later date, was largely Catholic and conservative in nature. This division was detrimental to the consolidation of the co-operative model prior to the Civil War, and competition between co-operatives resulted in poor overall performance (Planas and Valls-Junyet, 2011).[3] Second, a lack of state support also had a negative impact (Garrido, 2007; Planas and Medina-Albaladejo, 2017) – the only exception was the Catalan regional government, which supported the formation and development of these organisations (Planas, 2016).

As a result of these factors, Spanish agrarian co-operatives were small and under-capitalised organisations, with poor solvency; they were thus ephemeral and unable to consolidate. They focused their activities on acquiring supplies and providing credit for their members instead of industrial processing of raw materials and marketing of the final product. This was due to the fact that the initial investment to build the facilities to produce wine was quite high for these weak and small companies, and the state did not help them from a financial point of view (Saumell, 2002; Planas, 2003; Garrido, 2007).

Medina-Albaladejo and Menzani (2017), following Cook's (1995) agrarian co-operative life cycle institutional approach, established the different organisational stages of Spanish co-operative wineries. The first stage corresponds to the 'economic justification' of these organisations and the defensive nature of the model. Co-operative wineries were conceived as a mechanism which could be used to deal with a critical moment caused by the fall of wine prices and agrarian rents driven by over-production (Medina-Albaladejo, 2016). These early co-operatives were poorly consolidated and socially homogenous organisations (which prevented internal conflict), and they largely operated on a local scale; their organisational structure was simple, their financial position precarious and their management non-professional. The earliest attempt to regulate the operation of co-operatives was the Agrarian Co-operatives Act,[4] enacted in 1906. Previously, co-operatives operated within the framework of the 1885 Commercial Code,[5] which required the use of double-entry book-keeping, through books such as *libro de diario* (journal book), *libro mayor* (ledger), *libro de inventarios y balances* (inventories and balances book)[6] and *libro de actas* (minute book) and the annual preparation of balance sheets. The 1906 Act maintained the obligation to maintain the accounting systems imposed by the 1885 Commercial Code.[7] In addition, in order to monitor the tax exemptions granted by the new act, co-operatives were compelled to submit copies of their annual balance sheet to public regulators.[8] The 1906 Act was in force until the Second Republic (1931–1936). The Special Co-operatives Act was enacted on 8 September 1931,[9] but this new act brought about virtually no changes to accounting requirements.

All the mentioned legislation did not specify the accounting method that co-operatives, which were formed by small landowners and were typically lacking a professional management team, had to implement. In this context, co-operative wineries started introducing accounting methods, particularly double-entry bookkeeping (although the 1906 Act did not make this compulsory). By the late 19th century, the double-entry method was widespread across commercial organisations in Spain and was present in several contemporary texts on accounting published around that time: Castaño (1876), Oliver (1884) and Torrents (1885) (Benito and Portella, 2013; Donoso et al., 2006; Santos et al., 2014). The accounts of co-operative wineries were recorded in inventories and balances books. The *libro de diario* (journal book) and *libro mayor* (ledger) collected detailed information of all transactions of the co-operative. In order to ensure that the information recorded in the *libro de diario* and *libro mayor* was correct, account balances were checked by an accountant within the co-operative. These records compiled information concerning accounts, assets and financial position in general, but they chiefly focused on transaction recording, rather than on other items such as cost estimates. Table 13.1 presents a balance sheet for San Isidro in the 1930s. The records were not particularly sophisticated and were based on simple groupings of items, but they provided a relatively accurate idea of liquidity, inventories, fixed assets, debt and share capital.

During this period, co-operatives also took their first steps in developing techniques for the estimation of costs (though there was no legal obligation to do this).

Table 13.1 Balance sheet of the co-operative winery San Isidro, at the time known as El Progreso, 31 December 1937

Assets		*Liabilities*	
	Pesetas		*Pesetas*
Cash	27,668.35	Current accounts	13,300.20
Current accounts	249,280.25	Grapes 1937–1938	675.65
Inventories (vinegar)	1,586.35	Winery section 1937–1938	223,700.60
Sales section	29,569.70	Mandatory contributions	13,125.00
Alcohol factory section, 1937–1938	9,130.85	Non-mandatory contributions	1,028.65
Oil mill section, 1937–1938	668.20	Rural saving bank section	1,307.70
Machinery and equipment	4,696.50	Winery section capital	9,704.80
Laboratory	135.40	Sales section capital	17,422.25
Furniture	8,083.15	Machinery	15,680.00
Current account rural saving bank	25.00	Share capital	34,898.90
Total	330,843.75	Total	330,843,75

Source: Archive of the co-operative winery San Isidro. *Libro de inventarios y balances* (inventories and balances book).

This was largely undertaken for internal control purposes, and no general rules were applied. As such, co-operatives carried out this exercise in pursuance of their own specific interests, especially as a guide for pricing. This information was calculated in a very aggregate manner using data collected in the *libros de diario* (journal book) and *libro mayor* (ledger), focusing on such items as products (i.e., wine and other related products), labour costs, facility rent, transport, repairs of machinery and facilities, taxes and administration. However, while this may seem like an introduction of management accounting, at this stage the focus of accounting seemed to remain on legal requirements – for example, to monitor fiscal obligations towards the state – rather than as an instrument to inform decision making (i.e., management accounting). For example, the minute books of the board of directors' meetings and the general assembly hardly mentioned accounting documents in the decision-making process; only the more general aspects were mentioned.[10]

These co-operative wineries produced low-quality wine, which was generally commercialised in bulk. Because they lacked their own distribution networks, their retail sales were very low. As a consequence of this, their pricing policies bore little relation to costs, which could be related with their underdeveloped cost/management accounting methods. Prices were determined by the overcrowded conditions of the market and the strong bargaining position of purchasers – wholesale merchants or consolidated mercantile firms. In addition to this, co-operatives needed to sell their stock as soon as possible to leave room to process and store the subsequent harvest. This undermined their bargaining position even further. Finally, co-operatives were often forced to pay prices higher than market prices for grapes as a way to make the co-operative more attractive to new members. That is, the prices of raw materials were driven by a particular market logic. As a result of such factors, the financial position of co-operative wineries was precarious, and they were vulnerable to the threats posed by internal and external pressures and the lack of direct state support (Medina-Albaladejo, 2011).

In conclusion, the accounting practices used by co-operative wineries before the 1940s directly reflected the characteristics of these organisations – small organisations composed of small and medium-sized landowners with no training in accounting, who followed simple administrative procedures and adopted accounting methods which were dictated by external state pressures in the form of legislation. Despite these shortcomings, the fact is that this sector witnessed the earliest adoption of accounting methods, rudimentary as they were, in wine-producing regions dominated by small landowners.

Francoist interventionism (1939–1971)

The expansion of the co-operative model to most wine-producing areas, especially major regions such as Castilla-La Mancha which the model had not reached previously, took place after the Civil War. This was due to the financial support of the state. In 1954, there were 324 co-operative wineries, accounting for 16% of overall production. By 1969 the number of co-operatives had soared to 780 and represented 50% of the national production. In 1980, the proportion of production controlled by these organisations reached 60%, and in 2008, 70% – a percentage that has remained stable since. During the second half of the 20th century, the expansion of the co-operative model in Spain was similar to that in other countries such as France, where this movement had begun earlier and had firmer foundations (Medina-Albaladejo and Menzani, 2017).

This process of expansion also involved the end of the traditional ideological division between progressive and conservative co-operatives. The 1940s witnessed a process of ideological purging, a restructuring and homogenisation of all the Spanish co-operative movement. Co-operatives came under the control of public bodies, and in this way they instituted a mechanism of social control in the countryside and became a means to intervene in the wine market which suffered from endemic problems stemming from overproduction (Lanero, 2011; Cabana and Díaz-Geada, 2014). The state provided financial support for the construction of industrial facilities and for day-to-day operations, either by direct subsidies or by offering soft loans (i.e., with better conditions than those available in market for similar situations). Public aid was also provided for the purchase of machinery and supplies, and any part of the harvest which was difficult to sell in the open market was bought by the state (Planas and Medina-Albaladejo, 2017).

Spanish co-operative wineries then entered the second (organisational design) and third (growth and consequences) organisational stages. During these years, the organisational design of co-operative wineries was marked by isomorphism, which was promoted by the coercive pressures applied through the new Co-operatives Act, enacted in 1942, and the close control exercised by public agencies. Simultaneously, the model entered a rapid process of state-sponsored expansion. Article 3 of the 1942 Act was very clear: "As long as they do not contravene this Act, co-operative societies will be allowed to act autonomously according to their statutes, which will follow the guidelines of [. . .] the State".[11] Article 6 emphasised this point: "co-operative societies will be part of the *Obra Sindical de Cooperación* [National Trade Union of Co-operation], and will follow its guidelines".[12] Public agencies were given the power to dissolve co-operatives should it considered to be in the national interest.[13]

The development of co-operatives during Francoism facilitated mass production and the industrialisation of the wine sector in Spain (Pan-Montojo, 2001). However, the support provided by the Francoist regime did not contribute to the implementation of sound management policies, despite growth in the number of co-operatives triggered by state financial support. Some literature points out that these institutions suffered from severe financial and operational shortcomings (Saumell, 2004; Planas, 2013). They were economically and financially inefficient and were heavily dependent on external funding due to long-term debt to both the state and private banks (Medina-Albaladejo, 2015). These shortcomings also applied to operational aspects such as production management. The operational problems largely stemmed from the co-operatives' lack of autonomy in the decision-making process, due to forced integration into a corporate system backed by a dictatorial regime and the increasing heterogeneity of members. These associations no longer emerged spontaneously, but were rather promoted by the government and had no ideological foundations or social homogeneity which would ensure the cohesion of members. As a result of this lack of commitment, members were more interested in furthering their individual interests by seeking maximum short-term profit, thus undermining the co-operatives' ability to make new investments and hindering the daily operations of the society. In addition, they espoused an openly production-oriented attitude, regardless of market conditions. All raw material provided by members had to be bought (at inflated prices) and processed, with no consideration for the quality of the final product. Many co-operative wineries needed short-term loans from the state to continue operating. These problems were compounded by a political regime which was unable to manage the potential of a sector that controlled a very significant proportion of domestic wine production (Medina-Albaladejo, 2015).

Spanish co-operative wineries operated at regional and local levels and generally marketed a single product (low- to medium-quality wine, sold in bulk). In comparison to what happened in other countries, such as France and Italy, these co-operatives did not engage in integration processes, either vertical or horizontal. Their organisational structure remained simple and had no professional management. Legislation did not help in this regard. For example, Article 8 of the 1942 Act said that "no administrative function will be permanently entrusted to any given person or institution".[14] Positions were renewable and had to be occupied by members regardless of their ability to carry out administrative, management or marketing tasks. Appointments were controlled by public agencies, who reserved the power to veto appointees. In addition, managers had responsibility for decisions that were deemed to be against the spirit of co-operative action according to legislation.[15]

Forced organisational isomorphism[16] increased the development and homogenisation of accounting methods in co-operative wineries as an extra control mechanism. Homogenisation, however, was not total, as the legislation did not give detailed instructions on the sort of information that had to feature in accounting records. The 1942 Act, and its attached regulations, published in 1943, established accounting systems that differed little from those that had already been put in place in the preceding decades. Single- or double-entry bookkeeping was required, depending on the complexity of the operations carried out by each co-operative, as well as annual balance sheets.[17] The regulations also recommended producing annual reports, but this was optional.[18] These records were to be submitted every year to the public regulators.[19] The production of an annual balance sheet, reflecting the economic and financial position of co-operative societies, was by then widespread among Spanish co-operative wineries. Although double-entry bookkeeping was generalised, the lack of common criteria in accounting methods persisted. Generally, accounting practices attempted to follow the guidelines set by the public regulators, but they were managed by people with no specific accounting training. As a result, accounting criteria changed over time even within a single organisation. Entries that featured in the accounts for a number of years could later disappear, having been integrated into more general entries, or indeed be disaggregated into other items. For example, this was very usual in the case of the grouping of items in balance sheets, such as Receivable, Realisable, Fixed assets, etc.[20] Table 13.2 illustrates an example of a balance sheet from the 1950s. Compared to that from before the

Table 13.2 Balance sheet of the co-operative winery San Isidro, 31 December 1958

Assets		*Liabilities*	
	Pesetas		*Pesetas*
Cash and bank deposits	**1,361,798.34**	**Miscellaneous accounts**	**1,009,451.90**
Furniture and equipment	**38,846.90**	Guarantee	1,000,000.00
Machinery and tools	**1,786,178.75**	Social insurances balance	7,276.25
Wine tanks	**803,728.05**	Department treasury	2,175.65
Buildings	**601,808.20**	**Accounts payable**	**4,075,500.00**
Tractors	**455,794.37**	CA loan	425,000.00
Hidro-Nitro SA stocks	**27,400.00**	DGA loan	1,742,500.00
Fuels and oils	**26,912.10**	Other pending payments	1,908,000.00
Stock fertilisers	**196,458.35**	**Current accounts**	**8,812,324.66**
Improve facilities	**1,598,830.31**	Banks	3,858,592.60
Waste machinery	**75,900.35**	Customers, suppliers and others	1,744,363.66
Miscellaneous accounts	**1,193,177.37**	CCEV	1,250,000.00
Guarantee	1,000,000.00	SNCA	1,265,000.00
Expenses loan vine	49,894.31	Members	694,368.40
Results 1858	35,618.67	**Retained capital**	**2,313,255.95**
Grape, 1958–59	86,813.89	Feed mill section contributions	14,400.40
By-products, 1958–59	8,200.50	Alcohol factory section contributions	10,304.50
Oil mill section, 1958–59	12,650.00	Mandatory contributions	21,368.10
Current accounts	**8,552,516.67**	Assembly 1946 contributions	284,845.00
Loans vines	1,173,250.00	Assembly 1954 contributions	1,982,337.95
Customers, suppliers and others	346,696.74	**Funds for social causes**	**508,817.25**
Members	7,032,569.93	Reserve fund	84,332.55
		Social works	56,221.75
		Prevision fund	30,226.30
		Amortisations	338,036.65
Total	**16,719,349.76**	**Total**	**16,719,349.76**

Source: Archive of the co-operative winery San Isidro. *Libro de inventarios y balances* (inventories and balances book).

Civil War, the grouping of items is more sophisticated and more concepts are specified. However, certain groupings such as fixed assets are still absent, and the associated items have been disaggregated in different entries, such as machinery and tools, wine tanks, buildings, furniture and equipment.

The distribution of profits was determined by law.[21] Co-operatives had to create a reserve fund (to act as a security net against losses) and another fund for social causes (to aid members in need), which were extracted from the profit margin (a minimum of 25%). The rest of the profit was distributed among members. The public regulator ensured that this allocation of profit was respected, and this regulator had the power to fine and sanction if it was not.[22]

The Francoist period also witnessed the introduction of more developed cost and management accounting. Internal accounting documents, such as extracts of overhead costs or production costs, became common, although they were not required by any regulation. These documents demonstrate the growing complexity of management and production policies among co-operative wineries, though we should bear in mind that these accounting practices were adopted later by the co-operative wine sector more than by other Spanish firms (Donoso et al., 2006). From a methodological perspective, in any case, accounts were still poorly developed. As illustrated in Table 13.3, the managers of Pinoso made no distinction between fixed and variable costs, limiting themselves to recording the different expenses incurred by the society. The accounts of San Isidro and Rosario followed a similar practice.[23] Accounting documents were rarely used to inform strategic decisions, to a large extent because of the societies' small margin for manoeuvre, which was constrained by organisational features and their dependence on the public bodies. As was the case before the Civil War, co-operative wineries and their non-professional management adopted accounting practices in order to comply with the external pressure posed by the state, rather than to aid decision-making processes. The main purpose of cost estimates was to inform pricing, of both the wine sold and the grapes purchased from members. The co-operatives' capacity for making autonomous decisions in this regard was very limited due to market conditions and the strong bargaining position of purchasers and members. Again, management were generally in a rush to sell the wine to make room for the following harvest, which weakened their bargaining position even more. Profit allocation was to a large degree decreed by the administration, until investment during the 1960s was directed towards increasing the size of facilities with the aid of the state (a move which also allowed for the incorporation of new members).

Another type of document that was not legally compulsory was end-of-season reports, containing detailed information about production and commercialisation, which the co-operatives circulated internally. Total production of wine and by-products, market sale prices, liquidation prices, volume of product sold by types of product and overall, gradation of the grape by the Baumé scale[24] and the average alcoholic content of the wine were among the usual entries in these reports. Annual reports were also not compulsory.[25] These annual documents provided general information concerning the position of the society in qualitative and quantitative terms. The information provided covered internal and external issues, such as the number of members, the size of the agricultural property owned by members, global perspectives of the season and liquidation prices, total production, sales and turnover, investments in real estate and

Table 13.3 Extract of overhead costs and production costs of the co-operative winery Pinoso, 1965–1966

Overhead costs		*Production costs*	
	Pesetas		*Pesetas*
Taxes	11,994.95	Accident insurance	10,249.79
Telephone	3,000.05	Lighting	17,899.11
Office employees' wages	82,213.81	Fuels and oils	1,823.00
Administrator bonus	45,200.00	Winery temporary employees' wages	117,250.00
Social insurance	14,273.23	Winery employees' wages	161,120.53
Mail	1,530.30	Winery employees' bonus	23,975.00
Office supplies	7,170.45	Other wages	7,310.00
Weighing machine	19,759.00	Machinery repairs	102,143.67
Lighting	11,768.92	Cleaning products	5,187.00
Heating	1,725.50	Transport	3,926.00
Business expenses	9,036.00	Taxes	5,534.67
First aid kit	232.30	Oenological products	108,259.35
Accident insurance	2,211.21	Forms	1,863.78
Journals subscriptions	780.00	Social insurance	35,794.61
Donations	255.00	Business expenses	3,050.00
Building repairs	11,954.50	Advertising	1,500.00
Miscellaneous expenses	5,871.61	Laboratory	3,947.00
		Miscellaneous expenses	5,439.50
Total	228,976.83	Total	616,273.01
Wine production (litres)	3,746,820	Unit cost per litre of wine	0.2256

Source: Archive of the co-operative winery Pinoso. *Memorias Anuales 1965–66* (Annual Report, 1965–66).

equipment, financial position and management strategy. These reports also kept the members informed on who occupied the different management positions, and included general- and production-expense reports and profit statements.

The end of Francoism and the democratic period (1971–1980)

During the 1970s and 1980s, Spanish co-operative wineries entered Cook's (1995) fourth stage, 'crisis and recognition of conflicts'. This was a difficult time for the societies, as they entered a severe crisis due to their limited ability to adapt to radical changes within the market. Timid attempts were made to restructure and adapt to the new market conditions, but these attempts are still underway, and stage 5 has not been reached yet; this is in stark contrast to other countries, such as France and Italy (Medina-Albaladejo and Menzani, 2017).

The mid-1970s witnessed substantial changes in the wine market. Consumer preferences adopted a new pattern: instead of low-quality wine to be consumed daily as part of the Mediterranean diet, consumers began demanding smaller quantities of better-quality wines, which were bottled and better presented in general. Alongside other factors, this contributed to reduce the per-capita consumption of wine – a trend that persists to this day (Martínez-Carrión and Medina-Albaladejo, 2010). This change in consumption patterns posed a severe challenge to co-operative wineries, which specialised in the production of low-quality wine and adopted an unqualified production-oriented policy instead of a market-oriented one. In addition, the co-operatives' production capacity was overinflated, due to the growth process of the previous period with the support of the state. The fact that they were compelled to sell as fast as possible to make room for the following harvest did not help their bargaining position or the setting of sound pricing policies, as already mentioned. As such, the production of co-operative wineries was a good fit for the consumption patterns that prevailed in the 1940s, 1950s and 1960s. However, the co-operatives found it difficult to adapt to increasing competition and the decrease in consumption characteristic of the 1970s and 1980s. The market began exerting strong external pressures, selling prices in the domestic market stagnated and the co-operatives found it increasingly difficult to sell the wine produced with all grapes brought in by their members. These members in turn kept demanding a high price for their raw materials.[26]

The most common reaction to these pressures among co-operative wineries was to maintain their traditional management structures. This again demonstrates that these societies were still not market-oriented – this was the outcome of the interventionism practiced by the state during the previous period and internal organisational inertia. This left co-operative wineries at a clear disadvantage in the face of capitalist firms, increasingly competitive markets and decreasing consumption (Planas and Medina-Albaladejo, 2017). Some moderate reforms were undertaken, which were partially driven by public initiative. A new decree (2369/1971) was enacted in 1971 – that is, 28 years after the previous one – establishing a new set of regulations for co-operatives. These new regulations permitted the setting up of semi-professional management, and many co-operative wineries began hiring managers who, for the first time, used accounting to inform decision-making processes – especially those concerning investments to improve productivity and adapt to demand. This process of normative isomorphism, however, was only undertaken tentatively by some societies and not in all regions.

From the point of view of accounting, the state tried to adapt the existing legislation to the new conditions and bring it closer to European regulations (Romero, 1981). The 1971 decree made double-entry bookkeeping compulsory, regardless of region and the scale of operations,[27] and also demanded that co-operatives submit a profit and loss account to the public regulators,[28] along with the balance sheet and the annual report, which was no longer optional.[29]

In addition, the new decree gave members the right, for the first time, to request information on administrative issues and accounts. The outcome of this decree was the homogenisation of accounting practices among Spanish co-operative wineries. Official models for the balance sheet, the profit and loss account and extracts of production costs were created for societies to complete and submit (see Tables 13.4 and 13.5). Concerning the balance sheet, the grouping of items was more developed, and was similar to that which commercial regulators demanded of the rest of mercantile society. As illustrated in Table 13.6 (an example from San Isidro), the balance sheets submitted by co-operatives tried to respond to the new demands posed by the public regulator. This was, however, not the case of the profit and loss account and the extracts of production costs. As suggested by a sample of this kind of document belonging to 75 co-operatives, which are currently held in the archives of the Spanish Labour Ministry (General Administrative Archive), societies began to record these data only

Table 13.4 Official balance sheet model established by the Spanish Ministry of Labour

Assets	*Liabilities*
Liquid assets	**Current liabilities**
Cash	Creditors
Bank deposits	Accounts payable
Receivable	Un-subscriptions
Debtors	Fund for social causes
Prepaid expenses	**Long-term liabilities**
Realisable	Creditors
Stocks	Amortisations
Inventories	**Contingency accounts**
Fixed assets	Guarantee
Buildings	**Shareholders' equity**
Facilities	Share capital
Machinery and tools	Reserve funds
Vehicles	
Animals	
Furniture	
Containers	
Fund for social causes	
Financial fixed assets	
Contingency accounts	
Guarantee	

Source: General Administrative Archive, (14) 001.004, *Balances de cooperativas* (Balance sheets of co-operatives).

Table 13.5 Official profit and loss account and extract of production costs models established by the Spanish Ministry of Labour

Profit and loss account	*Extract of production costs*
Inventories	**Previous inventories**
Sales	**Purchases**
Interests	**Chemical products**
Membership fees	**Transport**
Amortisations	**Employees' transport**
Overhead costs	**Freights**
Business expenses	**Wages**
Wages	**Social insurance**
Extraordinary payments	**Containers**
Bonus	**Fuels**
Production expenses	**Driving force**
Taxes and insurances	**Facilities repairs**
Donations	**Rentals**
Water, lighting, cleaning and heating	**Water**
Social insurance	
Mail, telephone, telegraph	**Inventories**
Travels	**Sales**
Facilities repairs	By-products
Office supplies	Warehouse products
Journals subscriptions	Wine
Miscellaneous expenses	
Total	**Total**
Net profit	**Gross profit**
Reserve fund (15%)	**Loss**
Fund for social causes (10%)	
Dividend (75%)	
Loss	

Source: General Administrative Archive, (14) 001.004, *Balances de cooperativas* (Balance sheets of co-operatives).

because it was legally required. Recording was undertaken in a very aggregate manner, and they left most entries in the official models blank.[30]

The General Co-operatives Act was enacted in 1974, but this brought no changes to accounting practices.[31] The General Co-operatives Act of 2 April 1987 (3/1987)[32] and the Co-operatives Act of 16 July 1999 (27/1999),[33] both of which incorporated European regulations, involved the final modernisation of the Spanish legal framework and accounting practices. Also, new regional regulations have contributed to update business practices among these societies in recent years. These recent developments are beyond the temporal scope of this chapter.

Table 13.6 Balance sheet of the co-operative winery San Isidro, 31 December 1977

Assets		*Liabilities*	
	Pesetas		*Pesetas*
Liquid assets	**45,450,165.98**	**Payables**	**88,823,339.19**
Cash	776,794.01	CRPM loans	88,823,339.19
Bank deposits	44,673,371.97	**Deposits Rural Saving Bank section**	**261,229,027.67**
Realisable	**570,329.20**	**Short-term loans**	**65,000,000.00**
Hidro-Nitro SA stocks	53,700.20	Banco Hispano-Americano	15,000,000.00
Ajavin stocks	516,629.00	Banco Exterior de España	15,000,000.00
Receivable	**299,424,928.77**	Caja Rural Provincial Murcia	35,000,000.00
Current accounts	299,424,928.77	**Export credits**	**42,799,243.00**
Fixed assets	**359,004,287.62**	Banco de Vizcaya	40,000,000.00
Buildings	700,000.00	Banco de Vizcaya	677,243.00
Old winery facilities	12,334,942.52	Banco Exterior de España	2,122,000.00
New winery facilities	214,942,836.10	**BCA loan**	**100,000,000.00**
Real estate	1,117,347.95	**Fixed equity**	**38,664,196.01**
Furniture	2,776,233.76	Grapes balance	18,271,792.77
Machinery and tools	102,305,356.46	Alcohol factory balance	8,472,116.00
Wine tanks	5,768,976.68	Bottling balance	11,920,287.24
Vehicles	1,535,090.00	**Funds for social causes**	**37,844,086.88**
Hydraulic wells	864,715.85	Commercial growth	77,737.02
Households	16,158,788.30	Social work	2,464,415.58
Warehouse	500,000.00	Reserve fund	2,932,216.05
Deferred charges	**1,024,891.00**	Amortisations	21,330,918.23
Social insurances	1,024,891.00	Admission fees	38,800.00
Administrative Accounts	**10,598,666.37**	Investments	11,000,000.00
Oil mill inventories	2,660,218.75	**Retained capital**	**82,422,876.19**
Bottling	6,261,528.17	Feed mill section contributions	14,357.60
Containers	1,676,919.45	Alcohol factory section contributions	10,138.55
Voluntary contributions	**709,500.00**	Mandatory contributions	34,785.60
Retained capital equities CRP	709,500.00	Contributions assembly 1946	284,238.00
		Contributions assembly 1954	82,079,356.44
Total	**716,782,768.94**	**Total**	**716,782,768.94**

Source: Archive of the co-operative winery San Isidro. *Libro de inventarios y balances* (inventories and balances book).

Concluding comments

Historically, Spain has held a leading position in the production and exportation of wine worldwide. Co-operative wineries played a key role in the evolution and industrialisation of the sector during the second half of the 20th century. This chapter has analysed the main organisational changes undergone by these societies informed by an institutional lens and how these changes and the external pressures posed by the state affected accounting practices.

Three chronological periods have been distinguished in this chapter. The first period stretches from the emergence of co-operative wineries in Spain to the beginning of the Spanish Civil War (late 19th century to 1936). This period was characterised by small, simple and financially weak co-operatives, which were governed by non-professional managers. Legislation compelled these societies to keep accounting records (inventories and balances book, journal book and ledger), although the methodology used to keep these records was not specified. This prompted co-operative wineries to adopt the most common accounting practices at the time, and so they used simple double-entry bookkeeping techniques and poorly developed cost estimation practices. The second period spans most of the Francoist period (1939–1970). This period witnessed the expansion of Spanish co-operative wineries and a process of growth that was triggered by the financial support of the state (which also imposed strict legal controls on the operation of co-operative societies). This contributed to the homogenisation of accounting practices and in some developments in management and cost accounting. It is argued that, during the first two periods, co-operative wineries, which followed production-oriented instead of market-oriented policies and were run by non-professional management, adopted accounting practices more as a response to legal requirements and institutional control – especially during Franco's dictatorship – than as an instrument for decision making. The third period dates from the end of Francoism to the early years of the democratic period (1970–1980). During this period, co-operative wineries took the first steps to modernise and adapt to external pressures posed by new market conditions, although these reforms were only moderate, owing to the organisational inertia and the outcome of decades of state control. Legislation which was adapted to European standards was implemented, as well as minor organisational changes, including the professionalisation of managers. As a result, accounting began to be considered a useful tool in decision making, in an incipient process of normative isomorphism, at the same time that a process of homogenisation of accounting practices also developed across co-operatives.

Notes

1 This chapter has been written within the framework of research projects: HAR2015–64076-P (MINECO/FEDER, EU) and HAR2016–76814-C2–1-P (MINECO/FEDER, EU). I would like to thank Professors Amparo Ruiz Llopis and Salvador Calatayud (University of Valencia, Spain) for their helpful comments and suggestions.

2 Until 1939 this society was called El Progreso. Francoist officials purged the co-operative after the Spanish Civil War and changed its name to San Isidro.
3 O'Rourke (2007) and Galassi (2001) refer to this same phenomenon when discussing the failure of co-operative dairies in Ireland and rural credit co-operatives in Southern Italy.
4 *Ley de Sindicatos Agrícolas* (Agrarian Co-operatives Act), 28 January 1906.
5 *Código de Comercio* (Commercial Code), 22 August 1885, arts. 25–26.
6 This document shows the assets and liabilities of the business in detail. The annual balance sheets summarise the information of this book.
7 *Código de Comercio* (Commercial Code), 22 August 1885, arts. 25–26.
8 *Ley de Sindicatos Agrícolas* (Agrarian Co-operatives Act), 28 January 1906, art. 12.
9 *Ley Especial de Cooperativas* (Special Co-operatives Act), 8 September 1931.
10 Archives of the co-operative wineries San Isidro and Pinoso. *Libros actas de la asamblea general y la junta rectora* (minute books of general assembly and board of directors).
11 *Ley de Cooperación* (Co-operatives Act), 2 January 1942, art. 3.
12 *Ley de Cooperación* (Co-operatives Act), 2 January 1942, art. 6.
13 *Ley de Cooperación* (Co-operatives Act), 2 January 1942, art. 29.
14 *Ley de Cooperación* (Co-operatives Act), 2 January 1942, art. 19.
15 *Ley de Cooperación* (Co-operatives Act), 2 January 1942, art. 26.
16 The policies of the Italian Fascist government were similar in this regard, as pointed out by Doni et al. (2016) and Antonelli et al. (2016), who analysed two breweries.
17 *Reglamento de Cooperación* (Co-operatives Regulation), 11 November 1943, arts. 8 and 73.
18 *Reglamento de Cooperación* (Co-operatives Regulation), 11 November 1943, arts. 21, 22 and 73.
19 *Reglamento de Cooperación* (Co-operatives Regulation), 11 November 1943, art. 73.
20 Archives of the co-operative wineries San Isidro, Rosario and Pinoso. *Libro de inventarios y balances* (inventories and balances book).
21 *Reglamento de Cooperación* (Co-operatives Regulation), 11 November 1943, art. 13.
22 *Reglamento de Cooperación* (Co-operatives Regulation), 11 November 1943, art. 13.
23 *Memorias* (Annual Reports), Archives of the co-operative wineries San Isidro and Rosario.
24 This unit measures the sugar content of grapes. After fermentation, these sugars become alcoholic. Traditionally, this variable has been used as the main criteria to establish the quality of the wine and the price paid by co-operatives to associates for their grapes.
25 *Reglamento de Cooperación* (Co-operatives Regulation), 11 November 1943, art. 73.
26 Archives of the co-operative wineres San Isidro, Rosario and Pinoso. *Libro de actas de la asamblea general* (minute book).
27 *Reglamento de Cooperación* (Co-operatives Regulation), 13 August 1971, art. 8.
28 This accounting tool did not become generalised among Spanish firms until the reform of the Commercial Code in 1973.
29 *Reglamento de Cooperación* (Co-operatives Regulation), 13 August 1971, art. 10.
30 Archivo General de la Administración (Spanish General Administrative Archive), (14) 001.004, *Balances de cooperativas* (balance sheets).
31 *Ley General de Cooperativas 52/1974* (General Co-operatives Act 52/1974), 19 December 1974.
32 *Ley General de Cooperativas 3/1987* (General Co-operatives Act 3/1987), 2 April 1987.
33 Ley de Cooperativas 27/1999 (Co-operatives Act 27/1999), 16 July 1999.

Sources

Archival sources

Archive of the co-operative winery San Isidro:

- *Balances generales* (balance sheets), 1942–1981.
- *Correspondencia* (mail), several years.

- *Estatutos y reglamentos internos* (internal rules), several years.
- *Informes liquidación de campaña* (end-of-season reports), 1934–2002.
- *Libros actas de la asamblea general* (minute books of general assembly), 1939; 1952; 1960–1983.
- *Libros balances, diario y mayor* (inventories and balance books, journal books and ledger), several years.
- Memorias anuales (annual reports), 1941; 1960–1972; 1974–1975.

Archive of the co-operative winery Rosario:

- *Balances generales* (balance sheets), 1950–1975; 1994–2006.
- *Correspondencia* (mail), 1950–2006.
- *Estatutos y reglamentos internos* (internal rules), several years.
- *Informes liquidación de campaña* (end-of-season reports), 1950–2006.
- *Libros actas de la asamblea general* (minute books of general assembly), 1950–2006.
- *Libros actas de la junta rectora* (minute books of board of directors), 1964–1993.
- *Libros balances, diario y mayor* (inventories and balance books, journal books and ledger), several years.
- Memorias anuales (annual reports), 1952; 1954–1971; 1976–1977; 1979.

Archive of the co-operative winery Pinoso:

- *Balances generales* (balance sheets), 1932–1939; 1947–1954; 1961–1993.
- *Correspondencia* (mail), several years.
- *Estatutos y reglamentos internos* (internal rules), 1945.
- *Informes liquidación de campaña* (end-of-season reports), 1971–1982.
- *Libros actas de la asamblea general* (minute books of general assembly), 1935–1943; 1945–1984; 1999–2008.
- *Libros actas de la junta rectora* (minute books of board of directors), 1936–1990.
- *Libros balances, diario y mayor* (inventories and balance books, journal books and ledger), several years.
- Memorias anuales (annual reports), 1965–1966; 1979–1980; 1981–1982.

Archivo General de la Administración (Spanish General Administrative Archive):

- *Balances de cooperativas* (balance sheets of several co-operative wineries). Several years.

Legislation

Código de Comercio (Commercial Code), 22 August 1885.

Ley de Sindicatos Agrícolas (Agrarian Co-operatives Act), 28 January 1906.

Ley Especial de Cooperativas (Special Co-operatives Act), 8 September 1931.

Ley de Cooperación (Co-operatives Act), 2 January 1942.

Reglamento de Cooperación (Co-operatives Regulation), 11 November 1943.

Reglamento de Cooperación (Co-operatives Regulation), 13 August 1971.

Ley General de Cooperativas 52/1974 (General Co-operatives Act 52/1974), 19 December 1974.

Ley General de Cooperativas 3/1987 (General Co-operatives Act 3/1987), 2 April 1987.

Ley de Cooperativas 27/1999 (Co-operatives Act 27/1999), 16 July 1999.

Secondary sources

Antonelli, B., D'Alessio, R. and Cafaro, E. M. (2016). 'I will be your beer!' Contexts, organization and accounting practices of Birra Peroni. An institutional perspective (1896–1946). In: L. D'Amico, R. Di Pietra and M. Sargiacomo, eds. *Accounting and Food: Some Italian Experiences*. New York and London: Routledge, pp. 1–22.

Benito, H. and Portella, J. (2013). Del comercio a la industria harinera: la sociedad Vilaplana, Ensesa y Cía. en la fábrica de Campdorà (Girona), 1893–1897. *De Computis, Spanish Journal of Accounting History*, 10(19), pp. 205–229.

Cabana, A. and Díaz-Geada, A. (2014). Exploring modernization; agrarian fascim in rural Spain, 1936–1951. In: L. Fernández-Prieto, J. Pan-Montojo and M. Cabo, eds. *Agriculture in the Age of Fascism: Authoritarian Technocracy and Rural Modernization, 1922–1945*. Turnhout: Brepols, pp. 189–217.

Castaño, F. (1876). *La verdadera contabilidad*. Madrid: Imprenta de Alejandro Gómez Fuentenebro.

Cook, M. L. (1995). The future of U.S. agricultural cooperatives: A neo-institutional approach. *American Journal of Agricultural Economics*, 77(5), pp. 1153–1159.

Di Maggio, P. J. (1983). State expansion and organizational fields. In: R. H. Hall and R. E. Quinn, eds. *Organizational Theory and Public Policy*. Beverly Hills: Sage Press, pp. 147–161.

Di Maggio, P. J. and Powell, W. W. (1983). The iron case revisited: Institutional isomorphism and collective rationality in organizational fields. *American Sociological Review*, 48(2), pp. 147–160.

Doni, F., Frausin, A. and Gasperini, A. (2016). Exploring sustainability practices and reporting in the brewery industry: The case of Birrificio Angelo Poretti-Calsberg Italia (1877–1980). In: L. D'Amico, R. Di Pietra and M. Sargiacomo, eds. *Accounting and Food: Some Italian Experiences*. New York and London: Routledge, pp. 69–97.

Donoso, R., Giner, B. and Ruiz, A. (2006). La contabilidad de costes a finales del s. XIX: el caso de la empresa española Trenor y Cía. (1838–1926). *De Computis, Spanish Journal of Accounting History*, 3(4), pp. 42–67.

Fernández, E. and Simpson, J. (2017). Product quality or market regulation? Explaining the slow growth of Europe's wine cooperatives, 1880–1980. *The Economic History Review*, 70(1), pp. 122–142.

Galassi, F. (2001). Measuring social capital: Culture as an explanation of Italy's economic dualism. *European Review of Economic History*, 5(1), pp. 29–59.

Garrido, S. (2007). Why did most cooperatives fail? Spanish agricultural cooperation in the early twentieth century. *Rural History*, 18(2), pp. 183–200.

General Committee for Agricultural Cooperation in the European Union (2010). *Agricultural Cooperatives in Europe*. Brussels: Cogeca.

Lanero, D. (2011). Sobre el encuadramiento de los campesinos y la agricultura en el tiempo de los fascismos: una comparación entre nazismo y franquismo. *Ayer*, 83, pp. 53–76.

Martínez-Carrión, J. M. and Medina-Albaladejo, F. J. (2010). Evolution and recent developments of Spanish wine sector, 1950–2008. *Journal of Wine Research*, 21(1), pp. 77–95.

Medina-Albaladejo, F. J. (2011). *Cooperativismo y sector vitivinícola en España durante la segunda mitad del siglo XX*. Unpublished PhD thesis, Universitat Autònoma de Barcelona.

Medina-Albaladejo, F. J. (2015). Co-operative wineries: Temporal solution or efficient firms? The Spanish case during the late Francoism, 1970–1981. *Business History*, 57(4), pp. 589–613.

Medina-Albaladejo, F. J. (2016). Intervención estatal del sector vitivinícola español durante el franquismo: las bodegas cooperativas. In: N. M. Girbal-Blacha, M. I. López Ortiz and S. Regina de Mendonça, coords. *Agro y política a uno y otro lado del Atlántico. Franquismo, salazarismo, varguismo y peronismo*. Buenos Aires: Imago Mundi, pp. 31–54.

Medina-Albaladejo, F. J. and Menzani, T. (2017). Co-operative wineries in Italy and Spain in the second half of the Twentieth century: Success or failure of the co-operative business model? *Enterprise & Society*, 18(1), pp. 32–71.

Oliver, E. (1884). *El consultor del tenedor de libros*. Barcelona: Jaime Molinas.

O'Rourke, K. (2007). Culture, conflict and cooperation: Irish dairying before the Great War. *The Economic Journal*, 117(523), pp. 1357–1379.

Pan-Montojo, J. (2001). Las industrias vinícolas españolas: desarrollo y diversificación productiva entre el siglo XVIII y 1960. In: J. Carmona, J. Colomé, J. Pan-Montojo and J. Simpson, eds. *Viñas, bodegas y mercados. El cambio técnico en la vitivinicultura española, 1850–1936*. Zaragoza: Prensas Universitarias de Zaragoza, pp. 313–334.

Planas, J. (2003). Cooperativismo y difusión del cambio técnico en la agricultura. La contribución de las cámaras agrícolas (Cataluña, 1890–1930). *Historia Agraria*, 30, pp. 87–117.

Planas, J. (2013). El cooperativismo vitivinícola en tiempos de crisis: el Sindicato de Viticultores de Igualada (1921–1936). *Investigaciones de Historia Económica*, 9(3), pp. 155–164.

Planas, J. (2016). The emergence of winemaking cooperatives in Catalonia. *Business History*, 52(2), pp. 264–282.

Planas, J. and Medina-Albaladejo, F. J. (2017). Too little intervention or too much? The contribution of the state to the development of wine cooperatives in Spain. *Revista de Historia Industrial*, 70, pp. 77–107.

Planas, J. and Valls Junyet, F. (2011). Por qué fracasaban las cooperativas agrícolas? Una respuesta a partir del análisis de un núcleo de la Cataluña rabasaire. *Investigaciones de Historia Económica*, 7, pp. 310–321.

Powell, W. W. (1988). Institutional effects on organizational structure and performance. In: L. G. Zucker, ed. *Institutional Patterns and Organizations: Culture and Environment*. Cambridge: Ballinger, pp. 115–136.

Powell, W. W. (1991). *Expanding the Scope of Institutional Analysis*. Chicago: University of Chicago Press.

Powell, W. W. and Di Maggio, P. J. (1991). *The New Institutionalism in Organizational Analysis*. Chicago: University of Chicago Press.

Quinn, M. (2014). Stability and change in management accounting over time: A century or so of evidence from Guinness. *Management Accounting Research*, 25(1), pp. 76–92.

Romero, C. (1981). De la Ley de Cooperativas de 1942 al Reglamento de Sociedades Cooperativas de 1978: un análisis crítico. *Agricultura y Sociedad*, 18, pp. 33–63.

Santos, B., Fidalgo, E. and Santos, M. (2014). The origins of the Spanish railroad accounting model: A qualitative study of the MZA's operating account (1856–1874). *De Computis, Spanish Journal of Accounting History*, 11(21), pp. 73–103.

Saumell, A. (2002). *Viticultura i associacionisme a Catalunya. Els cellers cooperatius del Penedés (1900–1936)*. Tarragona: Diputació de Tarragona.

Saumell, A. (2004). El cooperativisme vitivinícola i els processos de modernització agrària al Penedès (1960–2002). *Recerques*, 49, pp. 97–132.

Torrents, A. (1885). *Tratado completo teórico-práctico de contabilidad mercantil, industrial y administrativa*. Barcelona.

14 The Monastery of Silos and its wine cellar in Ribera del Duero through its accounting books (14th, 18th and 19th centuries)

Lorenzo Maté, Begoña Prieto and Alicia Santidrián

Introduction

The Benedictine monastic order came into existence in Italy in the 6th century, founded by Saint Benedict of Nursia, who lived in Subiaco, Vicovaro and Montecasino (Italy) – the latter being his resting place. From there, the order would extend principally across southern Europe, mainly in the Mediterranean area where inhabitants cultivated cereals, vines and olives. The Benedictine Order follows the Rule of Saint Benedict (*Regula Benedicti*), which consists of 73 chapters, and its subsequent additions or "constitutions". These are promulgated by general chapters, who have a role similar to parliaments in political institutions (Prieto et al., 2006).

The characteristic of monasteries and the monastic orders in general, as opposed to the orders of mendicant friars, is that all monasteries are autonomous, existing independently from each other and without organised centralised orders. This aspect also implies economic independence, and these communities typically exist alone in rural environments, cultivating cereals, vines and tending to livestock. It is a subsistence economy that produces what is necessary for self-sufficiency, within confined areas that are not always the most appropriate for agricultural activity. The patrimonial expansion of monastery lands, linked to this independence, would become the motive for their decadence, as the nobles, patrons or founders of the monasteries would begin to express interest in their assets, going so far as to usurp and to enjoy such produce. In doing so, using their status as patrons or founders, they placed one or another family member as abbot, with the end purpose of ensuring that such assets were produced for the founder or patron. In such situations, it appears evident that there would neither be concern for the observance of the Rule of Saint Benedict, nor for the life in the community.

Congregations were formed to defend monasteries from these interventions and to return to regular observance of the Rule of Saint Benedict. The term "congregation" is used to refer to the federation of monasteries, united with each other because of the same reforms, each one keeping its own autonomy, but with a certain dependence on the abbot of the monastery at the head of the reforms. One of these congregations, and without doubt the most extensive and well known, was the Cluniacensian. Cluny was founded at the start of the 10th century, in the Bourgogne; as a monastery, it was directly linked to the Papacy in Rome.

Different aspects relating to the governance of the Benedictine Order have been explored in the accounting history literature. Several papers by Alistair Dobie have contributed to this field. A sample of accounts from the bursar's office at Durham Cathedral Priory describing sources of receipts, types of expenditure and the format of these accounts are examined by Dobie (2008). At the mentioned priory, Dobie (2011) explored the manner in which grain, bread and ale were accounted for, reflecting the manufacturing process of baking and brewing and the control over this process. The analysis of the statues issued by the general and provincial chapters relating to accounting, financial and management controls within Benedictine houses can be found in Dobie (2015). Some papers have studied reasons that could explain the lifespan of Benedictine abbeys. Governance structures relying heavily on internal control and supportive external control were the key elements suggested by Inauen et al. (2010) and Rost et al. (2010). Unlike these findings, Feldbauer-Durstmüller et al. (2012) emphasised the decisive influence of political power on the viability and long-term survival of Benedictine abbeys in Austria. Considering the important role played by the cellarer, who is responsible for the monastery's finances, Hiebl and Feldbauer-Durstmüller (2014) compared aspects of this task with those of a contemporary chief financial officer (CFO). Among others, the authors mentioned the cellarer's stewardship behaviour and his long-term orientation, although they also identified the downsides of the Benedictine governance that should be avoided for corporate CFOs. Nevertheless, the transferability of monastic governance structures is not easy, as monasteries and the corporate world differ decisively in their fundamental aims (Feldbauer-Durstmüller et al., 2012). In this sense, Payer-Langthaler and Hiebl (2013) provided a framework to define "performance" in the context of a Benedictine abbey, taking into account three basic intentions and six key actions the authors identified in their analysis of the Rule of Saint Benedict.

The works of both Prieto et al. (2006) and Maté et al. (2008) described the economic development of a Spanish monastery, the Monastery of Silos, from the end of the 17th century until the beginning of the 19th century, and analysed the sophisticated accounting practices of the Benedictine monks that served both accountability and decision-making purposes. This monastery is also the subject of our research in this chapter. The monastery is located in the district of Quintana del Pidio (Spain), on the banks of the River Duero. This district is today an important productive zone forming part of the Ribera del Duero denomination, globally recognised for the quality of its wines. The aim of this chapter is to detail the activities at the Monastery of Silos relating to wine and its production, control and consumption through its accounting books and other manuscripts deposited in its archive for periods of time during the 14th, 18th and 19th centuries. To achieve this goal, the chapter analyses the norms that refer to the consumption of wine that applied to the Benedictines, in general, and accounting documents of the wine cellar of the Monastery of Silos, during the previously mentioned centuries.

The remainder of this chapter is structured as follows. References to wine found both in the Rule of Saint Benedict and in the uses and customs of the congregation are described in the following section. The focus of the two subsequent sections concerns the Monastery of Silos and its accounting records in relation to wine, both before and after the monastery formed part of the Congregation of Valladolid. An overview of the method of rendering the accounts at the monastery is provided in the penultimate section and, finally, some concluding points are given.

The rule of Saint Benedict and wine

Chapter XL of the Rule of Saint Benedict "Of the Quantity of Drink" establishes that:

> Everyone hath his proper gift from God, one after this manner and another after that" (1 Cor 7:7). It is with some hesitation, therefore, that we determine the measure of nourishment for others. However, making allowance for the weakness of the infirm, we think one *hemina*[1] of wine a day is sufficient for each one. But to whom God granteth the endurance of abstinence, let them know that they will have their special reward. If the circumstances of the place, or the work, or the summer's heat should require more, let that depend on the judgment of the Superior, who must above all things see to it, that excess or drunkenness do not creep in. Although we read that wine is not at all proper for monks, yet, because monks in our times cannot be persuaded of this, let us agree to this, at least, that we do not drink to satiety, but sparingly; because "wine maketh even wise men fall off" (Sir 19:2). But where the poverty of the place will not permit the aforesaid measure to be had, but much less, or none at all, let those who live there bless God and murmur not. This we charge above all things, that they live without murmuring.

From its reading, it may be seen that it defines general rules on the moderate consumption of wine, without establishing a rigid norm that sets its consumption, while leaving increments to the established quantity at the discretion of the superior – due to conditions of the location, summer heat waves or type of work.

All congregations seek a certain uniformity of uses, customs, habits, religious practices (divine office), ceremonies, selection of work roles, organisation of the monastery, etc. The communication of these uses and customary practices to other monasteries was done in writing, copied and dispatched forthwith by messenger. These uses and customs also had the end purpose of interpreting or adapting passages from the Rule of Saint Benedict to specific circumstances. The uses and the customs of the congregations that were formed subsequent to the Congregation of Cluny inform us that the wine cellarer, assistant to the cellarer, takes in and records the wine harvest and places it in storage. The task of the refectioner was to place bread and wine on the tables of the refectory for the monks. The refectioner distributed the wine according to the established measure; this measure went by the name *poculum justiciae*. An equal quantity was also poured for the supper; in other words, two established measures per day. The refectioner also had the task of preparing the *pigmentum* (a type of liquor based on wine, cinnamon, honey and other spices), which was served in small cups (*modiolis*). The Rule of Saint Benedict also establishes that monks keep their peace at table, eating meals in community in profound silence, requesting items they might need with signs. According to the rule, signs were preferable at table and the sign to ask for wine was done by bending the thumb and moving it to the lips. In accordance with the uses and customs of the Congregation of Valladolid – of which the Monastery of Silos was part, as we shall see later – wine was requested by raising the index finger to touch the tip of the nose.

The first accounting records

The mediaeval documentation of the Benedictine Monastery of Silos since its foundation in the 11th century by Saint Domingo of Silos records the donation of landed property on the part of benefactors for the sustenance of the monks. In exchange, the monks had to offer up intercessory petitions and prayer for the salvation of the donors. On occasions the impression is given that these documents portray stereotyped notarial formalisms, such as land and vineyards, kitchen gardens and orchards, meadows and threshing grounds, springs and rivers, mountains, canals, mills, gateways and cultivated and fallow lands. The first document referring to the Priory of Quintana del Pidio is from King Alfonso VIII of Castile, dated 14 October 1190. The king gifted the town of Quintana with its lands, vines and vassals to the Monastery of Silos. In exchange, the monastery expressed its gratitude bequeathing the village of Santo Domingo de Nunno Faniz, situated alongside the River Duero, close to Tordesillas (Spain). There were some more donations, such as the one from Don Pedro González de Roa, who in 1312 gave all properties in his possession in Quintana to the Abbot of Silos, among which the vineyards (Férotin, 1897).

With regard to the production of wine, accounts of the Monastery of Silos, registered on 20th April 1338 (see Table 14.1), are of interest. This date was also the occasion of a Papal Bull on reform of the Benedictine Order issued by Pope Benedict XII. These accounts are the first available to us with information on the harvests of wheat and wine production. In this type of account, the incoming (*recebta*) and outgoing (*despensa*) of goods in kind (bread, wine) were noted first; and then income and expenditure in monies.

With a view to facilitating an understanding of these accounts, we include a brief explanation in Table 14.2 of the calculation of the shortfall. Also, on the basis of the accounts, we can establish the total cost of the wine in that year (1338), in maravedis[2] (see Table 14.3). The consumption of wine per monk can also be calculated. The accounts tell us that each monk consumed 70 pitchers of wine per year – multiplied by 16 litres per pitcher gives us 1,120 litres. Divided by 365 day gives us a daily intake of about 3.1 litres per day per monk.

Table 14.1 Accounts of 1338

[a]

All of Quintana de Arpidio is our farmstead, and we hold there our estate, vineyards and vassals; and rents [*of*] the estate 150 *almudes* [7 bushels] of mixed cereals for bread, 50 of wheat, 50 of rye and 50 of barley.	150
In Ribicela, close to this village of Quintana, we have estates of cereals and vineyards, and the vineyards are lost by reason of the wars; and the estate is worth 2 cart-loads of cereal, which are 6 *almudes* [1.12 pecks], half of wheat and half of barley.	6

[b]

Receipts of pitchers of wine	*Pitcher (16 lt.)*
From Puentedura	200
From Pedrosa	100
From Quintana	400
From Estrella	150
From Abendo and Arroyales	100
From vineyards close to the monastery	600
Sum of incoming pitchers	1,550
Sum of outgoing pitchers	3,620
And so the outgoings amount to more than the incoming pitchers	2,070

[c]

Abbey's expenses	*Maravedis*
The costs of labourers on the vineyards that we had done in Quintana, Puentedura, Pedrosa, Estrella, Abendo, Arrojales and close to the monastery	1,477
The costs of bringing 200 cart-loads from Puentedura, at 4.5 Noveles the load, that amounts to	90
The costs of bringing 100 cart-loads from Pedrosa, at 3 Noveles the cart-load, that amounts to	30
The costs of bringing 400 cart-loads from Quintana, the cart-load at 7 Noveles, that amounts to	280
The costs of the grape harvest in these places, with the carts and journeying	200
We gave to 30 monks, to each one, on each day, 2 servings [*justicias*], that are 3 quarts [*tres medinelos*], that amounts to 68 pitchers [*cántaras*] and 3 quarters for each monk each year, and with the measures that we give in the year, the provision of wine for each one amounts to 70 pitchers; and to 30 monks in the year it all amounts to	[pitchers] 2,100
We gave to 5 men of the convent, to 3 porters (of the door to the abbey, and to the cloisters, and the main door), to a young man who cuts wood, to 2 who bake the bread of the convent, to 3 vineyard labourers, to the carter, to the cook, to the muleteer of the abbot, to 8 family members, to 8 men of the abbot and to 4 men who cared for the vestments; that is together 33 men; and we gave to each the half of that to a monk, that amounts to 35 [pitchers] to each one each year, and so it amounts to	[pitchers] 1,155

Abbey's expenses	*Maravedis*
We gave to guests each day a pitcher that amounted in the year to 365 pitchers.	Maravedis
And so this wine, that is necessary in the monastery, amounts to 3,620 pitchers. Taking out the 1,550 pitchers that we had of ours, we had to buy 2,070 pitchers, and the pitcher bought at 2 Maravedis amounted to	4,140

Source: Archive of the Monastery of Silos.

Note: The measures quoted in this chapter are not exact equivalences. The *cántara* [pitcher] is defined in the Dictionary of the Royal Academy of Spanish as equivalent to 16.133 litres and an *almud* as varying between 1.75 litres and 5.68 litres (by dry weight), whence the previously mentioned equivalences of pecks and bushels.

Table 14.2 Calculation of shortfall (in pitchers and *Maravedis*), 1338

Pitchers produced	1,550
Pitchers delivered	3,620 (2,100 + 1,155 + 365)
Pitchers that have to be purchased (shortfall)	2,070
Cost of purchasing pitchers, in Maravedis (at 2 Maravedis per pitcher)	4,140

Table 14.3 Total cost of the wine, 1338

Production costs	2,077 (1,477 + 90 + 30 + 280 + 200)
Acquisition costs	4,140 (2,070 * 2)
Total	6,217

The monastery bought various vineyards in the 14th century, which shows an interest in siting its wine cellar in Quintana, having noted that the land was more suited to vineyards – something which holds to the present day.[3] For the same reason, the vineyards in and around Silos would be progressively abandoned. In 1346, the monastery bought two vineyards from Martín Pérez, from the neighbouring area of Aranda, Quintana, and in 1359 it purchased another vineyard for 200 maravedis. At the commencement of the 15th century, in 1406, the monastery once again bought another vineyard at a cost of 850 maravedis.

Accounting records within the Congregation of Valladolid

The Monastery of Silos officially became part of the Congregation of San Benito of Valladolid on 27 March 1512, although the first contacts for this reform and union with Valladolid date back to 1502. As from that time, the government, administration and organisation of the community were adapted to provisions established in the Constitutions of this Congregation.

The documentation from this time is much more abundant with reference to the boundaries of the properties (AMS documents of 1590 and 1622), purchases of vineyards (AMS documents of 1589) and exchanges of vineyard inheritances (AMS documents of 1695–1699). In 1700, 4,000 vines were planted and auctions were held to adjudicate assets belonging to people who had not paid the interest and principal of contracted loans (1715–1727). A more important purchase was in 1804 – some 11,000 vines, managed by Father Liciniano Sáez. In the 19th century there were around 60,000 vines tended by the monastery in Quintana, as may be seen in Table 14.4.

Table 14.4 Inventory of vines (1818)
i) Vines that the Father Prior of Quintana tends. The amount and their condition upon the departure of Father Romano (1818).
[a]

El Monte	6,000
El Pocho (purchased from Manuel Carpintero)	1,200
From Val de la Yegua to Fuente Espino	500
La Laguna	2,000
Tres Caminos	400
Carra Gumiel	600
Tarumba (by auction)	1,200
Las Adoveras	4,000
El Soto or San Millán	4,000
La Castellana	1,400
Thomás de Casas	700
Palos Blancos	900
Palos de Vázquez and Núñez (in two parcels)	3,000
Porquera	500
Palos del Santo, two thousand (manured)	2,000
El Peral	700
Largo	2,300
María Roa (half-manured)	3,000
San Clemente	2,000
El Cristo	2,400
Gramal	8,000
El Porcón	130
Revillas	1,000
Total	47,930

ii) Vines that are producing and were purchased with the testament of José Vega as the father of friar Liciniano
[b]

El Prado	2,000
Palos de la Manuela	1,200
Peña Ynglés	300
Laderón	1,100
Montecillo	2,200
León o Burro	750
Valdesantos (in two parcels)	3,000
Total	10,550

iii) Vines lost
[c]

Valdesanto	800
La Travesaña	1,200
San Miguel	500
Total	2,500

Source: Archive of the Monastery of Silos, Wine Cellar book 103, ff. 41v – 42

The administration of the monastery fell to the cellarer, while money was controlled by the depositors, who held it in the coffer of the monastery and painstakingly noted all income and expenditure. The obligation of noting everything in corresponding books was established for greater clarity (Prieto et al., 2006). With regard to the wine cellar, the cellarer was responsible for keeping a Wine Cellar Book with the rents of each year as a heading and where the grape harvests were paid. This book would be used to render accounts in June (festival of Saint John) and in December (Christmas). A standard charge/discharge accounting method was used. All operations were classified under two broad headings: income, receipts or "charges"; and expenditure or "discharges". These, in turn, were subdivided into relevant headings as necessary. The procedure consisted, first, in noting down all incoming items in the corresponding accounting book as entries under "charges", whether in cash and/or in kind; second, all outgoings in cash and/or kind were noted down as discharges of goods or cash. Finally, the resulting balance or shortfall was calculated, which generally showed a positive balance and which became the first entry under charges for the following period. In the less frequent case when discharges exceeded charges, the shortfall had to be made up by whoever had received the cash or goods in kind. However, in the case of ongoing transactions, the shortfall could also be noted down as the first entry under discharges for the following period. Using this method, the cellarer or his assistants and the depositors exchanged charges and discharges in such a way that the discharges made by the cellarer appeared as charges in the books of the depositors and vice versa (Prieto et al., 2006).

Tables 14.5 and 14.6 show the preparation of accounts employing this method at two points in time with two sorts of records – day and age, in kind and in monies. Table 14.5 presents in some detail entries relating to the wine of the Priory of Quintana del Pidio, as an excerpt from the accounts drawn up at year end 1700. The number of accounting entries recorded in Table 14.6 is much greater than in the Table 14.5, which gives an idea of the growing economic importance that viticultural activities had acquired at the Monastery of Silos at the time (leading up to the confiscation of church lands in Spain, which began in the late 18th century). The accounts appear, in keeping with the day and age and the aforementioned method, linked to the people who managed them settling differences between each other (cellarer or other officials and depositors), and not in the name of the monastery.

Table 14.5 The Wine Cellar Book: Christmas Accounts (1700)
"On 1st January 1701 on instructions of our very Reverend Father Juan de Castro, Abbot of this house, the accounts were taken in this book in the following way":

[a]

Charge	*Pitchers*
The Father Administrator owing what was carried forward in the balance of the last accounts	1,932
Pitchers that were bought in Gumiel de Izán on account of some debts	325
Pitchers from the harvest of this year	3,350
Sum	5,607

[b]

Discharge	*Pitchers*
The Father Administrator has as an asset that he has given for the expenditure of the Holy Convent, guests, servants and other obligations of the house, over these 6 months	564
Expended in the Priory on this person, and other obligations	42
Four young men, a maid servant and a boy	230
Spent on the pruning of the vines	10
Different labourers available to mulch, weed and other works	20
Spent on grape harvests with treaders and pullers and harvesters	30
Spent on filling the tuns, dregs, losses and spillage	260
Spent on the Priory and on some gratifications, 8 pitchers of wine that turned to vinegar	8
Given to the Brotherhoods for the Deceased	10
Sold to the officials in this house	61
Sum	1,235

[c]

Balance	*Pitchers*
This account is balanced with four thousand three hundred and seventy-two pitchers owing to the Father Administrator, and he has them to discharge	4,372

Source: Archive of the Monastery of Silos, Wine Cellar book 101, f. 46v

Table 14.6 The Wine Cellar Book: Accounts of 1814–1816
"On 15 July 1816 by instruction of our Father Domingo de Silos Moreno, Abbot of this monastery of Santo Domingo de Silos, I Friar Domingo Romano Prior of the Priory of Quintana del Pidio drew up the accounts of this administration, comprehensive since such day in the past year of 1814 up until the present when they were read before his Fatherliness and Fathers of the Council in the following form":

[a]

Charge	*Reals*	*Maravedis*
Five hundred and eighty-nine pitchers of wine, sold at 8 and a half Reals per pitcher, five thousand and six Reals and a half	5,006	17
One hundred pitchers of wine from the harvest in 1814 that were sold in 1815, at 18 Reals per pitcher, one thousand eight hundred Reals	1,800	
One thousand and forty-four pitchers of wine from the harvest of 1815 in 1816 at seven Reals per pitcher, seven thousand eight hundred and thirty Reals	7,830	
Total	14,636	17

[b]

Discharge		*Reals*	*Maravedis.*
Wine cellar	One thousand and fifty and a half Reals that the Master with the three officials spent inspecting the tuns of the cellars and who were employed in this operation 16 days, counting in this expense the work and the food	1,050	17
	To the blacksmith and his officials, for the work of repairing arches, as well as the food	80	
	Five new trees for the tuns at 9 Reals each one	45	
	A cask (8 Reals), a pitcher (6 Reals), 6 jugs (three and a half Reals): all in all thirty-five Reals, and eight more for the person and horses that brought it from Roa	43	
	Four Reals for twice closing the breathing hole of the wine-cellar of the cellar of Leon	4	
	A quarter of wine from Peralta	15	
	A bottle of rancid wine	10	
	Two pounds of chocolate	26	
	Four packs of parchment	9	14

(*Continued*)

Table 14.5 (Continued)

Discharge		*Reals*	*Maravedis.*
Grape harvest of 1814	Spending on 12 labourers washing the tuns in 1814 at 4 Reals and at 5	54	
	Labourers and horses to fetch water	28	
	76 labourers to harvest at different prices	316	22
	2 labourers to load the grape	40	
	The unloader of the wine press	20	
	9 mules at 39 Reals each one	351	
	2 labourers to clean the lagar [wine vat] and remove the dregs from it, and the wine press	10	
	Treading, pressing, filling the pitchers, removing the wine pomace, with 44 labourers	214	
	Hiring of 2 wineskins	26	
	One quarter of an outer wheel hoop	00	24
	Brushes to clean the tuns	28	
Grape harvest of 1815	17 baskets that were bought for the grape harvest this year	61	30
	Construction of three basket holders	36	
	Washing and cleaning the 2 lagars of the Lagar of José Vega, lagar and press of the Lagar of León and wine-cellar, 4 labourers	20	
	Large brushes for this task	28	
	224 harvesters at different prices	890	
	8 labourers to unload into the lagars	40	
	20 mules at 33 Reals the mule	660	
	Washing and cleaning the tuns, carrying the water	191	
	Treading, trampling, filling the pitchers, removing the wine pomace, with 64 labourers	320	
	Rental of three wineskins	2	4
Vineyards 1815	Four mattocks were purchased in 1815 at 48 Reals each one	192	
	Repair of another, and a pruning hook	26	
	8 mattocks purchased in Valladolid to cultivate the vines	48	
	A sickle for pruning the vines	10	
	Pruning with 121 labourers at 9 Reals the day	1,089	
	Weeding and digging overgrown vines, cleaning them and erecting fencing, with 65 labourers	553	17
	Digging all the vines in a day, with 305 labourers at 8 and a half Reals	2,592	17
	Digging and extending soil with 313 workers at 9 Reals each one	2,817	
	Forty Reals that were given to refresh the labourers on the last day of their work as an afternoon snack, that it is customary to give	40	
Vineyards 1816	Pruning this year with 123½ labourers at 9 Reals each one	1,111	17
	Digging on one day with 308½ labourers at 8 Reals and a half	2,622	8
	Levelling soil and digging with 332 labourers at 9 Reals each one	2,988	
	15 labourers who were employed to erect the fence of del Cristo, and to repair those of Adoveras and Soto, at 8 Reals and a half	127	17

Discharge		*Reals*	*Maravedis.*
	Mattock heads in the season with the labourers	120	
	Pick heads for the mattocks of the house	45	
	A small grubbing mattock for the kitchen garden	4	
	To dig at Marirrota 300 planting holes at the top of this vineyard	19	
	The mule that was employed for two days in carrying the crushed grape skins from the Lagar to the corral, and drink	46	
	The labourers, who helped to load it	10	
	A labourer to mix the crushed grape skins with the manure that the servant had cleared from the pigsties	7	
	Another labourer who cleaned the working area	6	
	2 cart-loads of straw that were purchased for manure and mixed with the crushed grape skin	130	
	One day and a half to employ a carter in carrying the manure to Marirrota	34	17
	2 women and a labourer to spread manure at Marirrota	7	
	A worker to prepare the land	8	17
	6 boots that were bought for grape harvesting and digging	72	
Balance	The balance was in favour of the Father Preacher Gamazo in the last accounts, two thousand eight hundred and eighty-five Reals.	2,885	
	Total	22,231	17

[c]

Balance	*Reals*	*Maravedis.*
This account is balanced at eight thousand seven hundred and sixty-nine *Reals*, and thirty Maravedis, that the Father Prior owes to the Priory.	8,769	30
Signed. Domingo Romano and Domingo de Silos Moreno. Read in public Council and approved, to which I bear witness. Friar Yldefonso Troncoso. Secretary		

Source: Archive of the Monastery of Silos, Wine Cellar book 103, ff. 30v–37v.Note: This balance was obtained from the difference between the total figures for charge and discharge of the accounts over the period 1814–1816, among which were found numerous other accounts such as bread, coal, meat and wood, as well as those relating to wine. We have excluded accounts under those other headings here.

Figure 14.1 summarises the account books of the monastery as per Prieto et al. (2006). The upper portion of Figure 14.1 shows a schematic diagram of the different accounting books, who was responsible for each book and their interrelations. As may be appreciated, the Wine Cellar Book was included in the group of books detailing income of rents in kind, in the same way as the Granary Book and the books of other kinds of income – which were under the responsibility of the cellarer. The headings of the accounting books declared what would supposedly be collected in the period and the charges and discharges for what was effectively charged and delivered to the depositors. The books noted as an opening balance any rents carried forward from previous years.

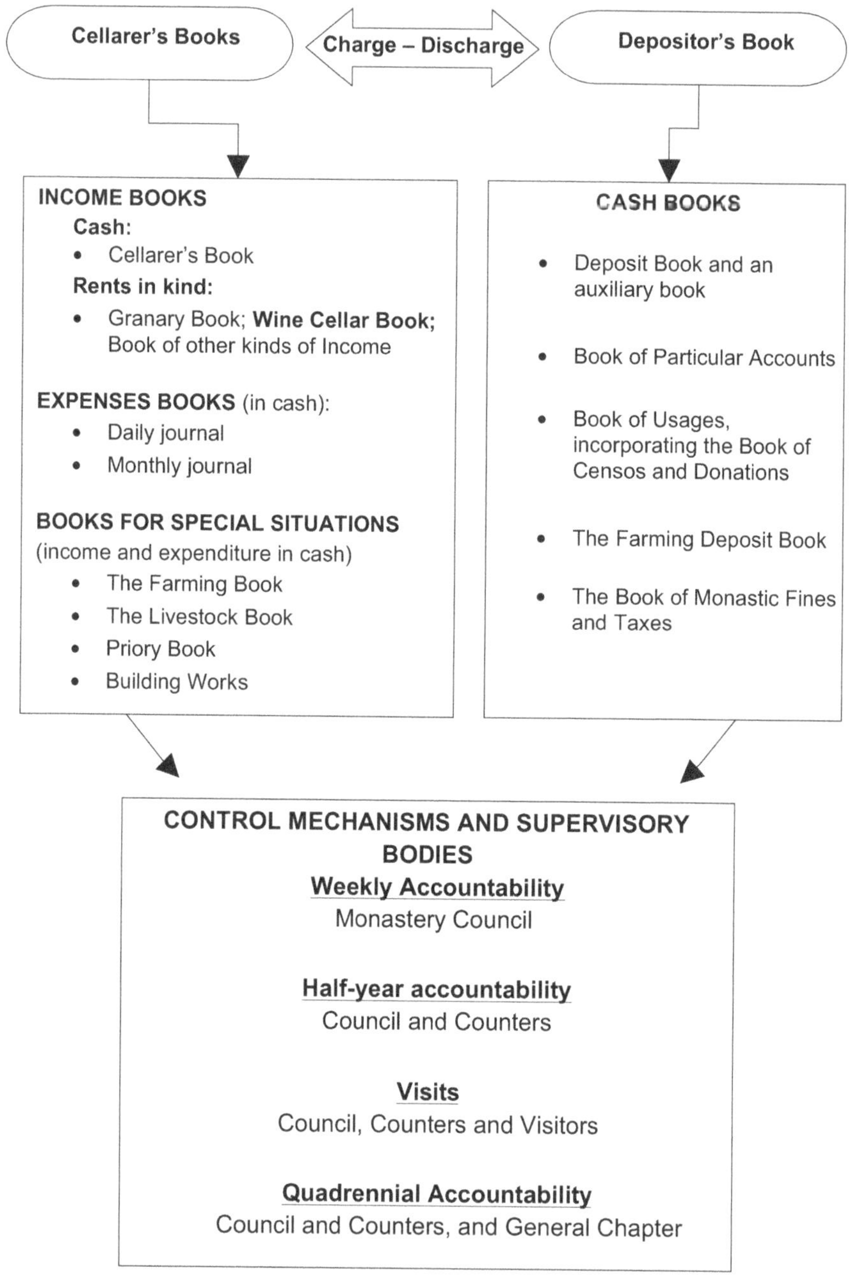

Figure 14.1 Accounts books of the Monastery of Silos

Source: Prieto et al. (2006)

The rendering of accounts and accountability

At the Congregation of Valladolid, abbots and other posts from the community were initially for three years and as from 1613, for four years. Control was achieved by means of different mechanisms, shown in the lower part of Figure 14.1. The rendering of the accounts of the monastery was done on a weekly basis. On a biannual basis (at Christmas and on the Day of St. John) accounts were rendered on the occasion of the visits of the Father General of the congregation, and every four years also on the occasion of the Chapter General.

Control of cash movements within the monastery, with subsequent deposits and withdrawals from the depositary coffer, took place every Saturday in the presence of the depositors, who controlled all withdrawals and their corresponding accounting records. Monks also had to make a full account before the abbot and the Fathers of the Council. To that end, the abbot appointed two monks with "intelligence in accounts" to the council (counters), whose task was to audit the accounts held by the depositors and by the cellarer twice *per annum*, coinciding with the festivals of Saint John (June) and Christmas. In addition, the Father General was obliged to make at least two ordinary visits to each monastery during his term of office, with extraordinary visits also possible. The following is a transcription of comments made as a result of the visit of the Father General in June 1826 in which irregularities were detected with regard to the upkeep of the Wine Cellar Book.[4]

Visit of the Father General (1826)

In these accounts the Cellarer leaves out ninety bushels as a charge that in the Granary Book was entered as a discharge of wheat carried to Quintana. Neither are six bushels of rye entered under charges, which they left to him in flour in the accounts of October 1824. And excessive expenditure on flour for the oxen, and bread and wine for the servants are noted. And he is charged to arrange it in all things as set down in the Visit. [Signed: The General of San Benito].

(AMS, the Wine Cellar Book 103, folio 95)

Visit of the Council (1826)

On the twenty-eighth day of June of the year one thousand eight hundred and twenty-six, the Council Visit took place of His Most Very Reverend Father General, in accordance with the provisions of our Constitutions. And having asked the Visitors of Offices and the Counters if they had anything to say of their commissions, or tasks, and they having answered no, His Most Reverend Father said that he had found the accounts so full of confusion, that they could not be approved, but should be produced again, because charges had been entered as discharges, sums were mistaken, numbers corrected, and there was no correspondence between the particular and the general balances. And in consequence, the real state in which the Monastery was found could not be deduced with clarity; so new general accounts of charge and discharge of all the books from the last Visit up until the present must be drawn up, and he instructed the Cellarer that henceforth the accounts be written neatly and precisely as our Constitutions recommend; and he instructed the Abbot, Depositors and Counters, never to sign the accounts without reviewing the sums, and wait until satisfied that they are right, to avoid in this way the many mistakes and errata that are seen in the present accounts. That equally he had observed that the expenditure in community was most excessive, singularly on the bread, in which he found a very notable difference, if compared month by month, and account by account, as in those of this Visit, that include from 26 December of the past year until the first of April, three months, it gives expenditure of thirty bushels, and in the six earlier ones it puts one hundred and thirty, and in those preceding one hundred and fifty-nine; a very exorbitant quantity for a community such as the one that is in the monastery, and the servants that it maintains. That an equal disproportion is found in the matter of barley, the same comparison once done, and likewise, the expenditure in monies over the two years. Hence he forewarned the Cellarer forthwith to regulate his accounts. And he did instruct the Abbot and the Counters to be vigilant and not to permit expenses that were not reasonable.

He also said that he had observed that the expenditure of the Priory of Quintana, that is administered by the Cellarer, is very excessive, and he saw no charge for the ninety bushels of wheat in the accounts that had been presented, that were discharged in the Granary Book, nor of the six of rye in flour, that his predecessor had left him in October of the year 1824, for which he had to answer.

That in the discharge of the wine, it put in summary what was brought to the monastery, and as in this place there is no Wine Cellar Book, in which by law it should be noted, in detail, what the community spends, and equally what the servants and day workers consume, etc., or is given for sale, the door was left open for any crookedness; and for that same reason he ordered that the Wine Cellar Book be opened and the expenditure be noted as is set down in our Constitutions, and that had before been practiced in this house. Finally, His most very Reverend Father General said that the administration from the house of the Priory of Quintana was a new project, needful of much exactitude, care and vigilance, to see what result it had, and to avoid extravagance and altercations in the Administration, because it happens that the plans foreseen are of utility, and those entrusted with their implementation are harmed out of carelessness; and for the same reason, and because he desired the best for this House, he could do no less than enliven the zeal of the Abbot, Fathers of the Council and the Cellarer, under whose charge it is. With which he closed the Council, and signed it his most very Reverend. [Signed.] The General of San Benito.

(AMS, Monastery Council Book (1777–1835), ff. 226–227v)

These comments from the visit in 1826 point not only to some poor record keeping, and possibly to some misrepresentations, but also clearly reveal that the accounts were not being prepared as set down by the constitutions of the order. At the same time, it is also evidence that the control mechanisms shown in Figure 14.1 were utilised, that is, that the monastery was held accountable for actions as revealed through its accounts.

Finally, in relation to the fourth mechanism of control, the abbot of the monastery had to render accounts before the Chapter General, which is the collegiate body charged with the governance of the congregation. This body meets every four years, is presided over by the Father General and constituted by the abbots of the monasteries and by the principal positions of the congregation. The counters had to draw up accounts for the abbot to take to the Chapter General in April to May every four years, usually coinciding with the end of his term of office. The new abbot, within a month after having taken possession of his office, had to draw up a new (quadrennial) statement of the house – in other words, he had to examine the earlier statement of accounts left to him by his predecessor. The new abbot, the previous abbot – if he was present – the counters and the cellarer would all sign this statement of accounts. If he found that the statement of accounts of his predecessor did not reflect the current state of the accounts, he had to inform the Abbot General on the first visit.

Final comments

This chapter reminds of the importance of the accounting documentation in the reconstruction of relevant aspects of business history. In the case of interest, the Wine Cellar Book of the Monastery of Silos offers important and interesting data on aspects such as the procedures of preparing the accounts, the people who were involved, the economic amounts at stake in the viticultural tasks of the monks and the different sources of income and expenditure related to wine harvesting and production. In addition, this analysis has given us the opportunity to reconstruct the relation of the Benedictine monks with the consumption of wine. This consumption was on the basis of general provisions that appear to be flexible in view of the different situations and circumstances – wine constituting an essential sustenance for the monastic community in a similar way to the importance of ale at Durham Cathedral Priory noted by Dobie (2011). Regarding this flexibility, according to the accounting books of the Monastery of Silos, the consumption of wine per monk was three times what the rule set. Nevertheless, it does not seem an excessive amount taking into account the low alcohol content of the wine at the time and the hard agricultural tasks performed by the monks. Moreover, the documentation presented provides an understanding of the viticultural heritage and its exploitation by the Monastery of Silos from its origin up until the ecclesiastical expropriations. Both this patrimony and the production of wine acquired a degree of importance in absolute terms throughout the history of the monastery. The fact that the wine cellar was situated in the municipal district, which today has the most wineries in Ribera del Duero, highlights the extraordinary entrepreneurial vision of these monks seven centuries ago.

Notes

1 According to the text of the Rule of Saint Benedict translated into Spanish in 1571, a *hemina* is equivalent to half an *azumbre* – about a litre of wine.
2 A maravedí was the name of various Iberian gold and then silver coins used between the 11th and 14th centuries.
3 At present, eight wineries may be found in this municipal district: Cillar de Silos, Bodega los Olmos, Pagos de Quintana, J. A. Calvo Casajús, Marqués de Valparaíso, Valle de Monzón, Prado de Olmedo, Alto Miraltares.
4 These visits took place in the years before confiscations of the lands of the monastery.

References

Primary sources

Accounts of the 1338 wine-cellar
Archive of the Monastery of Silos (AMS).
Monastery Council Book (1777–1835).
Wine Cellar book 101 of the Monastery of Silos, in Quintana del Pidio.
Wine Cellar book 103 of the Monastery of Silos, in Quintana del Pidio.

Secondary sources

Dobie, A. (2008). An analysis of the bursars' accounts at Durham Cathedral Priory, 1278–1398. *Accounting Historians Journal*, 35(2), pp. 181–208.
Dobie, A. (2011). A review of the granators' accounts of Durham Cathedral Priory 1294–1433: An early example of process accounting? *Accounting History Review*, 21(1), pp. 7–35.
Dobie, A. (2015). The role of the general and provincial chapters in improving and enforcing accounting, financial and management controls in Benedictine monasteries in England 1215–1444. *The British Accounting Review*, 47, pp. 142–158.
Feldbauer-Durstmüller, B., Sandberger, S. and Neulinger, M. (2012). Sustainability for centuries: Monastic governance of Austrian Benedictine abbeys. *European Journal of Management*, 12(3), pp. 83–92.
Férotin, M. (1897). *Recueil des Chartes de l'Abbaye de Silos*. Paris.
Hiebl, M. R. W. and Feldbauer-Durstmüller, B. (2014). What can the corporate world learn from the cellarer? *Society and Business Review*, 9(1), pp. 51–73.
The Holy Rule of St. Benedict. Available at: www.documentacatholicaomnia.eu/03d/0480-0547,_Benedictus_Nursinus,_Regola,_EN.pdf [Accessed 10th Jan. 2018].
Inauen, E., Rost, K., Osterloh, M. and Frey, B. (2010). Back to the future: A monastic perspective on corporate governance. *Management Revue*, 21(1), pp. 38–59.
Maté, L., Prieto, B. and Tua, J. (2008). Contabilidad, información y control en un contexto de actividades económicas diversificadas en la Edad Moderna: el Monasterio de Silos y su sofisticado sistema contable. *De Computis*, 9, pp. 136–229.
Payer-Langthaler, S. and Hiebl, M. R. W. (2013). Towards a definition of performance for religious organizations and beyond. *Qualitative Research in Accounting & Management*, 10(3/4), pp. 213–233.
Prieto, B., Maté, L. and Tua, J. (2006). The accounting records of the monastery of Silos throughout the XVIII century: The accumulation and management of its patrimony in the light of its accounts books. *Accounting History*, 11(2), pp. 221–256.
Rost, K., Inauen, E., Osterloh, M. and Frey, B. S. (2010). The corporate governance of Benedictine Abbeys. *Journal of Management History*, 16(1), pp. 90–115.

15 Accounting in the Port wine Chartered Trade Company (1756–1826)

João F. Ribeiro, José M. Oliveira and Maria F. Brandão

Introduction

The Chartered Trading Companies (henceforth, CTCs) of the *Ancien Régime* emerged in the context of European mercantilist policies, which led to the joining of forces between governments and the private sector in the search for the development of economic activities (Chaudhuri, 1965, p. 208; Anderson et al., 1983, p. 227; Gaastra, 2003, pp. 164 170; Ekelund and Tollison, 1997, p. 194). Given their size and complexity, CTCs led to the development of new and more sophisticated accounting systems, and double entry was their typical accounting technology (Baladouni, 1983, p. 75; Lemarchand, 1995, pp. 162–164). The Portuguese *Companhia Geral da Agricultura das Vinhas do Alto Douro* (hereafter, *Companhia*) was founded in 1756 and can be seen as a belated example of CTCs in the European context.

The present chapter seeks to describe the nature and uses of the accounting system of the *Companhia* between 1756 and 1826 in the broad framework provided by other Portuguese and European CTCs' accounting systems. To do so, we draw mostly on primary sources, including the information kept in the archive of the *Companhia* in Vila Nova de Gaia – annual reports, general ledger and sub-ledgers, records of meetings, copies of incoming and outgoing mail, legislation, statistics and other *ad hoc* documents, all considerably well preserved and organized (Sousa, 2003, pp. 17–25). The analysis of these documents, alongside the analysis of other printed sources, such as the *Companhia* by-laws and internal regulations, allowed us to reconstitute the *Companhia*'s accounting system key features and usages.

Although the *Companhia* had special prerogatives in the period between 1756 and 1834, information for the period 1827–1834 is scarce and hence our decision to conclude our analysis in the year 1826. Of particular interest is the evidence of an income-smoothing practice, particularly evident after 1784, which we discuss in light of the multiple groups of interest that form the complex institutional framework of the *Companhia*. In order to do so, our work was immensely facilitated by the fact that the history of the

Companhia has been the subject of some previous research (Marcos, 1997; Sousa, 2003 and 2006; Sousa and Pereira, 2008). This literature constituted an important secondary source for our study, as it supported the brief characterization of the *Companhia*'s history, organization and activities presented in the next section.

The *Companhia Geral da Agricultura das Vinhas do Alto Douro*: a chartered company and a regulator

The immediate motive for the creation of the *Companhia* was the need to overcome a wine price crisis that emerged in the 1750s in the Portuguese Douro Valley region, motivated by a sharp decrease of demand and consequently wine prices, due to poor quality and oversupply of wines – including second-class wines that came from regions outside the Douro valley.

At this time, production, blending and sale of wines was not properly regulated. To overcome this, a group of Douro valley farmers with the support of the Portuguese Crown established the *Companhia*, which specified general statutory rights and duties similar to those of two other contemporaneous Portuguese CTCs: *Companhia Geral de Comércio de Pernambuco e Paraíba* and *Companhia Geral de Comércio do Grão-Pará e Maranhão*, both of which mainly focused in trading with Brazil and African Portuguese colonies (Marcos, 1997, pp. 261–262, p. 370, p. 751). The *Companhia* acquired a series of concessions and rights and, in exchange, it took on obligations related to the control and development of an important sector of the Portuguese economy: the production and sale of the wine of the Douro Valley Region. The main concessions acquired by the *Companhia* were in the form of monopolies on the production and sale of several products. This included the sale of fortified wine ('Vinho de Embarque' which later on came to be known as Port wine), brandy and vinegar to the main Brazilian ports, the sale of table wine (or 'Vinho de Ramo', i.e., literally, 'Branch wine') in the district of Oporto and surrounding areas (legitimized by a supposed lack of control over the number of taverns and the quality of the wine these taverns sold) and the production of brandy. The latter was necessary to fortify the wine in the three provinces of northern Portugal – a privilege that was added in 1760 and which, in practice, implied a monopoly on the supply of other exporters (Sousa, 2006, p. 107, p. 192). The management of these concessions was facilitated by several prerogatives, such as the right to request warehouses and ships on an as-needed basis. In addition to activities performed under a monopoly, the *Companhia* competed in other areas. An example was the sale of fortified wine to seaports in Northern Europe, including England. The *Companhia* was never hegemonic in this latter market, as it did not have access to the distribution network of the English companies. However, it did considerable business during and after the Napoleonic Wars, when English companies left Oporto. Another example was the trading of imported goods (often in exchange for the sale of wine), such as cereals or iron arches and rings for casks.

In exchange, the *Companhia* assumed several obligations. Among the most relevant ones was the collection of taxes. Importantly, the *Companhia* was a trustee of these state funds, which meant it could borrow them when it needed money. Also, the *Companhia* was responsible for the regulation of the Douro wine sector,[1] and consequently was entrusted with the demarcation of the wine producing region; the policing of its borders; the production of detailed statistics on quantity and quality of wine produced, stored and sold, with information on producers, intermediaries, storing locations, destination ports; etc. The *Companhia* acted as a regulator and was also obliged to buy production excesses, in accordance with the quantities determined by the Crown, to avoid lowering of prices in the market. Furthermore, the *Companhia* acted as a creditor, as it had to lend funds to local farmers at a subsidized annual interest rate of 3%. Finally, it supervised improvement works in roads and waterways in the region, making use of the collected taxes.[2] Summing up, the activities of the *Companhia*, by nature and location, are represented in Figure 15.1.

This business structure was subject to little change throughout the period under study. Crucially, the two main monopolies – production and sale of brandy and monopoly in Oporto's taverns – remained in place and virtually untouched until the 1820s (Sousa, 2006, p. 172). To perform tasks as diverse as the ones described earlier, and in accordance with its rulings, the *Companhia* was organized by '*incumbências*', that is, board tasks or stewardships, under the supervision of the president of the board of directors. The president and the board members were elected among the main shareholders of the *Companhia* for three-year mandates. However, the king had to confirm the names, a tradition that was inherited from French companies (Marcos, 1997, p. 105). The *Companhia* was subordinated to the secretary of state of the kingdom, whose head was, in practice, the prime minister of Portugal. When the *Companhia* was created, Pombal was the holder of the prime minister's office, and it was through him that all communication flowed between the state and the representatives of the *Companhia*. Importantly, Pombal and his successors could issue notifications that constituted binding instructions for the board. The *Companhia*'s shareholders were thus passive subjects to decisions made elsewhere. This situation, characterized as it was by the considerable power of the state on decision making, was again similar to that of other Continental European CTCs (Vries and Woude, 1997; Ekelund and Tollison, 1997; Marcos, 1997). In general, the administrative solutions adopted by the *Companhia* are similar and, in a sense, emulate those of other existing CTCs (Marcos, 1997). The same can be said of its accounting systems, which drew heavily from prior experiences of other European companies, especially the British East India Company, the Dutch East India Company and Colbert's French companies.

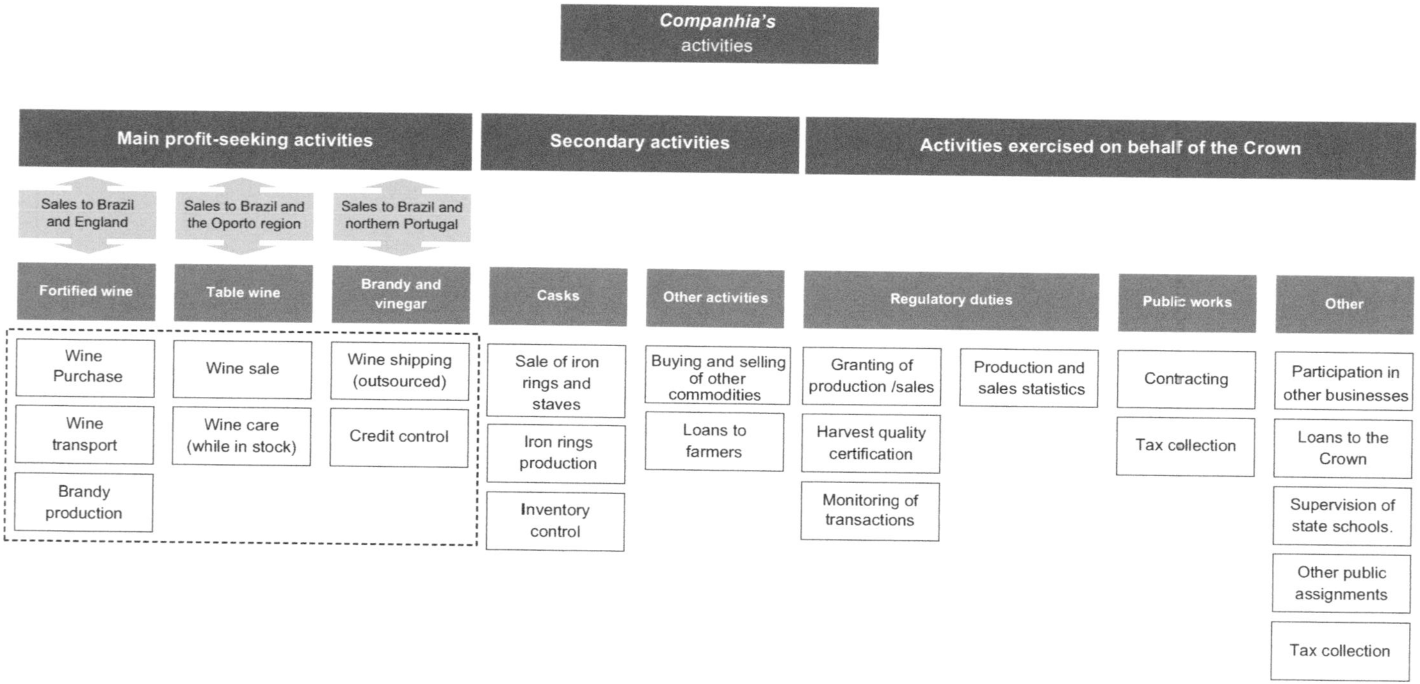

Figure 15.1 The activities of the *Companhia*, 1756–1826

Basic features of the *Companhia*'s accounting system

Notwithstanding the diversity of the *Companhia*'s activities, and the fact that all stewardships had their own accounting records and books, a unique set of accounts provided for the consolidation of the flows from all activities as well as an overall picture of the state of the *Companhia*, including its assets, liabilities, profits and losses. Figure 15.2 presents a synthesis of the archival evidence of the company's accounting books, in line with the list drawn up in the process of the inspection of its activities that started in June 1784.

This inspection was determined by the Crown, in the wake of the unrelenting opposition to Pombal's legacy with regard to chartered companies, which had already led in practice to the extinction of two other CTCs – the companies of Grão-Pará e Maranhão and Pernambuco e Paraíba. The inspection was conducted by Luís Pinto de Sousa Coutinho, a nobleman later to become prime minister, and aimed at assessing the company businesses and financial soundness, essentially on the basis of the scrutiny of its activities since the renewal of the company's charter for a second 20-year period. Worth mentioning for the purposes of this chapter are the list of accounts here referred to,[3] the list of the valuation criteria also referred to later in this section,[4] as well as the policy of earnings management dealt with later in the next section. The taxes collected on behalf of the Crown, as well as its allocation to some public uses, remained outside the consolidation perimeter illustrated by Figure 15.2. The *Companhia* duly kept records of its tax collection and the subsequent transferring to the Crown, but they were not part of its accounting system because the corresponding flows were not to be taken as a source of either profit or loss. The recording of the activities of the *Companhia* in the accounting books culminated in the elaboration of the Statement of the Financial Position of the *Companhia*, which was sent to the shareholders and the Crown. This statement consisted of a summary of the economic and financial position of the company and presented the calculation of profit and loss in the wider context of the calculation of the net equity value and the presentation of the respective assets and liabilities. At its conclusion there was a recommendation for the distribution of the available balance as dividends or their maintenance as retained earnings.

Throughout the years, no significant changes were found with regard to the layout of the Statement of the Financial Position of the *Companhia*. It invariably displayed, in an orderly fashion, the following components:

1. 'The Debit of the *Companhia*', which presented the net equity value of the previous year, the profits and the losses of the current year and the net difference between accounts receivable and accounts payable.
2. 'The Credit of the *Companhia*', which presented the values of the goods stored abroad and/or the trade receivables balances from the officials and agents of the *Companhia* in foreign countries, as well as the goods stored in the warehouses and the values of the fixed assets.

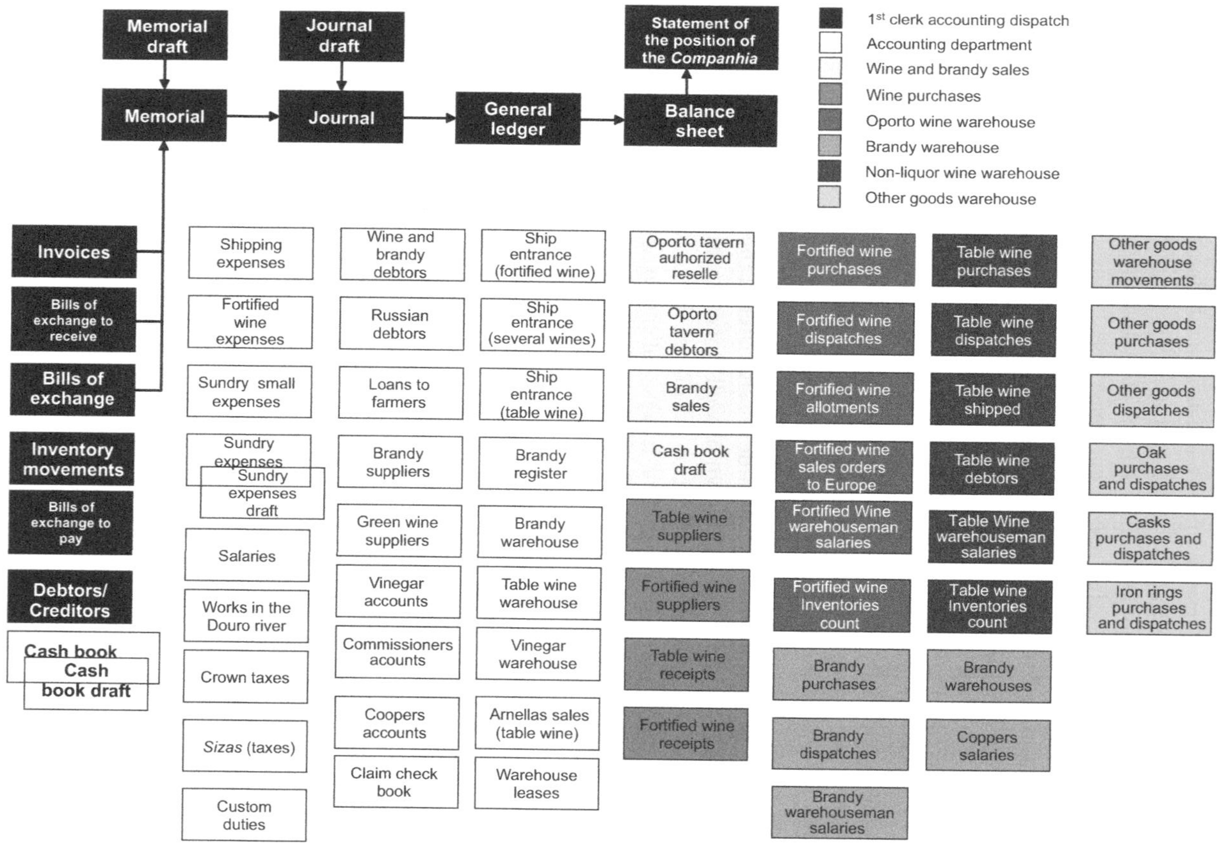

Figure 15.2 The accounting books of the *Companhia*, 1756–1826

3 'The Calculation of the return on capital', which comprised (i) a determination of an accounting rate of return – obtained by dividing the net income of the current year by the net equity value of the previous year; (ii) an indication of the value of the dividends to be distributed to shareholders; (iii) the ensuing new net equity value, considering the distribution of dividends; (iv) and, finally, the determination of the book value of each share.

For all the values indicated in the statements, there were cross-reference explanatory notes, with left-hand folios being reserved for the notes on corresponding values aligned in the right-hand folios. The notes were quite comprehensive, for example, in the case of commodities such as table wine, fortified wine, brandy, etc. In fact, the right-hand folios presented the net values of the margins each commodity gave rise to, that is, the sales revenues less the cost of the goods sold and other costs, for example, shipping and sales commissions. As a rule, the explanatory notes on the left-hand-folio not only mentioned the value of costs and revenues but also the amounts of the goods sold.

The *Companhia*'s bookkeeping was not based on a rigid chart of accounts, but evidence shows that its accountants duly followed the model of the statement of the financial position adopted by the first of the chartered companies created by Pombal – the *Companhia Geral de Grão-Pará e Maranhão.*[5] In the statements of the *Companhia* for the period 1756–1826, we have found a diversified set of accounts and a conceptual structure behind its articulation, as illustrated in Figure 15.3. The evidence available bears witness to no fewer than 166 accounts to record profits and losses and 59 accounts to record entries pertaining to the company's 'debit' (equivalent to the contemporary concepts of equity and liabilities) and 'credit' (equivalent to the contemporary concept of assets) balances. However, in Figure 15.3, this diversity has been reduced by us to a list of aggregate accounts in order to provide a summary view of all the accounts used in the Statements of the Financial Position of the *Companhia.*[6]

This bookkeeping model is in harmony with the teachings of João Henrique de Sousa, the first teacher of the *Aula de Comércio* – the Portuguese Public School of Commerce created by Pombal in 1759.[7] João Henrique de Sousa advocated that the aim of the double-entry method "was to give account of the capital value, increased or reduced by the profit or the loss incurred in the business on the one hand, and of the assets that make up the capital value on the other hand".[8]

The statutes of the *Companhia* do not refer to valuation criteria, but the report of the 1784 inspection contains relevant evidence in this regard. In fact, when it mentions the method adopted to calculate the accounting value of each of the shareholder's shares, the inspector gives account of the criteria behind the determination of the values of the various items that composed the shareholders' equity. These criteria, together with the explanatory notes in the left-hand folios of the statements of the position of the *Companhia*, rendered possible a reconstruction of the summary view of the valuation criteria, as well as the moment of account registration, which is presented in Figure 15.4.

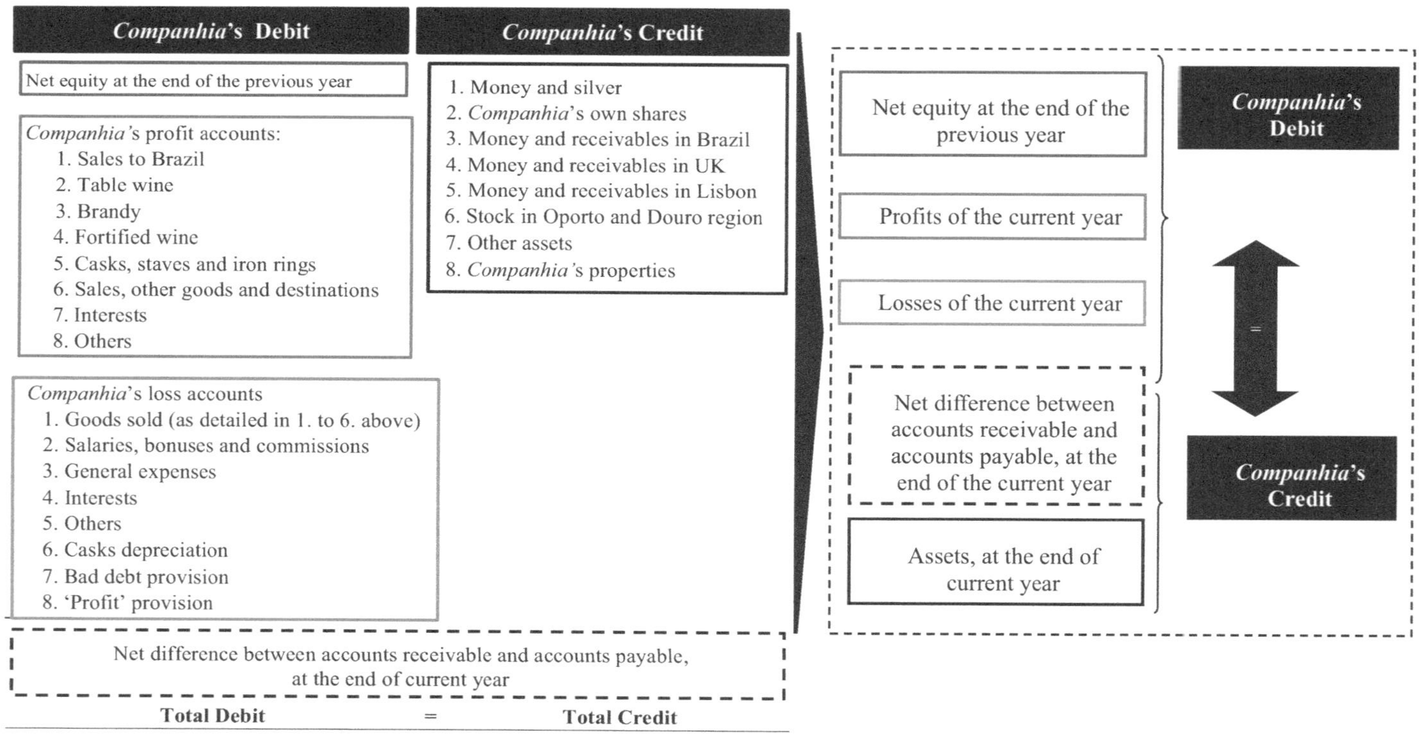

Figure 15.3 Accounts used and conceptual structure, Statements of the Financial Position of the *Companhia,* 1756–1826

Source: Summary view, on the basis of the information available in the Arquivo da CGAVAD, "*1º e 2º livro de balanços*" – cotas 6.2.005.10 lvs. 1 e 2 de 5.

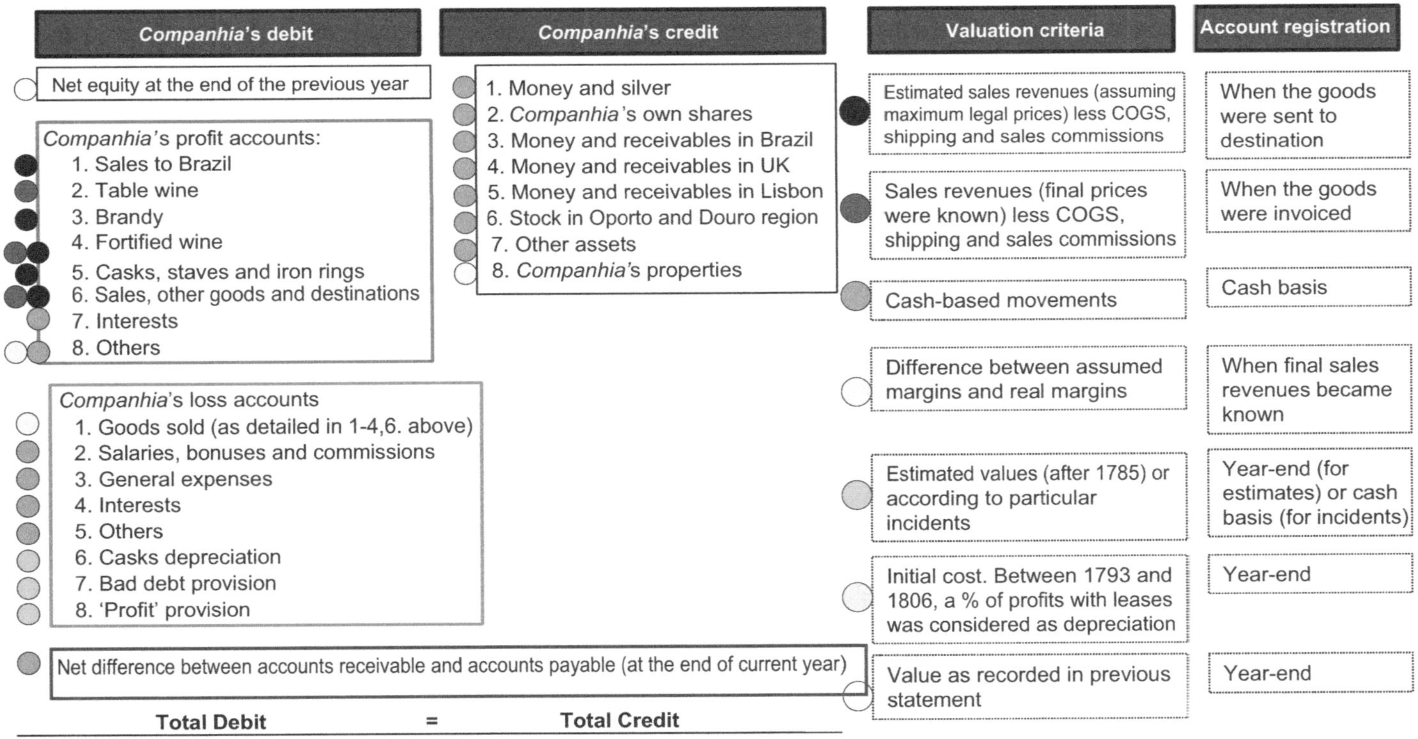

Figure 15.4 Valuation criteria and moment of account registration, Statements of the Financial Position of the *Companhia*, 1756–1826

Sources: ACGAVAD, Cotas 6.2.005.10, lvs. 1 e 2 de 5, *Livros de Balanços*; *Informação* . . ., 1999, pp. 186–187.

According to the information shown in Figure 15.4, we may conclude that the accounting system of the *Companhia* was essentially based on historical cost, as most of the values recorded in its accounts were determined according to this criterion, the notable exceptions being sales to Brazil and other regions where the *Companhia* placed their own agents; consequently the sales, gross margins and accounts receivable balances from those regions were based on estimates.

Companhia's accounting system key features – comparison to other notable CTCs

In this section we seek to explore how the *Companhia*'s accounting system – whose technical features were described in the previous section – was enacted. We were able to gather rich evidence on how the system was operated and used, and one word encapsulates our findings: diversity. The system had diverse purposes and served diverse actors. Not surprisingly, this can be understood in the light of technical-economic explanations and also with a set of institutional explanations.

The technical-economic explanations are related to the need to control credit flows in an essentially commercial business, where large volumes of information circulate; the need to control the flows of wine, brandy and other goods in the Douro region; and the need to calculate profits and other key performance indicators in order to determine the income available to satisfy the demands of creditors, shareholders and the Crown. The *Companhia*'s response to those needs was the adoption of a double-entry accounting system, based on the classical set of memorial, diary and ledger books, as well as the opening of as many auxiliary accounting books as required by the recording division; and to prepare comprehensive annual accounts, including a balance sheet and a profit and loss account. As would be expected (de Roover, 1956, p. 115; Littleton, 1966, pp. 361–368), the double-entry accounting system appears as a natural option, considering in particular the need to calculate the annual profit or loss and net equity. The literature on accounting systems of other CTCs, such as the British East India Company, the Dutch East India Company and Colbert's chartered companies (Marcos, 1997; Chaudhuri, 1965; Gaastra, 2003), although scarce in detail, confirms the existence of accounting systems similar to the one we have found in the *Companhia*. It can thus be said that the *Companhia*'s accounting system was part and parcel of the model adopted by European CTCs.

Institutional explanations provide a rationale for the very configuration of the system and the technical solutions it entailed. The evidence gathered suggests a case in which mimetic, coercive and normative isomorphism (DiMaggio and Powell, 1983) can be found. First, the *Companhia*'s accounting system was a close copy of the system that had been adopted in the *Companhia do Grão-Pará e Maranhão* in 1755 (Marcos, 1997). Furthermore, that system corresponded perfectly to the ideal of modernity that Pombal tried to implement in the accounting systems of certain sectors of the Portuguese economy and certain organizations of the Portuguese state itself (Rodrigues et al., 2003, 2004 and 2007). Pombal used to make comprehensive rulings with regard to accounting procedures and practices in order to ensure the implementation and the stabilization of the model he himself had envisaged. Things did not change after the fall of Pombal in 1777, and the boards of directors kept on complying with the central government's rulings. Finally, professional and educational pressures were evident: for instance, the Portuguese School of Commerce established in 1759 (*Aula do Comércio*) was an important influence on the bookkeeping model that was adopted.[9] Thus, in general, there was a 'fit' between the configuration of the *Companhia*'s accounting features and the institutional context and pressures it faced. More important however, was the way the *actual uses* of the system also served to ensure such a 'fit'. In short, the *Companhia*'s accounting system contributed to legitimatize and balance the interests of the Crown with those of its shareholders, governors and creditors, in such a way as to promote the continuity and financial sustainability of the *Companhia* itself. This was our key finding, and to its analysis and discussion we now turn.

The importance of the accounting system was manifest with regard to the relationship between the *Companhia* and the Crown, since it disclosed the usages of the privileges awarded. The annual Statements of the Position of the *Companhia* were drawn up in view of such requirements and quite often the government requested additional explanations, usually related to the nature and the margin of particular dealings, or to the financial soundness of the company.[10] In turn, the board of directors often used the accounts to claim better margins,[11] additional privileges or the territorial extension of existing privileges. The accounting system also played an important role in the transition from one board to the following board. As a rule, incoming boards conducted a thorough verification of the accounts prepared by outgoing boards, casting doubts on whatever procedures and matters they thought appropriate, and thereby sometimes extending the transition period for quite a long period.[12]

No less important was the role played by the accounting system in the relationship between the boards and the shareholders, as it provided the means for the calculation and the control of the commissions awarded to the members of the board, in accordance with the determinations of the Crown. The formula for calculating the commissions changed several times throughout the period under study, namely when the Crown accepted the claims of their insufficiency put forward by the boards, on the basis of detailed evidence gathered in the relevant accounting records. Commissions were awarded to board members on the basis of a fixed percentage of either the sales or the receivables of traded goods, always in accordance with the specific rulings of the Crown, as shown in Table 15.1 for the year of 1766.

The accounting system also served to present and justify earnings allocated annually to the payment of dividends to shareholders. The final section of the annual Statements of the Position of the *Companhia* consisted of the board's proposal for the distribution of dividends to shareholders, and this proposal had to be approved by the Crown as part of the approval of the annual statements. Delays in the preparation and submission of the annual statements

Table 15.1 Commissions of the board of directors of the *Companhia,* 1766

Values in réis	*Amounts*	*Commission fee*	*Commission amount*
Table wine sales to Lisbon – I	15 189 577	2%	303 792
Brandy sales to Lisbon	3 914 800	2%	78 296
Sales to Rio de Janeiro	10 933 395	2%	218 668
Port wine sold to other traders	102 687 058	2%	2 053 741
Brandy sales to other traders	36 018 032	2%	720 361
Table wine sold in Oporto and Douro region taverns	194 657 460	1%	1 946 575
Money received from Brazil – I	36 649 386	2%	732 988
Money received from Brazil – II	8 615 380	2%	172 308
Table wine sales to Lisbon – II	-	2%	31 614
Total			**6 258 341**
Expenses paid by the board of directors to the bookkeepers and clerks			**–2 919 650**
Net			**3 338 691**
Commissions due to each of the nine board members			**370 966**

Source: Adapted from Table number 28 "Rendimento das Comissões da Junta da Companhia, conforme resolução régia de 14 de Maio de 1766" in Sousa (2006, p. 123).

did not prevent the regular payment of dividends, given the willingness of the Crown to authorize their payment even before the annual closing and approval of accounts. The proposal duly reflected the rulings of the Crown on the minimum value of dividends and on the respective method of calculation. In accordance with the *Aviso Régio* issued on August 31st 1761, the *Companhia* considered a minimum yield of 4%, calculated on the basis of the net equity value of the previous year, and thereafter all the annual statements we reviewed followed this reference value. This minimum value, with express reference to the same calculation formula, always appeared in the annual statements of the Companhia. At the same time, an additional dividend value was always added in order to make up for a percentage on the shareholders' initial investment, that is, on the initial value of their subscriptions, as summarized in Figure 15.5.

The metrics used, that is, (i) dividends distributed as a proportion of the invested capital in circulation, (ii) ratio of distributed dividends to the minimum yield of 4% per annum and (iii) ratio of retained earnings to capital invested, are typically reported in the literature as reference ratios of the so-called transitional capitalism, which have been found in several European CTCs (Toms, 2008, pp. 5–7).

Last, but no less important, the accounting system also played a crucial role in the presentation of the annual earnings. In themselves, the annual earnings

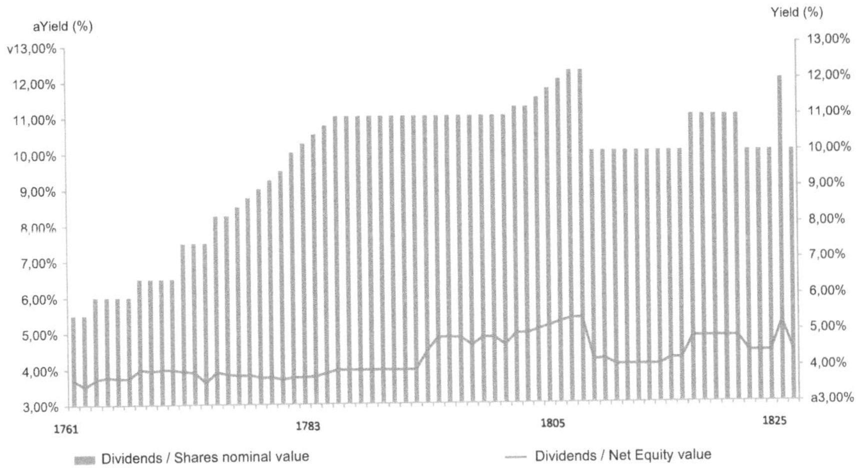

Figure 15.5 Rates of returns on capital, 1756–1826

Source: ACGAVAD, Cota 6.2.005.10, lvs. 1 e 2 de 5, Livros de Balanços . . .

were an important parameter in the actual balancing of all the interests involved in the activities of the *Companhia*, as well as in the assuaging of its critics. If annual earnings were too low, doubts would certainly be raised regarding the soundness of the company, whereas if they were too high, doubts would certainly be raised regarding the disproportion of the privileges granted to it. In this regard, we have found evidence of the practice of earnings smoothing, which we now outline.

Table 15.2 presents an overview of the earnings reported in the annual Statements of the Position of the *Companhia* between 1756 and 1826, taking into consideration the main sources of the profits and the losses generated in the period and the corresponding aggregate accounts that have been created by us to provide a summary view of the diversity of the accounts actually used in the statements.[13] As we can see in Table 15.2, most of the profits of the *Companhia* were generated by the fortified wine sales to England, the brandy produced and sold as a monopoly in the Portuguese northern region and the table wine sold as a monopoly to the taverns of the city of Porto and the surrounding areas.

From a different perspective, Figure 15.6. shows the evolution of the annual earnings reported in the accounts, the annual dividends distributed to shareholders and years when a delay in the closing of the accounts of the *Companhia* can be observed. As shown in Figure 15.6, after 1784 the accounts of the *Companhia* reported equal earnings in several consecutive years, the earnings reported thereafter coincided with dividends and dividends were distributed to shareholders before the closing date of the accounts. This was especially so in the last two

Table 15.2 Overview of the *Companhia*'s reported earnings, 1756–1826

Aggregate accounts	*Profits*	*Losses*	*Earnings*	*%*
Sales to Brazil	1.584.693	–798.377	786.316	15,4%
Table wine sales	2.546.247	–257.820	2.288.427	44,9%
Brandy	2.556.472	–451.116	2.105.356	41,3%
Fortified wine (mainly to England)	3.491.177	–205.864	3.285.313	64,4%
Casks, staves and iron rings	196.882		196.882	3,9%
Sales, other goods/destinations	170.382	–171.441	–1.059	0,0%
Other costs/income		–1.691.686	–1.691.686	–33,2%
Interests	718.611	–590.853	127.758	2,5%
Casks' depreciation		–367.771	–367.771	–7,2%
Bad debt provision		–772.221	–772.221	–15,1%
'Profit' provision		–544.366	–544.366	–10,7%
Extraordinary income/costs	301.572	–615.557	–313.985	–6,2%
Total (thousand *réis*)	**11.566.036**	**–6.467.072**	**5.098.964**	**100,0%**

Source: ACGAVAD, Cota 6.2.005.10, lvs. 1 e 2 de 5, *Livros de Balanços* . . .

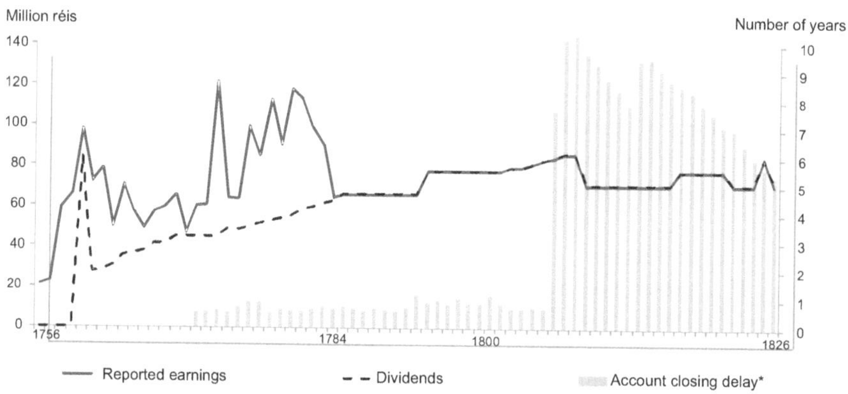

Figure 15.6 Reported earnings, dividends and account closing delay, 1756–1826

Source: Our reconstruction on the basis of the information gathered in ACGAVAD, Cota 6.2.005.10, lvs. 1 e 2 de 5, *Livros de Balanços* . . .

*Prior to 1770, no evidence was found with regard to account closing dates.

decades of the period, when delays of five or more years became quite common. This 'perfect coincidence' between reported earnings and dividends after 1784, we propose, came about as a consequence of the deliberate smoothing of the annual earnings, that is, the earnings presented in the accounts of the *Companhia* are in conformity with the fixing *a priori* of dividends to be distributed to shareholders. In line with Eckel (1981, p. 29), the evidence gathered shows a case of earnings artificially smoothed by the boards. The income-smoothing

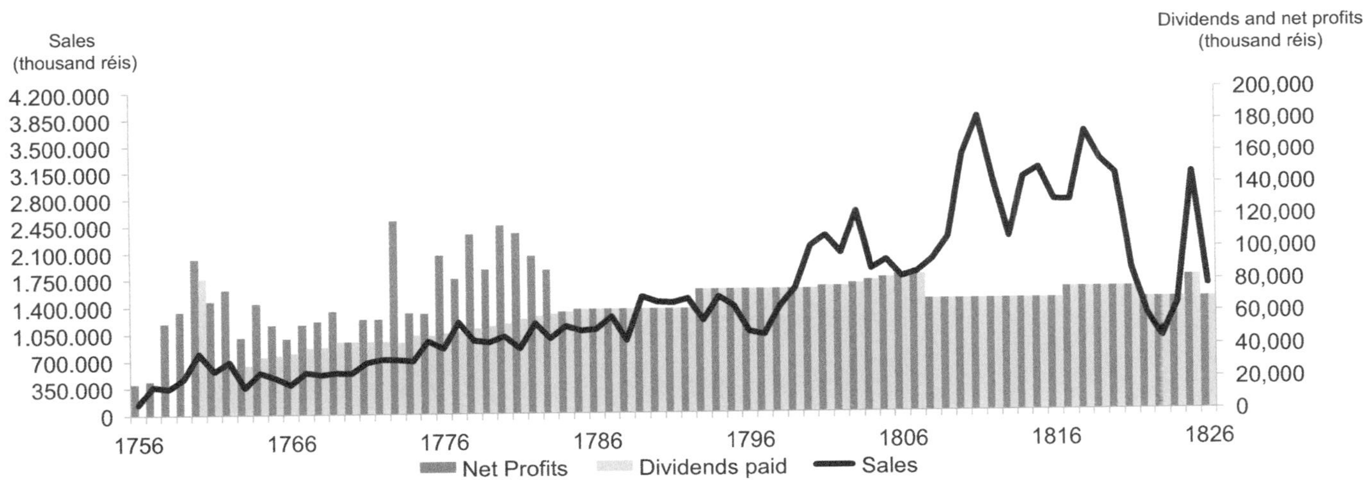

Income smoothing test according to Eckel (1981) model

1756-1826 period		
Values in thousand réis	Sales	Net profits
Average	1 462 054	71 816
Standard deviation (σ2)	909 877	16 972
Coefficient of variation (CV)	0,62	0,24
CV Income/sales		0,38

1756-1783 sub-period		
Values in thousand réis	Sales	Net profits
Average	672 625	71 299
Standard deviation (σ2)	256 414	25 939
Coefficient of variation (CV)	0,38	0,36
CV Income/sales		0,95

1784-1826 sub-period		
Values in thousand réis	Sales	Net profits
Average	1 976 101	72 153
Standard deviation (σ2)	808 764	6 099
Coefficient of variation (CV)	0,41	0,08
CV Income/sales		0,21

Figure 15.7 Annual sales, net profits and dividends, 1756–1826

Sources: ACGAVAD, Cota 6.2.005.10, lvs. 1 e 2 de 5, *Livros de Balanços . . .*; Sousa (2006, pp. 61–62).

Table 15.3 Test of income-smoothing hypothesis

1756–1826 period			*1756–1783 sub-period*		*1784–1826 sub-period*	
Values in thousand réis	*Sales*	*Net profits*	*Sales*	*Net profits*	*Sales*	*Net profits*
Average	1 462 054	71 816	672 625	71 299	1 976 101	72 153
Standard deviation (σ2)	909 877	16 972	256 414	25 939	808 764	6 099
Coefficient of variation (CV)	0,62	0,24	0,38	0,36	0,41	0,08
CV Income/sales		0,38		0,95		0,21

Year	*Revenues*	*Net profits*	*Year*	*Revenues*	*Net profits*	*Year*	*Revenues*	*Net profits*
1 756	139 824	19 162	1 780	996 577	116 038	1 804	1 841 579	80 840
1 757	370 350	20 774	1 781	844 167	111 129	1 805	1 958 094	82 560
1 758	342 975	56 597	1 782	1 164 764	97 031	1 806	1 742 951	84 280
1 759	466 929	63 674	1 783	970 226	88 424	1 807	1 805 723	84 280
1 760	796 199	95 989	1 784	1 122 998	62 694	1 808	1 963 824	68 800
1 761	566 637	70 102	1 785	1 068 182	64 152	1 809	2 244 303	68 800
1 762	686 094	76 887	1 786	1 083 872	64 152	1 810	3 330 449	68 800
1 763	355 064	47 685	1 787	1 248 160	64 152	1 811	3 832 048	68 800
1 764	544 544	68 621	1 788	939 363	64 152	1 812	2 983 543	68 800
1 765	470 856	55 229	1 789	1 496 389	64 152	1 813	2 247 969	68 800
1 766	389 635	46 965	1 790	1 428 170	64 152	1 814	3 024 977	68 800
1 767	539 780	55 449	1 791	1 419 813	64 152	1 815	3 147 476	68 800
1 768	511 157	57 423	1 792	1 471 923	64 152	1 816	2 727 977	68 800
1 769	538 803	63 650	1 793	1 193 653	75 680	1 817	2 719 898	75 680
1 770	531 315	44 720	1 794	1 491 454	75 680	1 818	3 628 793	75 680
1 771	669 174	58 460	1 795	1 373 278	75 680	1 819	3 252 706	75 680
1 772	711 451	58 580	1 796	1 042 558	75 680	1 820	3 064 866	75 680
1 773	701 323	119 393	1 797	1 001 222	75 680	1 821	1 824 555	75 680
1 774	684 435	62 369	1 798	1 360 155	75 680	1 822	1 240 645	68 800
1 775	938 439	62 039	1 799	1 590 720	75 680	1 823	942 878	68 800
1 776	849 033	97 608	1 800	2 137 279	75 680	1 824	1 364 389	68 800
1 777	1 183 438	83 203	1 801	2 275 523	77 400	1 825	3 074 992	82 560
1 778	945 826	110 645	1 802	2 050 443	77 400	1 826	1 620 493	68 800
1 779	924 475	88 529	1 803	2 592 039	79 120			

practice was a constant throughout the whole period we have studied, but it is particularly noticeable after 1784.

The income smoothing was made with the approval of the Crown,[14] by means of accounting manipulations that shifted costs and/or revenues from one period to another, in order that reported earnings might be identical to the amount fixed *a priori* as dividends to be distributed to shareholders. The manipulations essentially took place by means of adjustments recorded in several accounts, namely Casks Depreciation, Bad Debt Provision, 'Profit' Provision and Extraordinary Income/Costs, as shown in Figure 15.8. The column 'Net earnings' shows the earnings reported – quite steady and always a profit figure – and the remaining columns show the impact that Casks Depreciation, Bad Debt Provision, 'Profit' Provision and Extraordinary Income/Cost had in each year to reach the desired 'Net earnings' figures. Until 1820, the *Companhia* had higher 'Current' profits than that reported, so the board used accounting adjustments to downgrade the earnings reported; the opposite occurred between 1821 and 1826.

As can be seen in further detail in Table 15.4, some adjustments were even made to add 'positive' results in the last years of the period, when the current earnings of the *Companhia* became negative. For instance, the 1823 earnings (68,800 thousand réis profit) greatly benefited from an 'income provision' accounting entry of 130,264 thousand réis. If this entry had not been recorded, the *Companhia* would instead have reported a loss of 61,464 thousand réis. The impact of these adjustments in the profit and loss accounts were made against balance sheet debtor/creditor accounts. For instance, in 1826 we find a liability account named *Lucros para amortizar* (meaning 'profits to use') that shows with

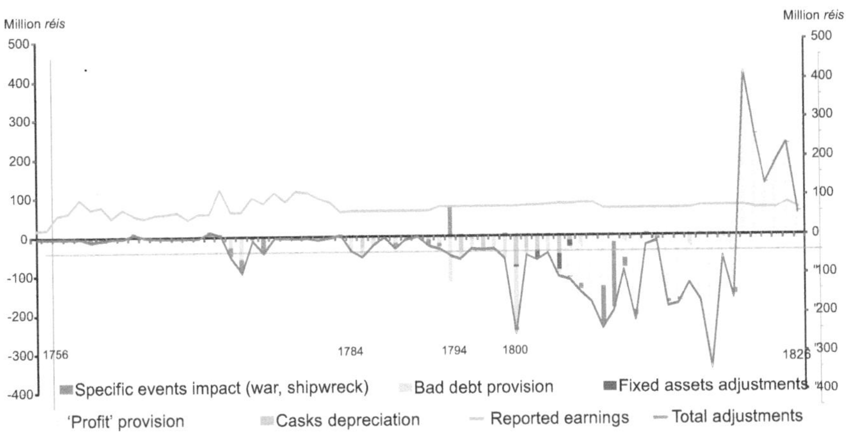

Figure 15.8 Smoothing of the earnings of the *Companhia*, 1756–1826

Source: Our reconstruction, based on the information gathered in ACGAVAD, Cota 6.2.005.10, lvs. 1 e 2 de 5, *Livros de Balanços* . . .

Table 15.4 Accounting adjustments evolution (1756–1826)

Thousand réis

Year	*Net earnings*	*Casks depreciation cost*	*Dab debt provision costs/income*	*Year*	*Net earnings*	*Casks depreciation cost*	*Fixed assets impaired*	*Bad debt provision costs/income*	*Profit provision costs/income*
1756	19 162			**1791**	64 152	–1 893			
1757	20 774			**1792**	64 152			–10 694	
1758	56 597			**1793**	75 680	–332		–19 963	
1759	63 674			**1794**	75 680	–8 232		–110 480	
1760	95 989			**1795**	75 680	–42 650		–12 000	
1761	70 102			**1796**	75 680	–9 358		–20 218	
1762	76 887			**1797**	75 680	–32 299			
1763	47 685			**1798**	75 680			–29 193	
1764	68 621			**1799**	75 680			–59 353	
1765	55 229			**1800**	75 680	–77 553	–6 285	–153 320	
1766	46 965			**1801**	77 400	–35 311		–12 628	
1767	55 449			**1802**	77 400	–40 054	–20 000		
1768	57 423			**1803**	79 120	–1 150		–42 154	
1769	63 650			**1804**	80 840	–50 094	–40 000	–9 223	
1770	44 720			**1805**	82 560	–14 000	–18 000	–5 509	–69 391
1771	58 460			**1806**	84 280			–33 293	–93 613
1772	58 580			**1807**	84 280			–3 529	–155 875
1773	119 393			**1808**	68 800			–5 438	–127 116
1774	62 369		–28 349	**1809**	68 800				–19 079

1775	62 039		–58 584	**1810**	68 800			–19 566	–41 944
1776	97 608			**1811**	68 800				–193 129
1777	83 203			**1812**	68 800				–24 576
1778	110 645			**1813**	68 800				–6 048
1779	88 529			**1814**	68 800				–167 159
1780	116 038			**1815**	68 800				–163 660
1781	111 129			**1816**	68 800			–34 118	–86 274
1782	97 031		–6 690	**1817**	75 680				–160 459
1783	88 424			**1818**	75 680			–24	–332 673
1784	62 694			**1819**	75 680			–10 284	–41 801
1785	64 152	–3 623	–33 436	**1820**	75 680			–3 215	–137 235
1786	64 152	–31 097	–19 265	**1821**	75 680			–17	414 271
1787	64 152	–10 000	–12 435	**1822**	68 800			–35	255 560
1788	64 152			**1823**	68 800				130 264
1789	64 152	–8 812	–10 207	**1824**	68 800				187 999
1790	64 152	–1 314	–4 000	**1825**	82 560				230 934
				1826	68 800				56 636
Total	**2 443 979**	**–54 845**	**–172 967**		**2 654 984**	**–312 926**	**–84 285**	**–599 254**	**–544 366**

Source: ACGAVAD, Cota 6.2.005.10, lvs. 1 e 2 de 5, *Livros de Balanços . . .*

a minor difference of 1,000 réis the exact balance of all previous years 'profit provision' adjustments accounted for (see the accounting entry marked with an arrow in Figure 15.9).

Another perspective of the smoothing of the earnings that underlies the Statements of the Position of the *Companhia* may be gained from Figure 15.10. This figure also displays the reconstruction of what may be called the current earnings, that is, the earnings that might otherwise have been presented in the annual statements in the absence of the adjustments recorded in several accounts, in view of the distribution of predetermined dividends. This shows that the *Companhia*'s current performance on annual earnings (profits and losses) was significantly different from the reported annual earnings. As a complement, Figure 15.11 displays the aggregate components of the reconstructed current earnings.

p

Ref.		Debit	Ref.		Credit
3	Miguel Dias de Faria in London	12 508$772	2	*Companhia* Equity	1 556 734$656
	Shipment to London	29 636$494	3	Manuel Vieira in London	20 709$709
(...)	(...)	(...)	(...)	(...)	(...)
			22	Profit provision	54 336$298
			(...)	(...)	(...)
Total		**4 884 304$890**	Total		**4 884 304$890**

Figure 15.9 Evidence of 'profit provision' balance in 1826 balance sheet

Source: ACGAVAD, Cota 6.2.005.03, lv. 5 de 5, Livros de Balanços . . . (summarized and translated).

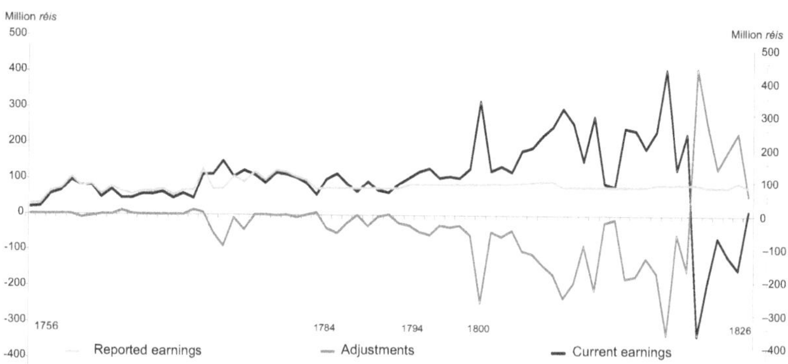

Figure 15.10 Reported earnings, current earnings and accounting adjustments, 1756–1826

Source: Our reconstruction, based on the information gathered in ACGAVAD, Cota 6.2.005.10, lvs. 1 e 2 de 5, *Livros de Balanços* . . .

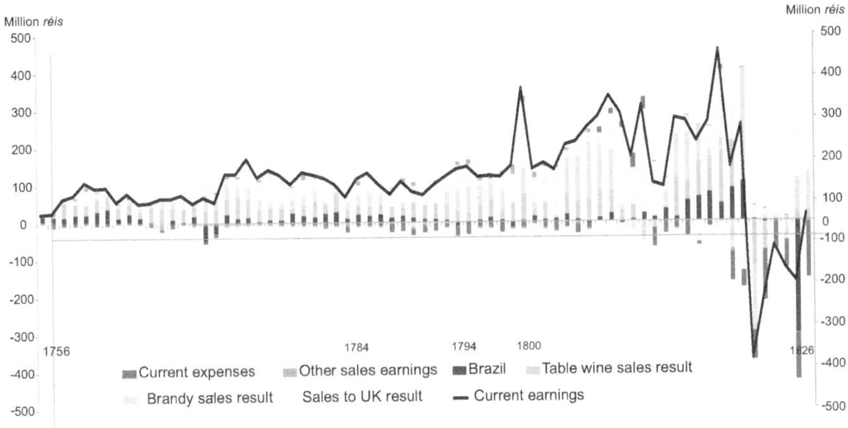

Figure 15.11 Reconstruction of the composition of the current earnings of the *Companhia*, 1756–1826

Source: Our reconstruction, based on the information gathered in ACGAVAD, Cota 6.2.005.10, lvs. 1 e 2 de 5, *Livros de Balanços . . .*

Why earnings smoothing?

The contrast between the irregularity of earnings and dividends, together with the accumulation of reserves, up to 1784, and the regularity and coincidence of earnings and dividends after 1784, may have been facilitated by two events. The first event was the fall of Pombal in 1777, which brought to an abrupt end the power he exerted over the *Companhia* and its staunch critics since it came into existence in 1756. He had the ways and means to enforce his views on the members of the successive boards and impose the creation of a reserve fund with the annual earnings not distributed to shareholders, as a measure of prudent management.

The second event may have to do with the outcome of the 1784 inspection, which was ordered to ascertain the situation of the *Companhia* two years after Pombal's death in 1782. The inspection was on the basis of scrutiny of its activities as the renewal of its charter was due at the beginning of 1777 – just a month before Pombal's fall. As mentioned earlier in this chapter, the inspection took place in the wake of the unrelenting opposition to Pombal's legacy, but the inspector's report in no way advocated the extinction of the *Companhia*, as was claimed by its detractors. In the closing remarks, the inspector even went so far as to assert that "notwithstanding the company's omissions, shortcomings and abuses (which the law must curb), the Agriculture of the Douro region and the prosperity of the Nation are dependent upon its existence".[15] Some of the comments and recommendations found in the inspector's report may have contributed to the emergence of the intentional smoothing of the annual earnings after 1784. This seems to have been the case in relation to the inspector's reaction to the false statement of accounts receivable, as no evidence had been found regarding provisions for bad debts. He had no doubts that bad debts should be recorded as losses, but he carefully recommended that "such a reform cannot be implemented at one stroke, because its action would considerably diminish the distributed profits; instead, the company should amortise an adequate portion of bad debts every year".[16] This seems to have also been the case with regard the comments made on the calculation of the equity capital of the company, which overall convey the idea that a decent remuneration should be guaranteed to shareholders.[17]

The intentional smoothing of the earnings of the *Companhia* after 1784 seems to have worked in favour of the interests of its main stakeholders. As a matter of fact, the members of the board of directors, who also were shareholders, viewed the *a priori* fixing of dividends (and therefore of the corresponding earnings) as a way to reduce the possibility of the scrutiny of their governance by the remaining shareholders. The providing for regular and adequate dividends to all shareholders could help directors hold on to offices, which were much sought after on account of the salary, information, influence and honours that were characteristic of high officialdom.

Common shareholders were also interested in the smoothing of the earnings. The privileges granted to the *Companhia* had been questioned since the very beginning by outsiders who considered the situation of the *Companhia* as unjust and excessive, and the stability of earnings and dividends contributed to tone down the opposition to the company. In addition, shareholders also benefited from the stability of dividends, as it contributed to a more secure livelihood. This was particularly important when dividends were necessary to service the shareholders' debts, whether or not debts had been incurred to buy the respective shares. Apparently dividends came to be regarded by shareholders as a source of a fixed income, rather than as a source of a variable income subject to the uncertainty of the annual earnings, as if shareholders behaved like rent-seekers rather than investors.[18] The Crown was mostly interested in the stability of the Douro wine production trade, and therefore in the stability of the company created to regulate this important sector of the Portuguese economy. Excessive earnings might excite the antagonism of all those who had been excluded from the seemingly lucrative activities of the company. Wide fluctuations in the annual earnings reported by the company might bring about instability in its shareholder base. Neither excessive nor erratic earnings were in the best interests of a Crown for whom this wine sector provided an important basis for tax collection, which incidentally was entrusted to the company itself. The convergence of the interests of the company's main stakeholders paved the way for the mask of stability of the annual earnings and the accounting system fulfilled the mission of providing the accounting records that gave shape to that mask.

Discussion and conclusions

This chapter sought to describe and explain the nature and uses of the accounting system of the *Companhia Geral da Agricultura das Vinhas do Alto Douro* between 1756 and 1826. As demonstrated, the *Companhia* adopted a double-entry accounting system based on the classical set of memorial, diary and ledger books, as the nature of business at this time demanded the preparation of summary comprehensive annual accounts, including a balance sheet and a profit and loss account.

The evidence analysed throughout this study demonstrated that the *Companhia*'s accounting system played several important roles, which included monitoring the movement of wines and brandy in the Douro region; controlling the collection of tax revenues on behalf of the state; registering the economic activity developed for its own gain; reporting economic and financial information to shareholders and creditors; and, finally, providing the information necessary for the dialogue between the company shareholders and the Portuguese governors about the loans granted to the *Companhia* as well as its privileges.

According to literature on this subject (Marcos, 1997; Chaudhuri, 1965; Gaastra, 2003), the configuration of the *Companhia*'s accounting system matches what one might call an expected model under a technical-economic perspective. That is, there was a need to control the credit flows in an eminently commercial business, where large volumes of information circulate, to control the flows of wines, brandy and other goods in the Douro region and finally to calculate the profits and other key performance indicators necessary to determine the income available to pay money to the creditors, shareholders and the state. All this justifies double-entry accounting as the most appropriate accounting system (de Roover, 1956, p. 115; Littleton, 1966, pp. 361–368).

However, such explanations – if satisfactory in explaining some aspects of our case – would fail to capture the richness of motives for the adoption of such solutions and, particularly, the way such solutions were put into practice. In fact, institutional and symbolic reasons are key to understand the nature and uses of the *Companhia*'s accounting system. The latter was consistent with a rhetoric of modernity according to the ideas of Enlightenment rationality – it legitimized privileges and it contributed to sustain a positive public opinion about the *Companhia* and to safeguard amounts invested.[19]

Indeed, the very nature and configuration of the system can be understood under the light of the isomorphic – mimetic, coercive and normative – pressures that the *Companhia* faced. The accounting system emulated that of other Portuguese and foreign CTCs, namely EIC, VOC and Colbert companies and most of the practices of the contemporary Portuguese companies of *Grão-Pará e Maranhão* and *Pernambuco e Paraíba*. There was also evidence of pressures – from the part of Pombal and his followers – for the adoption of specific procedures, and academic and professional influences were also apparent, namely the teachings of the *Aula do Comércio* (the Portuguese Public School of Commerce). Perhaps more importantly, the system was brought to life in a manner that can only be understood if one considers the institutional context of the *Companhia* and the multiple interests and powers surrounding it. The need to legitimize privileges obtained appeals to a compliance with expected patterns of behaviour (Richardson, 2005, p. 106). For instance, the *Companhia* needed to show that the maximum legal margins were being followed, that the flow of wines and brandy in the Douro region was being efficiently policed, that its profits were sufficient to pay dividends but no more than 'decent' and that its solvency ratios were adequate.

Over the period that we have analysed, the earnings-smoothing trend and the crystallization of the dividend distribution ratio at certain levels was achieved at the expense of arrangements whose 'neutral' declared intention was to add truth to the accounts, but in fact it extended a protective cloak to the distortion 'purpose' of those arrangements. This evidence of earnings smoothing over such a long period is quite a novel contribution of this chapter. In other important CTCs (EIC, VOC, Colbert companies), the scarcity of surviving accounting records is an obstacle to similar discussion. This finding could be interpreted as a worsening of the accounting practices, but we could also claim that it served well the purposes of the stakeholders in the *Companhia*, to the extent that a decrease in the *Companhia*'s returns/dividends volatility suited well the shareholders' desire for predictable cash inflows, and tended to minimize the public speech around the excesses of the *Companhia*'s monopolies. It is understandable that the practice of advancing the payment of fixed dividends based on fixed accounting earnings – before the annual accounts formal approval – contributed to generate a more 'peaceful' environment around the *Companhia*. In this way, the *Companhia* was not criticized by its creditors, largely made up by the state itself or by public and private funds controlled by the state; or by small and medium farmers that possessed little power and knowledge to denounce such practices.

In conclusion, the *Companhia*'s accounts and the subsequent use of the accounting information by its stakeholders can only be explained in view of what truly mattered to these actors in the long term: their will to receive dividends; and which ultimately depended on the best interests of the Portuguese government to maintain the *Companhia* as a major player in the Portuguese economic policy.

Notes

1 On account of the dual nature of the *Companhia* as a regulator and a trading company, Duguid and Lopes (1999) characterize it as an ambiguous company.
2 Besides these obligations, the *Companhia* was often asked by the Crown to support other projects alien to its object, such as the participation in the Fishing Company of Algarve, the building of warships to escort Oporto's merchant vessels, the promotion of trade with Baltic countries and the war effort against the French, among others.
3 See AHOP, Catálogo do Ministério do Reino, MR 35, *Negócios da Companhia. . . .*, Doc. N.° 22.
4 See *Informação do Estado . . .*, pp. 186–187.
5 In a 1761 ruling (*AHOP, MR 35 Negócios da Companhia:* Copia do Avizo), Pombal determined that the accountant of the *Companhia* should follow in the steps of his colleague at the *Companhia do Grão-Pará e Maranhão* with regard to the accounting procedures underlying the preparation of its annual statements.

6 See Oliveira (2013, pp. 310–316) for the criteria underlying the creation of the list of aggregate accounts.
7 On the relevance of this school for the emergence of the accounting profession in Portugal, see Rodrigues et al. (2007, 2004, 2003).
8 See *Arte da escritura*, pp. 130–131, as well as Carqueja (2010, p. 46, p. 49).
9 According to Rodrigues et al. (2007), the Portuguese School of Commerce was Europe's first official, government-sponsored school to offer formal instruction in commerce, including in double-entry bookkeeping. See also Rodrigues et al. (2004).
10 See, for example, the requests concerning the explanatory notes of the goods traded in the 1765 Statement (ACGAVAD, Cota 6.1.007.04, liv 7 of 17, *Letters from Frei João Mansilha . . .*, written on August 2nd. 1766, fl. 96).
11 In 1760, the board complained about the lengthy cycle of the Brazilian trade, which extended for more than two years, and asked for an increase in the respective margins. The argument was that the delay in the collection of sales revenues greatly increased the costs and risks of the company, therefore justifying an increase from 15% to 16% to 20% to 22% (Sousa, 2006, pp. 161–162).
12 No less than 23 months went by until the second board accepted the accounts transmitted by the first board (ACGAVAD, Cota 2.2.001, lv. 9 de 14, *Actas das sessões . . .*, Acta of 26.11.1762, fl 101 ff.).
13 See Oliveira (2013, pp. 310–316) for the criteria underlying the creation of the list of aggregate accounts.
14 For instance, in 1786 the Crown issued a notice to the *Companhia,* arguing that bad debt provisions were clearly necessary, but recommending this accounting adjustment should not be done on a single year in order not to jeopardize the *Companhia* credit and in order also not to cause public alarm. Instead the Crown recommended that bad debt provisions should be recorded annually according to the *Companhia*'s strength. (AHOP, Ministério do Reino, MR 5, *Aviso Régio de 28 de Janeiro de 1786,* Fls 160–165).
15 See, *Informação . . .*, p. 195.
16 See, *Informação . . .*, p. 188.
17 Cf. *Informação . . .*, pp. 158–161.
18 For evidence denoting the prevalence of this attitude in Portuguese society, see ACGAVAD, Cota 6.1.007.04, lv. 5 de 17, *Cartas de Frei João Mansilha . . .*, Letter written on March 3rd 1764, fl. 21 and Letter written on April 7th 1764, fls. 33–34.
19 In accordance with Scott (1987, p. 498), "organizations do not necessary conform to a set of institutionalized beliefs because they 'constitute reality' or are taken for granted, but often because they are rewarded for doing so through increased legitimacy, resources and survival capabilities".

Sources

Primary sources

Arquivo Histórico de Obras Públicas (AHOP)
Public Works Historical Archive, Lisbon, Portugal
Catálogo do Ministério do Reino
MR 5 *Aviso Régio de 28 de Janeiro de 1786* (Royal Notice of January 28, 1786).
MR 35 *Negócios da Companhia (Companhia affairs). Document 22: Rellacão dos Livros que actualmente servem nos Escritorios e contadoria da Comp.ª Geral da Agricultura das vinhas do Alto Douro, desde o primrº de Janeiro de 1777 primeiro da reforma dos segundos vinte annos da duração da mesma Companhia concedida por Sua Mag.de* (Index of the Books that currently serve in the offices of the Company since January 1st, 1777, first of the second twenty years charter of the Company granted by His Majesty).

Arquivo da Companhia Geral da Agricultura das Vinhas do Alto Douro (ACGAVAD)
Companhia's Archive, Oporto, Portugal

Manuscript 2.2.001 lv. 9 of 14 *Actas das sessões da Administração* (Minutes of board meetings).

Manuscript 6.1.007.04 (17 books) Letters from João de Mansilha – to the Company Board

Manuscript 6.2.005.10 lv. 1 of 5 *Livro de Balanços* (Annual balance sheet book), also mentioned as *Balanços e demonstrações de balanços.*

Manuscript 6.2.005.10 lv. 2 of 5 *Livro de Balanços* (Annual balance sheet book), also mentioned as *Balanços e demonstrações de balanços.*

Printed sources

Informação do Estado da Companhia do Douro no ano de 1784, elaborada por Luís Pinto de Sousa, depois Visconde de Balsemão, e dirigida ao Secretário de Estado, Visconde Vila Nova de Cerveira *(report of the State of the Companhia in the year 1784, prepared by Luís Pinto de Sousa, later Balsemão Viscount, and addressed to the Secretary of State, the Vila Nova de Cerveira Viscount)*. In Pereira, G. (1999). A Companhia Geral das Vinhas do Alto Douro em 1784, segundo um relatório de Luís Pinto de Sousa Coutinho. *Douro – Estudos & Documentos*, IV(8), pp. 157–195.

Instituição da Companhia Geral da Agricultura das Vinhas do Alto Douro (1756). In: Sousa, F. (2006). *A Real Companhia Velha: Companhia Geral da Agricultura das Vinhas do Alto Douro (1756–2006).* Porto: Cepese, pp. 433–442.

Secondary sources

Anderson, G., Mckonrmick, R. and Tollison, R. (1983). The economic organization of the English East India Company. *Journal of Economic Bahavior and Organization*, 4(2/3), pp. 221–238.

Baladouni, V. (1983). Accounting in the early years of the East India Company. *The Accounting Historians Journal*, 10(2), pp. 63–80.

Carqueja, H. (2010). '*Arte da Escritura Dobrada* que ditou na Aula de Comércio João Henrique de Sousa (1765)' – Um Comentário. In: *Arte da escritura dobrada que ditou na Aula do Comércio João Henrique de Sousa copiada para instrução de José Feliz Vanâncio Coutinho no ano de 1765*, Facsimile edition by H. O. Carqueja 2010. Lisbon: Ordem dos Técnicos Oficiais de Contas, pp. 10–66.

Chaudhuri, K. (1965). *The English East India Company: The Study of an Early Joint-Stock Company 1600–1640.* London: Frank Cass & Co Ltd.

de Roover, R. (1956). The development of accounting prior to Luca Pacioli according to the account-books of medieval merchants. In: A. C. Littleton and B. S. Yamey, eds. *Studies in the History of Accounting*. London: Sweet & Maxwell Ltd, pp. 114–174.

DiMaggio, P. and Powell, W. (1983). The iron cage revisited: Institutional isomorphism and collective rationality in organizational fields. *American Sociological Review*, 48(2), pp. 147–160.

Duguid, P. and Lopes, T. (1999). Ambiguous company: Institutions and organizations in the Port wine trade, 1814–1834. *Scandinavian Economic History Review*, XLVII(1), pp. 84–102.

Eckel, N. (1981). The income smoothing hypothesis revisited. *Abacus*, 17(1), pp. 28–40.

Ekelund, R. and Tollison, R. (1997). *Politicized Economies: Monarchy, Monopoly, and Mercantilism.* College Station: Texas A&M University Economics Series.

Gaastra, F. (2003). *The Dutch East India Company: Expansion and Decline.* Zutphen, The Netherlands: Walburg Press.

Lemarchand, Y. (1995). Style mercantile ou mode des finances. Le choix d'un modèle comptable dans la France d'Ancien Régime. *Annales. Histoire, Sciences Sociales. 50e année*, 1, pp. 159–182.

Littleton, A. (1966). *Accounting Evolution to 1900*. New York: Russell & Russell.
Marcos, R. (1997). *As Companhias Pombalinas – Contributo para a História das Sociedades por Acções em Portugal*. Coimbra: Livraria Almedina.
Oliveira, J. (2013). *A Contabilidade e o equilíbrio de interesses: O caso da Companhia Geral da Agricultura das Vinhas do Alto Douro (1756–1826)*. PhD Dissertation in Business Sciences – Accounting, Faculty of Economics, University of Porto.
Richardson, A. (2005). Accounting as a legitimating institution. In: N. Macintosh and T. Hopper, eds. *Accounting, the Social and the Political*. Oxford: Elsevier, pp. 105–114.
Rodrigues, L., Craig, R. and Gomes, D. (2007). State intervention in commercial education: The case of the Portuguese School of Commerce, 1759. *Accounting History*, 12(1), pp. 55–84.
Rodrigues, L., Gomes, D. and Craig, R. (2003). Corporatism, liberalism and the accounting profession in Portugal since 1755. *Accounting Historians Journal*, 30(1), pp. 95–128.
Rodrigues, L., Gomes, D. and Craig, R. (2004). The Portuguese School of Commerce, 1759–1844: A reflection of the 'enlightenment'. *Accounting History*, 9(3), pp. 53–71.
Scott, W. (1987). The adolescence of institutional theory. *Administrative Science Quarterly*, 32(4), pp. 493–511.
Sousa, F. (2003). *O Arquivo da Companhia Geral da Agricultura das Vinhas do Alto Douro – Real Companhia Velha*. Porto, CEPESE – Centro de Estudos da População, Economia e Sociedade.
Sousa, F. (2006). *A Real Companhia Velha: Companhia Geral da Agricultura das Vinhas do Alto Douro (1756–2006)*. Porto: CEPESE Centro de Estudos da População, Economia e Sociedade.
Sousa, F. and Pereira, C. (2008). *O Brasil, o Douro e a Real Companhia Velha (1756–1834)*. Porto: CEPESE – Centro de Estudos da População, Economia e Sociedade.
Toms, S. (2008). *Calculating Profit: A Historical Perspective on the Development of Capitalism*. University of York, Working Paper No. 4.
Vries, J. and Woude, A. (1997). *The First Modern Economy: Success, Failure and Perseverance of the Dutch Economy, 1500–1815*. Cambridge: Cambridge University Press.

Name index

Page numbers in italics indicate figures and in bold indicate tables on the corresponding pages.

Subject index

Page numbers in italics indicate figures and in bold indicate tables on the corresponding pages.

For Product Safety Concerns and Information please contact our EU representative GPSR@taylorandfrancis.com Taylor & Francis Verlag GmbH, Kaufingerstraße 24, 80331 München, Germany